CW01024176

CONTEMPORARY JAPANESE ARCHITECTURE

Philip Jodidio

CONTEMPORARY JAPANESE ARCHITECTURE

TASCHEN

ENTS

CONTENTS

Philip Jodidio

JAPAN METABOLIZING

The contemporary architecture of Japan has long been one of the most inventive in the world. No fewer than seven Japanese architects have won the Pritzker Prize, such figures as Tadao Ando stand out among the best-known and most admired architects in the world. The creativity of Japanese architecture is the fruit of a very particular situation that includes high population density, a modern, efficient economy, a long history, and the continual presence of disasters in the form of earthquakes. Today, economic stagnation, an aging population, and catastrophes like the Fukushima Daiichi meltdown have brought even greater pressure on the circumstances that form the very basis of architecture. As always, Japan has responded with energy and invention, but today's buildings are surely greener, smaller, and less expensive than those of another era. This is a time of shrinking expectations, as opposed to the decade between 1960 and 1970, when Japan emerged on the international architectural scene, leading the way to what seemed like a new world.

The Ultimate Metropolis

Even the most casual visitor to Japan is impressed by the vitality and density of the country, particularly in the great cities of Tokyo and Osaka. Although statistics may seem dry, in the case of Japan, they are essential to understanding the present and future of its architecture. Slightly smaller than California, Japan has a much larger population, estimated at 126.168 million in July 2018. It also has the highest median age of any major country (47.7 years, just ahead of Germany).[1] In fact, Japan now has a negative population growth rate (-0.24 %, 2018 est.) because its birth rate ranks 223rd in the world (7.5 births / 1000 population, 2018 est.).[2] Clearly stated, the population

of Japan is aging rapidly. Nor are these statistics without profound significance. In 2017, the Japanese Ministry of Health, Labor, and Welfare estimated that the country's population will decline to 87 million in 2060.[3] Greater Tokyo forms the largest urban concentration in the world. Including the peripheral prefectures of Kanagawa, Saitama, and Chiba, the overall population of Tokyo is no less than 37.468 million people. The central Tokyo Metropolitan Area, with only 0.6 % of the total land of Japan, is home to 13.491 million people, creating an extreme density of 6158 people per square kilometer as of October 1, 2015.[4] A large part of the eastern seaboard of the country, between Tokyo and Osaka, is almost continuously urbanized, while to the west, more mountainous and less densely settled areas exist. These facts, and in particular the urban density of the country (91.6 % of total population lived in urban areas in 2018[5]), are important in understanding its architecture. The Japanese are accustomed to conditions of crowding.

Catastrophe and Change

Another significant factor in Japanese architecture is the underlying sense of fragility born of catastrophes. Successive disasters, some natural and some man-made, have shaped the contemporary face of Tokyo. The first of these in the 20th century was the Great Kanto Earthquake of 1923, measuring 7.9 on the Richter scale, which may have killed 200 000 and left 64 % of the remaining population homeless. The second, even more radical in its destruction, was the American firebombing of the city between March and May of 1945. More people died in these months than in the instantaneous devastation of Hiroshima. By September 1945, the population of Tokyo, which had exceeded

6.9 million in 1942, had dropped through death and emigration to 2.777 million. Incendiary devices, dropped on a city constituted mostly of wooden structures, were particularly devastating. For this reason, it can be said that the largest city on earth has been rebuilt almost entirely since 1945. At the outset, this construction went forward with limited means. As in war-torn Europe, it was essential to build cheaply and fast. In more recent times, an implacable commercial logic, which has little to do with the canons of aesthetics, has been a dominant influence. In a sense, this tidal wave of bad architecture is the second man-made disaster of Tokyo's recent history. It has swept before it much of the beauty of centuries-old tradition. Disasters such as the 9.1 magnitude Tohoku earthquake of March 11, 2011, which left nearly 20 000 persons dead or missing, and a further 73 000 still without homes in 2018,[6] were surely the occasion for a profound rethinking of the role of architecture and its place in society. Nothing is certain in Japan, it seems, except for change.

The Infinite Jumble

Particularly for the Western visitor, Tokyo at first glance is an almost infinite jumble of unsightly electrical wires and small, ugly buildings. Aside from aesthetic considerations, there are two good reasons for the unusual appearance of Tokyo, and indeed of other large Japanese cities. One is that it is forbidden for any two buildings to share a structural wall. A tiny passageway between walls naturally limits the danger that the collapse of one building during an earthquake will cause a chain reaction. The second is *"nisshōken,"* which means "a right to sunlight." This practice, long observed in Japan, requires that any new building not deprive its neighbors of more

than a certain amount of their light. This rather humane approach results in the odd positions of many structures in their lots. In fact, though reference has often been made to "sunshine laws," legal protection as such is rather complex and may often be ignored, especially as cities have built more and more tall buildings.[7]

Bursting Bubble

After economic growth averaging 10 % a year in the 1960s, and 5 % a year in the 1970s and 1980s, the formidable Japanese economic machine practically ground to a halt in 1992 and 1993, partially because of contradictory domestic policies intended to wring speculative excesses from the stock and real-estate markets. The "bubble" years that preceded this time of reckoning saw the price of land in Japan reach incredible heights. In the late 1980s, it was said that the land of the Imperial Palace in central Tokyo had the theoretical market value of the whole of Manhattan. In the reigning speculative climate, banks saw no objection to lending large sums at very low interest rates to finance the purchase and construction of often extravagant buildings. In the boom years, Japan became an enormous laboratory for the development of contemporary architecture. Naturally, a majority of the new structures were without considerable aesthetic merit, but, in other cases, talented young architects were given a chance to realize their dreams, or those of their clients. Building an unusual structure, such as "La Flamme d'Or," Philippe Starck's 1989 restaurant for the Asahi Breweries (Sumida, Tokyo) was considered a perfectly reasonable public-relations gesture for a large company. The Japanese thirst for new architecture even included a call to foreigners, like the Frenchmen Starck and Christian de Portzamparc, Steven Holl and

Peter Eisenman from the United States, the Italian Aldo Rossi, and many others. This was also the period when Japanese millionaires or corporations were astonishing the art world by paying record prices for Impressionist and Post-Impressionist paintings at auction in New York or London. A wave of museum building swept across the archipelago, and clients, both private and public, often had the good sense to call on talented architects. Despite the excessive nature of the real-estate speculation that characterized this period and the economic havoc that it was to wreak afterwards, it might be said that the bubble years were a fruitful time for contemporary architecture in Japan. Money and clients were available in abundance, and the high quality of Japanese construction made it possible for some of the most innovative and interesting architecture in the world to be built. Naturally though, this euphoria had to come to an end. As Arata Isozaki, one of the leading figures of the profession in Japan and 2019 Pritzker Prize winner, explained: "The recession started in 1991. It was called the bursting of the bubble here. At first, private activity sponsored by private developers stopped. The result that there were to be no more crazy little buildings. The taxes kept coming in for public authorities though, so they had money for new projects. After the private side dropped out, the public side remained a good client for architects. In 1995, the public authorities began to complain about these projects. But then, many people in the administration believed that the only way to get Japan out of the recession was to promote construction. Housing was benefiting from this trend. There were no longer many cultural projects. There was a wave of art museum construction which began in the bubble years, and then theaters and concert halls were built. It seems to me that this cycle has

ended. Lately there has been a fashion for sports arenas, for example."[8] In 1996, Arata Isozaki, whose considerable architectural talents are matched by a keen sense of humor, laid out two simple rules for understanding the impact on contemporary architecture of the post-bubble economic climate. The first of these was: "No more crazy little buildings;" and the second: "No more *gaijins*."[9] *Gaijin* is, of course, the rather derogatory Japanese word for foreigners, who are not universally appreciated by the comparatively homogeneous population. The prescience of Isozaki's comments can even be measured today by the relative absence of foreign architects, even famous ones, on the Japanese architectural scene.

Lost Generation

In 1994, the Japanese economy began to experience a modest recovery, with an economic growth of 0.6 %. Yet somehow, the assurance presiding over the triumph of the 1980s had been lost, replaced by new doubts. As Lionel Barber wrote in *The Financial Times* in 1996: "…Even a partial view of Japanese society points to far-reaching political and economic change… The reality is that Japan is becoming a 'normal' country. Just as Americans and Europeans suffer from job insecurity and economic dislocation, so the Japanese are struggling to adapt to global competition. Unemployment is edging upwards. The population is aging. For the first time since 1945, the Japanese public is having doubts about the prospects for growth. The fashionable term is: stagnant prosperity. Some of this pessimism is exaggerated, the legacy of nearly five years of zero growth following the collapse of the bubble economy… The crash has been a searing experience."[10] And the impact of this period

Opposite: *Yoji Watanabe, New Sky Building, Tokyo, 1972. Roof water tower inspired by ship design.*

Kunio Maekawa, Prefectural Youth Center, Yokohama, Kanagawa, 1962.

continued long after the fact. The period between 1990 and 2010 is often referred to as the "Lost 20 Years" *(ushinawareta nijūnen)*, with GDP and wages falling in nominal terms. The fact that this time of stagnation was followed by the international economic crisis of 2007–09 has implied that many of the psychological barriers against a resurgence of extravagant contemporary architecture have remained in effect to this day. An attention to economic factors and a more general aesthetic conservatism have been the rule.

European Style

The emergence of modern Japanese architecture can be viewed in terms of a progressive liberation from Western influences. When the American Commodore Matthew Perry viewed the city of Edo during his 1853–54 expedition, he described it as an "extensive plain with a magnificent background of mountains and wooded country." Japan had been in willful isolation from the rest of the world for the previous 220 years. The far-reaching consequences of the Perry Expedition have often been analyzed, but, as early as 1872, the Meiji government called on the British architect and planner Thomas Waters (1842–98) to rebuild the sector to the southeast of the Imperial Palace, destroyed in that year by fire. Along a broad avenue, Waters laid out Neoclassical brick buildings forming the precursor of modern Ginza. Another Englishman, Josiah Conder (1852–1920), built numerous Second Empire-style masonry buildings, such as the National Museum in Ueno Park (1882), which became the symbols of the Japanese establishment until the Ministry of the Cabinet decided to call on the Germans Hermann Ende (1829–1907) and Wilhelm Böckmann (1832–1902). Their plan for a Prussian-style building for the Japanese

Diet, capped with a pagoda-like form, met with concerted opposition and calls for a resolution to the conflict between indigenous and Western architectural styles.[11]

Perhaps the first modern Western architect to leave his mark on Japan was Frank Lloyd Wright, who worked between 1916 and 1922 on the Imperial Hotel in Tokyo. "There was sixty to seventy feet of soft mud below the upper depth of eight feet of surface soil on the site," he wrote. "That mud seemed a merciful provision—a good cushion to relieve the terrible shocks. Why not float the building upon it? A battleship floats on salt water…"[12] Demolished in 1967, this eccentric structure famously survived the devastating earthquake of 1923, adding to Wright's reputation, not least of all in Japan.

In Tradition, the Roots of Modernity

On November 4, 1935, the German architect Bruno Taut (1880–1938) wrote in his journal: "I can truly claim to be the discoverer of Katsura." This affirmation, concerning the 17th-century imperial residence near Kyoto, is of considerable importance for the evolution of contemporary Japanese architecture. While the Japanese had in various ways absorbed the Western influences to which they were subjected after the Perry Expedition, they had come to reject many aspects of their own tradition. Thus, the rise of fascism in Japan was accompanied by a certain rejection of Western-inspired modernity in favor of an architecture called *teikan yoshiki* or the "Imperial roof style," which featured heavy cubic structures capped by equally ungainly "Japanese" roofs. Having arrived in Japan in May 1933, Taut spent three and a half years writing about Katsura, linking its elegant simplicity to the goals of the Modern Movement and calling it

an "eternal monument." As Arata Isozaki pointed out, other Western architects, such as the German Gustav Prattz, had visited Katsura even earlier than Taut, and had integrated its lessons into "the renewal of world architecture."[13] The rediscovery of the fundamental links between the purity of Japanese tradition and modernism itself occurred only after the trauma of World War II, partially because the very idea of calling on tradition had been misappropriated by a largely discredited political ideology.

In an interesting parallel, 1933 is also the year when the Japanese author Jun'ichirō Tanizaki first published his influential work *In Praise of Shadows*. Speaking of the specificity of Japanese architecture, he wrote: "A light room would no doubt have been more convenient for us, too, than a dark room. The quality that we call beauty, however, must always grow from the realities of life, and our ancestors, forced to live in dark rooms, presently came to discover beauty in shadows, ultimately to guide shadows towards beauty's ends."[14] This kind of thought, or that of Bruno Taut, who found "modernity" in Katsura, are the groundwork for fundamental aspects of contemporary Japanese architecture, where Western influences have been absorbed and deeper connections to tradition assimilated.

Frank Lloyd Wright was, of course, not the only Western architect to have exerted a direct influence on the development of modern Japanese architecture. Le Corbusier, for example, who continues to fascinate many Japanese architects, made his presence felt through projects like the National Museum of Western Art in Ueno Park in Tokyo (1959), and through the work of figures like Kunio Maekawa (1905–86) who worked in Le Corbusier's atelier in France from 1928 to 1930, before establishing his own office in Tokyo in 1935. Having

Kenzo Tange, Yoyogi National Gymnasium, and Second Gymnasium, Tokyo, 1964.

Opposite: *Kisho Kurokawa, Sony Tower, Osaka, 1976.*

Following double page: *Kenzo Tange, Embassy of Kuwait, Tokyo, 1970.*

supervised the construction of the original building, Maekawa completed the 1979 addition to the museum, symbolically reaffirming the importance of Le Corbusier in Japan. The postwar discovery of how Japanese tradition could give life to contemporary architecture by the Japanese themselves was spearheaded by the architect Kenzo Tange (1913–2005). Tange had worked in the late 1930s in the office of Kunio Maekawa, but his Yoyogi National Gymnasium, built for the 1964 Tokyo Summer Olympics, announced the emergence of an indigenous modernity with a quality and inventiveness on par with the West's. As Fumihiko Maki wrote: "The National Gymnasium for the Tokyo Olympics of 1964 was a magnificent product of 20th-century structural technology, as well as a bold and original conception of space. It is one of the landmarks of modern architectural history and assured the highest international reputation for Tangé."[15] Author of the Hiroshima Peace Park and Museum, a moving testimony to the horrific impact of the atomic bomb, Tange, who died in 2005, remains a symbol of modern Japanese architecture, though his late work, like Tokyo City Hall, a 243-meter-tall double tower that occupies three full blocks in the Shinjuku area (1991), is considered by many to be a symbol of the excesses of the so-called bubble years.

Floating Cities and Capsule Towers

A number of the leading figures in Japan's contemporary architecture scene emerged from the office of Kenzo Tange, among them Arata Isozaki (born in 1931) and Yoshio Taniguchi

along with Kiyonori Kikutake (1928–2011) and others, in the manifesto *Metabolism: The Proposals for New Urbanism*, published in 1960 at the time of the World Design Conference (WoDeCo) in Tokyo. The conference was presided over by Kenzo Tange, who presented his Plan for Tokyo 1960 at the same time. Developing from their work and from Kenzo Tange's MIT studio, the Metabolist movement combined ideas about organic biological growth and architectural megastructures, imagining floating cities and capsule towers. Metabolism might be considered a response to the human and environmental catastrophes of the war, as well as the continuing vulnerability of Japan to natural disasters. Architecture was imagined as a vehicle for the transformation of Japanese society toward spatial and organizational patterns that would be resilient and adaptable to change. Architecture was defined in technical terms but likened to biological regeneration. The actual buildings that emerged from this influential movement were not numerous, but they notably include Kurokawa's Nakagin Capsule Tower, which was built in just 30 days in 1972 (Shimbashi, Tokyo). Kenzo Tange also developed the concept of expandable architecture with his Yamanashi Broadcasting Press Center (Kofu, Yamanashi, 1966). Perhaps the most visible manifestation of Metabolism and also coincidentally its final significant act of presence was the 1970 World Exposition in Osaka, organized under the theme "Progress and Harmony for Mankind," with a master plan by Kenzo Tange and the Marxist Uzo Nishiyama. Tange designed the main pavilion called the Festival Plaza while Kikutake conceived

Buddhist Thought and Shinto Tradition

For a time, it seemed as though contemporary Japanese architecture had taken center stage in the world, inventing new ideas that were in harmony with the unique circumstances in Japan, a densely populated new world at the epicenter of war and earthquakes. Despite its resolutely forward-looking intent, Metabolism led some to rethink Japanese tradition in the light of modern change. Educated by Buddhist monks, Kisho Kurokawa was one of these. According to Rem Koolhaas and Hans Ulrich Obrist: "Witnessing the firebombing of Japan's cities in World War II was also fundamental: it made devastatingly clear to Kurokawa the impermanence of architecture. … Kurokawa insist(ed) that this apparently modern revelation—and a trigger for Metabolism—is actually a seamless continuation of Buddhist thought and Shinto Japanese tradition, evident in the reconstruction of Ise Shrine every 20 years since the seventh century."[16] The kind of connection that Kurokawa drew, at least in theory, between Japanese tradition and the modern world is an underlying fact and a strength of contemporary Japanese architecture; it brings the past, present, and future together in a continuum that is difficult to imagine in other countries.

Recognition on the World Stage

Emerging from the shadow of Kenzo Tange over time, such figures as Arata Isozaki and Yoshio Taniguchi began, in more recent years, to impose a Japanese presence on the world architectural stage. Isozaki, winner of the 2019

Kiyonori Kikutake, Sky House, Tokyo, 1958.

Opposite: *Kiyonori Kikutake, Hotel Tokoen, Yonago, Tottori, 1964.*

one of the first new museums to be designed by a foreign architect in the United States, and Taniguchi's more recent Museum of Modern Art reconstruction (2004) in New York showed that Japanese architects had been accepted, even within the art establishment's "inner sanctum." In the generation of Isozaki and Taniguchi, Fumihiko Maki, another survivor of Metabolism, is a figure of international importance, whose recent projects include 4 World Trade Center in New York (see page 260), and buildings for the Aga Khan in Canada. Like Taniguchi, Maki, winner of the 1993 Pritzker Prize, was in part educated in the United States and has a full mastery of English, which is still not the case with all of Japan's major architects.

Tadao Ando and Toyo Ito

To date, seven Japanese architects have won the Pritzker Prize. This list traces a path of influence and change, leading from one architect to the next, and surely announcing the profile of future Japanese winners.

1. Kenzo Tange 1987
2. Fumihiko Maki 1993
3. Tadao Ando 1995
4. SANAA 2010
5. Toyo Ito 2013
6. Shigeru Ban 2014
7. Arata Isozaki 2019

Tadao Ando may be the best known contemporary architect in the world, and it is, indeed, with Ando that Japan itself has reached the highest levels of international notoriety in this field. Born in Osaka in 1941, Tadao Ando was self-educated as an architect, largely through his travels in the United States, Europe, and Africa (1962–69). He received the 1995 Pritzker

Prize, and, aside from his prodigious buildings in Japan, he has recently completed the Pulitzer Foundation for the Arts (St. Louis, Missouri, USA, 2001) and the Modern Art Museum of Fort Worth (Texas, USA, 2002). Working for the French billionaire François Pinault, Ando completed renovations of Palazzo Grassi (2006) and Punta della Dogana (2009) in Venice (Italy) for the exhibition of contemporary art. A scheme to design a museum of contemporary art in Paris again for François Pinault was cancelled in the spring of 2005, but the same client commissioned Ando to renovate the Bourse du Commerce in the Halles area of the French capital (2021). Ando's powerful drawings and equally strong, usually concrete buildings have been admired and imitated by architecture students the world over for a number of years. It would seem that he has succeeded in building the long-sought bridge between East and West, creating astonishing sanctuaries of silence and light with an intentionally limited vocabulary of geometric forms. What seems clear in much of Ando's architecture is that he has sought out something more than a mastery of space. As he said in his acceptance speech for the Pritzker Prize: "I believe that there are two separate dimensions coexisting in architecture. One is substantive and concerns function, security, and economy, and inasmuch as architecture accommodates human living, it cannot ignore these elements of the real. However, can architecture be architecture with this alone? Since architecture is a form of human expression, when it steps out of the exigencies of sheer construction toward the realm of aesthetics, the question of architecture as art arises… What I have sought to achieve is a spatiality that stimulates the human spirit, awakens the sensitivity and communicates with the deeper soul."[17]

Born the same year as Ando, Toyo Ito may not have achieved the kind of international celebrity reserved to the Osaka architect, but he is clearly one of the leading figures of his generation in architecture, as confirmed by his 2013 Pritzker award. Usually attached to extremely light designs, as opposed to the more solid concrete of Ando, Toyo Ito completed two structures that won him considerable media attention in this century's early years. One is the Mediatheque in Sendai (2001). Making use of 13 white structural steel tubes that undulate through the structure like "seaweed" to hold up the building and carry its technical conduits, Ito innovated both at the most basic level of structural integrity and the architectural aesthetics. His 2002 Summer Pavilion in London's Kensington Park for the Serpentine Gallery was more ephemeral: a 309-square-meter single-story structure covered in aluminum panels and glass. His concept was to create a columnless structure that was not dependent on an orthogonal grid system, creating an open space to be used during the summer months as a café and event space. An algorithm derived from the rotation of a single square determined the seemingly random structure. Each piece of the structure functioned not only as a beam but also to absorb vibrations so that all elements combined to form a complex, mutually interdependent whole. The point, as explained by the architect, was "to render visible again the systems that make the most basic conditions of architecture."

Ito's thoughts about nature in the highly urbanized environment of Japanese cities are of considerable interest. Like most Japanese people, he was profoundly impacted by the catastrophic Tohoku earthquake and tsunami (2011). It was after that event that he wrote:

Opposite and this page: *Tadao Ando, Church of the Light, Osaka, 1989.*

"I can't help sensing a more fundamental disruption between our norm and reality. I think we design things in a mechanical manner as a 'complete machine,' complying with nature defined in quantities or abstract definitions; we do not engage with the natural environment as something constantly affected by the varying forces of ground, sea, or wind. In public architecture or private houses, we design strictly within an abstract framework. I think our task now is to rethink how we 'assume' design conditions, rather than reviewing the conditions. We need to start by questioning the way we relate to nature."[18] The path of this thinking may bear comparison to the origins of Metabolism, and yet, Ito has taken into account the intervening period and calls here for architecture that is more in harmony with the earth than the mega-architecture of an earlier generation.

Kazuyo Sejima, Kengo Kuma, and Shigeru Ban

Toyo Ito's office, like that of Tange before him, has been effective in developing talent. One of the most famous of his former employees is Kazuyo Sejima, who worked with him between 1981 and 1987 before forming her own office. Sejima, now a partner of Ryue Nishizawa (SANAA), has leapt to international prominence with work such as the New Museum of Contemporary Art (New York, USA, 2007) or the Louvre-Lens (Lens, France, 2012) and their 2010 Pritzker Prize. It might be said that Sejima, like her mentor, makes frequent use of impressions of extreme lightness or plays on reflection and transparency, which sometimes make it difficult to know where a building ends and where it begins. Such is the case of her 21st Century Museum of Contemporary Art (Kanazawa, 2004).

There, within a basic, simple round plan, she created a series of galleries and a variety of visitor experiences that defy what one might expect of modern architecture. Sejima's generation in Japanese architecture is especially rich in talent. Kengo Kuma (born in 1954), Shigeru Ban (1957), and Shuhei Endo (1960) offer a remarkable panorama of styles and innovative architecture that would be the envy of most countries. The best known of these figures is Shigeru Ban, winner of the 2014 Pritzker Prize, who made himself known outside of Japan with works like the Centre Pompidou-Metz (Metz, France, 2010) and apartment projects in New York. Kengo Kuma completed the very visible One Omotesando building in Tokyo in 2003 and the Nagasaki Prefectural Art Museum in 2005. Recently Kuma has completed one of his most symbolic and significant projects, the Japan National Stadium in Tokyo (with Taisei Corporation, Azuka Sekkei Co., Ltd.; see page 256), intended for the planned 2020 Tokyo Summer Olympic Games and successor to the ill-fated competition-winning scheme by Zaha Hadid. Making extensive use of Japanese wood and plants, Kuma ensures that the stadium will serve as a statement toward a gentler kind of architecture related to nature, even in the midst of Tokyo's urban sprawl. Importantly, Kuma's scheme is considerably lower and less expensive than the Hadid design, which had a retractable roof of considerable complexity.

A Generational Shift

Perhaps following in the footsteps of figures like Tange, Isozaki, and Toyo Ito, younger architects have successfully developed new directions in Japanese architecture that are surely more "modest" on the whole, and often connected to Japanese tradition in more or less subtle ways. As it happens, one of the precursors of a real exploration of tradition has been an architect from the generation of Ando and Ito: Professor Terunobu Fujimori (born in 1946) is an architectural historian who actually built his first building in 1991. With works like his Takasugi-an Teahouse (Chino, Nagano, 2004), he brought the ancient tradition of the Japanese teahouse to new heights, as it were, by perching the structure in trees six meters off the ground. Known for his eccentricity and sense of humor, Fujimori uses natural materials in a context that is always informed by his deep knowledge of the architectural history of his country.

Four architects born in the 1960s, Masaki Endoh (1963), Takaharu Tezuka (1964), Yui Tezuka (1969), and Hiroshi Sambuichi (1968) offer different visions of the present and future of their art. Masaki Endoh, working often with the engineer Masahiro Ikeda, has created a series of unusual houses. He usually gives his designs the name "Natural"—as in "Natural Ellipse" (Shibuya, Tokyo, 2002). He explains that this is because he believes that architecture must be based on "common sense and empirical knowledge." He goes on to say: "I believe that the design process is similar to evolution. Design that incorporates new concepts will survive into the future. Design that does not change over time will disappear. It is important to constantly challenge the established norms for this architectural evolution to continue." Takaharu and Yui Tezuka certainly also believe in challenging accepted norms, as their surprising Matsunoyama Natural Science Museum (Niigata, 2003) proves. This structure, essentially a Corten-steel tube designed to resist snow loads of up to 2000 tons, meanders over a length of 111 meters, following the topography and allowing visitors to "experience the light and colors under the

Introduction

Kengo Kuma, Hojo-an after 800 Years, Kyoto, 2012.

Opposite: *Terunobu Fujimori, Beetle's House, London, UK, 2010.*

different depths of snow, from four meters deep to 30 meters above the ground." Hiroshi Sambuichi designed two buildings published in this volume, the Miyajima Misen Observatory (Miyajima, Hiroshima, 2013, see page 338) and the Naoshima Hall (Naoshima, Kagawa, 2015, see page 344), both of which seek connections to local custom and tradition, their natural settings, and materials that have always been used in Japanese architecture. His work, however, remains clearly modern, despite its search have designed open pavilions in tradition.

Younger and Closer to Nature

The generation of Japanese architects born in the 1970s testifies to a high degree of innovation and, indeed, promises to break even further with the heritage of figures like Le Corbusier in favor of distinctively Japanese solutions, which are nonetheless sufficiently universal to gain acceptance and approval in many architectural circles. The best known of these figures are Sou Fujimoto (1971) and Junya Ishigami (1974). Ishigami, in particular, has sought to bring nature into his work in a way that is more than cosmetic—he searches rather for a "nature beyond nature," or perhaps "a nature never before seen." These ideas are developed in two of his projects published here, the Botanical Garden Art Biotop/Water Garden (Nasu, Tochigi, 2018, see page 198) and the Serpentine Gallery Summer Pavilion 2019 (Kensington Gardens, London, UK, 2019, see page 204). Both of these can be said to be at the limit of what has generally been considered architecture. The Water Garden is an astonishing creation that appears to be totally natural, when it has, in fact, been fabricated by Ishigami using plants, trees, and water.

His Yamaguchi House & Restaurant (Yamaguchi, 2016–), another unique project, is being created by simply digging into the earth and pouring concrete into the openings. When the earth around these forms is removed, it forms a "natural" space that is also obviously artificial. Junya Ishigami, as seen in his remarkable 2018 exhibition at the Fondation Cartier in Paris—"Freeing Architecture," seeks nothing less than a fundamental rethinking of the art of building. Here nature neither takes a back seat nor acts as an ornament; rather it becomes architecture's *raison d'être:* a deep, fundamental change.

Sou Fujimoto is also in the business of breaking down architectural barriers— something that he seeks to do even when as he works on a very small scale. As is frequently the case in his work, the Public Toilet in Ichihara (Chiba, Japan, 2012) challenges some of the most fundamental assumptions of architecture. Often viewed as leftover, yet necessary, spaces, most public toilets are architecturally indigent. Working near a train station in an area of Japan known for the beauty of its scenery, Fujimoto enclosed a space of 209 square meters with a log fence and actually dared to leave the toilets in a remarkably open, visible place within the perimeter he was assigned. The architect explains: "This multi-layered divergence of internal and external boundaries blends together public and private, the sense of openness and protection, nature and architecture, internal and external, large and small while retaining their ambiguity." The Japanese do have an unusual interest in toilets, as the highly sophisticated products of manufacturers such as Toto attest, and yet the idea of placing such a facility in an open garden is truly astonishing. The Public Toilet in Ichihara is no temporary installation, but Fujimoto also tried

his hand in 2013 at an ephemeral design, the Serpentine Gallery Summer Pavilion. The list of those who have designed these pavilions in London from year to year reads like a Who's Who of contemporary architecture. Architectural firms such as SANAA and most recently Herzog & de Meuron have designed open pavilions in the space near the Serpentine's Georgian gallery in Kensington Gardens. Once again, Fujimoto took an entirely different approach to the assignment, creating a web of 20-millimeter white steel poles erected in a latticework pattern. In its green park setting, this structure, which housed a café, was conceived as an invitation to consider the environment. Fujimoto states: "It is a really fundamental question, how architecture is different from nature, or how architecture could be part of nature, or how they could be merged… what are the boundaries between nature and artificial things."

Lifting and Expanding

Less well-known than his compatriots Ishigami and Fujimoto, Tsuyoshi Tane (1979) has taken a different approach to his profession, intentionally distancing himself from the architectural environment of Tokyo to install his office in Paris. Working with a firm he cofounded, Dorell.Gotmeh.Tane /Architects, he designed the Estonian National Museum (Tartu, Estonia, 2016) and had the highly unusual idea of using an abandoned Soviet-era airfield as the actual point of departure for a structure, with a roof that appears to be "lifting and expanding toward 'infinite space.'" Tsuyoshi Tane has, of course, also worked in Japan and is considered one of the "up and coming" figures in contemporary architecture within his age group. Closer to home, Tsuyoshi Tane

22

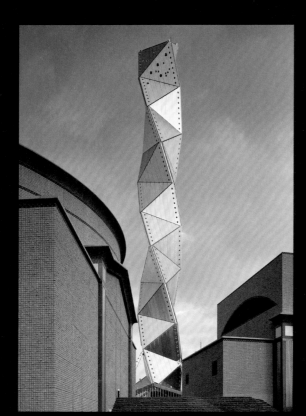

Arata Isozaki, Art Tower Mito, Mito, Ibaraki, 1990.

Opposite: Shigeru Ban, Centre Pompidou-Metz, Metz, France, 2010.

completed the Todoroki House in Valley (Setagaya, Tokyo, 2018, see page 412). With a relatively modest floor area of 188 square meters, this house is located in an unusual forested ravine in the midst of the city. Managing to live with nature despite the extreme urban density of Tokyo, the house looks out in eight directions, in touch with its unexpected environment.

Corrugated Metal and Plywood

Another young Japanese architect of note is Takashi Suo, born in 1980. His small (188 m²) Ishihara Dental Clinic (Okayama, 2017, see page 406) might be considered emblematic of current architecture in the country. Built for a modest €480 000 budget, it has an unlikely roadside site and looks to be a bit of a jumble, like much of the cityscape in urban and peri-urban Japan. The architect himself says: "It seems to be the result of inorganic and chaotic planning, but it is, in fact, in harmony with the environment." With its slightly shifted volumes designed for a certain amount of interior privacy for patients, and a structure that privileges corrugated sheet aluminum and plywood, this dental clinic is the result of intelligent and innovative design—almost uniquely Japanese in its assimilation of the neighborhood; "cheap" in the good sense of the word, it shows that contemporary Japanese architecture is stronger than the heavy constraints of urban density, or even a culture inured to continual upheaval and gradual aging. Nor is it an accident that the promising younger Japanese architects of today are building such small, yet inventive buildings. Their work is the clear consequence of existing conditions, such as the scarcity of urban land, a thirst for nature where there is almost none, the fact that it is forbidden for any two buildings to share a structural wall, economic

stagnation, and a general uncertainty about the future. This is not to say that, even as this book goes to press, there are no longer any massive projects under construction in Tokyo. Aside from Kuma's Japan National Stadium, which can seat up to 80 000 people, other preparations for the planned 2020 Tokyo Summer Olympic Games are transforming well-known parts of the city. Thus the area around Shibuya Station is the theater for a massive redevelopment, including several large new towers, designed partially by SANAA and, again, Kengo Kuma. In the hands of large corporate building and design firms like Tokyu Land Corporation and Nikken Sekkei, these projects are indicative of an overall trend toward taller buildings in the Japanese capital. Deeply integrated into the city's complex transportation system, such projects go beyond the specific expertise of individual architects. Thus, the Japan National Stadium is not the work of Kengo Kuma alone but that of a consortium (Taisei Corporation, Azusa Sekkei Co., Ltd., and Kengo Kuma & Associates). Close to earth in Tokyo, Jo Nagasaka (1971) and his firm Schemata have also innovated in the area of relatively modest and low-cost projects, such as the two published here—the rather rough conversion of the House in Sangenjaya (Setagaya, Tokyo, 2017, see page 286) and the °C (Do-C) Ebisu (Ebisu, Shibuya, Tokyo, 2017, see page 294) renovation of a "capsule" and sauna-based hotel. In both cases, Nagasaka makes use of modern buildings to create unexpected new spaces and uses for architecture. This is no longer the bright shining novelty of manga-style architecture that characterized the pre-bubble years, rather it is an unselfconscious reuse, where modesty and a degree of roughness are willfully embraced.

Unceasing Change

The architects presented in this volume, and others as well, have engaged Japan in a seemingly endless search for new forms in architecture. Even the house, the most fundamental unit of architectural design, is the object of constant exploration, with walls and floors and ceilings serving other purposes, freeing space to suit the needs of a modern, densely populated city. It has often been imagined that Tokyo could be considered a precursor to world-cities of the future, where extreme density engenders architectural innovation. In a thoughtful book called *Tokyo Metabolizing*, the commissioner of Japan's 2010 Pavilion for the Venice Architecture Biennale, Koh Kitayama, wrote: "Unlike the urban structures one finds in Europe that were created with a series of walls, Tokyo consists of an assemblage of independent buildings (grains). In other words, constant change is an inherent part of the system. In examining the unique aspects of this unceasing change, one realizes that the city of Tokyo is an incubator for new forms of architecture and architectural theories."[19]

Grain by Grain

This idea that the contemporary architecture of Japan is, indeed, metabolizing, but not in the ways foreseen by Tange, Kurokawa, and the others in the 1960s, is significant and is related to some of the very statistics laid out at the beginning of this text. The megastructures imagined by the Metabolists were a marriage between the mechanical and the organic, at a very large scale, a way, they thought, of dealing with Japanese society's inherent density and exposure to natural risk. Instead, today's Japanese architects are changing the city and the country grain by grain, with small

projects, often closer to nature and also to the country's ancient traditions. This does not mean that Japanese architecture has become less inventive, quite the contrary actually, but it is symptomatic of an aging society under constant threat, as the Fukushima disaster made clear. This is the new Metabolism, grain by grain, not such a brave new world, but one that responds to economic stagnation, a shrinking population, and disasters made worse by the failure of mechanical systems like the nuclear reactors that Japan relies on. Whether it be this younger generation that has yet to attain international fame, or in established figures ranging from Tadao Ando to Kazuyo Sejima, Japanese architecture has vanquished the difficulties it once faced in finding the appropriate juncture between national tradition and international modernity. As it happens, a good part of Japanese tradition, like the one exemplified at Katsura, has provided a way of approaching the link between past, present, and future that has eluded many Western architects. Accepting ambiguity, as seen in the evanescent reflections of Sejima's Kanazawa Museum, or constant change and the threat of catastrophe, is a key to understanding and appreciating what makes Japanese architecture different from that of Europe or America; but today ideas travel quickly. Delving into ancient traditions and open to the most contemporary thought and technical capacities, the Japanese are a force to be reckoned with in contemporary architecture.

1 https://www.cia.gov/library/publications/the-world-factbook/fields/343rank.html#JA accessed May 10, 2020.
2 https://www.cia.gov/library/publications/the-world-factbook/geos/ja.html accessed May 10, 2020.
3 Jonathan Abbamonte, "Japanese Government Says Shrinking Population Is the 'Biggest Challenge' for Economic Growth," Population Research Institute, October 24, 2017. https://www.pop.org/japanese-government-calls-population-shrinkage-biggest-challenge-economic-growth/ accessed May 10, 2020.
4 http://www.metro.tokyo.jp/english/about/history/history03.html accessed May 10, 2020.
5 https://www.cia.gov/library/publications/the-world-factbook/geos/ja.html accessed May 10, 2020.
6 Daisuke Kikuchi, "Japan Marks Seventh Anniversary of 3/11 with Moment of Silence," Japan Times, March 11, 2018. https://www.japantimes.co.jp/news/2018/03/11/national/japan-marks-seven-years-since-devastating-3-11-disasters/#.XBig7S2ZPhM accessed May 10, 2020.
7 Louis George Kittaka, "New Buildings can Take the Sunshine Out of Life," Japan Times, August 24, 2014. https://www.japantimes.co.jp/community/2014/08/24/how-tos/new-buildings-can-take-sunshine-life/#.XBd8Ty2ZPhM accessed May 10, 2020.
8 Arata Isozaki in conversation with the author Tokyo, April 1, 1996.
9 Idem.
10 Lionel Barber, "A Deeper Transformation," The Financial Times, April 10, 1996.
11 William Coaldrake, "Order and Anarchy: Tokyo from 1868 to the Present," in Tokyo, Form and Spirit, M. Friedman (ed.), Walker Art Center, Harry N. Abrams, New York, 1986.
12 Frank Lloyd Wright, An Autobiography, Duell, Sloan and Pearce, New York, 1943.
13 Arata Isozaki, "Katsura: A Model for Post-Modern Architecture," in Katsura Villa: Space and Form, A. Isozaki (ed.), Iwanami Shoten Publishers, Tokyo, 1983.
14 Jun'ichirō Tanizaki, In Praise of Shadows, trans. Thomas Harper and Edward Seidensticker, Leete's Island Books, Stony Creek, CT, 1977.
15 https://www.pritzkerprize.com/sites/default/files/inline-files/Fumihiko_Maki_Essay_1987_Tange.pdf accessed May 10, 2020.
16 Rem Koolhaas, Hans Ulrich Obrist, Project Japan: Metabolism Talks, Taschen, Cologne, 2011.
17 Tadao Ando, https://www.pritzkerprize.com/sites/default/files/inline-files/Tadao_Ando_Acceptance_Speech_1995.pdf accessed May 10, 2020.
18 Toyo Ito, "Postscript," in Rem Koolhaas, Hans Ulrich Obrist, Project Japan: Metabolism Talks, Taschen, Cologne, 2011.
19 Koh Kitayama, Yoshiharu Tsukamoto, Ryue Nishizawa, Tokyo Metabolizing, Toto Publishing, Tokyo, 2010.

JAPAN METABOLIZING

Schon seit Langem zählt Japan zu den architektonisch innovativsten Ländern der Welt. Nicht weniger als sieben japanische Architektinnen und Architekten wurden mit dem Pritzker-Preis ausgezeichnet. Persönlichkeiten wie Tadao Ando sind weltbekannt. Zurückzuführen ist die Originalität der japanischen Architektur auf ihre Entstehungsbedingungen. Das Land hat eine hohe Bevölkerungsdichte, verfügt über eine moderne und effiziente Wirtschaft, blickt auf eine lange und reiche Geschichte zurück und wird immer wieder aufs Neue von Erdbeben erschüttert. Das stagnierende Wirtschaftswachstum, die immer älter werdende Bevölkerung und die Katastrophe von Fukushima haben die Arbeitsbedingungen japanischer Architekten zusätzlich erschwert. Aber das Land stellt sich diesen Herausforderungen wie eh und je mit Verve und Erfindungsreichtum. Anders als früher wird heute eher klein, umweltverträglich und kostengünstig gebaut. Im Vergleich zu den 1960er-Jahren, als Japans Architekten zum ersten Mal die internationale Bühne betraten und mit ihren Arbeiten den Weg in eine neue Welt beschritten, werden an die Architektur heute andere Erwartungen gestellt.

Die ultimative Metropole

Es dürfte kaum einen Touristen geben, der von der Lebendigkeit und räumlichen Verdichtung Japans nicht beeindruckt ist, vor allem in den Großstädten Tokio und Osaka. Wer die Gegenwart und Zukunft japanischen Bauens verstehen will, muss sich die Zahlen des Landes vor Augen führen: Japan ist unwesentlich kleiner als Kalifornien, hat aber eine ungleich größere Einwohnerzahl: Laut einer im Juli 2018 erhobenen Schätzung leben hier 126,2 Millionen

größeren Nationen und liegt damit knapp vor Deutschland.[1] Das Bevölkerungswachstum ist rückläufig (-0,24 %; 2018). Die Geburtenrate liegt im weltweiten Vergleich auf Platz 223 (7,5 Geburten pro 1000 Einwohner; 2018).[2] Das heißt, die Bevölkerung altert rapide. Laut einer 2017 erhobenen Schätzung des japanischen Ministeriums für Gesundheit, Arbeit und Soziales wird die Bevölkerungszahl bis 2060 auf 87 Millionen gesunken sein.[3] Die Metropolregion Tokio ist der größte Ballungsraum der Welt. Zählt man die Präfekturen Kanagawa, Saitama und Chiba in der Peripherie dieses Gebiets hinzu, leben allein hier 37,5 Millionen Menschen. Der Kernbereich der Metropolregion, die Stadt Tokio selbst, nimmt zwar nur 0,6 % der Gesamtfläche Japans ein, trotzdem sind hier 13,5 Millionen Menschen zu Hause, was einer Bevölkerungsdichte von 6158 Einwohner/km² entspricht (Stand: 1. Oktober 2015).[4] Ein Großteil der Ostküste zwischen Tokio und Osaka ist nahezu lückenlos erschlossen, während es im Westen noch bergige, weniger dicht besiedelte Gebiete gibt. Um also Japans Architektur zu fassen, muss man diese Zahlen, vor allem aber die außerordentliche räumliche Verdichtung und Urbanisierung des Landes im Blick haben; 2018 lebten 91,6 % der Gesamtbevölkerung Japans in Städten.[5] Die Japaner sind an beengte Verhältnisse gewöhnt.

Katastrophe und Wandel

Ein weiterer wichtiger Aspekt für das Verständnis japanischer Architektur ist die Katastrophengeschichte des Landes. Das Erscheinungsbild Tokios beispielsweise ist einer Reihe desaströser Ereignisse geschuldet. Das erste seiner Art im 20. Jahrhundert war das Große

forderte es 200 000 Menschenleben und machte 64 % der Überlebenden obdachlos. Zwischen März und Mai 1945 wurden Brandbomben auf die Stadt abgeworfen, die noch zerstörerischer wirkten als das Erdbeben. Innerhalb dieser drei Monate starben mehr Menschen als unmittelbar nach dem Atombombenabwurf auf Hiroshima. Die Bevölkerungszahl Tokios, die 1942 noch bei 6,9 Millionen gelegen hatte, fiel aufgrund zahlreicher Todesfälle und einer Abwanderungswelle bis September 1945 auf 2,7 Millionen. Für eine überwiegend in Holzbauweise errichtete Stadt waren die Brandbomben verheerend. Die größte Stadt der Welt musste nach 1945 im Grunde komplett neu aufgebaut werden. Anfangs waren die Mittel begrenzt. Nicht anders als im kriegszerstörten Europa musste auch in Tokio schnell und billig gebaut werden. In jüngerer Vergangenheit dagegen hat sich eine kommerzielle Logik Bahn gebrochen, die mit gewachsenen ästhetischen Werten wenig gemein hat. Tokio wurde von schlechter Architektur geradezu überschwemmt. In gewisser Weise handelt es sich hierbei um die zweite menschengemachte Großkatastrophe in der jüngeren Geschichte der Stadt. Zudem haben Naturkatastrophen wie das Tohoku-Erdbeben vom 11. März 2011, das 20 000 Tote und Vermisste forderte, sowie zahlreiche Menschen obdachlos machte (bis heute sind 73 000 ohne Zuhause[6]), dafür gesorgt, dass die gesellschaftliche Bedeutung von Architektur von Grund auf neu gedacht werden musste. Nichts ist gewiss in Japan – nur die Veränderung.

Ein unendliches Durcheinander

Vor allem auf westliche Besucher wirkt Tokio auf den ersten Blick wie ein endloses Durch-

die zu dieser Zeit entstanden, ästhetisch wenig anspruchsvoll, aber es gab auch junge und äußerst talentierte Architekten, die ihre Träume oder die Träume ihrer Auftraggeber verwirklichten. Eines dieser Projekte, Phillippe Starcks Restaurant La Flamme d'Or für den Asahi-Brauereikonzern (Sumida, Tokio, 1989), fiel als PR-Maßnahme eines größeren Unternehmens seinerzeit durchaus nicht aus dem Rahmen. Das Verlangen der Japaner nach neuer Architektur führte neben den Franzosen Starck und Christian de Portzamparc auch die US-Amerikaner Steven Holl und Peter Eisenman, den Italiener Aldo Rossi und viele weitere Ausländer nach Japan. Japanische Millionäre und Unternehmen zahlten auf Auktionen in New York und London Rekordpreise für impressionistische und spätimpressionistische Gemälde und verblüfften damit die Kunstwelt. In Japan schossen Museumsneubauten aus dem Boden wie Pilze, und nicht selten waren es überaus begabte Architekten, die von privater oder öffentlicher Hand beauftragt wurden. Obwohl es die exzessiven Immobilienspekulationen jener Zeit gewesen sind, die den Grundstein für die Wirtschaftskrise gelegt haben, erwiesen sich die Jahre, bevor die Blase schließlich platzte, in architektonischer Hinsicht als äußerst fruchtbar. Es gab Geld und Auftraggeber im Überfluss. Der hohe bautechnologische Standard machte einige der innovativsten und interessantesten Projekte möglich. Aber irgendwann hatte die Euphorie ein Ende. Arata Isozaki, einer der führenden Architekten Japans und Gewinner des Pritzker-Preises 2019, sagte 1996: „Die Rezession nahm 1991 ihren Anfang. ‚Die Blase platzt‘, hieß es damals bei uns. Zuerst haben die privaten Bauunternehmer ihre Tätigkeit eingestellt, weswegen keine ausgefallenen Projekte mehr realisiert wurden. Da aber weiterhin Steuereinnahmen flossen, hatte die öffentliche

Hand noch Geld zu vergeben. Trotz des Wegfalls privater Investoren konnten Architekten also auf einen verlässlichen Auftraggeber setzen. Ab 1995 wurden auch die Behörden neuen Bauprojekten gegenüber eher skeptisch. Allerdings waren einige Regierungsvertreter davon überzeugt, dass man Japan nur aus der Rezession herausführen könne, indem man weitere Bauprojekte förderte. Vor allem der Wohnungsbau profitierte von diesem Trend. Im Kultursektor nahm die Bauaktivität dagegen allmählich ab, weil in den Jahren vor der Krise bereits Theater und Konzertsäle gebaut worden waren. Diese Entwicklung scheint jetzt an ihr Ende gekommen zu sein. In jüngster Zeit gibt es allerdings einen Trend zum Neubau von Sportstadien.“[8] Arata Isozaki ist nicht nur ein bemerkenswerter Architekt, er hat auch Sinn für Humor. Die Auswirkungen der Krise auf die Architektur in seinem Land fasste er wie folgt zusammen: „keine schrulligen kleinen Häuser mehr“ und „keine *gaijins* mehr“.[9] *Gaijin* ist eine abwertende Bezeichnung für Ausländer, die die vergleichsweise homogene japanische Bevölkerung nicht uneingeschränkt schätzt. Isozaki bewies damals große Weitsicht. Noch heute sind Architekten aus dem Ausland, auch die berühmten unter ihnen, nur selten in Japan anzutreffen.

Die verlorene Generation

Ab 1994 begann sich die japanische Wirtschaft allmählich zu erholen, mit einem bescheidenen Wachstum von 0,6 Prozent. Aber die triumphalen 1980er-Jahre waren vorbei, und die kollektive Selbstgewissheit war Gefühlen der Unsicherheit gewichen. Lionel Barber formulierte es 1996 in der Financial Times so: „[...] Ein flüchtiger Blick auf die japanische Gesellschaft genügt, und man versteht, dass alles auf einen tiefgreifenden politischen und

Isē d
in 4

Opp

Opp
Islar
vers.

wirtschaftlichen Wandel hindeutet […]. Die japanischen Verhältnisse ‚normalisieren' sich. Nicht anders als die Amerikaner und Europäer, die unter unsicheren Arbeitsplätzen und wirtschaftlichen Verwerfungen zu leiden haben, müssen sich nun auch die Japaner an den globalen Wettbewerb anpassen. Die Zahl der Arbeitslosen steigt. Die Bevölkerung altert. Zum ersten Mal seit 1945 sind die Wachstumsaussichten ungewiss. Freundlich ausgedrückt: Der Wohlstand stagniert. Aber der Pessimismus ist nur in Teilen gerechtfertigt und Folge eines beinahe fünfjährigen Nullwachstums nach dem Platzen der Blase … Der Absturz hat wehgetan."[10] Die Krise zog langfristige Folge nach sich: Die zwei Jahrzehnte zwischen 1990 und 2010 werden oft als die „zwei verlorenen Dekaden" bezeichnet *(ushinawareta nijūnen)* und waren durch ein sinkendes Bruttoinlandsprodukt und sinkende Löhne gekennzeichnet. Die Tatsache, dass zwischen 2007 und 2009 auf die japanische eine globale Wirtschaftskrise folgte, hat zu einer nach wie vor bestehenden Abneigung gegen unkonventionelle zeitgenössische Architektur beigetragen. Die Aufmerksamkeit für Kostenfaktoren und ein grundlegender ästhetischer Konservatismus sind seither die Regel.

Europäischer Stil

Die Herausbildung einer modernen japanischen Architektursprache ist als Ausdruck der Emanzipation von westlichen Einflüssen zu verstehen. Als der amerikanische Marineoffizier Matthew Perry 1853 im Rahmen der von ihm geleiteten Japan-Expedition Edo besichtigte, wie Tokio damals hieß, blickte er auf eine „weite Ebene vor einer prächtigen Wald- und Bergkulisse". Japan hatte sich in den 220 Jahren vor der Perry-Expedition vom Rest der

Welt abgeschottet. Die weitreichenden Auswirkungen der Expedition sind vielfach analysiert worden. Ohne sie wäre 1872 der britische Architekt und Ingenieur Thomas Waters (1842–1898) von der Meiji-Regierung nicht damit beauftragt worden, den Sektor südöstlich des Kaiserpalasts wiederaufzubauen, der im selben Jahr durch ein Feuer zerstört worden war. Waters ließ entlang einer breiten Allee klassizistische Backsteingebäude, die Vorläufer der modernen *Ginza*-Viertel, errichten. Josiah Conder (1852–1920), ebenfalls Engländer, entwarf zahlreiche Backsteingebäude im Stil des Second Empire, die zum Inbegriff des japanischen Establishments wurden, darunter das Nationalmuseum im Ueno-Park (1882). Darüber hinaus beauftragten die Kabinettsminister zwei Deutsche, Hermann Ende (1829–1907) und Wilhelm Böckmann (1832–1902), mit dem Entwurf eines Parlamentsgebäudes. Der Entwurf im preußischen Stil, der auf dem Dach mit einer pagodenartigen Konstruktion abschloss, sollte die japanische mit der westlichen Tradition versöhnen, stieß allerdings auf breiten Widerstand.[11]

Der vielleicht erste Architekt aus dem Westen, der Japan in architektonischer Hinsicht maßgeblich prägen sollte, war Frank Lloyd Wright (1867–1959). Wright arbeitete zwischen 1916 und 1922 am Imperial Hotel in Tokio. „Auf die erste, acht Fuß dicke Erdschicht folgten sechzig bis siebzig Fuß weichen Lehms, was eine glückliche Fügung war, taugte dieser doch dazu, heftige Erdstöße abzufedern. Warum nicht das Gebäude auf ihm schwimmen lassen? Ein Schlachtschiff, das auf dem Meereswasser schwimmt."[12] Der exzentrische Bau überstand das verheerende Erdbeben von 1923 und trug über Japans Grenzen hinaus zu Wrights gutem Ruf bei. Er wurde

Trac

Am
Arch
buch
der
Auss
liche
Näh
tung
Wäh
Einf
Expe
zu e
nen
des
mit e
ten
nann
sich
eben
rukti
nach
an s
in de
Best
verk
die E
hing
Arch
Deut
besi
„Ern
ren.
krieg
wanc
und
desh
fasc
Zwec
Im Ja

Werk *Lob des Schattens*, in dem es über die Besonderheit der japanischen Architektur heißt: „[...] ohne Zweifel wären auch für die Japaner helle Räume bequemer gewesen als dunkle. Das, was man als schön bezeichnet, entsteht in der Regel aus der Praxis des täglichen Lebens heraus. So entdeckten unsere Vorfahren, die wohl oder übel in dunklen Räumen wohnen mußten, irgendwann die dem Schatten innewohnende Schönheit, und sie verstanden es schließlich sogar, den Schatten einem ästhetischen Zweck dienstbar zu machen."[14] Diese Philosophie und Bruno Tauts Überzeugung, in der Katsura-Residenz die „Moderne" erkannt zu haben, sind grundlegend für die zeitgenössische japanische Architektur, die sich westliche Einflüsse zu eigen gemacht hat und auf einer tieferen Ebene der Tradition verbunden geblieben ist. Frank Lloyd Wright war natürlich nicht der einzige westliche Architekt, dessen Schaffen sich unmittelbar auf die moderne japanische Architektur ausgewirkt hat. Auch Le Corbusier (1887–1995) war in Japan präsent, beispielsweise durch sein Nationalmuseum für westliche Kunst im Ueno-Park (1959). Nach wie vor zeigen sich viele japanische Architekten von ihm fasziniert. Kunio Maekawa (1905–1986) wiederum arbeitete von 1928 bis 1930 im französischen Atelier von Le Corbusier, bevor er 1935 in Tokio sein eigenes Büro gründete. Er übernahm die Bauaufsicht über das Nationalmuseum und entwarf 1979 einen Anbau, der Le Corbusiers Bedeutung für Japan symbolisch bekräftigte.
Nach dem Krieg machten japanische Architekten die Entdeckung – allen voran Kenzo Tange (1913–2005), der Ende der 1930er-Jahre für Kunio Maekawa arbeitete –, dass sich der Gegenwart mithilfe der Tradition neues Leben einhauchen ließ. Mit Tanges Nationaler Sporthalle Yoyogi nahm eine spezifisch japanische

Moderne ihren Anfang, die sich mit der westlichen Moderne durchaus messen kann. Fumihiko Maki: „Die Nationale Sporthalle, die für die Olympischen Sommerspiele 1964 in Tokio gebaut wurde, ist ein herausragendes Ergebnis modernster bautechnischer Verfahren und zeichnet sich durch eine kühne und originelle räumliche Konzeption aus."[15] Tange, der 2005 starb, entwarf auch das Friedensmuseum in Hiroshima, das an die schrecklichen Folgen des Atombombenabwurfs der Amerikaner erinnert. Seine Arbeiten gelten nach wie vor als Inbegriff moderner japanischer Architektur – auch wenn sein Spätwerk, so zum Beispiel das Regierungsgebäude der Präfektur Tokio (1991), ein 243 m hoher Doppelturm, der im Stadtteil Shinjuku ganze drei Straßenzüge einnimmt, in den Augen vieler Menschen die Maßlosigkeit der Jahre vor der großen Krise symbolisiert.

Schwimmende Städte und Kapseltürme

Aus Kenzo Tanges Büro sind einige der führenden Architekten Japans hervorgegangen, darunter Arata Isozaki (geb. 1931) und Yoshio Taniguchi (geb. 1937). Fumihiko Maki (geb. 1928) und Kisho Kurokawa (1934–2007) wiederum studierten an der Universität Tokio unter Tange. Maki, Kurokawa und Kiyonori Kikutake (1928–2011) veröffentlichten 1960 anlässlich der World Design Conference (WoDeCo) in Tokio gemeinsam mit einer Reihe weiterer Architekten das Manifest *Metabolism: The Proposals for a New Urbanism*. Im Rahmen der Konferenz stellte Kenzo Tange seinen *Plan for Tokyo 1960* vor. Die Metabolisten kamen aus dem Umkreis von Tanges MIT-Studio, dachten biologische Wachstumsprozesse und architektonische Megastrukturen zusammen und imaginierten schwimmende Städte und „Kapseltürme". Die metabolische Bewegung

lässt sich als Antwort auf die menschliche und ökologische Katastrophe des Krieges einerseits und die Anfälligkeit Japans für Naturkatastrophen andererseits verstehen. Ihre Vertreter verstanden Architektur als Mittel zur Transformation der japanischen Gesellschaft durch die Entwicklung widerstands- und anpassungsfähiger raumorganisatorischer Muster. Trotz eines technisch geleiteten Architekturverständnisses ging es den Metabolisten um eine quasi-biologische Erneuerungsfähigkeit von Architektur. So einflussreich die Bewegung auch war, sehr viele Bauwerke hat sie nicht hervorgebracht. Zu nennen sind vor allem der Nakagin Capsule Tower von Kurokawa, erbaut 1972 in nur 30 Tagen (Shimbashi, Tokio), und das Yamanashi Broadcasting and Press Center (Kofu, Yamanashi, 1966), mit dem Kenzo Tange sein Konzept für erweiterbare Architektur verwirklichte. Ihren wichtigsten und zugleich letzten bedeutenden Auftritt hatten die Metabolisten im Rahmen der Weltausstellung 1970 in Osaka, die unter dem Motto „Fortschritt und Harmonie für die Menschheit" auf Grundlage eines Masterplans von Kenzo Tange und dem Marxisten Uzo Nishiyama (1911–1994) stattfand. Tange entwarf den Hauptpavillon (die sogenannte Festival Plaza) und Kikutake den Expo Tower, Kurokawa realisierte zwei Pavillons und konzipierte in Zusammenarbeit mit Maki die experimentellen Kapsel-Konstruktionen auf dem Dach der Plaza. Isozaki schuf zwei gigantische Roboter.

Buddhistische Überlegungen und schintoistische Traditionen

Eine Zeit lang galt den innovativen Entwürfen der Metabolisten, die in dem Bewusstsein um die traumatische Kriegsvergangenheit, die allgegenwärtige Erdbebengefahr und die hohe Bevölkerungsdichte des Landes entstanden

wurde, einer von sechs oder sieben japanischen „Stararchitekten", die weltweit Projekte
realisierten. Sein Museum of Contemporary
Art in Los Angeles (1986) war einer der ersten
US-amerikanischen Museumsneubauten, die
von einem Architekten aus dem Ausland entworfen wurden. Taniguchis Erweiterung des
Museum of Modern Art in New York (2004) wiederum hat deutlich gemacht, dass japanische
Architekten inzwischen auch willkommen sind,
an die „Heiligen Hallen" des globalen Kunst-
betriebs Hand anzulegen. In der Generation
von Isozaki und Taniguchi gehörte Fumihiko
Maki ebenfalls zu den Metabolisten und ist
inzwischen ein Architekt von Weltrang. Zu seinen jüngsten Projekten zählen das 4 World
Trade Center in New York (Seite 260) sowie
mehrere Gebäude für das Aga Khan Development Network in Kanada. Maki, der 1993 mit
dem Pritzker-Preis ausgezeichnet wurde,
erhielt seine Ausbildung zum Teil in den Vereinigten Staaten, wie auch Taniguchi. Maki
spricht fließend Englisch, was nicht für alle
großen Architekten Japans gilt.

Tadao Ando und Toyo Ito

Bis heute haben sieben japanische Architektinnen und Architekten den Pritzker-Preis ent-
gegengenommen. Sie repräsentieren das Ansehen und die Innovationsfähigkeit der japanischen Architektur und lassen vermuten, dass
auch in Zukunft wieder japanische Architekten
mit diesem Preis ausgezeichnet werden. Hier
eine Liste in chronologischer Reihenfolge:

1. Kenzo Tange, 1987
2. Fumihiko Maki, 1993
3. Tadao Ando, 1995

5. Toyo Ito, 2013
6. Shigeru Ban, 2014
7. Arata Isozaki, 2019

Es ist Tadao Ando gewesen, der womöglich
bekannteste zeitgenössische Architekt der
Welt, der der japanischen Architektur zu unge-
ahntem internationalem Renommee verholfen
hat. Er wurde 1941 in Osaka geboren und ist
Autodidakt. Sein Wissen hat er sich vornehmlich auf Reisen in die Vereinigten Staaten sowie
nach Europa und Afrika (1962–1969) angeeignet. Er wurde 1995 mit dem Pritzker-Preis ausgezeichnet und realisierte in den letzten zwei
Jahrzehnten außer Projekten in Japan auch die
Pulitzer Foundation for the Arts in St. Louis
(Missouri, USA, 2001) und das Modern Art
Museum in Fort Worth (Texas, USA, 2002). Für
den französischen Milliardär François Pinault
hat Ando zwei venezianische Ausstellungsräume für moderne Kunst umgebaut, den Palazzo
Grassi (2006) und die Punta della Dogana
(2009). Der Plan, für denselben Auftraggeber in
Paris ein Museum für zeitgenössische Kunst zu
bauen, wurde im Frühjahr 2005 fallengelassen,
stattdessen besorgte Ando für Pinault den
Umbau der Bourse du Commerce in Les Halles
(Paris, 2021). Andos ausdrucksstarke Zeich-
nungen und seine vornehmlich in Betonbauweise realisierten Entwürfe werden seit einigen
Jahren von Architekturstudenten auf der gan-
zen Welt bewundert und imitiert. Ihm ist es ge-
lungen, die lang ersehnte Brücke zwischen Ost
und West zu schlagen und mit einem bewusst
kleingehaltenen geometrischen Formenvoka-
bular bemerkenswerte Weihestätten des Lichts
und der Stille zu erschaffen. Ando geht es in
vielen seiner Projekte nicht vordergründig darum, den Raum zu beherrschen. In seiner Dan-

Architektur koexistieren meiner Ansicht nach zwei verschiedene Dimensionen nebeneinander: Die eine betrifft rein praktische Fragen der Funktionalität, der Wirtschaftlichkeit und der Sicherheit. Diese Aspekte der Wirklichkeit können nicht ignoriert werden, denn Architektur birgt menschliches Leben. Aber ist Architektur auch dann noch Architektur, wenn sie ausschließlich auf Grundlage dieser Aspekte entsteht? Architektur ist eine Form menschlichen Ausdrucks, und sobald sie die rein praktischen Erfordernisse des Bauens hinter sich lässt und in den Bereich des Ästhetischen vordringt, wird sie zur Kunst. Mir war daran gelegen, Räume zu erschaffen, die den menschlichen Geist stimulieren, die Sinne beleben und mit der Seele Zwiesprache halten."[17]

Toyo Ito wurde im selben Jahr wie Tadao Ando geboren. Er hat vielleicht nicht die gleiche internationale Berühmtheit erlangt wie der Architekt aus Osaka, ist aber ohne Zweifel einer der führenden Architekten seiner Generation. Der Pritzker-Preis, mit dem er 2013 ausgezeichnet wurde, bestätigt dies. Im Gegensatz zu Ando, der für kompakte Entwürfe in Betonbauweise steht, hat Ito eine Vorliebe für sehr leichte Konstruktionen. Anfang der Nullerjahre realisierte er zwei Projekte, die ihm große mediale Aufmerksamkeit bescherten: Eines davon ist die Mediatheque in Sendai (2001). Dreizehn weiße Stahlröhren, die sich wie „Seetang" durch den Baukörper winden, bilden das Tragwerk des Gebäudes und umschließen die Versorgungsleitungen. Mit dieser Konstruktion hat Ito nicht nur in statischer, sondern auch in ästhetischer Hinsicht Innovatives geleistet. Sein temporärer Sommerpavillon im Londoner Kensington Park für die Serpentine Gallery (2002) war ein 309 m² großer, eingeschossiger Bau mit einer Fassade aus Aluminiumplatten und Glas. Die Idee bestand darin, einen offenen Raum ohne ortho-

schaffen, der in den Sommermonaten als Café und für Veranstaltungen genutzt werden kann. Ein aus der Rotation eines Quadrats abgeleiteter Algorithmus bestimmte die nur scheinbar willkürliche Form. Jeder Teil des Baukörpers hat eine tragende und vibrationsdämpfende Funktion, alle Elemente sind abhängig voneinander und bilden ein komplexes Ganzes. Es se ihm darum gegangen, so der Architekt, „jene Prinzipien, die Architektur im Kern bestimmen, wieder sichtbar zu machen".

Ito war, wie die meisten Japaner, von dem Tohoku-Erdbeben und dem Tsunami (2011) zutiefst betroffen. Seine Gedanken über die Bedeutung der Natur für die räumlich hoch verdichteten japanischen Städte sind aufschlussreich. Nach der Katastrophe schrieb er: „Ich werde den Eindruck nicht los, dass zwischen unseren Standards und der Realität eine tiefe Kluft besteht. Wir entwerfen wie Maschinen, auf eine völlig mechanische Art und Weise und auf Grundlage einer quantitativ und abstrakt definierten Natur. Wir setzen uns nicht damit auseinander, dass die unsteten Kräfte der Erde, des Meers und des Winds fortwährend auf unsere Umwelt einwirken. Ganz gleich, ob es sich um öffentliche oder private Architektur handelt, wir entwerfen innerhalb eines unbeweglichen und abstrakten Bezugssystems. Unsere Aufgabe besteht meiner Ansicht nach nicht zuallererst darin, die Grundlagen unserer praktischen Arbeit einer Prüfung zu unterziehen, sondern zu überdenken, auf welchen Wegen wir zu diesen Grundlagen gekommen sind. Wir müssen zuallererst unser Verhältnis zur Natur hinterfragen."[18] Man mag angesichts solcher Überlegungen an die Ursprünge der metabolistischen Bewegung denken, aber die Zeit ist nicht spurlos an Ito vorübergegangen. Er fordert eine Architektur, die, anders als die Mega-Architektur der früheren Generation,

ab, das Japan National Stadium in Tokio (in Zusammenarbeit mit der Taisei Corporation und Azuka Sekkei Co., Ltd., Seite 256). Ursprünglich hatte Zaha Hadid die Ausschreibung für sich entschieden, aber ihr Entwurf stand unter keinem guten Stern und musste neu ausgeschrieben werden. Das Stadion wurde für die Olympischen Sommerspiele in Tokio, ursprünglich für 2020 geplant, konzipiert. Durch den extensiven Einsatz japanischer Hölzer und Pflanzen ist es trotz seines Standorts inmitten der Stadt beispielgebend für schonende und naturnahe Architektur. Kumas Entwurf ist zudem wesentlich niedriger und kostengünstiger als jener von Hadid, für den eine hochkomplexe, bewegliche Dachkonstruktion vorgesehen war.

Generationswechsel

Die jüngeren japanischen Architekten beschreiten, womöglich in der Nachfolge Tanges, Isozakis und Itos, andere und alles in allem „bescheidenere" Wege. Ihre Arbeiten weisen oft mehr oder weniger deutliche Bezüge zur japanischen Tradition auf. Einer der Wegbereiter für eine ernsthafte Auseinandersetzung mit japanischen Traditionen war jedoch ein Architekt und Architekturhistoriker aus der Generation Andos und Itos: Professor Terunobu Fujimori (geb. 1946) realisierte 1991 sein erstes Projekt und erneuerte mit Arbeiten wie dem Teehaus Takasugi-an (Chino, Nagano, 2004), das auf sechs Meter hohen Pfählen errichtet

1968) wiederum haben gänzlich verschiedene Vorstellungen von der Gegenwart und der Zukunft ihrer Kunst. Masaki Endoh, der oft mit dem Ingenieur Masahiro Ikeda zusammenarbeitet, hat eine ganze Reihe ungewöhnlicher Gebäude entworfen. Die meisten seiner Projektnamen enthalten den Begriff *natural*, so auch Natural Ellipse (Shibuya, Tokio, 2002). Endo erklärt, „natürlich" in seinem Sinne sei eine „auf gesundem Menschenverstand und empirischem Wissen" basierende Architektur – und weiter: „Ich glaube, dass dem Entwurfsprozess etwas Evolutionäres eigen ist. Architektur, die neue Ideen aufgreift, wird auch in Zukunft Bestand haben. Architektur, die sich im Verlauf der Zeit nicht verändert, wird eines Tages verschwinden. Und damit sie sich weiterentwickeln kann, müssen die Standards hinterfragt werden." Takaharu und Yui Tezuka sehen das offenbar ähnlich, wie ihr Naturkundemuseum Matsunoyama (Niigata, 2003) beweist. Bei diesem Projekt handelt es sich um eine 111 m lange Röhre aus Cortenstahl, die Schneelasten von bis zu 2000 Tonnen standhält, dem Geländeverlauf folgt und über einen Aussichtsturm verfügt. Besucher können hier „das Licht und die Farben des Schnees auf verschiedenen Höhenniveaus erleben – in vier Metern Tiefe oder in dreißig Metern Höhe".

Hiroshi Sambuichi ist in diesem Band mit zwei Projekten vertreten, dem Aussichtspunkt Miyajima Misen (Miyajima, Hiroshima, 2013, Seite 338) und der Naoshima-Halle (Naoshi-

Jünger und näher an der Natur

Die Arbeiten der Architekten, die i[n den] 1970er-Jahren geboren wurden[, zeugen von] großer Innovationskraft. In ihnen z[eichnet sich] ein noch deutlicherer Bruch mit de[n großen] Architekten wie Le Corbusier ab, z[ugunsten] unverkennbar japanischer Lösung[en. Diese] allerdings sind durch eine so allge[meingültige] Formensprache gekennzeichnet, [dass sie] in den unterschiedlichsten Archite[kturen] Akzeptanz und Zustimmung finde[n. Die be-] kanntesten Vertreter dieser Gener[ation sind] Sou Fujimoto (geb. 1971) und Juny[a Ishigami] (geb. 1974). Vor allem Ishigami will [die Natur] nicht nur oberflächlich in sein Wer[k einbezie-] hen, sondern nach einer „Natur je[nseits der] Natur", nach „einer noch nie zuvo[r gesehenen] Natur" suchen. An den beiden hie[r vorgestell-] ten Arbeiten Botanical Garden Art [Biotop/] Water Garden (Nasu, Tochigi, 2018[, Seite 322)] und dem Sommerpavillon der Ser[pentine] Gallery (Kensington Gardens, Lon[don, 2019,] Seite 204) wird dies sehr deutlich. [Seine Pro-] jekte bewegen sich an der Grenze [dessen,] was gemeinhin als Architektur ang[esehen] wird. Der außergewöhnliche Wass[ergarten mit] seinen vielen Pflanzen und Bäume[n, die ei-] nen naturwüchsigen Eindruck, wu[rde von] Ishigami entworfen. Seinem House [& Restau-] rant (Yamaguchi, 2016–), ein weite[res einzigar-] tiges Projekt, liegt ein Betongießv[erfahren zu-] Grunde, das eine „naturhaft" wirke[nde, aber] wohl künstliche Form entstehen lä[sst.]

Opposite: *Fumihiko Maki, Spiral Building, Tokyo, 1985.*

Fumihiko Maki, renovated Tokyo Metropolitan Gymnasium, Sendagaya, Tokyo, 1990.

Following double page: *Kiyonori Kikutake, Tokyo Edo Museum, Tokyo, 1993.*

Projekte. Sein öffentliches WC in Ichihara (Chiba, Japan, 2012) stellt architektonische Grundannahmen infrage. So notwendig öffentliche Toiletten auch sein mögen, architektonisch lassen sie oft zu wünschen übrig. In einer Region Japans, die für ihre reizvolle Landschaft bekannt ist, umzäunte Fujimoto unweit eines Bahnhofs eine Fläche von 209 m² mit einem Holzzaun und platzierte darin eine einzelne gläserne WC-Kabine. Der Architekt: „Das komplexe Divergieren verschiedener Innen- und Außengrenzen lässt Öffentlichkeit und Privatheit, Offenheit und Geschütztheit, Natur und Architektur, sowie Groß und Klein miteinander verschmelzen und unter Beibehaltung ihrer Ambivalenzen bestehen." Die Japaner schenken ihren Sanitäreinrichtungen außerordentlich viel Beachtung, die Produkte von Firmen wie Toto zeigen dies deutlich. Und doch überrascht die Idee, ein öffentliches WC in einem umzäunten Garten zu platzieren, zumal es sich nicht um eine temporäre Installation handelt. An einer ebensolchen hat sich Fujimoto im Jahr 2013 mit dem Londoner Serpentine Gallery Pavilion versucht, der üblicherweise unweit des georgianischen Domizils der Galerie in Kensington Gardens errichtet wird. Die Liste der Architekten, die den Serpentine Pavilion in den vergangenen Jahren entworfen haben, liest sich wie ein Who's who der zeitgenössischen Architektur. Während SANAA und Herzog & de Meuron sehr offene Pavillons konzipierten, ging Fujimoto die Aufgabe völlig anders an. Er schuf ein Gitterobjekt, bestehend aus 20 mm dünnen weißen Stahlkantprofilen. Fujimoto wollte die Besucher seines Entwurfs, in dem ein Café untergebracht war, dazu einladen, umgeben von der grünen Parklandschaft über die Umwelt nachzudenken. Der Architekt: „Die Frage, wodurch sich Architektur und Natur voneinander unterscheiden und wie Architektur ein Teil der Natur

werden oder mit ihr verschmelzen könnte, ist grundlegend … Wo verläuft die Grenze zwischen der Natur und künstlichen Objekten?"

In die Unendlichkeit des Raums

Tsuyoshi Tane (geb. 1979) ist weniger bekannt als Ishigami und Fujimoto. Er hat von der Tokioter Architekturszene bewusst Abstand genommen und sein Büro in Paris eröffnet. Zusammen mit Dorell.Gotmeh.Tane / Architects, einem von Tane mitbegründeten Büro, entwarf er das Estnische Nationalmuseum (Tartu, 2016). Er hatte die ungewöhnliche Idee, das Dach des auf einem stillgelegten Flugfeld aus der Sowjetzeit errichteten Museums „in die ‚Unendlichkeit des Raums'" streben zu lassen. Tane war auch in Japan tätig und gilt als einer der vielversprechendsten Architekten seiner Generation. Sein Todoroki House in Valley (Setagaya, Tokio, 2018, Seite 412) liegt in einem engen bewaldeten Tal inmitten der Stadt und ist mit 188 m² Wohnfläche nicht allzu groß. Obwohl es sich in einem sehr verdichteten urbanen Umfeld befindet, bietet es acht verschiedene Sichtachsen auf seine unvermutete Umgebung.

Wellblech und Sperrholz

Ein weiterer japanischer Architekt der jüngeren Generation ist Takashi Suo (geb. 1980). Seine 188 m² große Zahnarztpraxis Ishihara (Okayama, 2017, Seite 406) kann als repräsentativ für die aktuelle japanische Architektur angesehen werden. Sie wurde für ein überschaubares Budget von 480 000 Euro auf einem straßenseitigen Grundstück errichtet und macht zunächst, wie viele Häuser im urbanen und periurbanen Japan, einen regellosen Eindruck. Der Architekt: „Das Projekt wirkt wie das Ergebnis eines anorganischen und

chaotischen Planungsprozesses, tatsächlich aber steht es im Einklang mit seiner Umgebung." Die Praxis basiert auf einem intelligenten und originellen Entwurf, sie besteht vor allem aus Wellblech und Sperrholz und gewährt Patienten durch die leicht versetzten Baukörper eine gewisse Privatsphäre. So wie das Gebäude seine städtische Umgebung formal in sich aufnimmt, ist es auf eine geradezu singuläre Art und Weise japanisch. Das kostengünstige Bauprojekt beweist, dass zeitgenössische japanische Architektur über die Beschränkungen, die enge Städte, kulturelle Umwälzungen und eine alternde Gesellschaft mit sich bringen, erhaben ist. Es ist kein Zufall, dass die vielversprechenden jüngeren Architekten Japans so kleine und erfinderische Projekte entwerfen, schließlich müssen die verschiedensten Aspekte berücksichtigt werden: die Knappheit kommunalen Baulands, die Bestimmung, dass zwei Gebäude keine tragende Wand teilen dürfen, die stagnierende Wirtschaft, die allgemeine Zukunftsunsicherheit und die Sehnsucht nach mehr Natur, wo diese rar geworden ist.

Das heißt natürlich nicht, dass es in Tokio aktuell keine Großbaustellen gibt. Kengo Kumas neues Nationalstadion, das 80 000 Menschen Platz bieten wird, ist eine davon. Das Gesicht der Stadt hat sich im Vorfeld der geplanten Olympischen Sommerspiele 2020 jedoch auch an anderer Stelle verändert. So erfährt beispielsweise das Areal um den Bahnhof Shibuya eine weitreichende Umgestaltung, einschließlich mehrerer Hochhausneubauten, die unter anderem von SANAA und Kengo Kuma entworfen wurden. Projekte dieser Art gehen auf Großunternehmen wie die Tokyu Land Corporation oder Nikken Sekkei zurück und sind Ausdruck eines allgemeinen Trends zu höheren Gebäuden in der japanischen Hauptstadt. Da Bauvorhaben, die in das

Fumihiko Maki, 4 World Trade Center, New York, USA, 2013.

Opposite: Hiroshi Hara, Umeda Sky City, Osaka, 1993.

komplexe Verkehrssystem der Stadt einge-bunden werden müssen, die Expertise einzel-ner Architekten übersteigen, ist auch das neue Nationalstadion nicht die Arbeit von Kengo Kuma allein, sondern die eines Konsor-tiums, bestehend aus der Taisei Corporation, der Azusa Sekkei Co., Ltd. sowie Kengo Kuma & Associates.

Dem Erdboden näher und dennoch originell sind zwei eher kleine und weniger kosten-intensive Projekte, die Jo Nagasaka (geb. 1971) mit seinem Büro Schemata realisiert hat – zum einen der Umbau eines Hauses in Sangenjaya (Setagaya, Tokio, 2017, Seite 286) und zum anderen das Kapsel- und Saunahotel °C (Do-C) Ebisu (Ebisu, Shibuya, Tokio, 2017, Seite 294), ebenfalls ein Umbau. Nagasaka macht sich moderne Architektur zu eigen und ringt ihr neue Räume und Nutzungsmöglichkeiten ab. Dies ist kein Projekt, das durch seine Neuar-tigkeit besticht, wie die vor der Krise entstan-dene Architektur im Manga-Stil, sondern das Resultat eines Umnutzungskonzepts, das auf Bescheidenheit setzt.

Unaufhörlicher Wandel

Die hier versammelten Architektinnen und Architekten und viele ihrer Kolleginnen und Kollegen streben unaufhörlich nach neuen For-men des Ausdrucks. Auch die elementarste architektonische Gestaltungseinheit, das Wohnhaus, wird hierbei zum Gegenstand der Erneuerung. Böden, Wände und Decken wer-den über ihre grundlegenden Funktionen hinausgedacht, damit Raum entsteht für die Bewohner moderner, dicht bevölkerter Städte. Tokio wurde oft als Ort angesehen, der die Zukunft vieler Großstädte vorwegnimmt, in denen ohne architektonischen Erfindungs-reichtum der Prozess räumlicher Verdichtung schlicht nicht zu bewältigen sein wird.

Koh Kitayama, Kurator des japanischen Pavil-lons der Architekturbiennale Venedig von 2010, schreibt in *Tokyo Metabolizing*: „Im Gegensatz zu europäischen Städten mit ihren durch-gehenden Häuserfassaden besteht Tokio aus einer Ansammlung freistehender Gebäude (*grains*). Anders gesagt: Permanenter Wandel ist dem städtischen System inhärent. Betrach-tet man diesen einzigartigen und unaufhör-lichen Wandlungsprozess näher, wird Tokio zur Keimzelle für neue Architekturformen und Architekturtheorien."[19]

In kleinen Schritten

Die japanische Architektur der Gegenwart ist flexibel, wenn auch nicht auf die von Tange, Kurokawa und anderen Metabolisten der 1960er-Jahre imaginierte Weise. Ursächlich für diese Wandlungsfähigkeit sind gesellschaft-liche Veränderungen, die in den eingangs erwähnten Statistiken zum Ausdruck kommen. Die Megastrukturen der Metabolisten waren als Hybride konzipiert, in denen sich, als Ant-wort auf die räumliche Verdichtung und die Naturgefahren, denen die japanische Gesell-schaft ausgesetzt war und ist, das Mechani-sche und Organische verbinden. Heute sind es kleinere Projekte, mit denen die Architekten sowohl städtische als auch ländliche Räume in kleinen Schritten verändern, und nicht selten suchen sie dabei eine größere Nähe zur Natur und zu den Traditionen ihres Landes als die Metabolisten. Trotzdem mangelt es der japanischen Architektur keineswegs an Innovationskraft – das Gegenteil ist der Fall. Sie ist aber auch symptomatisch für eine Gesellschaft, die nicht nur immer älter wird, sondern – die Fukushima-Katastrophe hat es einmal mehr deutlich gemacht – in ständiger Gefahr lebt. Der Metabolismus unserer Tage träumt nicht von einer schönen neuen Welt,

sondern zeigt sich maßvoll angesichts wirt-schaftlicher Stagnation, sinkender Bevölke-rungszahlen und einer ständigen Bedrohung durch Naturkatastrophen, die noch dazu schwerwiegende Havarien an Kernkraftwerken auslösen können, von denen Japan abhängig ist. Sowohl die junge, noch weitgehend unbe-kannte Architektengeneration als auch etab-lierte Größen wie Tadao Ando und Kazuyo Sejima haben ein entscheidendes Problem der Vergangenheit überwunden: Sie haben einen Weg gefunden, die japanische Tradition mit der internationalen Moderne auf überzeu-gende Art und Weise zu verbinden. Dabei war es die Tradition selbst, die die entscheidenden Hinweise dafür geliefert hat, wie Vergangen-heit, Gegenwart und Zukunft ineinandergreifen können – die Katsura-Residenz ist hierfür ein gutes Beispiel. Möglicherweise unterscheidet sich die japanische von der europäischen und der amerikanischen Architektur im Kern durch die Fähigkeit zu akzeptieren, dass die Welt so unvorhersehbar ist wie die Spiegelungen des Lichts in Sejimas Museumsbau in Kanazwa. Durch ihre Offenheit für neue Ideen und Tech-nologien und ihre Bereitschaft, sich eingehend mit der Tradition ihres Landes auseinander-zusetzen, wird mit den Japanern, so viel ist sicher, auch in Zukunft zu rechnen sein.

Kazuyo Sejima + Ryue Nishizawa/SANAA,
21st Century Museum of Contemporary Art,
Kanazawa, Ishikawa, 2004.

Opposite: Kazuyo Seijima + Ryue Nishizawa/
SANAA, Louvre-Lens, Lens, France, 2006.

1 https://www.cia.gov/library/publications/the-world-factbook/fields/343rank.html#JA, Zugriff am 10. Mai 2020.
2 https://www.cia.gov/library/publications/the-world-factbook/geos/ja.html, Zugriff am 10. Mai 2020.
3 Jonathan Abbamonte, „Japanese Government Says Shrinking Population is the ‚Biggest Challenge‘ for Economic Growth", Population Research Institute, 24. Oktober 2017, https://www.pop.org/japanese-government-calls-population-shrinkage-biggest-challenge-economic-growth, Zugriff am 10. Mai 2020.
4 http://www.metro.tokyo.jp/english/about/history/history03.html, Zugriff am 10. Mai 2020.
5 https://www.cia.gov/library/publications/the-world-factbook/geos/ja.html, Zugriff am 10. Mai 2020.
6 Daisuke Kikuchi, „Japan Marks Seventh Anniversary of 3/11 with Moment of Silence", in: Japan Times, 11. März 2018, https://www.japantimes.co.jp/news/2018/03/11/national/japan-marks-seven-years-since-devastating-3-11-disasters/#.XBig7S2ZPhM, Zugriff am 10. Mai 2020.
7 Louis George Kittaka, „New Buildings can Take the Sunshine Out of Life", in: Japan Times, 24. August 2014, https://www.japantimes.co.jp/community/2014/08/24/how-tos/new-buildings-can-take-sunshine-life/#.XBd8Ty2ZPhM, Zugriff am 10. Mai 2020.
8 Arata Isozaki im Gespräch mit dem Autor, Tokio, 1. April 1996.
9 Ebd.
10 Lionel Barber, „A Deeper Transformation", in: The Financial Times, 10. April 1996.
11 William Coaldrake, „Order and Anarchy: Tokyo from 1868 to the Present", in: M. Friedman (Hrsg.), Tokyo, Form and Spirit, Walker Art Center, Harry N. Abrams, New York, 1986.
12 Frank Lloyd Wright, An Autobiography, Duell, Sloan & Pearce, New York, 1943.
13 Arata Isozaki, „Katsura: A Model for Post-Modern Architecture", in: A. Isozaki (Hrsg.), Katsura Villa: Space and Form, Iwanami Shoten Publishers, Tokio, 1983.
14 Jun'ichirō Tanizaki, Lob des Schattens, übersetzt von Eduard Klopfenstein, Manesse Verlag, Zürich, 1987.
15 https://www.pritzkerprize.com/sites/default/files/inline-files/Fumihiko_Maki_Essay_1987_Tange.pdf, Zugriff am 10. Mai 2020.
16 Rem Koolhaas, Hans Ulrich Obrist, Project Japan: Metabolism Talks, Taschen, Köln, 2011.
17 Tadao Ando, https://www.pritzkerprize.com/sites/default/files/inline-files/Tadao_Ando_Acceptance_Speech_1995.pdf, Zugriff am 10. Mai 2020.
18 Toyoo Ito, „Postscript", in: Rem Koolhaas, Hans Ulrich Obrist, Project Japan: Metabolism Talks, Taschen, Köln, 2011.
19 Koh Kitayama, Yoshiharu Tsukamoto, Ryue Nishizawa, Tokyo Metabolizing, Toto Publishing, Tokio, 2010.

Philip Jodidio

JAPAN METABOLIZING

L'architecture contemporaine au Japon a long-temps été l'une des plus imaginatives du monde. Pas moins de sept architectes nippons ont gagné le prix Pritzker et des personnalités comme Tadao Ando figurent parmi les bâtis-seurs les plus célèbres et admirés dans le monde entier. La créativité de l'architecture japonaise est le fruit d'un concours de cir-constances spécifiques, notamment d'une forte densité de population, d'une économie moderne et efficace, d'une longue histoire et de la succession ininterrompue de cata-clysmes sous forme de tremblements de terre. Aujourd'hui, la stagnation économique, le vieil-lissement de la population et des catastrophes comme l'accident nucléaire de Fukushima Daiichi exercent une pression plus forte que jamais sur ces circonstances à la base même de l'architecture. Comme toujours cependant, le Japon réagit avec force et inventivité, mais les bâtiments actuels sont sans aucun doute plus écologiques, plus petits et moins onéreux que leurs prédécesseurs d'une autre ère. L'heure est au rétrécissement des perspec-tives, ce qui n'était pas le cas pendant les dix années entre 1960 et 1970, lorsque le Japon a émergé sur la scène architecturale internatio-nale, ouvrant la voie vers ce qui paraissait alors un nouveau monde.

La métropole ultime

Tout visiteur, fût-il le plus désinvolte, ne peut qu'être impressionné par la vitalité et la densi-té du Japon, surtout dans les grandes villes que sont Tokyo et Osaka. En dépit de leur sé-cheresse apparente, les statistiques sont ici essentielles pour comprendre le présent et le futur de l'architecture au Japon. Légèrement plus petit que la Californie, le pays possède une population beaucoup plus importante, estimée à 126 168 millions en juillet 2018.

C'est aussi le grand pays industrialisé dont l'âge moyen de la population est le plus élevé (47,7 ans, juste devant l'Allemagne[1]). Le Japon présente même désormais un taux de crois-sance démographique négatif (-0,24 %, est. 2018), car son taux de natalité a chuté au 223e rang mondial (7,5 naissances/1 000 habitants, est. 2018[2]). Pour dire les choses clairement, la population japonaise vieillit rapidement. Ces statistiques ne sont donc pas dénuées d'une signification profonde. En 2017, le ministère japonais de la Santé, du Travail et des Affaires sociales estimait que la population japonaise déclinerait jusqu'à ne plus atteindre que 87 millions en 2060[3].

Le Grand Tokyo forme la plus grande concen-tration urbaine du monde. Avec les préfec-tures périphériques de Kanagawa, Saitama et Chiba, la population globale de Tokyo atteint pas moins de 37 468 millions d'habitants. La zone métropolitaine centrale de la ville, qui ne représente que 0,6 % de la surface totale du pays, est peuplée de 13 491 millions de personnes, soit une densité extrêmement élevée de 6158 habitants par kilomètre carré au 1er octobre 2015[4]. Une grande partie de la côte est du pays, entre Tokyo et Osaka, est presque entièrement urbanisée tandis qu'à l'Ouest, on trouve des régions plus monta-gneuses et moins densément peuplées. Ces faits, en particulier la densité urbaine du pays (91,6 % de la population totale vivait dans une zone urbaine en 2018[5]), sont importants pour comprendre l'architecture au Japon : les Japonais sont habitués à vivre entassés et à l'encombrement.

La catastrophe et le changement

Parmi les autres facteurs déterminants de l'ar-chitecture japonaise, on peut citer un senti-ment implicite de fragilité dû aux catastrophes

successives dont plusieurs, naturelles ou hu-maines, ont forgé les traits du Tokyo contem-porain. Le premier cataclysme du XX siècle est le grand tremblement de terre du Kanto de 1923, d'une magnitude de 7,9 sur l'échelle de Richter, qui a sans doute tué 200 000 per-sonnes et a laissé 64 % des survivants sans abri. Le deuxième, aux destructions encore plus radicales, ce sont les bombes incen-diaires déversées par les Américains sur la ville entre mars et mai 1945. Elles ont fait plus de morts que la dévastation instantanée d'Hiroshima. En septembre 1945, la popula-tion de Tokyo qui dépassait 6,9 millions en 1942 avait chuté à 2,777 millions du fait des morts et de l'émigration. Les engins incen-diaires jetés sur une ville constituée pour l'es-sentiel de constructions en bois ont été parti-culièrement dévastateurs. C'est pourquoi on peut affirmer que la plus grande ville du monde a été presque entièrement reconstruite après 1945. Une reconstruction qui a com-mencé avec des moyens limités – comme dans l'Europe déchirée par la guerre, il était alors essentiel de bâtir rapidement et à peu de frais. Plus récemment, une logique com-merciale implacable peu soucieuse de critères esthétiques a imposé son influence domi-nante. On peut presque dire que ce raz-de-marée d'architecture de mauvaise qualité a représenté la seconde catastrophe humaine dans l'histoire récente de Tokyo. Elle a balayé beaucoup de la beauté issue de traditions séculaires. Enfin, d'autres désastres comme le séisme du Tohoku du 11 mars 2011, d'une ma-gnitude de 9,1, qui a fait près de 20 000 morts ou disparus et 73 000 sans-abri – qui le sont toujours en 2018[6] –, ont certainement fourni l'occasion d'une réflexion approfondie sur le nouveau rôle de l'architecture et sa place dans la société. Rien n'est jamais certain au Japon, semble-t-il, sauf le changement.

La confusion sans fin

Aux yeux du visiteur occidental plus que tout autre, Tokyo paraît au premier regard dominé par un immense fouillis de fils électriques disgracieux et de petites constructions plutôt laides. Ces considérations esthétiques mises à part, deux bonnes raisons expliquent cet aspect insolite, qu'on retrouve par ailleurs dans d'autres grandes villes japonaises. L'une est l'interdiction des murs porteurs communs à deux constructions – un minuscule passage entre les parois limite naturellement le danger de réaction en chaîne après l'effondrement d'un bâtiment pendant un tremblement de terre. La deuxième raison porte le nom de *nisshōken*, ce qui signifie « le droit au soleil ». Cette pratique observée depuis longtemps au Japon exige que toute nouvelle construction ne prive pas ses voisins de plus d'une certaine quantité de lumière. Cette approche plutôt humaine se traduit par des positionnements parfois étranges des bâtiments sur les parcelles. Mais en réalité, malgré les références fréquentes aux « lois sur l'ensoleillement », la protection juridique est plutôt complexe et sans doute souvent ignorée, notamment avec les immeubles en hauteur que les villes construisent en nombre croissant[7].

L'éclatement de la bulle

Après avoir connu une croissance moyenne de 10 % par an dans les années 1960 et de 5 % par an dans les années 1970 et 1980, la formidable machine économique japonaise s'est presque totalement arrêtée en 1992 et 1993, en partie du fait de mesures de politique intérieure contradictoires visant à purger les excès de la spéculation sur les marchés boursiers et immobiliers. Les années de « bulle » qui ont précédé l'heure du bilan ont vu les prix du

foncier atteindre des sommets inimaginables au Japon. À la fin des années 1980, il se disait que le terrain du palais impérial, au Centre de Tokyo, avait une valeur marchande théorique équivalente à celle de tout Manhattan. Dans le climat de spéculation qui régnait alors, les banques ne voyaient aucune objection à prêter des sommes importantes à des taux d'intérêt extrêmement réduits pour financer l'achat et la construction de bâtiments souvent extravagants. Le Japon est ainsi devenu un immense laboratoire pour le développement de l'architecture contemporaine pendant ces années de prospérité. Bien sûr, la majorité de ces nouvelles constructions ne présentaient aucun mérite particulier sur le plan esthétique, mais dans d'autres cas, de jeunes architectes de talent ont eu la chance de transformer leurs rêves, ou ceux de leurs clients, en réalité. La construction d'une structure aussi originale que « La Flamme d'Or », le restaurant des brasseries Asahi (Sumida, Tokyo) par Philippe Starck en 1989 était alors considéré comme parfaitement raisonnable pour les relations publiques d'une grande société. La soif de nouvelle architecture des Japonais a même fait appel à des étrangers comme les Français Starck et Christian de Portzamparc, les Américains Steven Holl et Peter Eisenman, l'Italien Aldo Rossi, et bien d'autres. C'est aussi l'époque où les millionnaires japonais ou les entreprises japonaises stupéfiaient le monde de l'art en payant des prix records aux enchères de New York ou de Londres pour des peintures impressionnistes et post-impressionnistes. Une vague de constructions de musées a alors balayé l'archipel, et les clients, publics ou privés, ont souvent eu la présence d'esprit de faire appel à des architectes de talent. Malgré le caractère excessif de la spéculation immobilière qui a caractérisé cette période et les ravages qu'elle a causés à

l'économie ensuite, on est en droit d'affirmer que les années de la « bulle » ont été fructueuses pour l'architecture contemporaine au Japon. L'argent coulait à flots, les clients ne manquaient pas et la grande qualité de la construction japonaise a permis la réalisation d'une architecture parmi les plus innovantes et les plus intéressantes au monde. Mais bien sûr, cette euphorie devait prendre fin. Arata Isozaki, l'un des chefs de file de la profession au Japon et lauréat du prix Pritzker en 2019, le raconte en ces termes : « La récession a débuté en 1991. On a dit ici que la bulle éclatait. Pour commencer, l'activité privée sponsorisée par des promoteurs privés a cessé. Avec comme résultat l'arrêt des petites constructions spectaculaires. L'impôt continuait cependant de rentrer, de sorte que les pouvoirs publics avaient l'argent nécessaire à de nouveaux projets. Après le retrait du secteur privé, le secteur public est donc resté un bon client pour les architectes. En 1995, les autorités ont commencé à désavouer ces projets. Mais beaucoup de gens dans l'administration étaient alors convaincus que le seul moyen de faire sortir le Japon de la récession était de promouvoir la construction. Le logement a bénéficié de cette tendance. On ne voyait plus autant de projets culturels. Il y a eu une vague de constructions de musées d'art, qui avait commencé pendant la bulle, elle a été suivie par la construction de théâtres et de salles de concert. Il me semble que ce cycle a pris fin lui aussi. Dernièrement, la mode était aux équipements sportifs[8]. » En 1996, Arata Isozaki, dont l'immense talent architectural va de pair avec un profond sens de l'humour, a défini deux règles simples qui permettent de comprendre l'impact de la situation économique post-bulle sur l'architecture contemporaine. La première est « plus de petites constructions spectaculaires » et la deuxième « plus de *gaijins*[9] ». Le

terme japonais plutôt désobligeant de *gaijin*
désigne, bien sûr, les étrangers, qui ne font
pas l'unanimité dans la population relativement homogène. La clairvoyance des propos
d'Isozaki se mesure jusqu'à aujourd'hui à la
relative absence d'architectes étrangers,
même les plus connus, sur la scène architecturale japonaise.

La génération perdue

En 1994, l'économie japonaise entame une
modeste reprise avec une croissance de
0,6 %. Mais l'assurance qui dominait pendant
les triomphales années 1980 a disparu, rem-
placée par de nouveaux doutes. Lionel Barber
le décrit en ces termes dans *The Financial
Times* en 1996 : « [...] Même une vue limitée de
la société japonaise met en avant des change-
ments politiques et économiques d'une
grande portée... La réalité, c'est que le Japon
est en train de devenir un pays "normal". De
même que les Américains et les Européens
souffrent de l'absence de sécurité de l'emploi
et des troubles économiques, les Japonais
luttent pour s'adapter à la concurrence internationale. Le chômage est en hausse. La population vieillit. Pour la première fois depuis
1945, le public japonais doute des perspec-
tives de croissance. Le terme à la mode est :
prospérité stagnante. Ce pessimisme est parfois exagéré, mais c'est l'héritage de presque
cinq ans de croissance zéro après l'éclate-
ment de la bulle économique... Le crash a été
une expérience très violente[10]. » Et l'impact de
cette période dure encore, longtemps après.
Les années 1990-2010 sont souvent citées
comme les « 20 ans perdus » *(ushinawareta
nijūnen)* pendant lesquels le PIB et les salaires
ont chuté en termes nominaux. Comme par
ailleurs cette stagnation a été suivie de la
crise économique mondiale de 2007–2009,

bon nombre des barrières psychologiques
contre une résurgence de l'architecture
contemporaine extravagante existent encore
aujourd'hui. Une plus grande attention aux
questions économiques et une esthétique
plus généralement conservatrice sont aujourd'hui de rigueur.

Le style européen

L'émergence de l'architecture japonaise
moderne peut être considérée sous la forme
d'une libération progressive des influences
occidentales. Lorsque le commodore améri-
cain Matthew Perry aperçoit la cité d'Edo
(ancien nom de Tokyo) pendant son expédition
de 1853–1854, il la décrit comme une « vaste
plaine sur un superbe arrière-plan de montagnes et de campagne boisée ». Le Japon
s'était volontairement tenu isolé du reste du
monde depuis 220 ans. Les conséquences et
la portée considérable de l'expédition de Perry
ont fait l'objet de nombreuses analyses, mais
il est vrai que dès 1872, le gouvernement Meiji
fait appel à l'architecte et urbaniste britannique Thomas Waters (1842–1898) pour re-
construire la zone située au sud-est du palais
impérial, détruite par un incendie la même
année. Sur une large avenue, il érige des bâtiments néo-classiques en briques qui seront
les précurseurs du quartier moderne de Ginza.
Un autre Anglais, Josiah Conder (1852–1920),
construira de nombreux bâtiments en maçon-
nerie dans le style du Second empire – notamment le Musée impérial dans le parc d'Ueno
(1882) – qui deviendront les symboles de l'establishment japonais jusqu'à ce que le ministère du Cabinet décide de faire appel aux Alle-
mands Hermann Ende (1829–1907) et Wilhelm
Böckmann (1832–1902). Leur projet de style
prussien pour la diète japonaise, surmonté
d'une forme rappelant une pagode, se heurte à

une opposition concertée qui exige une réso-
lution du conflit entre les styles architecturaux
locaux et occidentaux[11].
Le premier architecte occidental moderne à
laisser son empreinte au Japon est peut-être
Frank Lloyd Wright (1867–1959) qui a travaillé
à l'hôtel Impérial de Tokyo de 1916 à 1922.
« Soixante à soixante-dix pieds de boue
meuble se trouvaient sous la couche supérieure de huit pieds du sol de surface du terrain, écrit-il. Cette boue m'a paru une disposition des plus heureuses – un bon coussin pour
amortir les chocs les plus terribles. Pourquoi
ne pas faire flotter le bâtiment dessus ? Un
cuirassé flotte sur l'eau salée[12]... » Démoli en
1967, l'édifice fantastique est célèbre pour
avoir résisté au tremblement de terre dévasta-
teur de 1923, ce qui a encore ajouté à la réputation de Wright, en particulier au Japon.

La tradition, les racines de la modernité

Le 4 novembre 1935, l'architecte allemand
Bruno Taut (1880–1938) note dans son journal : « Je peux véritablement affirmer que je
suis celui qui a découvert Katsura. » Une affirmation à propos de la résidence impériale du
XVIIe siècle près de Kyoto qui sera d'une importance considérable pour le développement
de l'architecture japonaise contemporaine.
En effet, si les Japonais avaient diversement
assimilé les influences occidentales auxquelles ils avaient été soumis après l'expédition de Perry, ils avaient aussi fini par rejeter
bien des aspects de leur propre tradition. La
montée du fascisme au Japon s'était cependant accompagnée d'un certain rejet de la
modernité d'inspiration occidentale en faveur
d'une architecture appelée *teikan yoshiki* ou le
« style de la couronne impériale », aux lourdes
structures cubiques surmontées de toits
« japonais » tout aussi disgracieux. Arrivé au

Japon en mai 1933, Taut passera trois ans et demi à écrire sur Katsura, dont il associe l'élégante simplicité aux objectifs du mouvement moderne et qu'il décrit comme un « monument éternel ». Arata Isozaki fait cependant remarquer que d'autres architectes occidentaux, notamment l'Allemand Gustav Prattz, ont visité Katsura avant Taut et en ont tiré les leçons pour « le renouvellement de l'architecture mondiale[13] ». La redécouverte des liens fondamentaux entre la pureté de la tradition japonaise et le modernisme n'interviendra qu'après le traumatisme de la Seconde Guerre mondiale, notamment parce que l'idée même du recours à la tradition avait été détournée par une idéologie politique désormais largement discréditée.

Pour faire un parallèle intéressant, c'est aussi en 1933 que l'auteur japonais Jun'ichirō Tanizaki publie pour la première fois son texte influent *Éloge de l'ombre.* Il y écrit à propos de la spécificité de l'architecture japonaise : « [...] Le Japonais, qui eût certainement préféré lui aussi une pièce claire à une pièce obscure, a été amené à faire de nécessité vertu. Mais ce que l'on appelle le beau n'est d'ordinaire qu'une sublimation des réalités de la vie, et c'est ainsi que nos ancêtres, contraints à demeurer bon gré mal gré dans des chambres obscures, découvrirent un jour le beau au sein de l'ombre, et bientôt ils en vinrent à se servir de l'ombre en vue d'obtenir des effets esthétiques[14]. » Ce type de réflexion, comme celle de Bruno Taut qui voyait une certaine « modernité » chez Katsura, est à l'origine de plusieurs éléments fondamentaux de l'architecture japonaise contemporaine qui absorbe les influences occidentales et tire parti de ses liens plus profonds à la tradition.

Frank Lloyd Wright n'est, bien sûr, pas le seul architecte occidental à avoir directement influencé le développement de l'architecture

japonaise moderne. Le Corbusier, par exemple, qui fascine encore aujourd'hui de nombreux architectes nippons, a manifesté sa présence dans des projets tels que le Musée national de l'art occidental du parc d'Ueno, à Tokyo (1959), et à travers le travail de personnalités comme Kunio Maekawa (1905–1986) qui a travaillé en France dans son atelier de 1928 à 1930 avant d'ouvrir son agence à Tokyo en 1935. Ce dernier a supervisé la construction du premier musée et en a achevé l'extension de 1979, réaffirmant ainsi symboliquement l'importance de Le Corbusier au Japon. La découverte après-guerre par les Japonais eux-mêmes de la manière dont leur tradition pouvait donner vie à l'architecture contemporaine est avant tout le fait de l'architecte Kenzo Tange (1913–2005). Il avait travaillé à la fin des années 1930 dans l'agence de Kunio Maekawa, mais son gymnase de Yoyogi construit pour les Jeux olympiques de Tokyo en 1964 annonce véritablement l'émergence d'une modernité nationale dont la qualité et l'inventivité n'ont rien à envier à celles de l'Occident. Fumihiko Maki écrit à ce propos : « Le gymnase des Jeux olympiques de Tokyo en 1964 est un superbe produit de la technologie structurelle du XXᵉ siècle, ainsi qu'une conception audacieuse et originale de l'espace. C'est une référence pour l'histoire de l'architecture moderne qui a assuré à Tange une immense réputation internationale[15]. » Auteur du parc et du musée du Mémorial de la paix à Hiroshima, témoignage émouvant de l'horreur atomique, Tange, mort en 2005, demeure un symbole de l'architecture japonaise moderne même si ses dernières réalisations, notamment l'hôtel de ville de Tokyo, deux tours de 243 m de haut qui occupent trois blocs du quartier de Shinjuku (1991), sont considérées par beaucoup comme le symbole des excès auxquels ont donné lieu les années de la bulle.

Des cités flottantes aux tours capsules

Bon nombre des chefs de file de l'architecture contemporaine au Japon sont issus de l'agence de Kenzo Tange, notamment Arata Isozaki (né en 1931) et Yoshio Taniguchi (né en 1937). De même, Fumihiko Maki (né en 1928) et Kisho Kurokawa (1934–2007) ont suivi les cours de Tange à l'université de Tokyo. Ces derniers ont tous les deux participé, avec Kiyonori Kikutake (1928–2011) et d'autres, au manifeste *Metabolism: The Proposals for New Urbanism* publié en 1960 pendant la Conférence mondiale du design (World Design Conference Tokyo, WoDeCo Tokyo) de Tokyo présidée par Kenzo Tange, qui présente alors aussi son « plan pour Tokyo 1960 ». Issu de leur travail et de celui du Studio MIT de Kenzo Tange, le mouvement métaboliste intègre des idées de croissance biologique organique à des mégastructures architecturales, imaginant notamment des villes flottantes et des tours capsules. Le métabolisme peut être considéré comme une réponse aux catastrophes humaines et environnementales de la guerre et une expression de la vulnérabilité persistante du Japon face aux catastrophes naturelles. Il imagine l'architecture comme le vecteur de transformation de la société japonaise, vers de nouveaux modèles d'espace et d'organisation, plus résistants et capables de s'adapter au changement, la définissant en termes techniques, tout en la comparant à la régénération biologique. Peu des projets de ce mouvement très influent ont été réellement construits, mais ils comprennent des exemples notables telle la tour capsules Nakagin de Kurokawa, construite en seulement 30 jours en 1972 (Shimbashi, Tokyo). Kenzo Tange développe aussi le concept d'architecture extensible avec notamment le Centre de communications de Yamanashi (Kofu, Yamanashi, 1966). Mais

Previous double page: Kenzo Tange, St. Mary's Cathedral, Tokyo, 1964.

Opposite: Kenzo Tange, Shizuoka Press and Broadcasting Center, Tokyo, 1967.

Kenzo Tange, Yamanshi Press and Broadcasting Center, Kofu, Yamanashi, 1967.

l'expression la plus visible du métabolisme, qui se trouve aussi être son dernier acte de présence significatif, est l'Exposition universelle d'Osaka en 1970 autour du thème « Progrès et harmonie pour l'humanité », dont le plan directeur a été réalisé par Kenzo Tange et le marxiste Uzo Nishiyama (1911–1994). Tange a créé le pavillon principal appelé Festival Plaza, tandis que Kikutake a conçu l'Expo Tower. Kurokawa a également construit deux pavillons, lui et Maki ont imaginé des capsules expérimentales placées sur le toit de la Plaza et Isozaki est l'auteur de deux robots géants.

**De la pensée bouddhiste
à la tradition shinto**

Un temps, l'architecture japonaise contemporaine a paru occuper le devant de la scène mondiale, inventant des idées nouvelles qui correspondaient à la situation très particulière du pays, épicentre des guerres et des séismes, monde nouveau densément peuplé. Malgré ses intentions résolument tournées vers l'avenir, le métabolisme a incité certains à repenser la tradition japonaise à la lumière du changement et de la modernité. Kisho Kurokawa, éduqué par des moines bouddhistes, est l'un d'eux. Selon Rem Koolhaas et Hans Ulrich Obrist : « Le bombardement des villes japonaises auquel il a assisté pendant la Seconde Guerre mondiale a été un élément fondamental : il a fait comprendre de manière implacable à Kurokawa le caractère éphémère de l'architecture. [...] Kurokawa a souligné que cette révélation *a priori* moderne – l'un des éléments déclencheurs du métabolisme – est en fait la continuation directe de la pensée bouddhiste et de la tradition japonaise shinto, telle qu'elle apparaît notamment dans la reconstruction du sanctuaire d'Ise tous les vingt ans depuis le VIIᵉ siècle[16]. » Le lien que Kurokawa a établi,

au moins en théorie, entre la tradition japonaise et le monde moderne sous-tend l'architecture japonaise contemporaine dont il constitue l'une des forces ; il réunit le passé, le présent et le futur dans un continuum difficilement imaginable dans d'autres pays.

La reconnaissance internationale

Certaines personnalités comme Arata Isozaki et Yoshio Taniguchi ont fini par sortir de l'ombre de Kenzo Tange et ont commencé plus récemment à imposer la présence japonaise sur la scène architecturale mondiale. Isozaki, lauréat du prix Pritzker en 2019, a longtemps été l'un des six ou sept architectes « stars » qui quadrillent le monde avec leurs projets. Son musée d'Art contemporain à Los Angeles (1986) a été l'un des premiers nouveaux musées construit par un architecte étranger aux États-Unis, tandis que la reconstruction plus récente du Museum of Modern Art de New York (2004) par Taniguchi a montré que les architectes japonais sont désormais acceptés jusque dans le « saint des saints » de l'establishment artistique. Dans cette génération, Fumihiko Maki, autre architecte rescapé du métabolisme, est aussi une personnalité reconnue dans le monde entier, dont les projets récents comprennent notamment la tour 4 du World Trade Center à New York (page 260) et des constructions pour l'Aga Khan au Canada. Comme Taniguchi, Maki, lauréat du prix Pritzker en 1993, a été formé en partie aux États-Unis et maîtrise parfaitement l'anglais, ce qui n'est pas toujours le cas de tous les grands architectes japonais.

Tadao Ando et Toyo Ito

À ce jour, sept architectes japonais ont gagné le prix Pritkzer. La liste de leurs noms marque

l'influence et le changement d'un architecte au suivant et augure sans doute le profil des futurs lauréats japonais.

1. Kenzo Tange 1987
2. Fumihiko Maki 1993
3. Tadao Ando 1995
4. SANAA 2010
5. Toyo Ito 2013
6. Shigeru Ban 2014
7. Arata Isozaki 2019

Tadao Ando est peut-être l'architecte contemporain le plus connu au monde et celui qui a permis au Japon d'accéder au plus haut niveau de notoriété internationale dans le domaine de l'architecture. Né à Osaka en 1941, Tadao Ando est autodidacte et doit sa formation d'architecte en grande partie à ses voyages aux États-Unis, en Europe et en Afrique (1962-1969). Il a reçu le prix Pritzker en 1995 et, outre ses fabuleuses constructions au Japon, il vient d'achever la Pulitzer Foundation for the Arts (St. Louis, Missouri, 2001) et le musée d'Art moderne de Fort Worth (Texas, 2002). Il a également travaillé pour le milliardaire français François Pinault à la rénovation du Palazzo Grassi (2006) et de la Punta della Dogana (2009) à Venise, destinés à des expositions d'art contemporain. Un projet de musée d'art contemporain à Paris, de nouveau pour François Pinault, a été annulé au printemps 2005, mais ce dernier a confié à Ando la rénovation de la Bourse de commerce dans le quartier des Halles de la capitale française (2021). La force d'expression des dessins d'Ando et la puissance égale de ses bâtiments, généralement en béton, sont admirées et imitées par les étudiants en architecture du monde entier depuis de nombreuses années. Il semble avoir réussi à jeter le pont longtemps attendu entre l'Orient et l'Occident avec ses

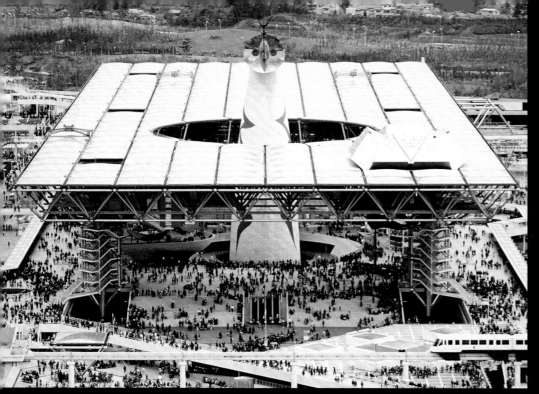

étonnants sanctuaires de silence et de lumière au vocabulaire de formes géométriques délibérément réduit. Mais ce qui semble surtout ressortir clairement de la plupart de ses réalisations, c'est qu'il recherche quelque chose de plus que la seule maîtrise de l'espace. Ainsi qu'il l'a exprimé dans son discours de réception du prix Pritzker : « Je crois que deux dimensions distinctes coexistent dans l'architecture. L'une est substantielle et concerne la fonction, la sécurité et l'économie, dans la mesure où l'architecture loge l'être humain, elle ne peut ignorer ces éléments du réel. Mais cela suffit-il à l'architecture pour être architecture ? Étant donné qu'elle est une forme d'expression humaine, la question de l'architecture en tant qu'art surgit dès qu'elle sort des exigences de la pure construction pour rejoindre le domaine de l'esthétique… Ce que j'ai cherché à réaliser, c'est une spatialité qui stimule l'esprit humain, éveille les sens et communique avec le plus profond de l'âme[17]. »

Né la même année qu'Ando, Toyo Ito n'a peut-être pas atteint la célébrité internationale dont jouit l'architecte d'Osaka, mais il est sans aucun doute l'une des personnalités dominantes de sa génération en architecture, ce qu'a confirmé le prix Pritzker en 2013. Générale-ment attaché à un design extrêmement léger, à l'opposé du béton plus massif d'Ando, deux de ses projets lui ont valu une attention considérable des médias au début de notre siècle. L'un est la médiathèque de Sendai (2001). À l'aide de 13 tubes de structure en acier blanc qui « ondulent » à travers le bâtiment comme des « algues » pour le soulever et loger ses câbles et canalisations techniques, Ito innove au niveau le plus fondamental de l'intégrité structurelle et de l'esthétique architecturale. Plus éphémère, son pavillon de l'été 2002 érigé

pour la Serpentine Gallery était une construction de 309 m² de plain-pied, couverte de panneaux d'aluminium et de verre. L'idée était de créer une structure sans colonnes qui ne dépende pas d'un système de grille orthogonal afin de former un espace ouvert destiné à abriter un café et diverses manifestations pendant l'été. La structure en apparence aléatoire a en fait été déterminée par un algorithme dérivé de la rotation d'un simple carré, chacun de ses éléments tenait lieu de poutre, mais servait aussi à absorber les vibrations afin de former un tout complexe et réciproquement interdépendant associé aux autres éléments : « L'idée, explique l'architecte, était de rendre de nouveau visibles les systèmes qui créent les conditions les plus fondamentales de l'architecture elle-même. »

Les réflexions d'Ito sur la nature dans l'environnement extrêmement urbanisé des villes japonaises sont d'un intérêt considérable. Comme la plupart des Japonais, il a été profondément choqué par le tremblement de terre et le tsunami dévastateurs de la région du Tohoku (2011), à la suite duquel il a écrit : « Je ne peux m'empêcher de voir un décalage fondamental entre notre norme et la réalité. Je pense que nous concevons les choses mécaniquement comme une "machine complète", en tenant compte de la nature définie par des quantités ou des définitions abstraites ; mais sans considérer l'environnement naturel comme constamment affecté par les forces variables du sol, de la mer ou du vent. Qu'il s'agisse d'architecture publique ou de maison particulière, nous les imaginons uniquement dans un cadre abstrait. Je pense que notre mission consiste désormais à repenser la manière dont nous "supposons" les conditions de la création, non de revoir les conditions

nous interroger sur la forme de notre relation à la nature[18]. » Ce cheminement dans la réflexion peut être rapproché des origines du métabolisme, c'est pourtant la période intermédiaire qu'Ito considère ici en appelant ici à une architecture davantage en harmonie avec la terre que les mégaréalisations de la génération précédente.

Kazuyo Sejima, Kengo Kuma et Shigeru Ban

L'agence de Toyo Ito, comme celle de Tange avant lui, a formé efficacement des talents. L'une de ses plus célèbres anciennes employées est Kazuyo Sejima, qui a travaillé avec lui de 1981 à 1987 avant d'ouvrir sa propre agence. Aujourd'hui partenaire de Ryue Nishizawa (SANAA), elle a rapidement gagné le devant de la scène internationale avec des réalisations telles que le nouveau musée d'Art contemporain (New York, 2007) ou le Louvre-Lens (Lens, France, 2012) et le prix Pritzker 2010. On pourrait dire de Sejima que, comme son mentor, elle a largement recours aux effets de légèreté extrême ou qu'elle joue sur les reflets et la transparence, ce qui rend parfois difficile de distinguer la fin ou le début d'un bâtiment. C'est le cas de son musée d'Art contemporain du XXIe siècle (Kanazawa, 2004) : sur un plan de base circulaire tout simple, elle est parvenue à créer plusieurs salles d'exposition, et autant d'impressions différentes pour les visiteurs, qui dépassent tout ce que l'on peut attendre de l'architecture moderne.

Au Japon, le groupe d'âge de Sejima est particulièrement riche en talents architecturaux. Kengo Kuma, né en 1954, Shigeru Ban (1957) et Shuhei Endo (1960) proposent un remarquable panorama de styles et une innovation

plupart des autres pays. Le plus célèbre d'entre eux est Shigeru Ban, lauréat du prix Pritzker 2014, qui s'est fait connaître hors du Japon avec des projets comme le Centre Pompidou-Metz (Metz, France, 2010) ou des appartements à New York. Kengo Kuma, quant à lui, a réalisé le musée d'Art de la préfecture de Nagasaki en 2005 et surtout l'immeuble très en vue One Omotesando à Tokyo en 2003. Au moment de la mise sous presse de ces pages, il était en train d'achever l'un de ses projets les plus symboliques et significatifs, le nouveau stade national à Tokyo (voir page 256), pour lequel il a succédé à l'infortunée gagnante du concours, Zaha Hadid. Kuma y fait un usage intensif du bois japonais et de la végétation, assurant que le stade prévu pour les Jeux olympiques de 2020 constituera un manifeste en faveur d'une architecture plus douce et proche de la nature, et ce, même au cœur de l'expansion urbaine de Tokyo. Autre point important, le projet de Kuma est considérablement moins haut et moins onéreux que celui de Hadid à la toiture rétractable extrêmement complexe.

La nouvelle génération

S'ils suivent peut-être les traces de personnalités telles que Tange, Isozaki et Toyo Ito, les jeunes architectes ont aussi ouvert avec succès de nouvelles voies à l'architecture japonaise, certainement plus « modestes » dans l'ensemble et souvent associées plus ou moins subtilement à la tradition japonaise. C'est un hasard, mais l'un des précurseurs de cette exploration sérieuse de la tradition est un architecte de la génération d'Ando et Ito : le professeur Terunobu Fujimori (né en 1946) est un historien de l'architecture qui a construit son premier bâtiment en 1990. Il a porté à de

nouveaux sommets la tradition ancestrale de la maison de thé japonaise avec des réalisations comme Takasugi-an (Chino, Nagano, 2004), perchée dans les arbres à six mètres au-dessus du sol. Connu pour son originalité et son sens de l'humour, Fujimori utilise des matériaux naturels dans un contexte toujours soigneusement défini par sa connaissance approfondie de l'histoire architecturale de son pays. Quatre autres architectes nés dans les années 1960, Masaki Endoh (1963), Takaharu (1964) et Yui Tezuka (1969) et Hiroshi Sambuichi (1968) proposent des visions différentes du présent et du futur de leur art. Masaki Endoh est l'auteur de plusieurs maisons originales, souvent construites en collaboration avec l'ingénieur Masahiro Ikeda. Beaucoup de ses projets portent le nom de « Natural » – tel « Natural Ellipse » (Shibuya, Tokyo, 2002) – justifié par sa conviction que l'architecture doit être fondée sur « le bon sens et la connaissance empirique ». Il explique notamment : « Je crois que le processus de création est semblable à l'évolution. Le design qui sait intégrer de nouveaux concepts survivra. Le design qui ne change pas avec le temps est appelé à disparaître. Pour que l'architecture poursuive son évolution, il est important de remettre constamment en question les normes établies. » Takaharu et Yui Tezuka sont eux aussi certainement convaincus de la nécessité de remettre en question les normes universellement admises, leur étonnant musée des Sciences de la nature Matsunoyama (Niigata, 2003) en est la preuve. La structure, faite pour l'essentiel de tubes d'acier Corten, est conçue pour résister à des poids de neige allant jusqu'à 2000 tonnes et serpente sur une longueur de 111 m, épousant la topographie du paysage et permettant aux visiteurs de « se faire une idée de la lumière et des couleurs sous différentes profondeurs de

neige, de 4 m de profondeur à 30 m au-dessus du sol ». Hiroshi Sambuichi, enfin, est l'auteur de deux édifices publiés ici, l'observatoire du mont Misen de Miyajima (Miyajima, Hiroshima, 2013, voir page 338) et le centre communautaire Naoshima Hall (Naoshima, Kagawa, 2015, voir page 344), qui cherchent tous les deux à se rapprocher des coutumes et traditions locales, de leurs cadres naturels et des matériaux utilisés depuis toujours dans l'architecture japonaise. Son travail demeure cependant résolument moderne malgré sa volonté de s'attacher à la tradition.

Plus jeunes et plus près de la nature

La génération d'architectes japonais nés dans les années 1970 témoigne d'un degré élevé d'innovation et promet de ce fait une rupture encore plus marquée avec l'héritage de personnalités comme Le Corbusier, en faveur de solutions spécifiquement japonaises mais néanmoins suffisamment universelles pour être acceptées et approuvées dans de nombreux cercles d'architecture. Les plus connus sont Sou Fujimoto (1971) et Junya Ishigami (1974). Ce dernier en particulier cherche à introduire la nature dans son travail au-delà de l'aspect purement cosmétique – en quête d'une « nature au-delà de la nature », ou peut-être d'« une nature encore jamais vue ». Il développe ces idées dans les deux projets publiés ici, Botanical Garden Art Biotop/Water Garden (Nasu, Tochigi, 2018, voir page 198) et House & Restaurant (Yamaguchi, 2016–, voir page 204), dont on peut dire qu'ils sont à la limite de ce que l'on considère généralement comme architecture. Le Water Garden est une étonnante création qui donne l'impression d'être parfaitement naturelle alors qu'en réalité, elle a été fabriquée par Ishigami à l'aide de

oposent certains fabricants tels que Toto, ais l'idée même de les placer dans un jardin vert est réellement stupéfiante. Si les toi- tes publiques d'Ichihara ne sont pas une stallation temporaire, Fujimoto s'est aussi say é en 2013 au design éphémère avec le avillon d'été de la Serpentine Gallery. La liste e ceux qui ont réalisé ces pavillons à Londres année en année est un véritable *Who's Who* e l'architecture contemporaine. Des pavillons ès ouverts ont été imaginés par des archi- ctes comme SANAA ou, plus récemment, erzog & de Meuron sur l'emplacement réser- é à cet effet à côté de la galerie géorgienne erpentine, à Kensington Gardens. Là encore, ujimoto a adopté une approche totalement ifférente et créé un tissu de piquets en acier lanc de 20 mm formant un motif treillissé. ans la verdure du parc environnant, la struc- ure qui abritait un café a été conçue comme ne invitation à réfléchir à l'environnement. ujimoto déclare : « La question de savoir à uel point l'architecture diffère de la nature est ne question véritablement fondamentale, ou omment l'architecture pourrait faire partie de a nature, ou comment elles pourraient être usionnées… Quelles sont les limites entre la ature et les éléments artificiels. »

e décollage et l'avancée

Bien moins connu que ses compatriotes shigami et Fujimoto, Tsuyoshi Tane (1979) adopte une approche différente de sa profes- sion et a pris délibérément ses distances avec l'environnement architectural de Tokyo lors- qu'il a installé son agence à Paris. En collabo- ration avec la société dont il est cofondateur, Dorell.Gotmeh.Tane / Architects, il a créé le Musée national d'Estonie (Tartu, Estonie, 2016)

militaire abandonnée de l'époque soviétique comme point de départ, au sens propre du terme, d'une structure dont le toit semble « décoller et s'avancer vers un "espace infi- ni" ». Bien sûr, Tsuyoshi Tane a aussi travaillé au Japon, et il est considéré comme un repré- sentant de l'architecture contemporaine « qui monte » dans son groupe d'âge. Plus près de chez lui, il a construit la Maison dans la vallée de Todoroki (Todoroki House in Valley, Setagaya, Tokyo, 2018, voir page 412). D'une surface au sol de 188 m² relativement mo- deste, elle est située dans un singulier creux forestier au cœur de la ville. Elle parvient à offrir une vie dans la nature malgré l'extrême densité urbaine de Tokyo et s'ouvre sur huit directions de son décor inattendu.

Le métal ondulé et le contreplaqué

Takashi Suo, né en 1980, est un autre éminent jeune architecte japonais. Sa petite (188 m²) clinique dentaire d'Ishihara (Okayama, 2017, voir page 406) peut être considérée comme emblématique de l'architecture actuelle au Japon. Construite pour un coût modeste de 480 000 euros, elle occupe un terrain impro- bable au bord de la route et donne une cer- taine impression de chaos, comme presque partout dans le Japon urbain et périurbain. L'architecte lui-même explique : « On a l'im- pression de voir le résultat d'un plan sans ordre ni logique, mais en réalité, il est parfaite- ment en harmonie avec le voisinage. » Avec ses volumes légèrement décalés les uns par rapport aux autres pour garantir une certaine intimité aux patients et une structure qui privi- légie les feuilles d'aluminium ondulé et le contreplaqué, la clinique dentaire est le fruit d'une conception intelligente et innovante –

intégration à son voisinage. « Bon marché »
dans le bon sens du terme, elle démontre que
l'architecture japonaise contemporaine résiste
aux contraintes les plus lourdes de densité
urbaine, et même à une culture aguerrie par les
cataclysmes permanents et le vieillissement
progressif. Ce n'est pas un hasard si les jeunes
architectes japonais prometteurs construisent
aujourd'hui des bâtiments d'aussi petite taille –
mais inventifs. C'est la conséquence évidente
des conditions actuelles, notamment la pénu-
rie de terrains en ville, la soif de nature là
où elle est quasiment inexistante, l'interdiction
à deux constructions d'avoir un mur porteur
en-commun, le marasme économique et une
incertitude généralisée quant à l'avenir.
Cela ne veut pas dire qu'on ne construisait
plus de projets de grande envergure à Tokyo
au moment de la mise sous presse de ce
livre. En plus du nouveau stade national de
80 000 places de Kuma, d'autres préparatifs
des Jeux olympiques de 2020 métamorphosent
des quartiers connus de la ville. Celui de
la gare de Shibuya est ainsi le théâtre d'un
réaménagement massif qui comprend la
construction de plusieurs nouvelles tours
imposantes, créées en partie par SANAA et,
là encore, Kengo Kuma. Ces projets confiés
à de grandes entreprises de construction et
de design telles que Tokyu Land Corporation
ou Nikken Sekkei témoignent d'une tendance
globale aux bâtiments plus hauts dans la
capitale japonaise. Parfaitement intégrés
au système complexe de transports urbains,
ces projets ne sont pas le fruit de la seule
expertise d'architectes isolés. Le nouveau
stade national n'est ainsi pas l'œuvre du
seul Kengo Kuma, mais d'un groupe (Taisei
Corporation, Azusa Sekkei Co., Ltd. et
Kengo Kuma & Associates).
Plus près du sol, Jo Nagasaka (1971) et son

projets plutôt modestes et peu onéreux
à Tokyo, comme les deux publiés ici – la
transformation sommaire d'une maison
à Sangenjaya (Setagaya, Tokyo, 2017, voir
page 286) et la rénovation de l'hôtel « capsule » et sauna °C (Do-C) à Ebisu (Shibuya,
Tokyo, 2017, voir page 294). Dans les deux
cas, il se sert de bâtiments modernes pour
créer de nouveaux espaces et des usages
inattendus pour l'architecture. On n'y retrouve
plus la nouveauté scintillante de l'architecture
« manga » caractéristique des années d'avant
la bulle, mais plutôt une réutilisation naturelle
de structures urbaines qui passe délibérément
par une certaine modestie et un certain degré
de « rugosité ».

Le changement permanent

Les architectes présentés ici, et les autres
autant qu'eux, ont engagé le Japon dans
une quête en apparence infinie de nouvelles
formes architecturales. Même la maison,
l'unité la plus fondamentale de la conception
architecturale, fait l'objet d'explorations
constantes où les murs, les sols et les plafonds remplissent d'autres objectifs en libé-
rant de l'espace pour répondre aux besoins
d'une ville moderne densément peuplée. On a
souvent pensé que Tokyo pourrait être considéré comme un précurseur des villes-mondes
du futur dans lesquelles une densité extrême
sera source d'innovation architecturale. Dans
son livre inspiré intitulé *Tokyo Metabolizing*,
le commissaire du pavillon du Japon à la
Biennale d'architecture de Venise 2010 Koh
Kitayama écrit : « Contrairement aux structures urbaines qu'on trouve en Europe et
qui ont été créées comme une série de murs,
Tokyo se compose d'un assemblage de

Opposite: *Arata Isozaki, Ceremonial Court, Education City, Doha, Qatar, 2012.*

Kohei Nawa, Throne, 2018, temporarily installed beneath I. M. Pei's Louvre Pyramid, Paris, France.

Following double page: *Kengo Kuma, Japan National Stadium, Tokyo, 2019.*

japonaise a désormais surmonté les difficultés auxquelles elle a été confrontée dans sa quête du lien le plus approprié entre tradition nationale et modernité internationale. C'est par hasard qu'une bonne partie de la tradition japonaise, notamment celle incarnée par Katsura, a fourni un moyen d'approcher le lien entre passé, présent et futur qui a échappé à de nombreux architectes occidentaux. Accepter l'ambiguïté, comme le font les réflexions fugitives du musée Kanazawa de Sejima, ou le changement permanent et la menace de catastrophe, telles sont les clés qui permettent de comprendre et d'apprécier ce qui différencie l'architecture japonaise de l'architecture européenne ou américaine – mais les idées voyagent vite aujourd'hui. Plongés dans les traditions anciennes et ouverts à la pensée la plus contemporaine et à la technologie, les Japonais sont une force avec laquelle il faut compter dans l'architecture contemporaine.

1   *https://www.cia.gov/library/publications/the-world-factbook/fields/343rank.html*, consulté le 10 mai 2020.
2   *https://www.cia.gov/library/publications/the-world-factbook/geos/ja.html*, consulté le 10 mai 2020.
3   *Jonathan Abbamonte, « Le gouvernement japonais affirme que la baisse de population est le "plus grand défi" pour la croissance économique », Population Research Institute, 24 octobre 2017. https://www.pop.org/japanese-government-calls-population-shrinkage-biggest-challenge-economic-growth/*, consulté le 10 mai 2020.
4   *http://www.metro.tokyo.jp/english/about/history/history03.html*, consulté le 17 décembre 2018.
5   *https://www.cia.gov/library/publications/the-world-factbook/geos/ja.html*, consulté le 10 mai 2020.
6   *Daisuke Kikuchi, « Japan Marks Seventh Anniversary of 3/11 with Moment of Silence », Japan Times, 11 mars 2018. https://www.japantimes.co.jp/news/2018/03/11/national/japan-marks-seven-years-since-devastating-3-11-disasters/#.XBig7S2ZPhM*, consulté le 10 mai 2020.
7   Louis George Kittaka, « New Buildings can Take the Sunshine Out of Life », *Japan Times*, 24 août 2014. *https://www.japantimes.co.jp/community/2014/08/24/how-tos/new-buildings-can-take-sunshine-life/#.XBd8Ty2ZPhM*, consulté le 10 mai 2020.
8   *Arata Isozaki en conversation avec l'auteur, Tokyo, 1ᵉʳ vril 1996.*
9   *Idem.*
10 *Lionel Barber, « A Deeper Transformation », The Financial Times, 10 avril 1996.*
11 *William Coaldrake, « Order and Anarchy: Tokyo from 1868 to the Present », in Tokyo, Form and Spirit, M. Friedman (éd.), Walker Art Center, Harry N. Abrams, New York, 1986.*
12 *Frank Lloyd Wright, An Autobiography, Duell, Sloan and Pearce, New York, 1943.*
13 *Arata Isozaki, « Katsura: A Model for Post-Modern Architecture », in Katsura Villa: Space and Form, A. Isozaki (éd.), Iwanami Shoten Publishers, Tokyo, 1983.*
14 *Jun'ichirō Tanizaki, Éloge de l'ombre, trad. René Sieffert, Verdier, Paris, 2011.*
15 *https://www.pritzkerprize.com/sites/default/files/inline-files/Fumihiko_Maki_Essay_1987_Tange.pdf*, consulté le 10 mai 2020.
16 *Rem Koolhaas, Hans Ulrich Obrist, Project Japan: Metabolism Talks, Taschen, Cologne, 2011.*
17 *Tadao Ando, https://www.pritzkerprize.com/sites/default/files/inline-files/Tadao_Ando_Acceptance_Speech_1995.pdf*, consulté le 10 mai 2020.
18 *Rem Koolhaas, Hans Ulrich Obrist,* Project Japan: Metabolism Talks, Taschen, Cologne, 2011.
19 *Koh Kitayama, Yoshiharu Tsukamoto, Ryue Nishizawa,* Tokyo Metabolizing, Toto Publishing, Tokyo, 2010.

MIKIO MIZUTA MEMORIAL HALL

HITOSHI ABE

Sakado, Saitama, 2017
Area: 1802 m²
Collaboration: Kume Sekkei Co. Ltd.
(Executive Architect)

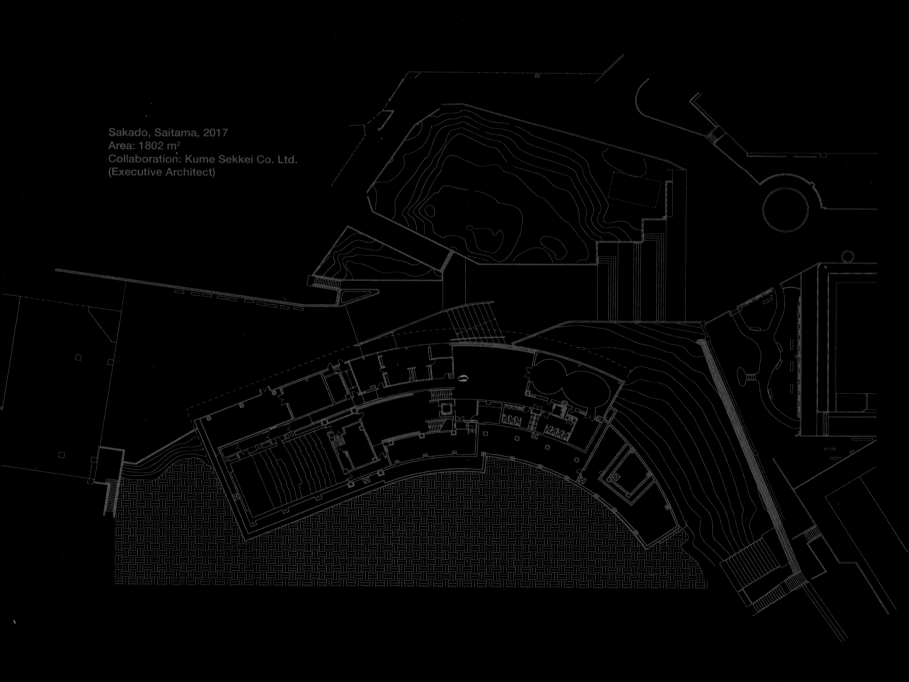

HITOSHI ABE was born in 1962 in Sendai. He worked from 1988 to 1992 in the office of Coop Himmelb(l)au, obtaining his M.Arch degree from SCI-Arc (Los Angeles, 1989) and a Ph.D. from Tohoku University (Sendai, 1993). He created his own firm, Atelier Hitoshi Abe, in 1992 and opened a second office in Los Angeles in 2008. Beginning in 1994, he directed the Hitoshi Abe Architectural Design Laboratory at the Tohoku Institute of Technology. He was a Professor at Tohoku University (2002–07), and then, in 2007, he was appointed Professor and Chair of the UCLA Department of Architecture and Urban Design. In 2010, he was appointed Paul I. and Hisako Terasaki Chair in the Study of Contemporary Japan as well as Director of the UCLA Terasaki Center for Japanese Studies (Los Angeles). His work includes the Miyagi Water Tower (Rifu, Miyagi, 1994); Miyagi Stadium (Rifu, Miyagi, 2000); Michinoku Folklore Museum (Kurikoma, Miyagi, 2000); Kanno Museum (Shiogama, Miyagi, 2005); KCH/Whopper Clinic and Residence (Saitama, Saitama, 2006); and the FRP Ftown Building (Sendai, Miyagi, 2007). His recent work includes Intilaq Tohoku Innovation Center (Sendai, Miyagi, 2016); the UCLA Terasaki Research Institute (Los Angeles, California, USA, 2017); and the Mikio Mizuta Memorial Hall (Sakado,

HITOSHI ABE, geboren 1962 in Sendai, arbeitete von 1988 bis 1992 im Büro von Coop Himmelb(l)au, absolvierte seinen M.Arch am SCI-Arc (Los Angeles, 1989) und promovierte an der Universität Tohoku (Sendai, 1993). Er gründete 1992 das Atelier Hitoshi Abe und eröffnete 2008 ein zweites Büro in Los Angeles. Ab 1994 leitete er das Hitoshi Abe Architectural Design Laboratory am Tohoku Institut für Technologie. Er war Professor an der Universität Tohoku (2002–2007) und wurde 2007 zum Professor und Vorsitzenden des UCLA Department of Architecture and Urban Design ernannt. Seit 2010 ist er Inhaber des Paul I. and Hisako Terasaki Lehrstuhls für zeitgenössische Japanstudien und Leiter des UCLA Terasaki Center für Japanstudien (Los Angeles). Zu seinen Projekten gehören der Miyagi Water Tower (Rifu, Miyagi, 1994), das Miyagi Stadium (Rifu, Miyagi, 2000), das Folkloremuseum Michinoku (Kurikoma, Miyagi, 2000), das Kanno Museum of Art (Shiogama, Miyagi, 2005), das Praxis- und Wohngebäude KCH/Whopper (Saitama, Saitama, 2006) sowie das FRP Ftown Building (Sendai, Miyagi, 2008). Jüngere Projekte sind das Intilaq Tohoku Innovation Center (Sendai, Miyagi, 2016), das UCLA Terasaki Research Institute (Los Angeles, 2017) und die Mikio Mizuta Gedenkhalle (Sakado, Saitama, 2017, hier vorgestellt).

HITOSHI ABE est né en 1962 à Sendai. Il a travaillé dans l'agence Coop Himmelb(l)au de 1988 à 1992 et a obtenu son M.Arch à SCI-Arc (Los Angeles, 1989), ainsi qu'un doctorat de l'université Tohoku (Sendai, 1993). Il a ouvert son agence, Atelier Hitoshi Abe, en 1992, puis un second bureau à Los Angeles en 2008. Il dirige depuis 1994 le laboratoire de design architectural Hitoshi Abe à l'Institut de technologie de Tohoku. Il a été professeur à l'université Tohoku (2002–2007), puis nommé professeur et président du département d'architecture et design urbain de l'UCLA en 2007. Il a été nommé à la chaire Paul I. et Hisako Terasaki d'étude du Japon contemporain et directeur du Centre d'études japonaises Terasaki de l'UCLA (Los Angeles) en 2010. Ses travaux comprennent notamment le château d'eau de Miyagi (Rifu, Miyagi, 1994) ; le stade de Miyagi (Rifu, Miyagi, 2000) ; le Musée folklorique de Michinoku (Kurikoma, Miyagi, 2000) ; le musée d'Art Kanno (Shiogama, Miyagi, 2005) ; la clinique et résidence KCH/Whopper (Saitama, Saitama, 2006) et l'immeuble FRP Ftown Building (Sendai, Miyagi, 2007). Parmi ses réalisations récentes figurent le Centre de l'innovation Intilaq de Tohoku (Sendai, Miyagi, 2016) ; l'Institut de recherches Terasaki de l'UCLA (Los Angeles, 2017) et le mémorial Mikio Mizuta (Sakado, Saitama, 2017, publié ici).

Opposite: *as can be seen in an aerial view, the roof of the building forms a notched arc that folds around existing forest land.*

Above: *a main feature of the design is the very low profile of the building. The drawing below shows the hill on which the structure is built.*

Previous double page: *despite appearing to be relatively closed from above, the building has ample glazed surfaces with views of the exterior. The leading edge of the building wraps around an exterior terrace facing the forest. Section drawings show the single slope of the main roof and the low profile of the structure.*

Interiors are high and airy, with natural light filtering in from several different angles.

This two-story MEMORIAL HALL includes an auditorium, a pre-function area, kitchen, offices, and a Founder's Room. Named after Mikio Mizuta (1905–76), the Japanese Minister of Finance from 1960 to 1962, it is located at the foot of Josai Hill, an important symbol for the campus of Josai University, a private institution founded in 1965. The architects explain that "a key concept was developing a solution which would be in symbiosis with the hill. A low-slung, gently arched roof mimics the topography of the hillside and minimizes the height of the building. Underneath the roof, three terraced levels follow the sloping terrain to create an expansive atrium space with framed views out of the forest to the south." Hitoshi Abe has sought to create a "bridge" between the landscape and his architecture. Inside the building, the key space is the double-height Founder's Room, which is adjacent to the main atrium and houses displays related to the history of the University and the life of Mikio Mizuta. Commissioned on the occasion of the 50th anniversary of Josai University, this reinforced-concrete and steel building was designed between January 2014 and May 2015 and built between November 2015 and March 2017.

Die zweigeschossige GEDENKHALLE verfügt über ein Auditorium, einen Empfangsbereich, eine Küche, Büros und einen sogenannten Gründersaal. Das Projekt wurde nach Mikio Mizuta (1905–1976) benannt, der von 1960 bis 1962 japanischer Finanzminister war. Es liegt am Fuß der Josai-Anhöhe, dem Erkennungszeichen des Campus der 1965 gegründeten Josai-Privatuniversität. Den Architekten zufolge „soll der Entwurf in einem symbiotischen Verhältnis zur Anhöhe stehen, ein niedriges, leicht geschwungenes Dach ahmt das Relief der Anhöhe nach und minimiert die Gebäudehöhe. Dem abschüssigen Gelände folgen drei terrassierte Ebenen und bilden ein großzügiges Atrium, von dem aus man auf den im Süden gelegenen Wald blickt". Hitoshi Abe wollte eine Brücke zwischen der Landschaft und der Architektur schlagen. Der größte und wichtigste Raum ist der doppelt hohe, an das Atrium grenzende Gründersaal, in dem eine Ausstellung über die Geschichte der Universität und das Leben von Mikio Mizuta präsentiert wird. Die in Stahlverbundbauweise errichtete Gedenkhalle wurde anlässlich des 50-jährigen Bestehens der Josai-Universität in Auftrag gegeben, von Januar 2014 bis Mai 2015 entworfen und von November 2015 bis März 2017 gebaut.

Ce MEMORIAL HALL à deux niveaux comprend un auditorium, un vestibule, une cuisine, des bureaux et la salle du Fondateur. Nommé d'après Mikio Mizuta (1905–1976), ministre japonais des Finances de 1960 à 1962, il est situé au pied de la colline Josai, point de repère symbolique du campus de l'université Josai, un établissement privé fondé en 1965. Les architectes expliquent que « l'un des concepts clés a été le développement d'une solution en symbiose avec la colline. Un toit surbaissé légèrement voûté reproduit la topographie du coteau et réduit la hauteur du bâtiment. En dessous, trois niveaux en terrasse épousent la pente du terrain afin de créer un vaste atrium aux vues encadrées sur la forêt en direction du sud ». Hitoshi Abe a voulu créer un « pont » entre le paysage et son architecture. À l'intérieur, le cœur du complexe est la salle du Fondateur avec son espace double hauteur, adjacente à l'atrium principal, qui accueille des expositions autour de l'histoire de l'université et de la vie de Mikio Mizuta. Commandé pour le 50ᵉ anniversaire de l'université Josai, ce bâtiment en béton armé et acier a été conçu entre janvier 2014 et mai 2015, puis construit entre novembre 2015 et mars 2017.

SHANGHAI POLY THEATER

TADAO ANDO

Jiading, Shanghai, 2014
Area: 55 904 m²

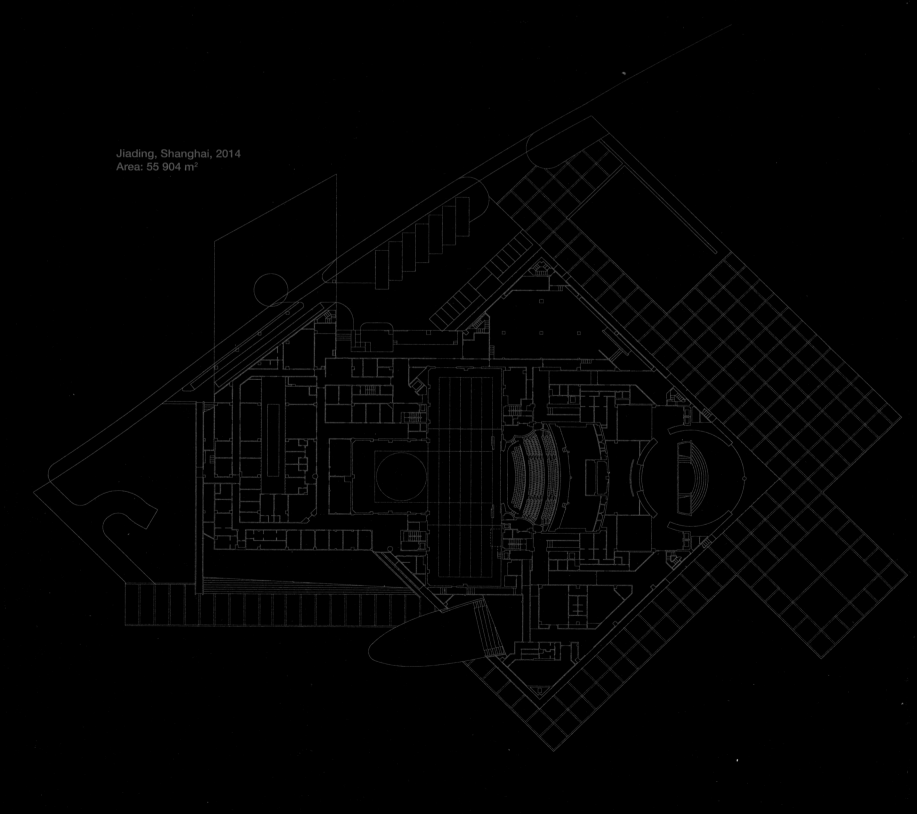

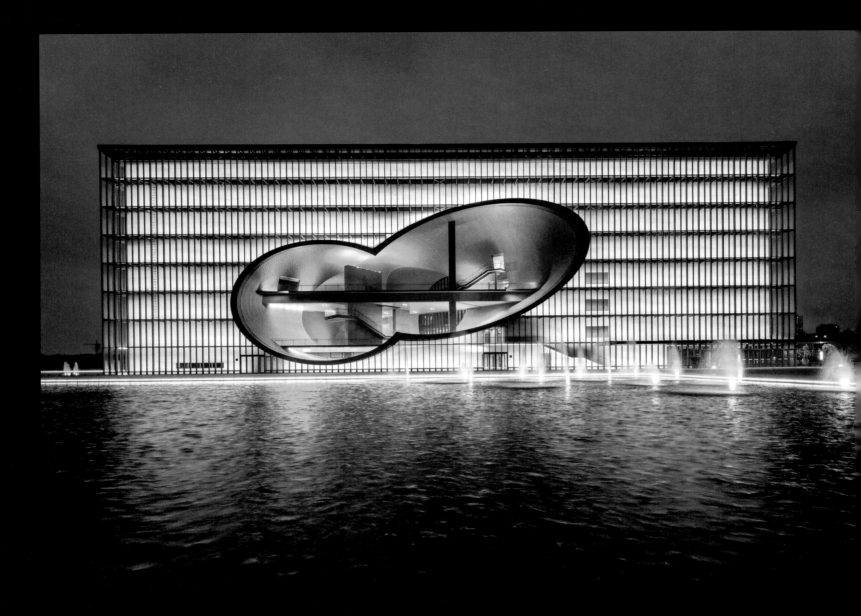

Born in Osaka in 1941, TADAO ANDO was self-educated as an architect, largely through his travels in the United States, Europe, and Africa (1962–69). He founded Tadao Ando Architect & Associates in Osaka in 1969. He has received the Alvar Aalto Medal (1985); the Medaille d'or, French Academy of Architecture (1989); the 1992 Carlsberg Prize; the 1995 Pritzker Prize; and the 1996 Praemium Imperiale. Notable recent buildings include the Modern Art Museum of Fort Worth (Texas, USA, 2002); Chichu Art Museum (Naoshima, Kagawa, 2004); Omote Sando Hills complex (Tokyo, 2006); 21_21 Design Sight (Tokyo, 2007); Tokyu Toyoko Line Shibuya Station (Shibuya, Tokyo, 2008); and the renovation of the Punta della Dogana (Venice, Italy, 2009). More recently, Ando has completed the Stone Sculpture Museum (Bad Münster am Stein, Germany, 2010); Château La Coste Art Center (Le Puy-Sainte-Réparade, France, 2011); the Roberto Garza Sada Center (University of Monterrey, Mexico, 2012); the Ando Museum (Naoshima, Kawaga, 2013); the Clark Center, Clark Art Institute (Williamstown, Massachusetts, USA, 2014); the Shanghai Poly Theater (China, 2014, published here); and the Anno Mitsumasa Art Museum (Kyotango, Kyoto, 2017, also published here). He is currently working on a new art exhibition venue for the Pinault Foundation (Bourse du Commerce, Paris, France, 2021).

TADAO ANDO wurde 1941 in Osaka geboren und ist Autodidakt. Sein Wissen hat er sich auf Reisen in die Vereinigten Staaten sowie nach Europa und Afrika (1962–1969) angeeignet. 1969 gründete er in Osaka die Firma Tadao Ando Architect & Associates. Ando wurde mit der Alvar-Aalto-Medaille (1985), der Medaille d'or der Französischen Akademie für Architektur (1989), dem Carlsberg-Architekturpreis (1992), dem Pritzker-Preis (1995) und dem Praemium Imperiale (1996) ausgezeichnet. Bedeutende Projekte der letzten zwei Jahrzehnte sind das Modern Art Museum in Fort Worth (Texas, USA, 2002), das Chichu Kunstmuseum (Naoshima, Kagawa, 2004), der Komplex Omotesando Hills (Tokio, 2006), 21_21 Design Sight (Tokio, 2007), der Bahnhof Shibuya für die Tokyu-Toyoko-Linie (Shibuya, Tokio, 2008) und ein Umbau der Punta della Dogana (Venedig, 2009). In jüngerer Vergangenheit hat Ando ein Steinskulpturenmuseum (Bad Münster am Stein, Deutschland, 2010) realisiert, das Centre d'Art Château La Coste (Le Puy-Sainte-Réparade, Frankreich, 2011), das Roberto Garza Sada Center an der Universität Monterrey, San Pedro Garza García, Mexiko, 2012), das Ando Museum (Naoshima, Kawaga, 2013), das Clark Center und das Clark Art Institute (Williamstown, Massachusetts, USA, 2014), das Shanghai Poly Theater (China, 2014, hier vorgestellt) und das Anno Mitsumasa Museum (Kyotango, Kyoto, 2017, ebenfalls hier vorgestellt). Derzeit arbeitet Ando an einem neuen Ausstellungsort für die Fondation Pinault (Bourse du Commerce, Paris, 2021).

Né à Osaka en 1941, TADAO ANDO est autodidacte et doit sa formation d'architecte en grande partie à ses voyages aux États-Unis, en Europe et en Afrique (1962–1969). Il a fondé Tadao Ando Architect & Associates à Osaka en 1969. Il a reçu la médaille Alvar Aalto en 1985, la médaille d'or de l'Académie française d'architecture en 1989, le prix Carlsberg en 1992, le prix Pritzker en 1995 et le Praemium Imperiale en 1996. Parmi ses constructions récentes les plus notables figurent le musée d'Art moderne de Fort Worth (Texas, 2002) ; le musée d'Art de Chichu (Naoshima, Kagawa, 2004) ; le complexe commercial Omote Sando Hills (Tokyo, 2006) ; le centre dédié au design 21_21 Design Sight (Tokyo, 2007) ; la station Shibuya de la ligne de métro Tokyu Toyoko (Shibuya, Tokyo, 2008) et la rénovation de la Punta della Dogana (Venise, 2009). Encore plus récemment, il a achevé le musée de la Sculpture en pierre (Bad Münster am Stein, Allemagne, 2010) ; le Centre d'art du château La Coste (Le Puy-Sainte-Réparade, France, 2011) ; le Centre Roberto Garza Sada (université de Monterrey, Mexique, 2012) ; le musée Ando (Naoshima, Kawaga, 2013) ; le Clark Center du Clark Art Institute (Williamstown, Massachusetts, 2014) ; le Poly Theater de Shanghai (2014, publié ici) et le musée Anno Mitsumasa (Kyotango, Kyoto, 2017, également publié ici). Il travaille actuellement à un nouvel espace d'exposition pour la Fondation François Pinault (Bourse du commerce, Paris, 2021).

The Jiading District, northwest of the center of
Shanghai, is near the Yangtze River. Ando's design
features an unusual façade with cylindrical voids
offering views of a man-made waterway.
Right: a sketch by Tadao Ando.

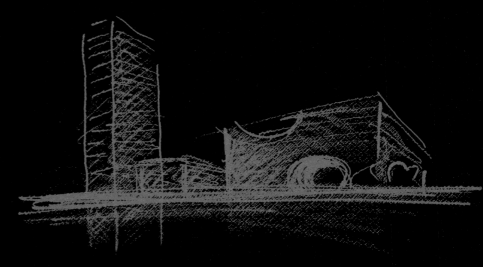

Previous double page: *the 1600-seat main theater. Here, Ando combines wood, concrete, and glass to create an almost Piranesian interpenetration of spaces.*

The SHANGHAI POLY THEATER is located 30 kilometers northwest of Shanghai in the suburban district of Jiading, a rapidly growing area that is host to the Shanghai International Circuit, a Formula One racetrack. Based around an opera house, the Shanghai Poly Theater is set on a lake and intended to form the core of a new cultural center. Its design makes use of structures in steel-reinforced concrete and a steel frame. As always with Ando, strong geometric forms, in particular its 100-meter-square volume and height of 30 meters, dominate. Yet the composition is a complex one, with unexpected elliptical cutouts in the main curtain wall, which is clad in clear laminated glass. Otherwise expressed as a strict grid, the façades correspond to the architect's clearly stated intentions. He says: "What we proposed was a building that asserts its presence through the intensity of its internal spaces rather than through overt symbolism in its external form."

Das SHANGHAI POLY THEATER liegt 30 km nordwestlich vom Zentrum Shanghais in Jiading, einem schnell wachsenden Stadtbezirk, in dem sich der Shanghai International Circuit, eine Formel-1-Rennstrecke, befindet. Der zentrale Punkt des Projekts, das an einen See grenzt und als Herzstück eines neuen Kulturquartiers konzipiert wurde, ist ein Opernhaus. Das Shanghai Poly Theater wurde in Skelettbauweise und aus Stahlbetonelementen errichtet. Wie immer bei Ando dominieren geometrische Linien, hier vor allem in Gestalt eines quaderförmigen Baukörpers mit einer Seitenlänge von 100 m und einer Höhe von 30 m, dessen Hauptvorhangfassade aus transparentem Verbundglas über elliptische Ausschnitte verfügt. Die streng gerasterten Fassaden spiegeln die Intention des Architekten wider: „Wir haben ein Gebäude vorgeschlagen, das sich durch die Eindringlichkeit der Innenräume und nicht durch eine offensichtliche Symbolik seiner äußeren Form behauptet."

Le SHANGHAI POLY THEATER est situé à 30 km au nord-ouest de Shanghai, dans le district suburbain de Jiading, une zone qui se développe rapidement et où se trouve notamment le Shanghai International Circuit, une piste de Formule 1. Articulé autour d'un opéra, le théâtre est construit sur un lac et a pour vocation de devenir le cœur d'une nouvelle zone culturelle. Le design fait appel à des structures en béton armé d'acier et à une charpente en acier. Comme toujours avec Ando, les formes géométriques strictes dominent, notamment le volume cubique de 100 m, haut de 30 m, mais la composition est complexe et comporte en particulier de surprenantes découpures en ellipse dans le principal mur rideau, revêtu de verre feuilleté clair. Les façades à la trame strictement quadrillées expriment les intentions clairement définies de l'architecte. Il le dit en ces termes : « Ce que nous avons proposé, c'est un bâtiment qui impose sa présence par l'intensité de ses espaces intérieurs plus que par un symbolisme trop évident dans sa forme extérieure. »

Inside the theater's foyer, large curving wooden ribs are transversed by doorways, a bridge, and a concrete wall, creating unexpected spaces generated by geometric volumes.

The 1600-seat main theater is aligned along a diagonal line that originates from the main entrance at the northeastern corner of the square plan. Confirming this concept, 18-meter-wide cylindrical voids have been inserted into the volume at different angles from all sides. It is the "collision" of these cylinders with the façade that creates the elliptical openings, thus underlining a strict relationship between exterior and interior. These three-dimensional spaces constitute the framework of the composition. Ando states: "The interplay between the solids and voids and the cubes and tubes produces a spatial sequence… We hope that the resultant public spaces will become alternative 'stages' that will encourage people to actively engage in cultural activities." Designed between 2009 and 2010, the project was built between March 2011 and August 2014. It was built on a 30 235-square-meter site.

Der Hauptsaal verfügt über 1600 Sitzplätze und orientiert sich an einer diagonalen Linie, die vom Hauptzugang am nordöstlichen Ende des quadratischen Grundrisses ausgeht. Dem Konzept entsprechend wurden von allen Seiten und in unterschiedlichen Winkeln zylindrische Hohlräume von 18 m Breite in das Volumen eingebracht. Die „Kollision" dieser Zylinder mit der Fassade erzeugt die elliptischen Öffnungen, unterstreicht das strenge Verhältnis von innen und außen und bestimmt die Komposition. Ando: „Das Zusammenspiel zwischen Masse, Leere, Quadern und Röhren bewirkt eine Abfolge verschiedenartiger Räume … Wir hoffen, dass die öffentlichen Bereiche, die dadurch entstehen, zu alternativen ‚Bühnen' werden, auf denen sich die Menschen dazu angeregt fühlen, Kultur aktiv mitzugestalten." Der Bau wurde zwischen 2009 und 2010 projektiert und zwischen März 2011 und August 2014 auf einem 30 235 m² großen Grundstück errichtet.

La grande salle de théâtre de 1 600 places suit une diagonale qui part de l'approche principale, à l'angle nord-est du plan carré. Le concept est renforcé par d'immenses alvéoles cylindriques larges de 18 m, insérées dans le volume à différents angles de tous les côtés. C'est la « collision » entre ces cylindres et la façade qui creuse les ouvertures en ellipses et souligne le rapport strict entre extérieur et intérieur. Ces espaces tridimensionnels forment la structure même de la composition. Ando explique : « L'interaction entre les masses solides et les vides, et entre les cubes et les tubes produit une séquence spatiale… Nous espérons que les espaces publics ainsi obtenus deviendront des « scènes » alternatives qui encourageront la participation active du public aux activités culturelles proposées. » Conçu entre 2009 et 2010, le projet a été construit entre mars 2011 et août 2014 sur un site de 30 235 m².

ANNO MITSUMASA ART MUSEUM

TADAO ANDO

Kyotango, Kyoto, 2017
Area: 442 m²

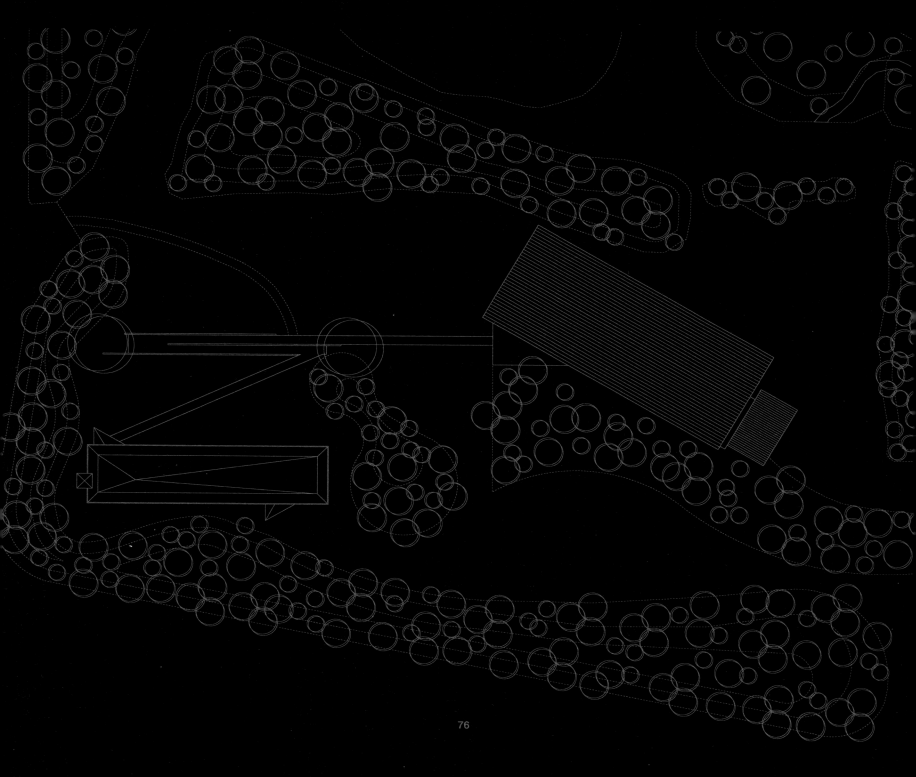

Ando's dark cedar façade brings to mind some Japanese temple repositories. No specific reference to traditional architecture is made, but the idea that this building contains something precious is clear.

Opposite: *an interior space is articulated in wood and metal, with a subtle combination of natural and artificial light.*

The building is nestled into the woods and its green coloration emphasizes its rapport with the natural setting.

Born in 1926, Anno Mitsumasa is an author and illustrator of children's books, winner of the 1984 Hans Christian Andersen Award. Located on a 4524-square-meter site in a forested rural area of northern Kyoto, the building is clad in cedar. As usual, Ando creates an indirect, diagonal approach path with a series of parallel concrete walls in front of the building. Stairs and a double-height space lead up to a second-floor gallery. Long and narrow (6 x 36 m), the relatively simple building uses wood inside with respect for the "delicate and tranquil watercolors of the painter," and has a faceted roof. Mounds of earth around the building were planted with seedlings that should create a forest environment within 10 years of the opening. Tadao Ando states: "I hope that this art museum will take root in the site and come to be embraced by the surrounding woods. We are anticipating that the architecture and landscape which reside within the forest will rouse the creativity of visitors and artists."

Anno Mitsumasa, geboren 1926, ist Kinderbuchautor sowie -illustrator und Gewinner des Hans-Christian-Andersen-Preises (1984). Das Gebäude befindet sich auf einem 4524 m² großen Grundstück in einer bewaldeten, ländlichen Gegend nördlich von Kyoto und ist mit Zedernholz verschalt. Wie üblich hat Ando einen indirekten, diagonal verlaufenden Zugangsweg angelegt, in diesem Fall mit parallelen Betonwänden. Aus einem doppelt hohen Raum führen Treppen zu einer Galerie in der zweiten Etage. Das relativ schlichte Gebäude mit Facettendach ist lang und schmal (6 x 36 m). Mit Rücksicht auf die „zarten und meditativen Aquarelle des Malers" kam im Inneren des Museums Holz zum Einsatz. Die Erdwälle um das Gebäude wurden mit Setzlingen bepflanzt, innerhalb von zehn Jahren nach der Eröffnung soll die unmittelbare Umgebung bewaldet sein. Tadao Ando: „Ich hoffe, dass das Kunstmuseum an diesem Ort Wurzeln schlägt und von Wald umgeben sein wird. Wir gehen davon aus, dass die Architektur und die Gartenlandschaft in ihrer waldigen Umgebung die Kreativität von Besuchern und Künstlern inspirieren."

Né en 1926, Anno Mitsumasa est un auteur et illustrateur de livres pour enfants, lauréat du prix Hans Christian Andersen en 1984. Construit sur un terrain de 4 524 m² dans une zone rurale de forêts au nord de Kyoto, le bâtiment est revêtu de cèdre. Comme à son habitude, Ando crée une voie d'approche indirecte en diagonale avec une série de murs parallèles en béton devant le bâtiment. Des escaliers et un espace double hauteur mènent à une galerie au premier étage. Longue et étroite (6 x 36 m), la construction relativement simple est en bois à l'intérieur par respect pour les « délicates et paisibles aquarelles du peintre » et possède un toit à plusieurs facettes. De jeunes arbres ont été plantés sur des remblais autour du bâtiment et devraient l'entourer d'une forêt d'ici dix ans. Tadao Ando explique : « J'espère que ce musée d'art s'enracinera sur le site et se trouvera un jour au milieu des bois. Nous espérons que l'architecture et le paysage au cœur de la forêt stimuleront la créativité des visiteurs et des artistes. »

LOUIS VUITTON MAISON OSAKA MIDOSUJI

JUN AOKI

Osaka, 2019
Collaboration: Peter Marino Architect,
H&A, TAISEI Corporation, A.N.D,
Louis Vuitton Malletier

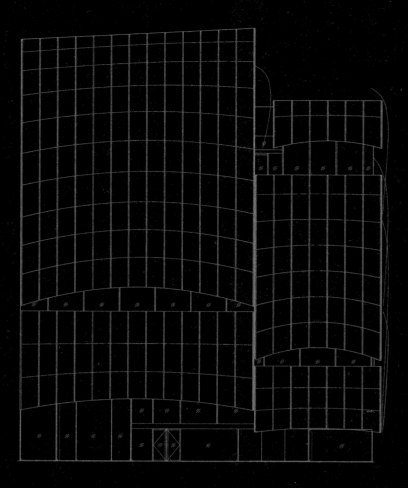
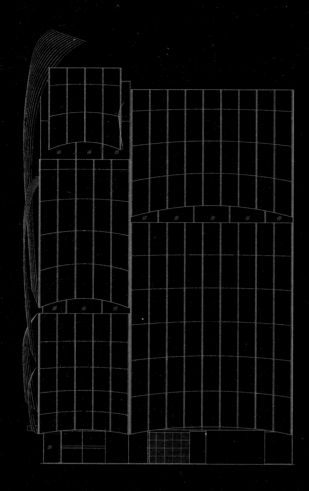

Above: *elevation drawings of the main façades.*
Opposite: *seen from above, the façades of the*
building are uniformly lit, recalling billowing sails.
A rooftop terrace can also be seen.

Born in 1956 in Yokohama, JUN AOKI graduated from the University of Tokyo in 1980, completed his Master's in Architecture two years later, and became a registered architect in 1986. He worked in the office of Arata Isozaki (1983–90) and created his own firm, Jun Aoki & Associates, in 1991. His built work includes the Fukushima Lagoon Museum (Toyosaka, Niigata, 1997); Aomori Museum of Art (Aomori, 2006); SIA Aoyama Building (Tokyo, 2008); L'Avenue Shanghai (Shanghai, China, 2013); Omiyamae Gymnasium (Tokyo, 2014); and the Miyoshi Civic Hall Kiriri (Hiroshima, 2014). He is a Professor at the Tokyo University of the Arts, and Director of Kyoto Municipal Museum of Art. He has completed a number of projects for the French fashion brand Louis Vuitton, including Louis Vuitton Nagoya (Nagoya, Aichi, 1999); Louis Vuitton Omotesando (exterior design, Omotesando, Tokyo, 2002); Louis Vuitton New York (exterior design, New York, USA, 2004); Louis Vuitton Matsuya Ginza (Tokyo, 2013); and the façades of the more recent Louis Vuitton Maison Osaka Midosuji (Osaka, 2019, published here).

JUN AOKI wurde 1956 in Yokohama geboren, schloss 1980 ein Studium an der Universität Tokio ab und absolvierte zwei Jahre später einen Master in Architektur. Aoki ist seit 1986 zugelassener Architekt. Er arbeitete im Büro von Arata Isozaki (1983–1990) und gründete 1991 seine eigene Firma, Jun Aoki & Associates. Zu seinen Projekten gehören das Fukushima Lagoon Museum (Toyosaka, Niigata, 1997), das Aomori Museum of Art (Aomori, 2006), das SIA Aoyama Building (Tokio, 2008), die L'Avenue Shanghai (Shanghai, 2013), die Omiyamae-Sporthalle (Tokio, 2014) und die Miyoshi Civic Hall Kiriri (Hiroshima, 2014). Er ist Professor an der Tokyo University of the Arts und Leiter des Kyoto Municipal Museum of Art. Er hat mehrere Projekte für das französische Modeunternehmen Louis Vuitton realisiert, darunter Louis Vuitton Nagoya (Nagoya, Aichi, 1999), Louis Vuitton Ginza (Fassade, Ginza, Tokio, 2000), Louis Vuitton New York (Fassade, 2001) und Louis Vuitton Matsuya Ginza (Tokio, 2013); darüber hinaus hat er zuletzt auch die Fassadengestaltung des Louis Vuitton Maison Osaka Midosuji (Osaka, 2019, hier vorgestellt) übernommen.

Né en 1956 à Yokohama, JUN AOKI a obtenu une licence auprès de l'université de Tokyo en 1980, puis une maîtrise en architecture deux ans plus tard. Il est architecte agréé depuis 1986. Il a travaillé dans l'agence d'Arata Isozaki (1983–1990) et créé sa propre entreprise, Jun Aoki & Associates, en 1991. Parmi ses constructions, figurent le Fukushima Lagoon Museum (Toyosaka, Niigata, 1997) ; Aomori Museum of Art (Aomori, 2006) ; SIA Aoyama Building (Tokyo, 2008) ; L'Avenue Shanghai (Shanghai, Chine, 2013) ; Omiyamae Gymnasium (Tokyo, 2014) ; et le Miyoshi Civic Hall Kiriri (Hiroshima, 2014). Il est professeur à la Tokyo University of the Arts, et directeur du Kyoto Municipal Museum of Art. Il a réalisé un certain nombre de projets pour la marque de mode française Louis Vuitton, notamment Louis Vuitton Nagoya (Nagoya, Aichi, 1999) ; Louis Vuitton Ginza (conception de l'extérieur, Ginza, Tokyo, 2000) ; Louis Vuitton New York (conception de l'extérieur, New York, États-Unis, 2001) ; Louis Vuitton Matsuya Ginza (Tokyo, 2013) ; ainsi que les façades de la plus récente Maison Louis Vuitton Osaka Midosuji (Osaka, 2019, publiée ici).

Jun Aoki was responsible for the façade design of this store in the heart of Osaka, which was inaugurated on February 1, 2020. The interiors are the work of Peter Marino. The façade design was inspired by the sails of traditional Edo period *Higaki-Kaisen* cargo ships. Osaka is known as Japan's City of Water and these ships were a basis of its trade for centuries. Metal fretwork detailing at ground level of the LOUIS VUITTON MAISON is intended to "give the impression of a ship floating on water." A ribbon-like liquid crystal sculpture by photographer Kenta Kobayashi enlivened the store windows at the time of the opening. The façade design relies on a steel-frame structure, visible from the exterior, that is covered with 10 3-D airfoil shapes made with curved glass panels. The architect explains that each double-glazed panel has two layers of highly transparent glass, one of which, facing out, is treated with a ceramic frit to create a "white cloth pattern on the surface," and to prevent it from appearing green, as the glass usually might. The use of glass permits uniform lighting from the interior, making the entire building glow from within after dark.

Jun Aoki war für das Fassadendesign dieses Geschäfts verantwortlich, das am 1. Februar 2020 im Herzen von Osaka eröffnet wurde. Die Innenarchitektur geht auf Peter Marino zurück. Das Fassadendesign ist von den Segeln der traditionellen *Higaki-Kaisen*-Handelsschiffe aus der Edo-Zeit inspiriert. Osaka gilt als Japans „Stadt des Wassers". Viele Jahrhunderte beruhten die hiesigen Handelsaktivitäten auf diesen Schiffen. Laubsägearbeiten aus Metall im Erdgeschoss sollen „den Eindruck eines auf dem Wasser schwimmenden Schiffes vermitteln". Zur Eröffnung belebte eine bandförmige Flüssigkristall-Skulptur des Fotografen Kenta Kobayashi die Schaufenster. Das Fassadendesign basiert auf einer von außen sichtbaren Stahlrahmenkonstruktion, die mit zehn 3D-Tragflächenformen aus gebogenen Glasscheiben verkleidet ist. Der Architekt erklärt, jedes Paneel bestehe aus zwei Schichten hochtransparenten Glases, von denen diejenige, die nach außen zeigt, mit einer keramischen Fritte behandelt sei, um ein „weißes Tuchmuster auf der Oberfläche" zu erzeugen und um zu vermeiden, dass das Glas grün erscheint. Der Einsatz von Glas ermöglicht eine gleichmäßige Lichtverteilung, die das gesamte Gebäude nach Einbruch der Dunkelheit von innen leuchten lässt.

Jun Aoki a été chargé de la conception de la façade de ce magasin situé au cœur d'Osaka, qui a été inauguré le 1er février 2020. Peter Marino en a conçu l'intérieur. La conception de la façade s'inspire des navires traditionnels *Higaki-Kaisen* de la période Edo. Osaka est surnommée la Cité de l'Eau du Japon, et ces navires ont permis pendant des siècles les échanges commerciaux. Les détails des éléments métalliques, au niveau du sol de la MAISON LOUIS VUITTON, sont destinés à « donner l'impression d'un navire flottant sur l'eau ». Une sculpture évoquant un ruban de cristal liquide du photographe Kenta Kobayashi a animé les vitrines du magasin pour son inauguration. La conception de la façade repose sur une structure en acier, visible de l'extérieur, recouverte de 10 formes d'ailes en 3D réalisées au moyen de panneaux de verre incurvés. L'architecte explique que chaque panneau à double vitrage se compose de deux couches de verre hautement transparent, la couche extérieure étant traitée par frittage céramique pour créer un « motif de tissu blanc sur la surface », et pour éviter d'apparaître vert, couleur normale du verre. L'utilisation du verre permet un éclairage uniforme qui fait briller tout le bâtiment de l'intérieur une fois la nuit tombée.

THE MASS

NOBUO ARAKI / THE ARCHETYPE

Harajuku, Tokyo, 2016
Area: 193 m²

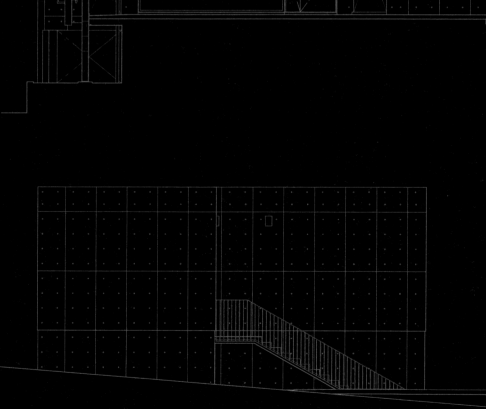

*Previous double page: the building appears to
be a solid block of concrete, with only its wooden
door suggesting an opening.*

*The upper level shows the same kind of minimal
abstraction but also deploys large windows, gray
metal doors, and projecting concrete canopies.*

NOBUO ARAKI was born in 1967 in Kumamoto.
He received his architecture degree from the
Nishinippon Institute of Technology (Fukuoka).
He created The Archetype in 1997, after
working in the office of Toyokawa Architects &
Associates. He is currently Visiting Professor
at the Nishinippon Institute of Technology.
His work includes numerous store and office
designs, like those for SOPH. in Hiroshima
(2016); Roppongi Hills (Tokyo, 2016); and
Ginza (Tokyo, 2017); AURALEE (Tokyo, 2017);
and the Sony PCL Office (Tokyo, 2018). He has
also designed the House in Oyamdai (Tokyo,
2015); The Mass (Harajuku, Tokyo, 2016,
published here); and the House in Mitatsunamachi (Tokyo, 2018).

NOBUO ARAKI wurde 1967 in Kumamoto
geboren und absolvierte ein Architektur-
studium am Nishinippon Institut für Technologie
(Fukuoka). Nachdem er im Büro von Toyokawa
Architects & Associates gearbeitet hatte,
gründete er 1997 The Archetype. Derzeit ist
er Gastprofessor am Nishinippon Institute
for Technology. Zu seinen Arbeiten gehören
zahlreiche Laden- und Büroeinrichtungen,
darunter die SOPH. Stores (Hiroshima, 2016),
Roppongi Hills (Tokio, 2016), Ginza (Tokio,
2017), AURALEE (Tokio, 2017) und das Sony
PCL Office (Tokio, 2018). Darüber hinaus hat
er entworfen: House in Oyamadai (Tokio, 2015),
The Mass (Harajuku, Tokio, 2016, hier vorgestellt) sowie House in Mitatsunamachi
(Tokio, 2018).

NOBUO ARAKI est né en 1967 à Kumamoto.
Il a obtenu son diplôme en architecture au
Nishinippon Institute of Technology (Fukuoka).
Il a créé The Archetype en 1997 après avoir
d'abord travaillé dans l'agence Toyokawa
Architects & Associates. Il est actuellement
professeur associé au Nishinippon Institute of
Technology. Il a conçu de nombreux magasins
et bureaux, parmi lesquels les boutiques SOPH.
d'Hiroshima (2016) ; Roppongi Hills (Tokyo,
2016) et Ginza (Tokyo, 2017) ; celle d'AURALEE
(Tokyo, 2017) et les bureaux de Sony PCL
(Tokyo, 2018). Il a également créé une maison
à Oyamdai (Tokyo, 2015) ; la galerie The Mass
(Harajuku, Tokyo, 2016, publiée ici) et la House,
à Mitatsunamachi (Tokyo, 2018).

Stairs lead to the upper level and the glazed
volumes. The in situ concrete is smooth but
undeniably powerful, imposing itself as a physical
presence even beyond its contents.

Designed beginning in June 2014, this "private and independent" art space was completed in November 2016. The rather unassuming concrete block structure is located in Harajuku near Omotesando on a side street off the main avenue, in the midst of a typical jumble of small shops and low-rise buildings. Where the heterogenous architectural environment makes it difficult to "stand out," the architect has opted instead for a spare, geometric austerity to make his work "exist." The basic concrete structure is combined with steel doors, brass and wood features. The entry points of the building have protruding eaves and entrance steps in order to "provide protection from seasonal weather damage." The architect collaborated with the artist Fumio Tachibana (born in 1968 in Hiroshima) for the visual identity of the project and to develope several small sculptures located on the exterior at ground level. Exhibitions have included the Swiss-born photographer Henry Leutwyler's *Document*, Hiroshi Fujiwara's *71-84 Punk Archive*, and, at the end of 2018, *Still*, floral

Die Entwurfsarbeiten für diesen „privaten und unabhängigen Kunstraum" begannen im Juni 2014, fertiggestellt wurde das Projekt im November 2016. Der eher zurückhaltende Betonquader befindet sich unweit der Omotesando-Allee in Harajuku, inmitten des typischen Gewirrs aus kleinen Geschäften und Flachbauten. Da es hier aufgrund des heterogenen architektonischen Umfelds schwierig ist, „aufzufallen", hat sich der Architekt dafür entschieden, das Projekt durch geometrische Strenge „zum Leben zu erwecken". Der schlichte Betonbau ist mit Stahltüren sowie Messing- und Holzelementen versehen. Die Gebäudezugänge sind „zum Schutz vor saisonalen Witterungsschäden" mit breiten Traufen und Vordächern ausgestattet. Araki hat mit dem 1968 in Hiroshima geborenen Künstler Fumio Tachibana zusammengearbeitet, um den visuellen Auftritt des Kunstraums und mehrere Kleinskulpturen zu entwerfen, die sich auf Bodenniveau außerhalb des Gebäudes befinden. Ausgestellt haben hier unter anderem der in der Schweiz geborene Fotograf Henry

La conception de cet espace « privé et indépendant » consacré à l'art a commencé dès juin 2014 et il a été achevé en novembre 2016. Formé d'un bloc de béton assez discret, il est situé à Harajuku, près d'Omotesando, dans une rue latérale à l'écart de l'avenue principale, au cœur d'un méli-mélo typique de petites boutiques et immeubles de faible hauteur. Dans cet environnement architectural hétérogène qui rend difficile de « sortir du lot », l'architecte a préféré une austérité géométrique sobre pour « faire exister » son œuvre. La structure de base en béton est associée à des portes en acier et des accessoires en bronze et bois. Les entrées du bâtiment possèdent des avant-toits et des marches destinés à « protéger des intempéries saisonnières ». L'architecte a collaboré avec l'artiste Fumio Tachibana (né en 1968 à Hiroshima) pour l'identité visuelle du projet et pour plusieurs petites sculptures à l'extérieur, placées au niveau du sol ou sur les murs. Parmi les expositions déjà présentées, on peut citer celle du photographe d'origine suisse Henry Leutwyler, *Document*, *71-84 Punk Archive*

PATH

ARTECHNIC

Tokyo, 2018
Area: 396 m²

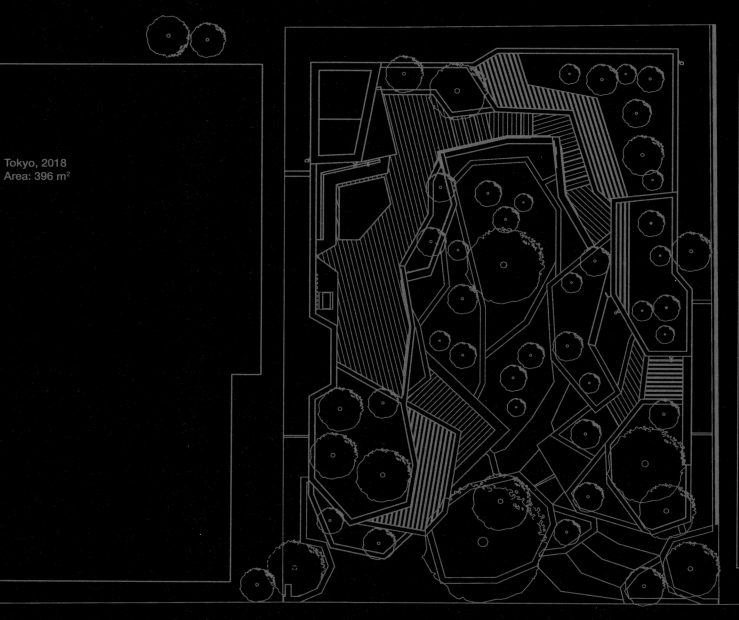

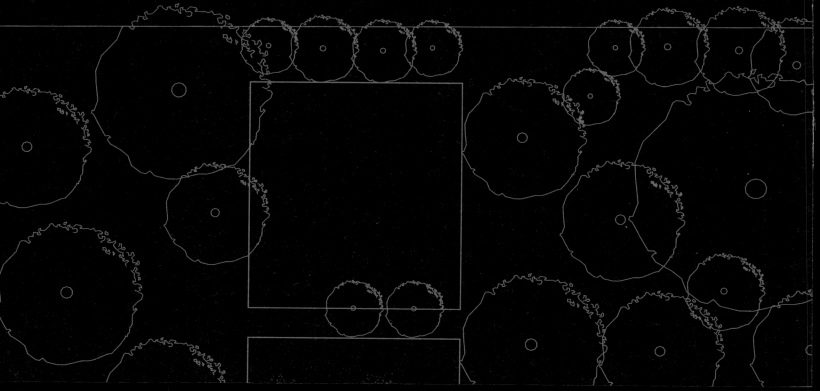

Although gray planar surfaces are the rule, the unusual angles of the building give it an organic appearance, emphasized by ample greenery.

KOTARO IDE was born in Tokyo in 1965 and graduated from the Department of Architecture at the College of Art and Design, Musashino Art University (Tokyo, 1989). He worked in the office of Ken Yokogawa Architects from 1989 to 1994 and estáblished his own office, ARTechnic Architects, in 1994. His work includes the SMD House (Zushi, Kanagawa, 1995); Oak Terrace Apartment Building (Oota, Tokyo, 1997); YMM House (Suginami, Tokyo, 1999); MSO House (Shibuya, Tokyo, 2000); Cherry Terrace Library (Shibuya, Tokyo, 2002); Manazuru Studio (Manazuru, Kanagawa, 2003); YMG House (Yokohama, Kanagawa, 2003); NKM House (Shibuya, Tokyo, 2005); Shell (Karuizawa, Nagano, 2008); M&M Rosie (Tokyo, 2009); YNO House (Tokyo, 2012); Breeze (Tokyo, 2012); the Ito Animal Hospital (Ito, Shizuoka, 2013); and PATH (Tokyo, 2018, published here).

KOTARO IDE wurde 1965 in Tokio geboren und ist Absolvent des Fachbereichs Architektur der Fakultät für Kunst und Design an der Kunsthochschule Musashino (Tokio, 1989). Er arbeitete von 1989 bis 1994 bei Ken Yokogawa Architects und gründete 1994 sein eigenes Büro – ARTechnic Architects. Zu seinen Projekten zählen SMD House (Zushi, Kanagawa, 1995), das Oak Terrace Apartment Building (Oota, Tokio, 1997), YMM House (Suginami, Tokio, 1999), MSO House (Shibuya, Tokio, 2000), Cherry Terrace Library (Shibuya, Tokio, 2002), Manazuru Studio (Manazuru, Kanagawa, 2003), YMG House (Yokohama, Kanagawa, 2003), NKM House (Shibuya, Tokio, 2005), Shell (Karuizawa, Nagano, 2008), M&M Rosie (Tokio, 2009), YNO House (Tokio, 2012), Breeze (Tokio, 2012), die Tierklinik Ito (Ito, Shizuoka, 2013) sowie PATH (Tokio, 2018, hier vorgestellt).

KOTARO IDE est né à Tokyo en 1965. Il est diplômé du département d'architecture du collège d'art et design à l'université d'art Musashino (Tokyo, 1989). Il a travaillé dans l'agence Ken Yokogawa Architects de 1989 à 1994 avant d'ouvrir la sienne, ARTechnic Architects, en 1994. Ses principales réalisations comprennent la maison SMD (Zushi, Kanagawa, 1995) ; l'immeuble d'appartements Oak Terrace (Oota, Tokyo, 1997) ; la maison YMM (Suginami, Tokyo, 1999) ; la maison MSO (Shibuya, Tokyo, 2000) ; la bibliothèque Cherry Terrace (Shibuya, Tokyo, 2002) ; le studio Manazuru (Manazuru, Kanagawa, 2003) ; la maison YMG (Yokohama, Kanagawa, 2003) ; la maison NKM (Shibuya, Tokyo, 2005) ; la villa Shell (Karuizawa, Nagano, 2008) ; M&M Rosie (Tokyo, 2009) ; la maison YNO (Tokyo, 2012) ; l'immeuble Breeze (Tokyo, 2012) ; l'hôpital vétérinaire d'Ito (Shizuoka, 2013) et le complexe résidentiel PATH (Tokyo, 2018, publié ici).

In the heart of the building, terraces and more
planting create agreeable open spaces enlivened
by an irregular plan.

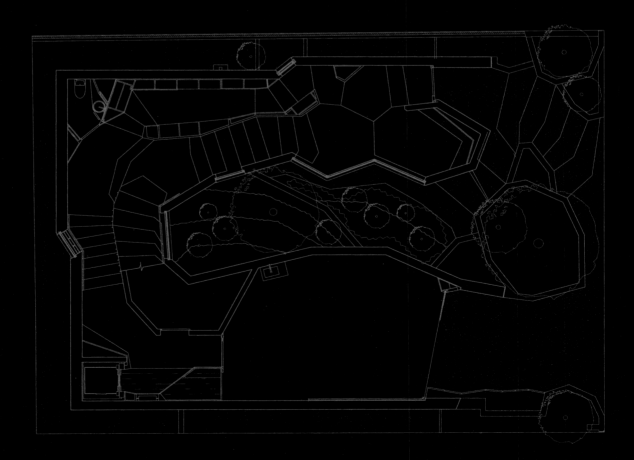

Previous double page: full-height glazing and gardens that will grow in more fully bring in both light and a green respite from the urban environment.

Above: a stairway and a view toward an apartment interior with its wooden floors ilustrate the warmth and intriguing spatial experience created by the architecture.

The architect explains his research in terms of creating "an abstract natural scenery" in concrete. Three sides of the site are closed off by other buildings, so an emphasis was placed on openings to the north alongside the road. The site is sloped and has half levels, meaning that "the whole volume, which resembles a rocky mountain, is set back at each layer." The name of the house, PATH, referring to the access to the "rocky mountain (valley?)," was provided by the design. Kotaro Ide explains that this concept of the mountain is related to visits he made to the works of Peter Zumthor in Switzerland (Vals), but also to his familiarity with the volcanic "columnar joints" seen in the area of the Izu Peninsula in Japan that he saw during his childhood. The gray, jutting appearance of the structure confirms this geological reference, although the suggestion that this is an "organic" design is more subliminal than it is apparent in the visual sense. In fact, plans for the building are more directly related to the "mountain valley" concept than the emerging forms, where straight, albeit angled lines are quite present.

Der Architekt wollte mit diesem Projekt eine „abstrakte Naturlandschaft" aus Beton entwerfen. Das Grundstück wird auf drei Seiten durch andere Gebäude begrenzt, sodass der Schwerpunkt auf die zur Straße hin offene Nordseite gelegt wurde. Der Standort ist abschüssig, und „das Volumen ähnelt in seiner Gesamtheit einem zerklüfteten Berg". Der Projektname PATH resultiert aus den Eigenschaften des Entwurfs und bezieht sich auf den Zugangsweg zu dem „zerklüfteten Berg". Kotaro Ide zufolge ging sein Berg-Konzept auf Besuche bei Peter Zumthor in der Schweiz (Vals) und auf die säulenförmigen Vulkangesteinsformationen zurück, die er als Kind auf der japanischen Izu-Halbinsel gesehen hat. Das graue, aufwärtsstrebende Erscheinungsbild des Gebäudes bekräftigt den geologischen Bezug, trotzdem bleiben die laut Ide „organischen Eigenschaften" des Entwurfs unterschwellig und offenbaren sich nicht auf den ersten Blick. Tatsächlich wird die Ähnlichkeit mit einem „Bergtal" eher in den Entwurfszeichnungen als in der finalen Formgebung selbst deutlich, in der gerade, wenn auch abgewinkelte Linienverläufe sehr präsent sind.

L'architecte explique sa recherche par la création d'« un décor naturel abstrait » en béton. Sur trois des côtés du site, la vue est obstruée par d'autres constructions, de sorte que les ouvertures vers le nord ont été privilégiées, du côté de la route. Le terrain est en pente, avec des demi-niveaux, de façon à ce que « le volume dans son ensemble, qui fait penser à une montagne rocheuse, présente des couches chacune en retrait par rapport à la précédente ». Le nom, PATH, évoque l'accès à la « montagne rocheuse (ou vallée ?) » et s'explique par le design lui-même. Kotaro Ide explique que ce concept de montagne vient des œuvres de Peter Zumthor qu'il a vues en Suisse (Vals), mais aussi des « colonnes basaltiques » d'origine volcanique dans la péninsule d'Izu, au Japon, qu'il a découvertes dans son enfance. Le gris et la structure en surplomb confirment cette référence géologique, même si l'idée d'un design « organique » est plus subliminale que réellement visible. En fait, les plans du bâtiment sont plus directement associés au concept de « vallée montagneuse » que les formes émergentes où les lignes droites, bien qu'anguleuses, restent très présentes.

Angled furniture seems to echo the forms of the
building. Views of the space, both interior and
exterior, fully characterize the design.

LA SEINE MUSICALE

SHIGERU BAN

Île Seguin, Boulogne-Billancourt, France, 2017
Area: 36 500 m²
Collaboration: Jean de Gastines

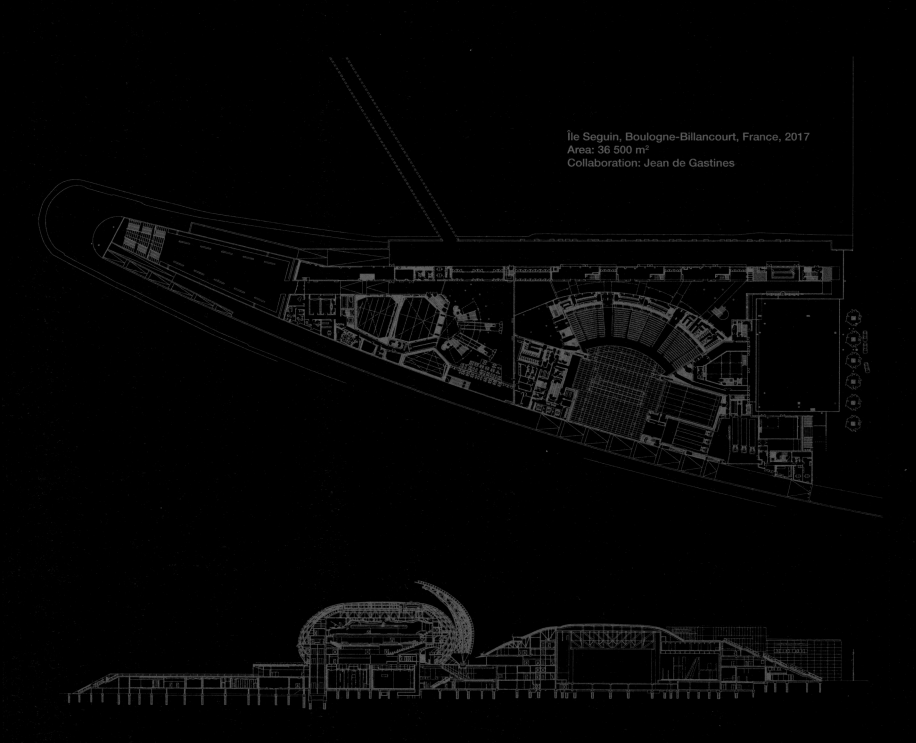

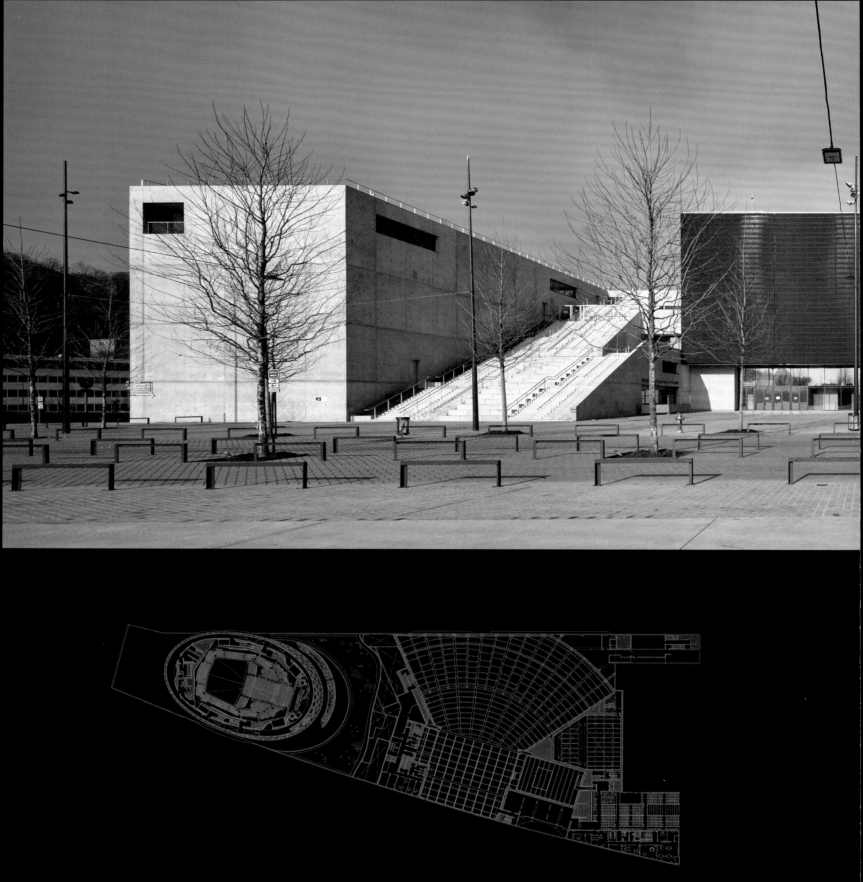
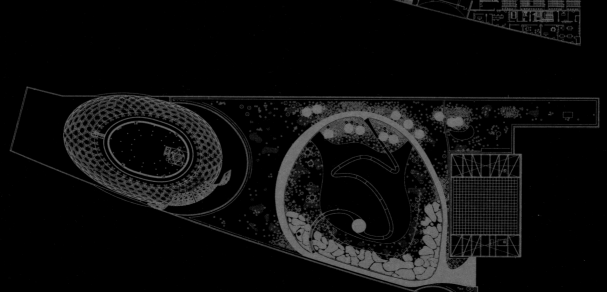

Born in 1957 in Tokyo, SHIGERU BAN studied in Los Angeles at SCI-Arc from 1977 to 1980. He then attended the Cooper Union School of Architecture, where he studied under John Hejduk (New York, 1980–82), returning to graduate in 1984 after working in the office of Arata Isozaki for a year. He then founded his own firm in Tokyo in 1985. Shigeru Ban was awarded the 2014 Pritzker Prize. He designed the Japanese Pavilion at Expo 2000 in Hanover. His more recent work includes disaster relief Post-Tsunami Rehabilitation Houses (Kirinda, Hambantota, Sri Lanka, 2007); Haesley Nine Bridges Golf Clubhouse (Yeoju, South Korea, 2009); and Metal Shutter House on West 19th Street in New York (USA, 2010). He installed his Paper Temporary Studio (2004) on top of the Centre Pompidou in Paris to work on the Centre Pompidou-Metz (Metz, France, 2010). Other work includes L'Aquila Temporary Concert Hall (Italy, 2011); Container Temporary Housing, disaster-relief project for the east Japan earthquake and tsunami (Onagawa, Miyagi, 2011); Tamedia (Zurich, Switzerland, 2013); Cardboard Cathedral (Christchurch, New Zealand, 2013); Aspen Art Museum (Colorado, USA, 2014); Oita Prefectural Art Museum (Oita, 2015); and Cast Iron House (New York, USA, 2017). Published here are La Seine Musicale (Île Seguin, Boulogne-Billancourt, France, 2017); Mount Fuji World Heritage Center (Shizuoka, 2017); and Shonai Hotel Suiden Terrasse (Tsuruoka, Yamagata, 2018).

SHIGERU BAN wurde 1957 in Tokio geboren und studierte von 1977 bis 1980 am SCI-Arc in Los Angeles, anschließend studierte er bei John Hejduk an der Cooper Union School of Architecture (New York, 1980–1982); an die er nach einjähriger Tätigkeit im Büro von Arata Isozaki 1984 zurückkehrte, um seinen Abschluss zu machen. Im Jahr darauf gründete er in Tokio eine eigene Firma. Shigeru Ban wurde 2014 mit dem Pritzker-Preis ausgezeichnet. Er entwarf den japanischen Pavillon für die Expo 2000 in Hannover. Neuere Arbeiten sind unter anderem der Wiederaufbau eines Dorfes, das durch einen Tsunami zerstört wurde (Kirinda, Hambantota, Sri Lanka, 2007), das Haesley Nine Bridges Golf Clubhouse (Yeoju, Südkorea, 2009) und das Metal Shutter House an die West 19th Street in New York (2010). Auf dem Dach des Centre Pompidou in Paris installierte er sein Paper Temporary Studio (2004), in dem er das Centre Pompidou Metz (Metz, Frankreich, 2010) entwarf. Weitere Projekte sind unter anderem ein temporärer Konzertsaal in L'Aquila (Italien, 2011), temporäre Containerbehausungen im Rahmen eines Katastrophenhilfeprojekts nach dem Tsunami in Ostjapan (Onagawa, Miyagi, 2011), Tamedia (Zürich 2013), Cardboard Cathedral (Christchurch, 2013), das Aspen Art Museum (Colorado, 2014), das Kunstmuseum der Präfektur Oita (Oita, 2015) und Cast Iron House (New York, 2017). Hier vorgestellt werden: La Seine Musicale (Île Seguin, Boulogne-Billancourt, Frankreich, 2017), Mount Fuji World Heritage Center (Shizuoka, 2017) sowie Shonai Hotel Suiden Terrasse (Tsuruoka,

Né en 1957 à Tokyo, SHIGERU BAN a fait ses études à Los Angeles au SCI-Arc de 1977 à 1980, puis à l'École d'architecture de la Cooper Union auprès de John Hejduk (New York, 1980–82). Il a ensuite travaillé un an pour Arata Isozaki avant de revenir passer son diplôme de fin d'études en 1984 Et de fonder son agence à Tokyo en 1985. Shigeru Ban a été lauréat du Pritzker Prize en 2014. Il a conçu le pavillon du Japon à l'Expo 2000 de Hanovre. Ses réalisations les plus récentes comprennent les maisons de réhabilitation dans le cadre des secours aux victimes du tsunami (Kirinda, Hambantota, Sri Lanka, 2007) ; le clubhouse du golf de Haesley Nine Bridges (Yeoju, Corée du Sud, 2009) et les Metal Shutter Houses de la 19e Rue Ouest à New York (2010). Il a installé son Studio temporaire en papier sur la terrasse du Centre Pompidou à Paris pour y travailler au Centre Pompidou-Metz (2010). Parmi ses nombreuses autres réalisations figurent la salle de concert temporaire de L'Aquila (Italie, 2011) ; le logement temporaire en containers, projet d'aide aux victimes du tremblement de terre et du tsunami dans l'est du Japon (Onagawa, Miyagi, 2011) ; le siège de Tamedia (Zurich, 2011–13) ; la Cathédrale de carton (Christchurch, Nouvelle-Zélande, 2013) ; le musée d'Art d'Aspen (Colorado, 2014) ; le musée d'Art de la préfecture d'Oita (Oita, Japon, 2015) ; et la Cast Iron House (New York, 2017) publiés ici ; La Seine musicale (île Seguin, Boulogne-Billancourt, 2017) ; le Mount Fuji World Heritage Center (Shizuoka, 2017) et le Shonai Hotel Suiden Terrasse (Tsuruoka, Yamagata, 2018).

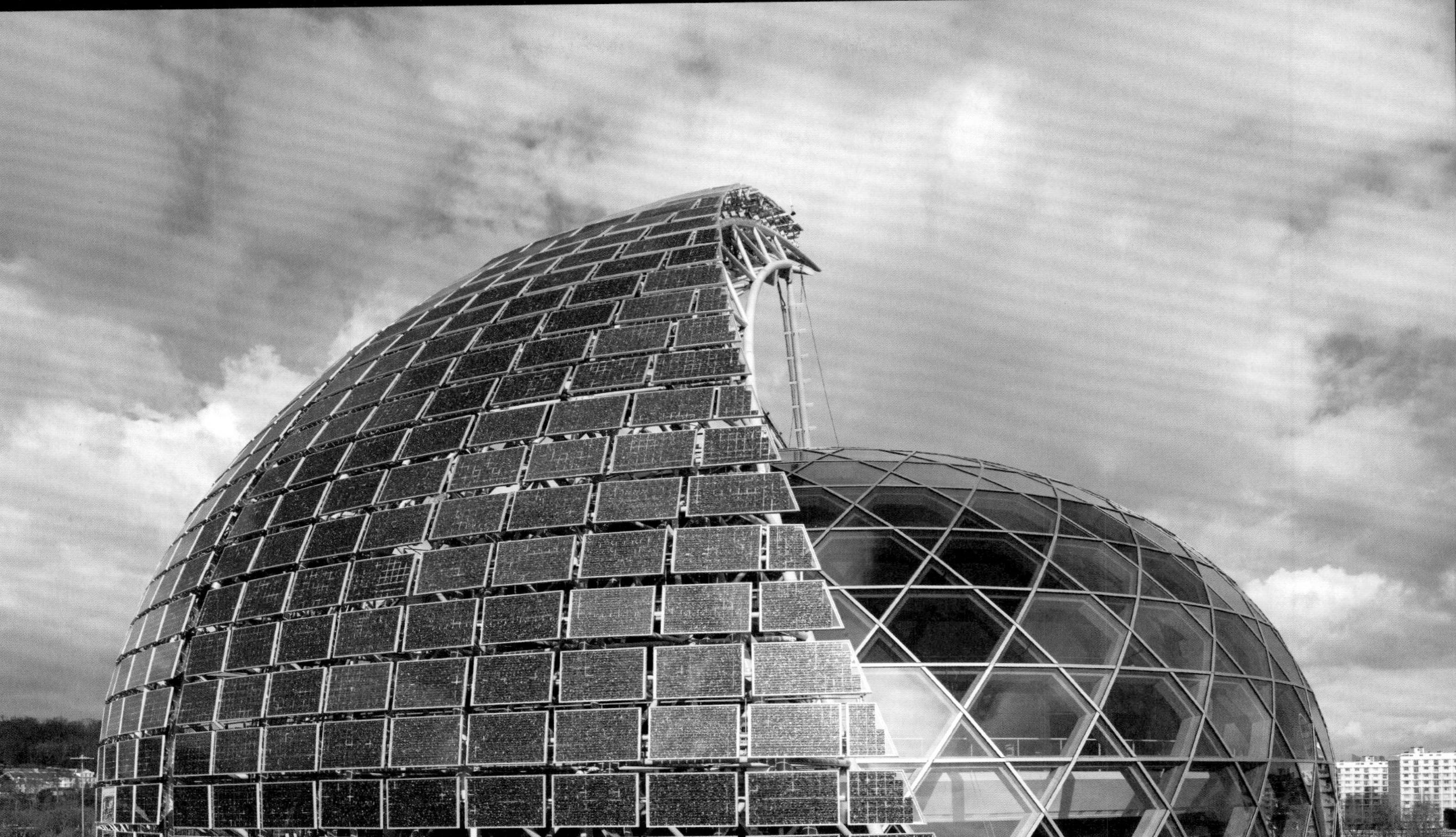

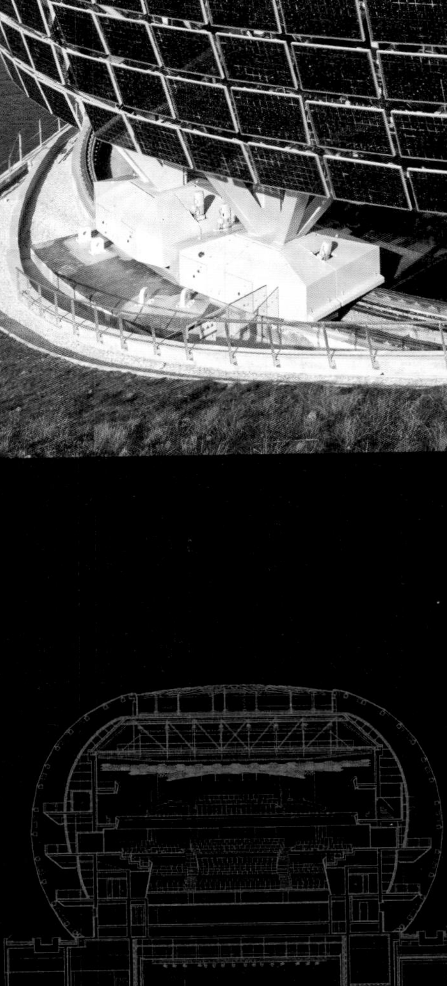

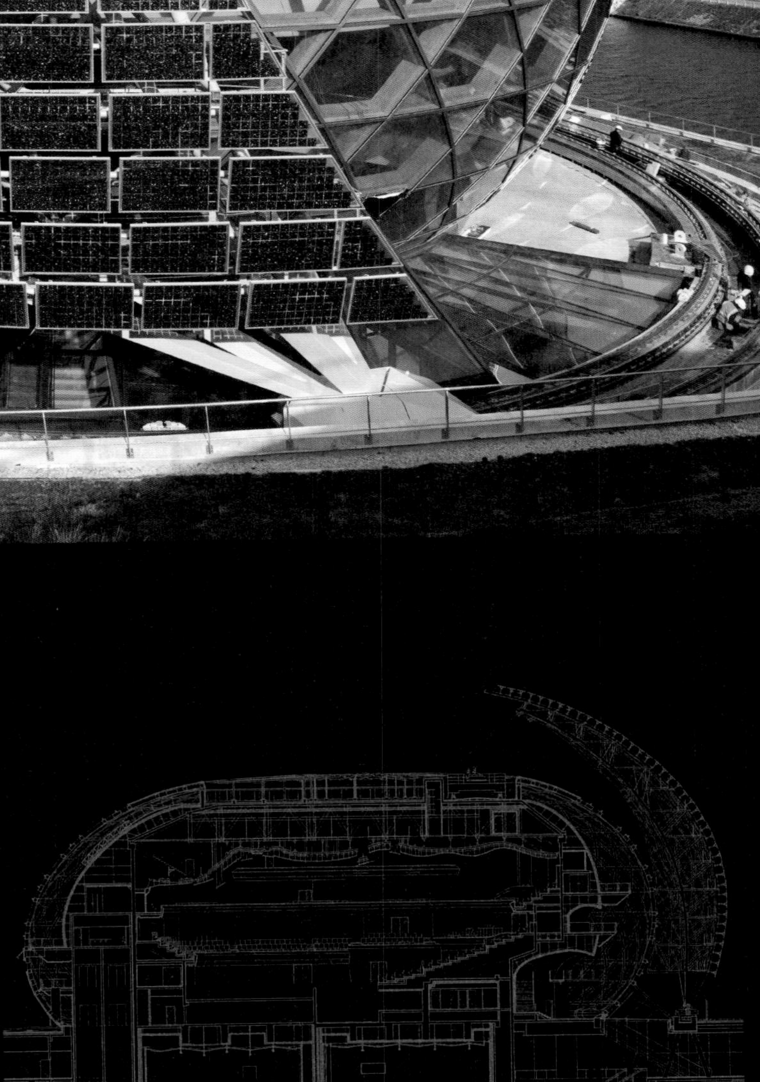

The concert hall has birch plywood walls, solid oak floors, while a ceiling with acoustic panels made from wood and paper tubes is suspended from an acoustic reflector to enhance acoustics.

Sitting on a 280-meter-long site originally intended for the François Pinault Foundation designed by Tadao Ando, the SEINE MUSICALE is inserted into an overall master plan conceived by Jean Nouvel. The most visible feature of the complex is its "sail," a semi-spherical form covered with 470 photovoltaic panels and designed to turn according to the orientation of the sun. Within the sail, behind a timber structure that carries glass hexagons, an egg-shaped acoustic shell covers the auditorium. According to Shigeru Ban: "Its color changes from emerald green to bronze red according to the lighting and the angle of vision. It is inspired by the Japanese *tamamushi* beetle." The multipurpose Grande Seine concert hall intended for amplified music has 4000 seats but can accommodate as many as 6000. The classical music concert hall has 1150 seats, birch plywood walls, solid oak floors, and a ceiling made of 916 wood hexagons filled with paper tubes and suspended from an acoustic reflector. The complex includes a choir school, a rooftop garden, rehearsal and recording rooms, an interior street, a giant screen at the main entrance, and a 1475-square-meter sculpture garden at the tip of the Île Seguin, originally the site of a Renault automobile factory. Constructed for the cost of €170 million, the facility opened in April 2017. Built by the Department of the Hauts-de-Seine, the complex is under the programmatic control of STS Evènements, a joint venture between the television station TF1 and Sodexo, a health services company.

LA SEINE MUSICALE wurde in einen Masterplan von Jean Nouvel eingefügt und liegt auf einem 280 m langen Grundstück, auf dem ursprünglich die von Tadao Ando entworfene Fondation Pinault gebaut werden sollte. Der Komplex ist durch das sogenannte Segel, eine halbsphärische, mit 470 Photovoltaikmodulen versehene Struktur, die sich dem Sonnenverlauf entsprechend ausrichten lässt, weithin sichtbar. Innerhalb des Segels, hinter einer Holzkonstruktion, in die sechseckige Glaselemente eingelassen sind, befindet sich die eiförmige Akustikumhüllung des Auditoriums. Ban: „Die Farben changieren je nach Beleuchtung und Blickwinkel zwischen Smaragdgrün und Bronzerot und sind durch den japanischen *tamamushi*-Käfer inspiriert." Der multifunktionale Konzertsaal ist für verstärkte Musik bestimmt, hat 4000 Sitzplätze und kann insgesamt bis zu 6000 Personen aufnehmen. Der Konzertsaal für klassische Musik hat 1150 Sitzplätze, verfügt über eine Birkenfurnierverschalung, Böden aus massiver Eiche und eine Deckenkonstruktion aus 916 Holzsechsecken, die mit papierenen Röhren gefüllt und an einem akustischen Reflektor aufgehängt sind. Zu dem Komplex gehören eine Chorschule, ein Dachgarten, Probe- und Aufnahmeräume, eine rue Intérieure, ein großer Bildschirm am Haupteingang und ein 1475 m² großer Skulpturengarten. Die Île Seguin war früher der Sitz der Renault-Werke. Die für 170 Millionen Euro erbaute Einrichtung wurde im April 2017 eröffnet. Federführend in der Programmgestaltung des vom Département Hauts-de-Seine in Auftrag gegebenen Komplexes ist STS Evènements, ein Joint Venture zwischen dem Fernsehsender TF1 und Sodexo, einem Gesundheitsunternehmen.

Occupant un terrain long de 280 m destiné au départ au bâtiment de la Fondation François Pinault créé par Tadao Ando, la SEINE MUSICALE s'insère dans un plan directeur global conçu par Jean Nouvel. L'élément le plus visible du complexe est sa « voile » de forme hémisphérique, recouverte de 470 panneaux photovoltaïques qui tournent pour suivre la course du soleil. À l'intérieur, derrière une structure en bois qui supporte des hexagones en verre, une coque acoustique ovoïde recouvre l'auditorium. Pour Shigeru Ban, « sa couleur passe du vert émeraude au rouge bronze selon l'éclairage et l'angle de vision. Elle s'inspire de la carapace du coléoptère japonais *tamamushi* ». La salle de concert polyvalente de la Grande Seine, destinée à la musique amplifiée, dispose de 4 000, places mais peut accueillir jusqu'à 6 000 spectateurs. La salle de musique classique, quant à elle, possède 1 150 fauteuils, des murs en contreplaqué de bouleau, de solides planchers de chêne et un plafond composé de 916 hexagones en bois emplis de tubes de carton et suspendus à un réflecteur acoustique. Le complexe accueille une maîtrise de chant, un jardin sur le toit, des salles de répétition et d'enregistrement, une allée intérieure, un écran géant à l'entrée principale, et un parc de sculptures de 1 475 m² à la pointe de l'île Seguin, site occupé à l'origine par une usine automobile Renault. La construction a coûté 170 millions d'euros et l'établissement a ouvert en avril 2017. Construit par le département des Hauts-de-Seine, le complexe doit sa programmation à STS Événements, une entreprise commune à la chaîne de télévision TF1 et à Sodexo, un prestataire de services dans le domaine de la santé

MOUNT FUJI WORLD HERITAGE CENTER

SHIGERU BAN

Fujinomiya, Shizuoka, 2017
Area: 3411 m²
Collaboration: Studio on Site (Landscape Design),
ARUP (Structural Engineer, MEP)

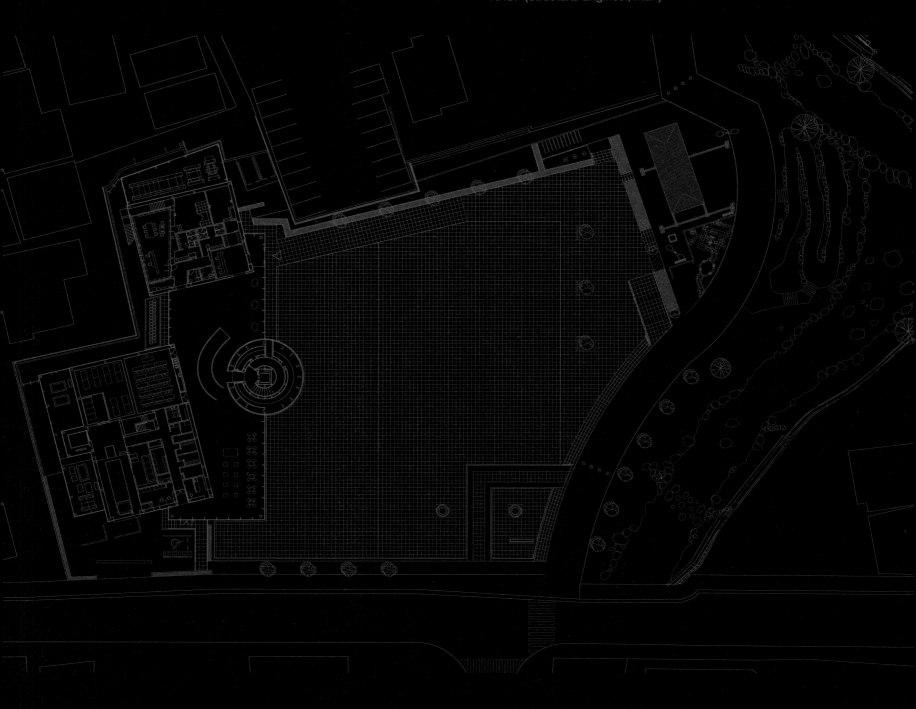

The latticed wood shape of this exterior volume recalls the inverted form of Mount Fuji, which becomes a right-side-up image when reflected in the pond.

The environmental scheme of this building includes "natural circulation created by Mount Fuji," including the use of spring water that is at 15 °C at all times of year for cooling, as well as a high-efficiency heat pump and water recycling. The building has exterior walls in latticed wood and its shape recalls the image of an inverted Mount Fuji. A large pond fed by the spring water used in the heating and cooling system is located in front of the building, thus reflecting this shape right-side up. A spiral ramp leads from the ground floor to the fifth level, allowing visitors to see exhibitions as they ascend. The observation hall on the fifth level features a very large window where visitors have a panoramic view of the real mountain. The use of an unusual shape, together with its wooden lattice and the overall sustainability of the building, make it one of Ban's more emblematic designs.

Das Energie- und Umweltkonzept des Gebäudes macht sich „die durch den Fuji hervorgerufene natürliche Luftbewegung" zunutze, verwendet zu Kühlzwecken Quellwasser, dessen Temperatur ganzjährig bei 15 °C liegt, und ist mit einer hocheffizienten Wärmepumpen- und Wasseraufbereitungsanlage ausgestattet. Das Projekt verfügt über eine Holzgitterfassade und soll an einen kopfstehenden Berg erinnern. Die Form des Berges spiegelt sich aufrecht in einem großen Teich, der von dem im Heiz- und Kühlsystem verwendeten Quellwasser gespeist wird. Eine spiralförmige Rampe führt aus dem Erdgeschoss bis in die fünfte Etage, Besucher können sich im Verlauf des Aufstiegs die Ausstellungen ansehen. Die Aussichtshalle im fünften Stock verfügt über ein sehr großes Fenster, von hier aus haben die Besucher freie und weite Sicht auf den Fuji. Die ungewöhnliche Form, das Holzgitter und das nachhaltige Konzept machen das Gebäude zu einem der emblematischeren Entwürfe des Architekten.

Le concept écologique du bâtiment tire profit de la « climatisation naturelle créée par le mont Fuji » lui-même, qui passe notamment par l'utilisation de l'eau d'une source à 15 °C toute l'année pour rafraîchir l'atmosphère, mais aussi par une pompe à chaleur à haut rendement et le recyclage de l'eau. Le bâtiment présente des murs extérieurs en treillage de bois et sa forme rappelle le mont Fuji à l'envers. Il se reflète à l'endroit dans un vaste bassin devant lui, alimenté par l'eau de la source utilisée pour le chauffage et la climatisation. Une rampe grimpe en spirale du rez-de-chaussée au cinquième étage, et traverse plusieurs expositions sur son passage. La salle d'observation au dernier étage dispose d'une immense fenêtre avec une vue panoramique sur le véritable volcan. Le choix d'une forme inédite, le treillage de bois et le caractère globalement durable de l'ensemble en font l'une des créations les plus emblématiques de Ban.

The torii gate of the Mount Fuji World Heritage Center is visible across the water in this image, as is the generous glazed interior space of the Center itself.

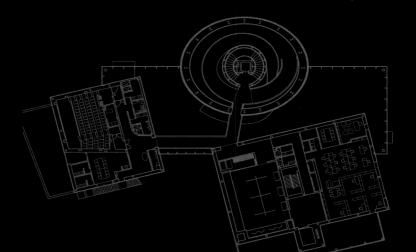

SHONAI HOTEL SUIDEN TERRASSE

SHIGERU BAN

Kitakyoden, Tsuruoka, Yamagata, 2018
Area: 9088 m²
Collaboration: Studio on Site (Landscape Design),
ARUP (Structural Engineer, MEP)

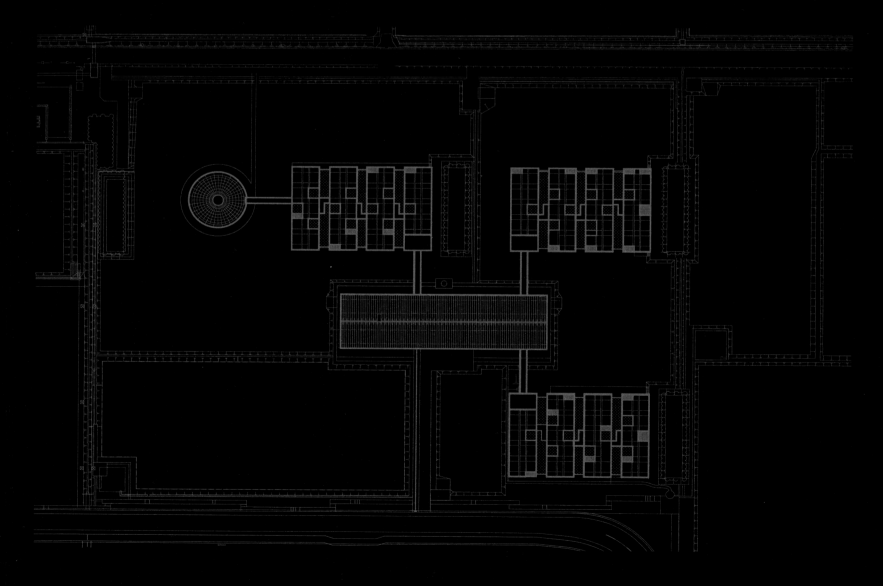

Known as a rice-growing region, the Shonai Plain is the location of this new hotel. The two-story wooden structure appears to float on rice paddies (*suiden* in Japanese). Further linking the design to the region, the wings of the hotel are named after three sacred mountains located in Yamagata Prefecture (the three mountains of Dewa: Mount Haguro, Mount Gassan, and Mount Yudono). These rectangular room blocks are grouped around a central elongated rectangular pavilion. The hotel, the first by Shigeru Ban, has 143 guestrooms and a natural hot spring bath. The spa fitness building has a roof made from laminated wood in a hexagonal woven pattern, covering the entire spa area. The central common area contains the reception, restaurant, library, and gift shops. Local food and sake is featured in the restaurant. The hotel is located five minutes by car from Tsuruoka station and was built for Yamagata Design in steel, concrete, and timber. The guestroom building is a column-beam timber structure. Using his trademark light design, the architect has also succeeded here in connecting this hotel both to its immediate site (the rice paddies) and to historic points of interest in the area.

Der Standort dieses Hotelneubaus ist die als Reisanbaugebiet bekannte Shonai-Ebene. Die zweigeschossige Holzkonstruktion scheint über den Reisfeldern (jap.: *suiden*) zu schweben. Die verschiedenen Flügel des Hotels sind nach den drei heiligen Bergen von Dewa in der Präfektur Yamagata benannt (Haguro, Gassan, Yudono). Die rechteckigen Zimmerblocks gruppieren sich um einen zentralen, länglichen, ebenfalls rechteckigen Pavillon. Dies ist Shigeru Bans erster Hotelbau, er verfügt über 143 Zimmer und ein Naturthermalbad. Das Gebäude, in dem sich der Spa- und Fitnessbereich befindet, ist im gesamten Wellnessareal von einer Deckenkonstruktion aus Schichtholz mit einer hexagonalen Webstruktur überdacht. Im zentral gelegenen Gemeinschaftsbereich befinden sich die Rezeption, das Restaurant, die Bibliothek und die Souvenirläden. Im Restaurant werden regionale Küche und Sake angeboten. Das Hotel liegt fünf Autominuten vom Bahnhof Tsuruoka entfernt und wurde für den Auftraggeber Yamagata Design unter Verwendung von Stahl, Beton und Holz gebaut. Das Gebäude, in dem sich die Zimmer befinden, ist eine Träger-Stützen-Konstruktion aus Holz. Durch die ihm eigene, klare und leichte Formensprache gelingt es dem Architekten, das Hotel mit den Reisfeldern in der unmittelbaren Umgebung und den historischen Sehenswürdigkeiten der Region in Bezug zu setzen.

C'est dans la plaine de Shonai, région rizicole connue, que se trouve ce nouvel hôtel. La structure en bois à deux niveaux semble flotter sur les rizières (*suiden* en japonais). Pour ancrer encore plus le complexe dans la région, les ailes de l'hôtel portent les noms des trois montagnes sacrées de la préfecture de Yamagata (les trois monts de Dewa : le mont Haguro, le mont Gassan et le mont Yudono). Les blocs rectangulaires contenant les chambres sont groupés autour d'un pavillon central allongé, également rectangulaire. L'hôtel, le premier construit par Shigeru Ban, possède 143 chambres et des bains alimentés par une source d'eau chaude naturelle. Le toit en bois lamellé du bâtiment, consacré à un centre de beauté et de bien-être, présente un motif tissé hexagonal qui recouvre tout l'espace spa. Au centre, la partie commune abrite la réception, le restaurant, la bibliothèque et la boutique de souvenirs. Le restaurant sert des produits locaux et du saké. L'hôtel est à 5 min en voiture de la gare de Tsuruoka et a été construit pour Yamagata Design en acier, béton et bois d'œuvre. Le bâtiment des chambres possède une structure en bois à poutres et colonnes. Avec le travail sur la lumière qui est sa marque de fabrique, l'architecte est parvenu ici aussi à associer l'hôtel à son environnement immédiat (rizières) et aux sites de la région présentant un intérêt historique.

Light-colored wood floors, ceilings, screens, and furnishings participate in the light, airy appearance of the dining area above.

Below: a guest room with an open sliding glass wall.

OMOTESANDO KEYAKI BUILDING

NORIHIKO DAN

Shibuya, Tokyo, 2013
Area: 955 m²
Collaboration: ARUP (Structural Engineer),
Setsubikeikaku (Electrical Engineer)

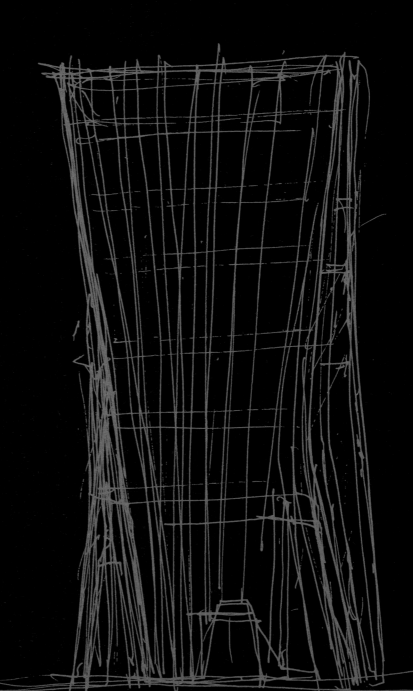

The shape formed by the columns of the building, which is located on a corner of Omotesando avenue, differentiates it completely from surrounding buildings, even those designed by very well-known architects.

NORIHIKO DAN was born in 1956 in Kanagawa Prefecture. He received his B.A. degree from Tokyo University (1979) and his M.A. from the same institution in 1982, working at that time in the Fumihiko Maki Laboratory. He founded Arch Studio in 1982 as well, before obtaining an M.A. degree from Yale University. He established Norihiko Dan and Associates in 1986. His recent work includes HOLON L/R (Shibuya, Tokyo, 2004); the N-Clinic (Saitama, 2005); M-Hall (Aichi, 2007); Sun Moon Lake Administration, Office of Tourism (Yuchi, Nantou, Taiwan, 2010); the Omotesando Keyaki Building (Shibuya, Tokyo, 2013, published here); and Taiwan Taoyuan International Airport Terminal 1 (Taiwan, 2014). More recent work includes the Convention Center in Ningbo (Zhejiang, China, 2019); Ginza 8 Chome Project (Tokyo, 2019); and North Aoyama Project (Tokyo, 2019).

NORIHIKO DAN wurde 1956 in der Präfektur Kanagawa geboren. Im Jahr 1979 machte er seinen B.A. an der Universität Tokio und 1982 seinen M.A., während des Studiums arbeitete er im Fumihiko Maki Laboratory. Bevor er an der Yale University einen zweiten Masterstudiengang absolvierte, gründete er 1982 Arch Studio. Norihiko Dan and Associates gründete er 1986. Zu seinen jüngeren Projekten zählen HOLON L/R (Shibuya, Tokio, 2004), N-Clinic (Saitama, 2005), M-Hall (Aichi, 2007), Unit J-5 (Shibuya, Tokio, 2009), HOLON II (Shibuya, Tokio, 2009), das Touristeninformationszentrum Sun Moon Lake (Yuchi, Nantou, Taiwan, 2010), das Omotesando Keyaki Building (Shibuya, Tokio, 2013, hier vorgestellt) sowie den Taiwan Taoyuan International Airport Terminal 1 (Taiwan, 2014). Weitere aktuelle Projekte sind unter anderem ein Tagungszentrum in Ningbo (Zhejiang, China, 2019), das Ginza 8-Chome Project (Tokio, 2019) und das North Aoyama

NORIHIKO DAN est né en 1956 dans la préfecture de Kanagawa. Il est titulaire d'un BA (1979) et d'un MA (1982) de l'université de Tokyo où il a travaillé dans le laboratoire de Fumihiko Maki. Il a fondé Arch Studio en 1982, avant d'obtenir un M.A. de l'université de Yale. Il a créé Norihiko Dan and Associates en 1986. Ses réalisations récentes comprennent HOLON L/R (Shibuya, Tokyo, 2004) ; la clinique N (Saitama, 2005) ; M-Hall (Aichi, 2007) ; Unit J-5 (Shibuya, Tokyo, 2009) ; HOLON II (Shibuya, Tokyo, 2009) ; l'administration de l'office de tourisme du lac du Soleil et de la Lune (Yuchi, Nantou, Taïwan, 2010) ; l'immeuble Omotesando Keyaki (Shibuya, Tokyo, 2013, publié ici) et le terminal 1 de l'aéroport international Taoyuan de Taïwan (Taïwan, 2014). Ses projets récents comprennent le palais des congrès de Ningbo (Zhejiang, Chine, 2019) ; le projet Ginza 8 Chome (Tokyo, 2019) ; et North Aoyama (Tokyo, 2019).

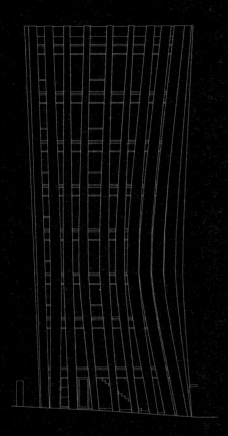
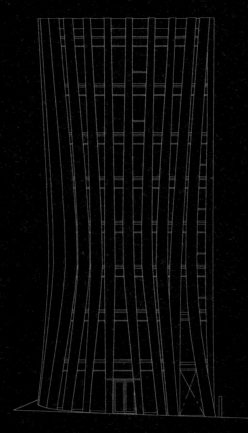
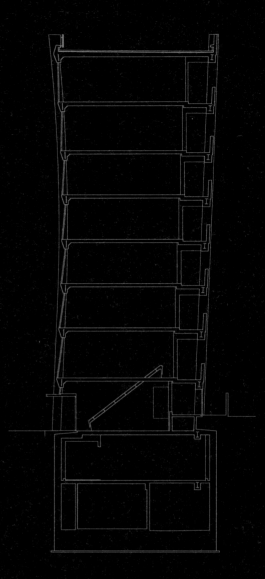

Opposite: *the angular appearance of the building's exterior is echoed in this image of a staircase, which opens onto the carefully composed concrete forms imagined by Norihiko Dan.*

Located directly next to Toyo Ito's Tod's Building (2004), in the middle of Omotesando avenue, this eight-story steel-frame, reinforced-concrete structure has a footprint of just 138 square meters. The architect explained that he willfully engaged the work of his colleague Toyo Ito "by creating a diagonal orientation with an irregularly shaped circle. This is to maximize the corner lot feature of the premises, and to accentuate the inner vertical façade of the adjacent Tod's building, in order to create a certain 'symbiotic' synergy." Although Norihiko Dan's building adds another element to the local architectural promenade, which also includes work by SANAA (Dior, 2004) nearby and Tadao Ando (Omotesando Hills, 2005) just opposite, the OMOTESANDO KEYAKI BUILDING, now a Hugo Boss store, is meant to contribute to the interrelation of the neighborhood rather than constitute a stand-alone statement. Dan further explains that the "leaf-shaped columns" have a texture that was created with the use of wooden molds for the poured-in-place concrete.

Diese achtgeschossige Stahlbetonkonstruktion mit einer Grundfläche von nur 138 m² befindet sich auf dem zentralen Abschnitt der Omotesando-Allee und in unmittelbarer Nachbarschaft zu Tod's Building (2004) von Toyo Ito. Der Architekt bezog den Entwurf seines Kollegen ganz bewusst mit ein und entschied sich für eine „diagonale Ausrichtung und einen unregelmäßig kreisförmigen Grundriss – auf diese Weise sollten das Eckgrundstück optimal ausgenutzt, die vertikale Innenfassade von Tod's Building akzentuiert und ‚symbiotische' Synergien freigesetzt werden." Zwar fügt Norihiko Dan der Omotesando-Allee, auf der sich ganz in der Nähe ein Bau von SANAA (Dior, 2004) und direkt gegenüber ein Bau von Tadao Ando (Omotesando Hills, 2005) befinden, ein weiteres architektonisches Element hinzu, aber das OMOTESANDO KEYAKI BUILDING, in dem sich ein Hugo Boss Store befindet, soll zum architektonischen Wechselspiel in der Nachbarschaft beitragen und kein selbstbezügliches Statement darstellen. Dan zufolge entstand die Oberflächenstruktur der „blattförmigen Säulen" mithilfe von Holzformen, in die sie vor Ort gegossen wurden.

Située juste à côté de l'immeuble Tod's créé par Toyo Ito (2004), au centre de l'avenue Omotesando, cette construction de huit niveaux en béton armé à charpente en acier occupe une empreinte de seulement 138 m². L'architecte explique qu'il a volontairement associé le travail de son collègue Toyo Ito au sien « en créant une orientation en diagonale avec un cercle de forme irrégulière. Cela permet d'optimiser la parcelle d'angle et de mettre encore plus en valeur la façade intérieure verticale de l'immeuble Tod's voisin afin de créer une certaine synergie "symbiotique" ». S'il ajoute un nouvel élément à la promenade architecturale locale qui comprend aussi des réalisations de SANAA (Dior, 2004) à proximité et de Tadao Ando (Omotesando Hills, 2005) juste en face, l'IMMEUBLE OMOTESANDO KEYAKI, aujourd'hui un magasin Hugo Boss, se veut plus une contribution aux liens étroits entre les bâtiments du voisinage qu'une expression autonome. Dan explique aussi que la texture des « colonnes en forme de feuille » a été obtenue avec des moules en bois pour le béton coulé en place.

LOOPTECTURE A

SHUHEI ENDO

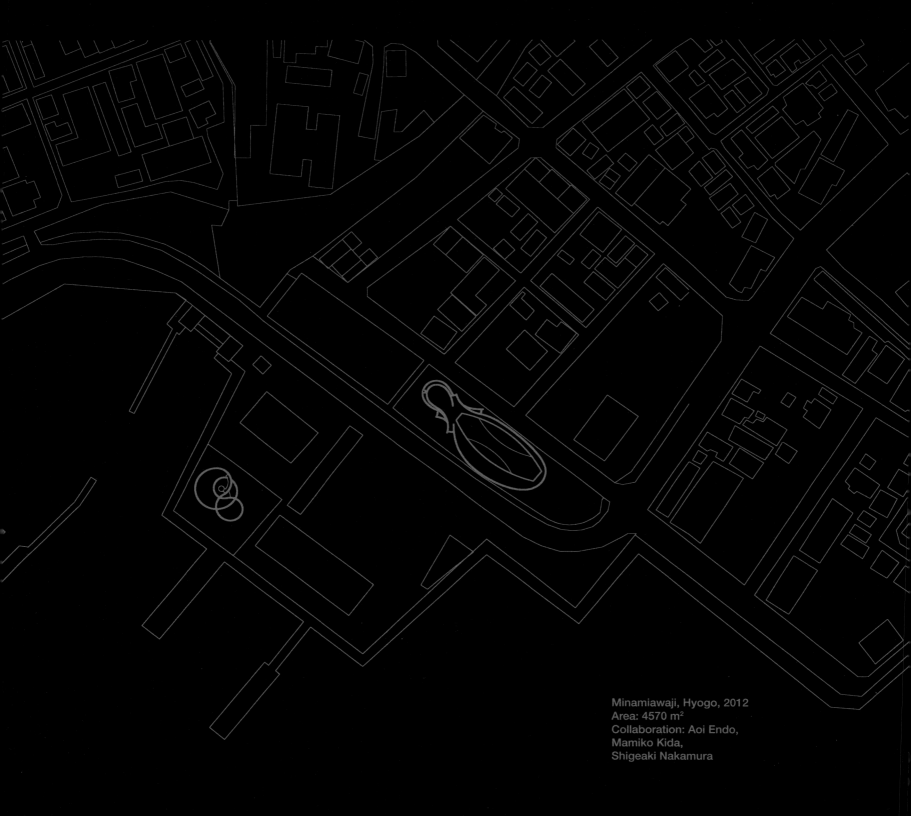

Minamiawaji, Hyogo, 2012
Area: 4570 m²
Collaboration: Aoi Endo,
Mamiko Kida,
Shigeaki Nakamura

The fish-like form of the building is clearly visible in this aerial view but so, too, is its unusual overall design, which appears in good part to be opaque.

Born in Shiga Prefecture in 1960, SHUHEI ENDO obtained his master's degree from the Kyoto City University of Arts in 1986. He worked after that with the architect Osamu Ishii and established his own firm, the Endo Shuhei Architect Institute, in 1988. His work has been widely published, and he has received numerous prizes, including the Andrea Palladio International Prize in Italy (1993). He is currently Professor at the Graduate School of Architecture, Kobe University. His work includes Slowtecture S (Maihara, Shiga, 2002); Growtecture S (Osaka, 2002); Springtecture B (Biwa-cho, Shiga, 2002); Bubbletecture M (Maibara, Shiga, 2003); Rooftecture C (Taishi, Hyogo, 2003); Rooftecture H (Kamigori, Hyogo, 2004); and Bubbletecture O (Maruoka, Fukui, 2004). In 2007, he completed Bubbletecture H (Sayo, Hyogo); Slowtecture M (Miki-city, Hygo); and Rooftecture M (Habikino City, Osaka). More recent work includes Looptecture A (Minamiawaji, Hyogo, 2012, published here); Rooftecture OT2 (Osaka, 2012); Arktecture M (Himeji, Hyogo, 2013); the Donald Keene Center of Japanese Culture (Kashiwazaki, Niigata, 2013); Growtecture B (Kashiwazaki, Niigata, 2015); and Rooftecture P (Nagahama, Shiga, 2017).

SHUHEI ENDO wurde 1960 in der Präfektur Shiga geboren und schloss 1986 sein Master-studium an der Städtischen Kunsthochschule Kyoto ab. Anschließend arbeitete er mit dem Architekten Osamu Ishii zusammen und grün-dete 1988 sein Büro Endo Shuhei Architect Institute. Seine Projekte wurden vielfach veröf-fentlicht und mit zahlreichen Preisen ausge-zeichnet, darunter der italienische Andrea Palladio International Prize (1993). Derzeit ist er Professor an der Graduiertenschule für Architektur der Universität Kobe. Zu seinen Arbeiten zählen unter anderem Slowtecture S (Maihara, Shiga, 2002), Growtecture S (Osaka, 2002), Springtecture B (Biwa-cho, Shiga, 2002), Bubbletecture M (Maibara, Shiga, 2003), Rooftecture C (Taishi, Hyogo, 2003), Roof-tecture H (Kamigori, Hyogo, 2004) und Bubble-tecture O (Maruoka, Fukui, 2004). Im Jahr 2007 realisierte er Bubbletecture H (Sayo, Hyogo), Slowtecture M (Miki-city, Hygo) und Roof-tecture M (Habikino City, Osaka). Neuere Arbeiten sind unter anderem Looptecture A (Minamiawaji, Hyogo, 2012, hier vorgestellt), Rooftecture OT2 (Osaka, 2012), Arktecture M (Himeji, Hyogo, 2013), das Donald Keene Center of Japanese Culture (Kashiwazaki, Niigata, 2013), Growtecture B (Kashiwazaki, Niigata, 2015) und Rooftecture P (Nagahama, Shiga, 2017).

Né dans la préfecture de Shiga en 1960, SHUHEI ENDO a obtenu son master de l'uni-versité des arts de Kyoto en 1986. Il a ensuite travaillé pour l'architecte Osamu Ishii et a fondé son agence, Endo Shuhei Architect Institute, en 1988. Son œuvre a été largement publiée et a reçu de nombreuses distinctions, dont le prix Andrea Palladio International en Italie (1993). Il enseigne actuellement à l'École supé-rieure d'architecture de l'université de Kobé. Parmi ses réalisations : Slowtecture S (Maihara, Shiga, 2002) ; Growtecture S (Osaka, 2002) ; Springtecture B (Biwa-cho, Shiga, 2002) ; Bubbletecture M (Maibara, Shiga, 2003) ; Roof-tecture C (Taishi, Hyogo, 2003) ; Rooftecture H (Kamigori, Hyogo, 2004) et Bubbletecture O (Maruoka, Fukui, 2004). Parallèlement à Bubbletecture H (Sayo, Hyogo, 2006–07), il a achevé Slowtecture M (Miki-city, Hyogo) et Rooftecture M (Habikino City, Osaka) en 2007. Ses créations plus récentes comprennent notamment Looptecture A (Minamiawaji, Hyogo, 2012, publié ici) ; Rooftecture OT2 (Osaka, 2012) ; Arktecture M (Himeji, Hyogo, 2013) ; le centre Donald Keene de la culture japonaise (Kashiwazaki, Niigata, 2013) ; Growtecture B (Kashiwazaki, Niigata, 2015) et Rooftecture P (Nagahama, Shiga, 2017).

Both a theater and a tsunami refuge for the local population, the building is lifted off the ground precisely because of potential high water. Its surface pattern gives it an almost archaic appearance.

The combination of wood and mesh-molded concrete gives a fairly rough and mysterious air to the interior spaces located near the theater, which is seen on the next double page.

According to tradition, Awaji Island, where this theater is located, is the birthplace of traditional Japanese puppet play, Ningyo-Joruri. A company of professional performers is even based in the building. Shuhei Endo employed exposed concrete in a corrosion-resistant steel-mesh mold, allowing the creation of a 3-D curved surface that appears to be "soft." According to the architect: "The texture of the concrete blends with the scenery of the port town." The plan of the structure resembles a slightly deformed figure eight, or perhaps a fish. The structure is, in fact, intended primarily as a tsunami refuge for local populations, and it is thus lifted on pilotis. Its main entrance is on the second floor. Opposite this entrance, the upper southern wall opens out in the direction of the sea. A curved interior wall finished in black wood leads to the 200-seat theater. Shuhei Endo explains: "Although the wood has a simple forceful expression when compared to the concrete surface of the wall in the mesh mold, the inherent feel of the material, the comfort of its familiarity and the composure has a feeling of opening similar to the outdoor alley. This is the beginning of the making of the space, which invites a visitor to a theater." There is little artificial light in this area. The interior walls of the auditorium are finished in 30-year-old traditional Kawara Japanese roof tiles.

Die Insel Awaji, auf der sich dieses Theater befindet, ist der Überlieferung nach der Ursprungsort des traditionellen Ningyo-Joruri-Figurentheaters, und tatsächlich ist in diesem Gebäude auch ein professionelles Puppenspielerensemble zu Hause. Shuhei Endo verwendet Sichtbeton in einer korrosionsbeständigen Stahlgitterform, wodurch eine geschwungene, dreidimensionale und „weich" anmutende Oberfläche entsteht. Der Architekt: „Die Textur des Betons fügt sich in die Umgebung der Hafenstadt ein." Der Grundriss erinnert an eine verformte Acht oder an einen Fisch. Auf einer Pilotis-Konstruktion gebaut, soll es im Falle eines Tsunami den Anwohnern zudem als Zufluchtsort dienen. Der Haupteingang liegt im zweiten Geschoss. Die meerseitige Südfassade des Gebäudes verfügt im oberen Bereich über eine Fensteröffnung. Der Weg in den Theatersaal mit seinen über 200 Sitzplätzen führt an einer geschwungenen, mit schwarzem Holz verkleideten Innenwand vorbei. Shuhei Endo: „Obwohl das Holz im Vergleich zur Betonoberfläche schlicht und kraftvoll anmutet, vermittelt es durch seinen Materialcharakter und seine Vertrautheit eine große Offenheit. Dies ist der Beginn der Entstehung des Raumes, der den Besucher in ein Theater einlädt." Hier gibt es nur wenig künstliches Licht. Die Innenwände des Theatersaals sind mit 30 Jahre alten, traditionellen *kawara*-Ziegeln verkleidet.

L'île d'Awaji où se trouve ce théâtre a traditionnellement donné naissance au spectacle de marionnettes japonais appelé Ningyo-Joruri, dont une troupe professionnelle est basée dans le bâtiment. L'architecte a utilisé du béton apparent et un moule à mailles en acier inoxydable qui lui a permis de créer une surface tridimensionnelle courbe d'apparence « douce ». Pour lui, « la texture du béton se fond dans le décor de la ville portuaire ». Le plan du bâtiment rappelle un 8 légèrement déformé, ou peut-être un poisson. Il a d'abord été conçu comme un refuge pour les populations locales en cas de tsunami, ce qui explique les pilotis sur lesquels il est surélevé. L'entrée principale est au deuxième niveau. En face, le haut mur sud s'ouvre vers la mer. Un mur intérieur incurvé aux finitions de bois noir mène au théâtre de 200 places. Shuhei Endo explique : « Malgré l'expression de force simple du bois par rapport à la surface en béton du mur aux mailles moulées, la sensation inhérente du matériau, le confort de son caractère familier et de sa composition confère un sentiment d'ouverture semblable à celui de l'allée extérieure. C'est le début de la création de l'espace qui invite un spectateur au théâtre. » La lumière artificielle est très réduite. Les parois de l'auditorium sont ornées de tuiles japonaises *kawara* vieilles de 30 ans, utilisées traditionnellement pour les toits.

CHILDREN'S PRACTICE PITCHING FIELD

MASAKI ENDOH

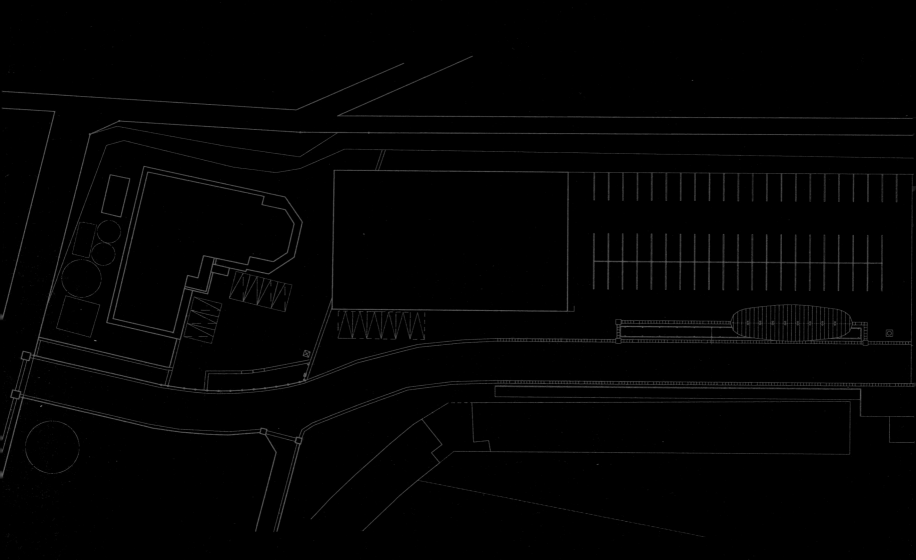

Minamiaizu, Fukushima, 2016
Area: 71 m²
Collaboration: Sei Haganuma,
Ejiri Structural Engineers

The building is, indeed, moveable and seems to be so in this parking lot setting. The angled panels and tapered roof emphasize the impression of movement.

MASAKI ENDOH was born in Tokyo in 1963. He graduated from the Science University of Tokyo in 1987 and completed an M.Arch in 1989, at the same University. He worked for the KAI-Workshop (1989–94) and established his firm, EDH Endoh Design House, in 1994. He has been a Professor at Chiba Institute of Technology since 2008. He was awarded the Tokyo House Prize for Natural Shelter in 2000; the Yoshioka Award for Natural Shelter in 2000; and the JIA "Rookie of the Year 2003" for Natural Ellipse in 2003. His body of work include Natural Shelter (Tokyo, 1999); Natural Illuminance (Tokyo, 2001); Natural Slats (Tokyo, 2002); Natural Ellipse (Tokyo, 2002); Natural Wedge (Tokyo, 2003); Natural Strata (Kawasaki, 2003); and, more recently, Natural Illuminance II (Tokyo, 2011); Natural Strip IV (Tokyo, 2011); and the Children's Practice Pitching Field (Fukushima, 2016, published here).

MASAKI ENDOH wurde 1963 in Tokio geboren, absolvierte 1987 ein Studium an der Naturwissenschaftlichen Universität Tokio und erhielt ebenda 1989 seinen M.Arch. Er arbeitete für den KAI-Workshop (1989–1994) und gründete 1994 EDH Endoh Design House. Seit 2008 ist er Professor an der Technischen Hochschule Chiba Kogyo Daigaku. Endoh erhielt den Tokyo House Prize für Natural Shelter (2000), den Yoshioka Award für Natural Shelter (2000) und den JIA Rookie of the Year 2003 für Natural Ellipse (2003). Zu seinen Arbeiten gehören unter anderem Natural Shelter (Tokio, 1999), Natural Illuminance (Tokio, 2001), Natural Slats (Tokio, 2002), Natural Ellipse (Tokio, 2002), Natural Wedge (Tokio, 2003) und Natural Strata (Kawasaki, 2003). In jüngerer Vergangenheit realisierte er Natural Illuminance II (Tokio, 2011), Natural Strip IV (Tokio, 2011) sowie einen Softball-Platz für Kinder (Fukushima, 2016, hier vorgestellt).

MASAKI ENDOH est né à Tokyo en 1963. Il est diplômé de l'Université des sciences de Tokyo (1987) où il a également obtenu un M. Arch en 1989. Il a travaillé pour KAI-Workshop (1989–94) et a ouvert son agence, EDH Endoh Design House, en 1994. Il est professeur à l'Institut de technologie de Chiba depuis 2008. Il a reçu le Tokyo House Prize pour Natural Shelter en 2000 ; et le prix Yoshioka pour Natural Shelter en 2000 et le prix du débutant « Rookie of the Year 2003 » du Japan Institute of Architects pour Natural Ellipse en 2003. Ses réalisations comprennent Natural Shelter (Tokyo, 1999) ; Natural Illuminance (Tokyo, 2001) ; Natural Slats (Tokyo, 2002) ; Natural Ellipse (Tokyo, 2002) ; Natural Wedge (Tokyo, 2003) ; Natural Strata (Kawasaki, 2003) et, plus récemment, Natural Illuminance II (Tokyo, 2011) ; Natural Strip IV (Tokyo, 2011) et le terrain de jeux de ballons couvert pour enfants (Fukushima, 2016, publié ici).

Despite being relatively small, the narrow, high, wooden structure does not declare its function and might perhaps be mistaken for a kind of church when seen from a distance.

Although it is modest by nature, this structure, sponsored by Nike for practice pitching, is part of broader effort to revive the area of Fukushima. It is intended mainly to be used in the winter season to allow children to practice throwing and pitching: softball is a popular sport in the region. The movable building is made with Tate log panels fabricated with locally harvested wood. The architect states: "The proposal for this new building shows that removing and rebuilding are one way to change the future of Fukushima." Masaki Endoh has been a consistent experimenter in building design and engineering. This new project, although quite small, shows a continued interest in structural and materials innovation, while creating an attractive and readily

Dieses bescheidene Projekt wurde vom Sporthersteller Nike finanziert und ist Teil weitreichender Anstrengungen, die Region Fukushima zu revitalisieren. Kinder sollen hier vor allem im Winter die Möglichkeit haben, Softball zu spielen. Die Sportart ist in der Gegend sehr beliebt. Die mobile Konstruktion wurde mit Platten aus regional geschlagenem Holz gefertigt. Der Architekt: „Der Entwurf zeigt, dass eine Möglichkeit, die Zukunft von Fukushima zu verändern, darin besteht, abzureißen und neu zu bauen." Im Hinblick auf die Gebäudeplanung und die Bauweise hat Masaki Endoh schon immer gern experimentiert. Trotz seiner eher geringen Größe steht dieser ansprechende und flexibel einsetzbare Übungsplatz für das anhaltende Interesse

Malgré son caractère naturellement modeste, la structure sponsorisée par Nike pour encourager la pratique du base-ball et du softball contribue à l'effort plus important entrepris pour redonner vie à la région de Fukushima. Elle est destinée à être surtout utilisée en hiver pour l'entraînement des enfants au lancer et au jet de balle : le softball est un sport très populaire dans la région. La construction mobile est faite de panneaux de rondins fabriqués à partir de bois récolté sur place. L'architecte déclare : « Cette proposition de nouveau bâtiment montre à quel point le déplacement et la reconstruction peuvent constituer l'une des solutions pour un nouvel avenir à Fukushima. » Masaki Endoh a toujours expérimenté en matière de conception et de construction. Ce nouveau projet, malgré

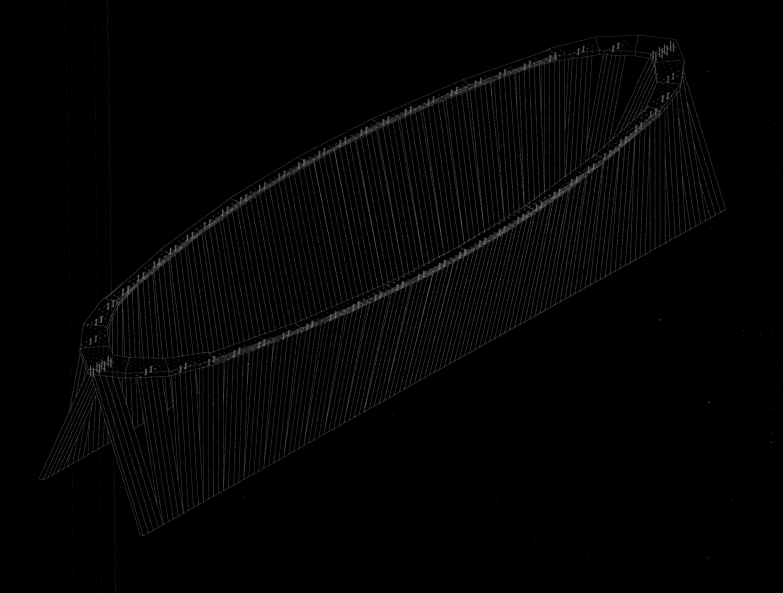

*The generous but simple columnless interior space
echoes its wooden exterior design and employs
a combination of natural and artificial light.*

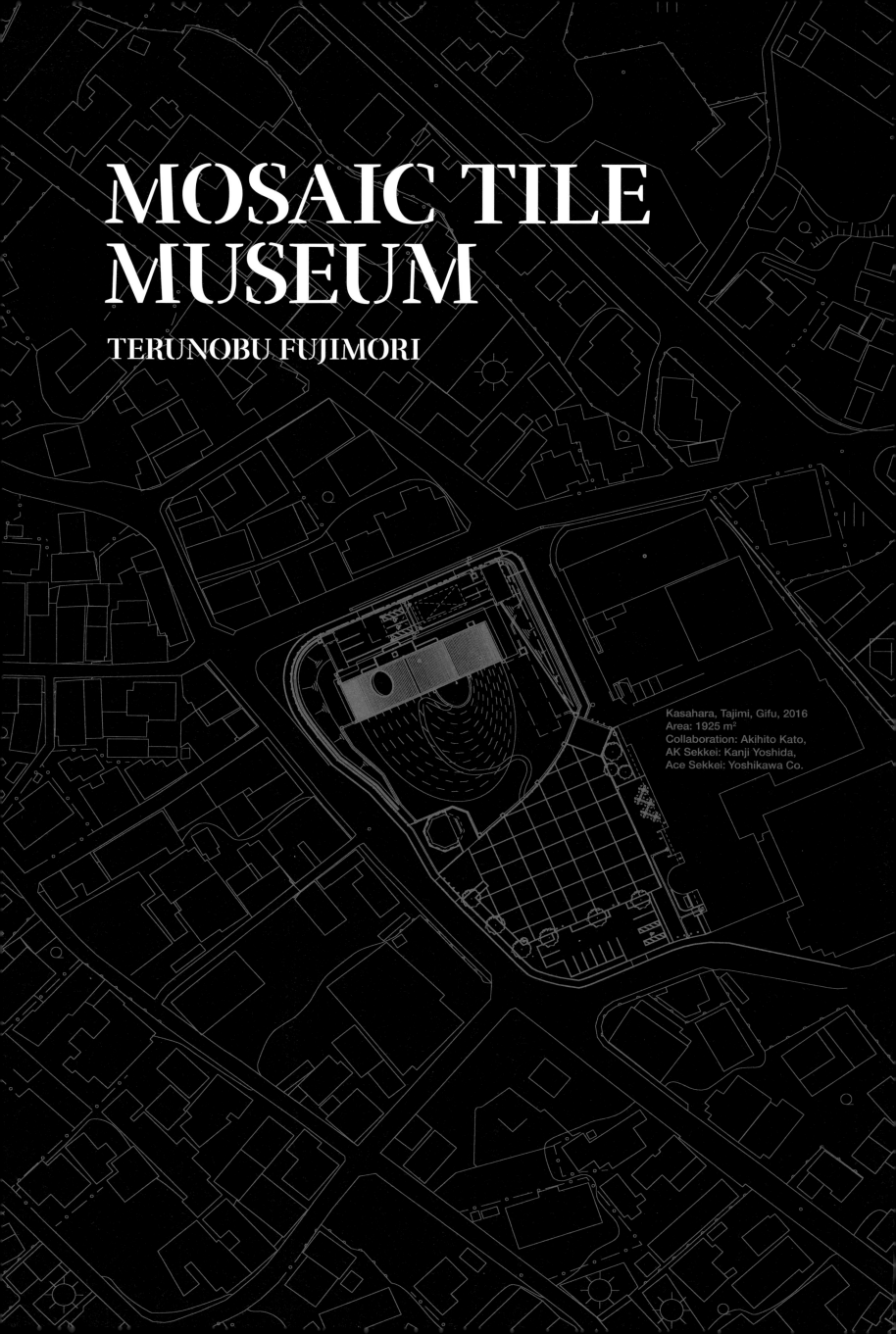

MOSAIC TILE
MUSEUM

TERUNOBU FUJIMORI

Kasahara, Tajimi, Gifu, 2016
Area: 1925 m²
Collaboration: Akihito Kato,
AK Sekkei: Kanji Yoshida,
Ace Sekkei: Yoshikawa Co.

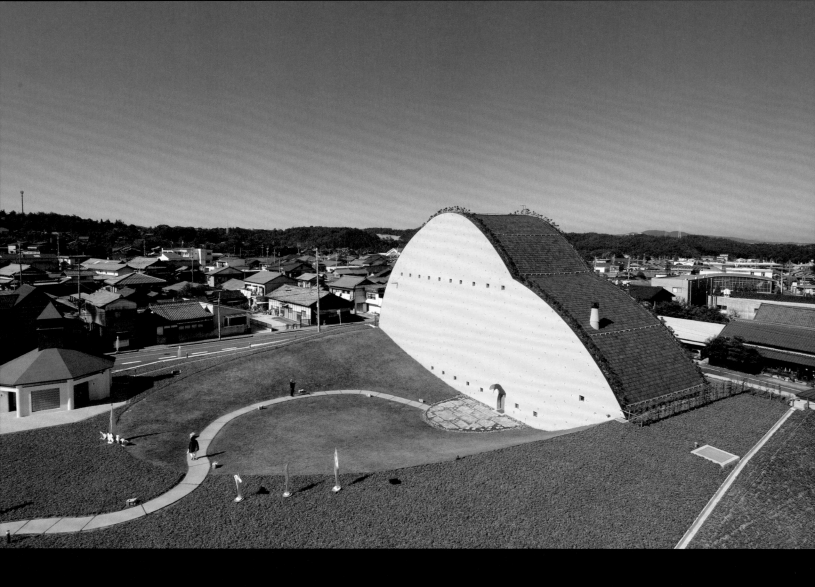

Born in Chino City, Nagano, in 1946, TERUNOBU FUJIMORI attended Tohoku University (1965–71) in Sendai before receiving his Ph.D. in Architecture from the University of Tokyo (1971–78). He is a Professor Emeritus at the University of Tokyo's Institute of Industrial Science. Although research on Western-style buildings in Japan from the Meiji period onwards remains his primary activity, he is also a practicing architect. His first built work was the Jinchokan Moriya Historical Museum (Chino City, Nagano, 1991). He has designed a number of unusual teahouses including Ichiya-tei (One Night Teahouse, Ashigarashimo, Kanagawa, 2003); Takasugi-an (Too-High Teahouse, Chino City, Nagano, 2004); and Chashitsu Tetsu (Teahouse Tetsu, Musée Kiyoharu Shirakaba, Nakamaru, Hokuto City, Yamanashi, 2005). He also designed the Charred Cedar House (Nagano City, Nagano, 2007); Roof House (Omihachiman, Shiga, 2009); and Copper House (Kokubunji City, Tokyo, 2009). His recent work includes the "Beetle's House" (Victoria & Albert Museum, London, UK, 2010); Hamamatsu House (Shizuoka, 2012); Storkhouse (Raiding, Austria, 2013); Soft-Hard Zinc House (Tokyo, 2014); Seminar House Pavilion, Dorich House Museum (Kingston, UK, 2016); and the Mosaic Tile Museum (Tajimi, Gifu,

TERUNOBU FUJIMORI wurde 1946 in Chino (Präfektur Nagano) geboren und studierte an der Universität Tohoku in Sendai (1965–1971), bevor er an der Universität Tokio in Architektur promovierte (1971–1978). Er ist emeritierter Professor am Institut für Industriewissenschaften der Universität Tokio. Obwohl er vor allem westliche Architektur in Japan seit der Meiji-Periode erforscht, entwirft er auch eigene Projekte. Sein erstes Projekt war das Historische Museum Jinchokan Moriya (Chino, Nagano, 1991). Fujimori hat eine Reihe ungewöhnlicher Teehäuser entworfen, darunter Ichiya-tei (One Night Teahouse, Ashigarashimo, Kanagawa, 2003), Takasugi-an (Too-High Teahouse, Chino, Nagano, 2004) und Chashitsu Tetsu (Tetsu-Teahouse, Kiyoharu-Shirakaba-Museum, Nakamaru, Hokuto, Yamanashi, 2005). Darüber hinaus entwarf Fujimori das Charred Cedar House (Nagano, 2007), das Roof House (Omihachiman, Shiga, 2009) und das Copper House (Kokubunji, Tokio, 2009). Zu seinen jüngsten Projekten gehören Beetle's House (Victoria & Albert Museum, London, 2010), Hamamatsu House (Shizuoka, 2012), Storchenhaus (Raiding, Österreich, 2013), Soft-Hard Zinc House (Tokio, 2014), der Seminarhauspavillon für das Dorich House Museum (Kingston, 2016) und ein Mosaikfliesenmuseum (Tajimi, Gifu, 2016,

Né à Chino City, Nagano (Japon) en 1946, TERUNOBU FUJIMORI a suivi les cours de l'université Tohoku (1965–71) à Sendai avant d'obtenir son doctorat en architecture à l'université de Tokyo (1971–78). Il est aujourd'hui professeur émérite de l'Institut des sciences industrielles de l'université de Tokyo. Il continue de pratiquer l'architecture, même si la recherche sur les bâtiments de style occidental au Japon à partir de la période Meiji reste son activité principale. Son premier projet construit a été le Musée historique Jinchokan Moriya (Chino City, Nagano, 1991). Il est aussi l'auteur de nombreuses maisons de thé originales, parmi lesquelles Ichiya-tei (Ashigarashimo, Kanagawa, 2003) ; Takasugi-an (Chino City, Nagano, 2004) et Chashitsu Tetsu (musée Kiyoharu Shirakaba, Nakamaru, Hokuto City, Yamanashi, 2005). Il a également créé la Maison de cèdre brûlé (Nagano City, Nagano, 2007) ; la Maison-toit (Omihachiman, Shiga, 2009) et la Maison de cuivre (Kokubunji City, Tokyo, 2009). Parmi ses projets récents figurent la Beetle's House (Victoria & Albert Museum, Londres, 2010) ; la maison Hamamatsu (Shizuoka, 2012) ; la Maison de la cigogne (Raiding, Autriche, 2013) ; la Soft-Hard Zinc House (Tokyo, 2014) ; le pavillon Seminar House du Dorich House Museum (Kingston, RU, 2016) et le musée du Carreau de mosaïque (Tajimi, Gifu, 2016,

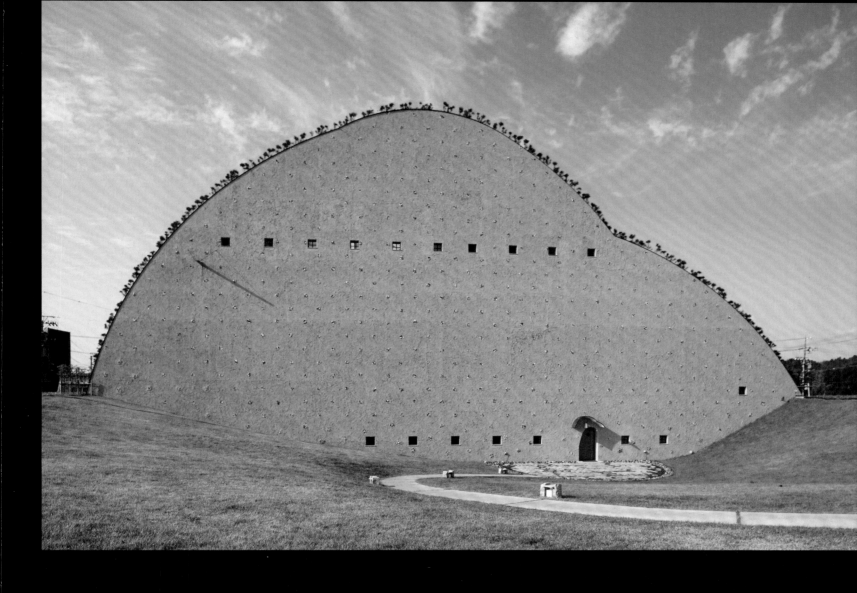

Fujimori is known for his unusual buildings, and this project is no exception. Photos and drawings emphasize the similarity of the structure to a natural land formation—a kind of artificial hill.

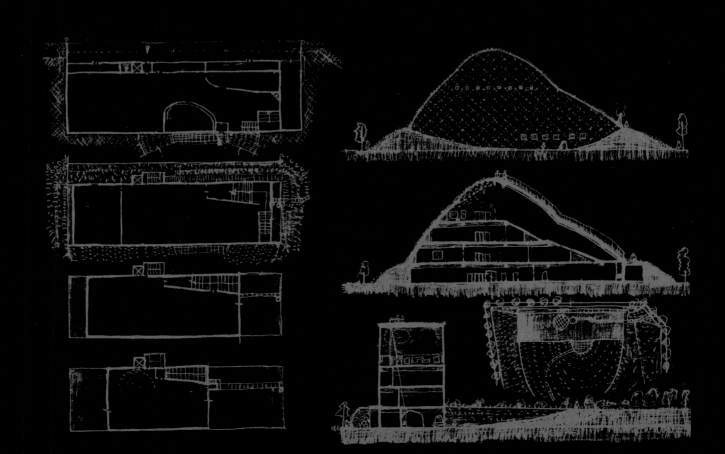

A clever vortex-shaped wire structure exhibits local
tiles beneath an oval skylight.

Soil-colored cement and plaster walls, together with wooden floors, give an earthy feeling to interiors; a kind of "primitive" form of modern architecture seems present in these images.

This four-story city-owned museum of tiles includes a shop and studio on the ground floor, a showroom for tile companies on the second level, an exhibition space on the third floor, and a tile showroom on the top level. The Tajimi area where it is located is known for its production of tiles. The building is in reinforced concrete, with soil-colored cement plaster walls and wooden floors: round 19-millimeter ceramic tiles are added to these surfaces. The building itself, seen in section, resembles a hill or a mountain. Its façade is intended to evoke associations with the earth. Roof tiles are used on the side elevations, and the contours are defined by pine trees. The site slopes gently toward the entrance in the form of an inverted cone. The museum building is set so that it appears to rise from the bottom of a pit. "In ancient times the human dwelling in its most reduced form has always been made of earth piled in the shape of a simple mound," says Fujimori. "Earth is the source of tiles, and so I gave the museum the appearance of an ancient mound."

Dieses viergeschossige, städtische Fliesenmuseum beherbergt einen Museumsshop und ein Studio im ersten, einen Showroom für Fliesenhersteller im zweiten, Ausstellungsräumlichkeiten im dritten und einen weiteren Showroom für Fliesen im obersten Geschoss. Die Region Tajimi, in der sich das Museum befindet, ist für ihre Fliesenproduktion bekannt. Die Stahlbetonkonstruktion verfügt über mit erdfarbenem Zement verputzte Wände sowie Holzböden. Sowohl Wände als auch Böden sind mit 19 mm-Keramikfliesen verziert. Der Querschnitt des Gebäudes hat die Form eines Hügels oder Bergs. Die Fassade soll erdige Assoziationen wecken. An den Seitenflächen werden Dachziegel verwendet, die Konturen werden durch eine Kiefernpflanzung begrenzt. Das Gelände fällt in Form eines invertierten Kegels in Richtung Eingang sanft ab. Das Museum wurde so positioniert, dass es aus der Senke herauszuwachsen scheint. „Zu Urzeiten waren menschliche Behausungen aufs Äußerste reduziert, sie bestanden aus Erdmaterial und hatten die Form eines einfachen Hügels", so Fujimori. „Fliesen bestehen ebenfalls aus Erdmaterialien, also habe ich dem Museum die Anmutung eines Erdhügels gegeben."

Ce musée municipal sur quatre niveaux comprend une boutique et un studio au rez-de-chaussée, un showroom pour les entreprises de céramique au premier étage, un espace d'exposition au deuxième et un showroom de carreaux au dernier étage. La région de Tajimi, où il est situé, est connue pour sa production de carreaux de céramique. La construction est en béton armé avec des murs plâtrés en ciment de la couleur de la terre et des sols en bois : des carreaux de céramique ronds de 19 mm ont été ajoutés sur ces surfaces. Le bâtiment vu en coupe fait penser à une colline ou à une montagne. La façade a été conçue pour évoquer la terre. Les élévations des côtés sont garnies de tuiles et les contours sont définis par des pins. Le terrain descend en pente douce vers l'entrée en forme de cône inversé. Le musée donne l'impression de sortir d'un puits ou d'un cratère. « Dans le passé, l'habitat humain, dans sa forme la plus rudimentaire, a toujours été fait d'un amoncellement de terre formant un simple monticule, explique Fujimori. La terre étant le matériau principal des carreaux de mosaïque, j'ai donc donné au musée l'apparence d'un ancien tertre. »

OMOTESANDO BRANCHES

SOU FUJIMOTO

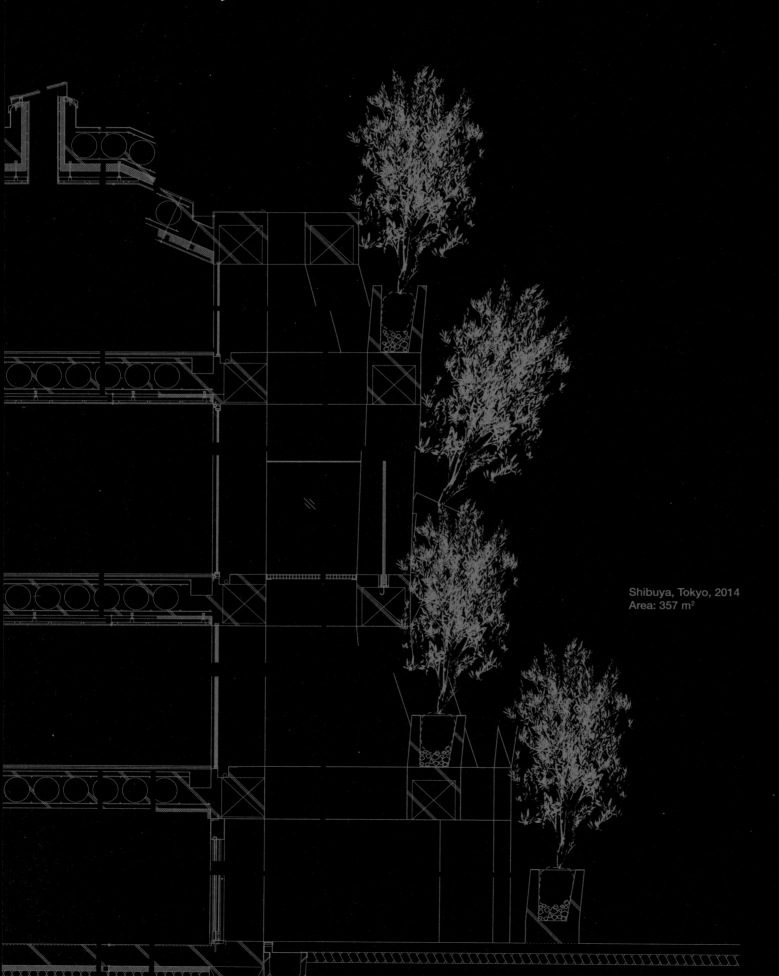

Shibuya, Tokyo, 2014
Area: 357 m²

OMOTESANDO BRANCHES

The trees start at ground level, which gives the unusual impression of a kind of vertical forest set on a street that otherwise has only a little greenery.

SOU FUJIMOTO was born in 1971. He received a B.Arch degree from the University of Tokyo, (Faculty of Engineering, Department of Architecture, 1990–94), and established his own firm, Sou Fujimoto Architects, in 2000. He is considered one of the most interesting rising Japanese architects, and his forms usually evade easy classification. His more recent work includes the Final Wooden House (Kumamura, Kumamoto, 2008); Musashino Art University Museum and Library (Tokyo, 2010); Tokyo Apartment (Tokyo, 2010); UNIQLO Shinsaibashi (Osaka, 2010); House NA (Tokyo, 2011); Public Toilet (Ichihara, Chiba, 2012); House K (Nishinomiya, Hyogo, 2012); the Serpentine Gallery Summer Pavilion 2013 (Kensington Gardens, London, UK, 2013); Omotesando Branches (Shibuya, Tokyo, 2014, published here); the Naoshima Pavilion (Naoshima, Kagawa, 2015, also published here); Rental Space Tower ("House Vision" exhibition, Tokyo, 2016); and L'Arbre Blanc (Montpellier, France, 2019). Currently, Sou Fujimoto has two other ongoing projects in France: Mille Arbres (Paris, 2014–); and the Learning Center of the École Polytechnique (Paris, 2015–).

SOU FUJIMOTO wurde 1971 geboren und absolvierte einen B.Arch an der Universität Tokio (Fakultät für Ingenieurwissenschaften, Fachbereich Architektur, 1990–1994). Im Jahr 2000 gründete er Sou Fujimoto Architects. Fujimoto gilt als einer der interessantesten aufstrebenden japanischen Architekten. Seine Entwürfe entziehen sich in der Regel einer einfachen Klassifizierung. Zu seinen jüngeren Projekten gehören das Final Wooden House (Kumamura, Kumamoto, 2008), ein Museum und eine Bibliothek für die Musashino Kunsthochschule (Tokio, 2010), Tokyo Apartment (Tokio, 2010), UNIQLO Shinsaibashi (Osaka, 2010), House NA (Tokio, 2011), Public Toilet (Ichihara, Chiba, 2012), House K (Nishinomiya, Hyogo, 2012), der Sommerpavillon der Serpentine Gallery 2013 (Kensington Gardens, London, 2013), Omotesando Branches (Shibuya, Tokio, 2014, hier vorgestellt), Naoshima Pavilion (Naoshima, Kagawa, 2015, ebenfalls hier vorgestellt), Rental Space Tower (Ausstellung „House Vision", Tokio, 2016) und L'Arbre Blanc (Montpellier, Frankreich, 2019). Aktuell arbeitet Sou Fujimoto an zwei weiteren Projekten in Frankreich: Mille Arbres (Paris, 2014–) und an einem Lernzentrum für die École polytechnique (Paris, 2015–).

SOU FUJIMOTO est né en 1971. Il est titulaire d'un B.Arch du département d'architecture de l'université de Tokyo, faculté d'ingénierie (1990–94). Il a créé sa société, Sou Fujimoto Architects, en 2000. Il est considéré comme l'un des architectes japonais les plus intéressants de la nouvelle génération et ses formes échappent souvent à toute classification. Parmi ses réalisations : la Final Wooden House (Kumamura, Kumamoto, 2008) ; le musée et la bibliothèque de l'université d'art Musashino (Tokyo, 2010) ; un appartement à Tokyo (2010) ; le magasin UNIQLO à Shinsaibashi (Osaka, 2010) ; la maison NA (Tokyo, 2011) ; Toilettes publiques (Ichihara, Chiba, 2012) ; la maison K (Nishinomiya, Hyogo, 2012) ; le pavillon d'été 2013 de la Serpentine Gallery (Kensington Gardens, Londres, 2013) ; l'immeuble Omotesando Branches (Shibuya, Tokyo, 2014, publié ici) ; le pavillon de Naoshima (Naoshima, Kagawa, 2015, également publié ici) ; une tour d'espaces locatifs (exposition « House Vision », Tokyo, 2016) et L'Arbre Blanc (Montpellier, France, 2019). Actuellement, Sou Fujimoto a deux autres projets en cours en France : Mille arbres (Paris, 2014–), et le bâtiment d'enseignements mutualisés de l'École polytechnique (Paris, 2015–).

The white, planted façades offer small balconies,
while interiors, for example the residential space
seen above, are bright and open.

This small four-story building with tilted planters for trees that seem to grow from its
façade is located in one of the small shopping
and residential streets just off Omotesando.
Although there are also trees that grow nearby,
the store stands out clearly in its densely
packed low-rise neighborhood. With a footprint of just 162 square meters, OMOTESANDO
BRANCHES contains a store, office area, and
residence. The 16 planters, each measuring
50 × 50 centimeters, hold Japanese maples
(*Acer palmatum*), European privet (*Ligustrum
vulgare*), Griffith's ash *(Fraxinus griffithii)*,
and Sapphire berry (*Symplocos paniculate*).
Despite its different planted varieties, the
overall structure is intended in its whole to
represent a kind of artificial tree, with branches that are actually alive. The architect explains: "The backstreet area of Tokyo is an
organic network of pathways with vegetation
and plants—it's a mix of everything. We tried
to recreate that kind of mixture in the architecture. The frame of Omotesando Branches
transforms into trees. The project is quite
small, but I like it because it reflects our
method—our strategy is to integrate different
things; sometimes nature and architecture, the
inside and outside of architecture, and other
things. Typically, these integrations happen
in the backstreets of Tokyo. It's my tribute to
Tokyo's crazy backstreets."

Dieses kleine, viergeschossige Gebäude
mit seinen geneigten Pflanzkübeln, in denen
Bäume wachsen, als wurzelten sie in der Fassade, liegt in einer der kleinen Einkaufs- und
Wohnstraßen abseits der Omotesando-Allee.
Zwar wachsen in unmittelbare Nähe weitere
Bäume, trotzdem sticht dieses Geschäft aus
der verdichteten und flach bebauten Nachbarschaft deutlich hervor. In dem Gebäude mit
einer Grundfläche von nur 162 m² befinden sich
ein Ladengeschäft, Büroräumlichkeiten und
eine Wohnung. In den 16 Pflanzgefäßen, die je
50 x 50 cm messen, wachsen Fächerahorn
(Acer palmatum), Liguster *(Ligustrum vulgare)*,
Esche *(Fraxinus griffithii)* und Saphirbeere
(Symplocos paniculate). So ähnelt OMOTE-
SANDO BRANCHES einem Baum mit lebenden
Ästen. Der Architekt: „Die Tokioter Nebenstra-
ßen sind ein organisches Wegenetz mit Pflan-
zen und Bäumen – hier gibt es nichts, was
es nicht gibt. Wir wollten, dass sich diese
Mischung auch in der Architektur wiederfindet.
Die Fassade von Omotesando Branches wird
zu Bäumen. Der Bau ist recht klein, aber er ge-
fällt mir, weil er unsere Methode widerspiegelt:
Die Strategie besteht darin, unterschiedliche
Dinge eins werden zu lassen – zum Beispiel
Natur und Architektur oder das Innere eines
Bauwerks mit seinem Äußeren und so weiter.
Es sind die kleinen Nebenstraßen Tokios, in
denen solche Verbindungen typischerweise zu
beobachten sind. Das Projekt ist meine Hom-
mage an Tokios aberwitzige Nebenstraßen."

Ce petit immeuble de quatre niveaux aux
jardinières inclinées dont les arbres donnent
l'impression de pousser sur la façade est situé
dans l'une des petites rues commerçantes
et résidentielles qui jouxtent Omotesando.
Malgré la présence d'arbres tout proches, le
magasin se détache nettement des bâtiments
très serrés de faible hauteur du voisinage.
Sur une empreinte au sol de seulement 162 m²,
OMOTESANDO BRANCHES abrite un magasin,
un bureau et un logement. Les 16 jardinières
de chacune 50 x 50 cm contiennent des érables
du Japon *(Acer palmatum)*, un troène *(Ligustrum vulgare)*, un frêne de l'Himalaya *(Fraxinus
griffithii)* et un *Symplocos paniculate*. Malgré
la différence des variétés plantées, l'ensemble
est destiné à représenter un arbre artificiel aux
branches bien vivantes. L'architecte explique :
« Les ruelles de Tokyo forment un réseau organique de sentiers garnis de végétation – c'est
un mélange de tout. Nous avons essayé de
recréer ce type de mélange dans l'architecture.
La charpente d'Omotesando Branches se t
ransforme progressivement en arbres. C'est un
petit projet, mais je l'aime bien car, il reflète
notre méthode – notre stratégie consiste à intégrer des choses différentes ; parfois la nature
et l'architecture, l'intérieur et l'extérieur, entre
autres. Ces intégrations sont typiques des
ruelles de Tokyo. C'est mon hommage au lacis
fou de venelles tokyoïte. »

NAOSHIMA PAVILION

SOU FUJIMOTO

Naoshima, Kagawa, 2015
Area: 64 m²

This work is the first by Sou Fujimoto on the island of Naoshima, known for its museums and hotels by Tadao Ando and SANAA, as well as a significant presence of contemporary art. NAOSHIMA PAVILION is set near the port of Honmura, where SANAA created their own cloud-shaped passenger terminal in 2017 using fiber-reinforced plastic spheres and a gridded wood frame. Fujimoto's irregular structure is seven meters high and is intended to allow visitors to enter just to see, or to shelter themselves from the sun. The angular structure is covered in white stainless steel mesh and was created at the occasion of the 2016 Setouchi International Art Festival, which occurs here and on neighboring islands every three years. Naoshima and nearby islands rise steeply from the Inland Sea and this Pavilion is likened by the architect to an "irregular stone, floating like an island on the ground." He also explains: "The interior space, cloaked in the translucent mesh, creates the sensation of a soft white spatial membrane, only allowing the wind, sounds, and smells of the port in. It is a kind of inverted island and a new form of space that is different from rigid architectural spaces made with conventional floors, walls, and ceilings. While our sense of vision is diminished, our sense of hearing, touch and smell are enhanced, allowing us to experience the place with all our senses. Though small, this is an ambitious work designed to provide a new architectural experience."

Dies ist Sou Fujimotos erstes Projekt auf der Insel Naoshima, die sowohl für ihre Museeen und Hotelbauten von Tadao Ando und SANAA als auch für die bemerkenswerte Präsenz zeitgenössischer Kunst bekannt ist. Der NAOSHIMA-PAVILLON befindet sich im Hafen von Honmura, für den SANAA 2017 einen auf einer Holzrahmenkonstruktion beruhenden, wolkenförmigen Passagierterminal aus faserverstärkten Kunststoffkugeln realisiert haben. Fujimotos Naoshima-Pavillon ist 7 m hoch, man kann einfach nur sein Inneres erkunden oder darin Zuflucht vor direkter Sonne suchen. Die weiße Edelstahlgitterkonstruktion entstand 2016 anlässlich des Setouchi International Art Festival, das alle drei Jahre auf Naoshima und den Nachbarinseln stattfindet. Naoshima selbst und die nahegelegenen Inseln ragen steil aus der Inlandsee, der Pavillon wiederum wird vom Architekten mit einem „kantigen Stein" verglichen, „der wie eine Insel auf dem Boden schwimmt". Fujimoto weiter: „Ein lichtdurchlässiges Netz umhüllt den Innenraum wie eine weiche weiße Membran, die nur den Wind und die Geräusche und Gerüche des Hafens passieren lässt. Es handelt sich um eine Art Insel auf dem Trockenen und eine neue Form des Raums, die sich von der Starrheit anderer Räume mit ihren konventionellen Böden, Wänden und Decken unterscheidet. Während unser Sehvermögen geschwächt wird, werden unser Gehör, unser Tastsinn und unser Geruchssinn gesteigert, sodass wir den Ort mit all unseren Sinnen erfahren können.

Ce pavillon est la première construction de Sou Fujimoto sur l'île de Naoshima, connue pour les musées et hôtels de Tadao Ando et SANAA et pour la forte présence de l'art contemporain. Le PAVILLON NAOSHIMA est situé près du port de Honmura où SANAA a aussi créé son terminal passagers en forme de nuage en 2017 avec des sphères de plastique armé de fibres et une ossature en treillis de bois. La construction irrégulière de Fujimoto est haute de 7 m et les visiteurs sont invités à y entrer simplement pour regarder ou pour s'abriter du soleil. La structure anguleuse est recouverte d'un maillage d'acier inoxydable blanc. Elle a été créée en 2016 pour la Triennale d'art de Setouchi qui se déroule ici et sur les îles voisines. Naoshima et les îles proches se dressent à pic dans la mer Intérieure du Japon, de sorte que le pavillon est comparé par l'architecte à un « caillou irrégulier, flottant comme une île sur le sol ». Il explique aussi que « l'espace intérieur, enveloppé dans le maillage translucide, crée la sensation d'une membrane spatiale souple et blanche qui ne laisse pénétrer que le vent, les sons et les odeurs du port. C'est en quelque sorte une île inversée et une nouvelle forme d'espace qui diffère des espaces architecturaux rigides aux sols, murs et plafonds classiques. Alors que notre vue est diminuée, notre ouïe, notre toucher et notre odorat sont exacerbés pour nous permettre d'appréhender le lieu avec tous nos sens. Il a beau être petit, c'est un travail ambitieux destiné à offrir une nouvelle expérience architecturale ».

Near the Ferry Terminal by SANAA in the Port of Honmura, the Pavilion is a new and unexpected presence in what remains otherwise a fairly sleepy fishing port.

HOUSE IN KAWASAKI

GO HASEGAWA

Kawasaki, Kanagawa, 2017
Area: 78 m²
Collaboration: Ohno Japan (Structural Engineer)

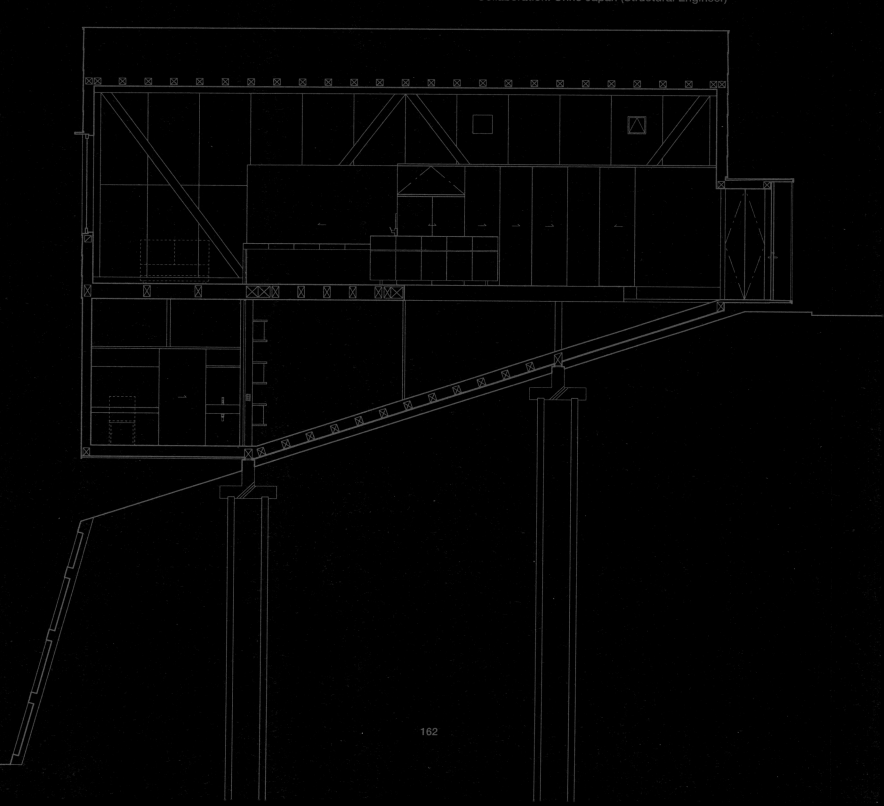

From the exterior, the house is surprisingly closed, although it does assume a typical double-sloped roof. Only the main wooden door breaks the gray color scheme of the whole.

GO HASEGAWA was born in 1977 in Saitama. He completed a Master's degree at the Tokyo Institute of Technology, Graduate School of Science and Engineering (2002), before working in the office of Tiara Nishizawa (2002–04). He founded Go Hasegawa & Associates in 2005, and received a Ph.D. in Engineering from the Tokyo Institute of Technology (2015) before working as a visiting professor at the University of California (Los Angeles, 2017) and at the Harvard GSD (Cambridge, MA, 2017 and 2019). In 2017, he won the Grand Prize in the Tokyo Gas House Design Competition for his House in a Forest (Nagano, 2006) and the 24th Shinkenchiku Award for his House in Sakuradai (Mie, 2006). His work also includes Pilotis in a Forest (Gunma, 2010); Townhouse in Asakusa (Tokyo, 2010); House in Komazawa (Tokyo, 2011); House in Yokohama (Kanagawa, 2016); Yoshino Cedar House (Yoshino, Nara, 2016); House in Kawasaki (Kanagawa, 2017, published here); a chapel in Guastalla (Italy, 2017); and Villa beside a Lake (Hamamatsu, Shizuoka, 2020, also published here).

GO HASEGAWA wurde 1977 in Saitama geboren, absolvierte an der Graduiertenschule für Natur- und Ingenieurwissenschaften der Technischen Hochschule Tokio ein Master-studium (2002) und arbeitete im Büro von Tiara Nishizawa (2002–2004). 2005 gründete er Go Hasegawa & Associates. Er promovierte an der Technischen Hochschule Tokio (2015), bevor er als Gastprofessor an der University of California (Los Angeles, 2017) und an der Harvard GSD (Cambridge, Massachusetts, 2017 und 2019) unterrichtete. Hasegawa gewann 2007 für House in a Forest (Nagano, 2006) den Hauptpreis eines von Tokyo Gas ausgeschriebenen Architekturwettbewerbs und den 24. Shinkenchiku Award für House in Sakuradai (Mie, 2006). Zu seinen Projekten gehören unter anderem Pilotis in a Forest (Gunma, 2010), Townhouse in Asakusa (Tokio, 2010), House in Komazawa (Tokio, 2011), House in Yokohama (Kanagawa, 2016), Yoshino Cedar House (Yoshino, Nara, 2016), House in Kawasaki (Kanagawa, 2017, hier vorgestellt), eine Kapelle in Guastalla (Italien, 2017) und Villa beside a Lake (Hamamatsu, Shizuoka, 2020, ebenfalls hier vorgestellt).

GO HASEGAWA est né en 1977 à Saitama. Il est titulaire d'un master de l'École supérieure de sciences et d'ingénierie de l'Institut de techno-logie de Tokyo (2002), et a ensuite travaillé dans l'agence de Tiara Nishizawa (2002–2004). Il a fondé Go Hasegawa & Associates en 2005 ; il a obtenu un doctorat d'ingénieur à l'Institut de technologie de Tokyo (2015), et il est depuis professeur associé à l'université de Californie (Los Angeles, 2017) et à la Harvard GSD (Cambridge, MA, 2017 et 2019). Il a remporté le grand prix du concours Gas House Design de Tokyo en 2007 avec sa Maison dans une forêt (Nagano, 2006), et la 24e édition du prix Shinkenchiku pour sa maison à Sakuradai (Mie, 2006). Parmi ses autres réalisations : la maison Pilotis dans une forêt (Gunma, 2010) ; une maison de ville à Asakusa (Tokyo, 2010) ; une maison à Komazawa (Tokyo, 2011) ; une maison à Yokohama (Kanagawa, 2016) ; la maison en cèdre de Yoshino (Yoshino, Nara, 2016) ; une maison à Kawasaki (Kanagawa, 2017, publiée ici) ; une chapelle à Guastalla (Italie, 2017) ; et une villa au bord d'un lac (Hamamatsu, Shizuoka, 2020, également publié ici).

Inside, the house belies the enclosed impression that it gives from the street: it is open and airy, with wood used for most surfaces.

This home was designed for a couple living with a mother. The site has an 8.5-meter slope from the top of the site to the bottom, which the architect dealt with using a system with a "structure consisting of four piles, with an inclined plane hanging from it for the garden space, which follows the slope of the site without touching it." This solution avoids costly excavation and foundation construction that might otherwise have been required. The narrow entrance is located at the top of the lot and shows only a narrow wooden door and a simple blank façade. The upper floor offers a view of Mount Fuji. The mother's room and terrace cantilever from the structure on the upper level. Gardens on the north and south sides can be seen from the lower floor, which is raised above the slope. In fact, the house adapts fully to the steep environment, seeming at one with its unusual situation. Gardens on the north and south sides of the house are accessible from the lowest level,

Dieses Haus wurde für ein Paar und die mit ihnen lebende Mutter entworfen. Das Grundstück weist zwischen dem höchsten und dem niedrigsten Punkt ein Gefälle von 8,5 m auf. Der Architekt entwarf „einen Bau mit vier Stützen, an denen eine geneigte Gartenebene aufgehängt ist, die dem Gefälle folgt, ohne den Boden zu berühren". Durch diese Konstruktion waren kostspielige Aushub- und Fundamentarbeiten, die andernfalls möglicherweise nötig gewesen wären, vermeidbar. Der begrenzte Eingangsbereich befindet sich am oberen Ende des Grundstücks und ist lediglich durch eine schmale Holztür und die schlichte schwarze Fassade zu erkennen. Aus der oberen Etage kragen das Zimmer der Mutter und die Terrasse vor, von hier aus sieht man den Fuji. Die Gärten auf der Nord- und Südseite sind vom Untergeschoss aus, das über den Hang hinausragt, zu sehen. Tatsächlich passt sich der Bau voll und ganz der steilen Umgebung an und scheint eins mit seiner ungewöhnlichen

La maison a été conçue pour un couple qui vit avec la mère de l'un des deux. Le terrain suit une pente de 8,5 m du haut en bas que l'architecte a exploitée avec un système composé d'une « structure sur quatre piliers d'où est suspendu un plan incliné pour le jardin, qui épouse la pente sans la toucher ». Cette solution permet d'éviter les frais élevés de terrassement et de creusement de fondations qui auraient été nécessaires sinon. L'entrée étroite est située dans la partie supérieure et ne donne à voir qu'une étroite porte en bois et une façade nue et simple. L'étage supérieur a vue sur le mont Fuji. La chambre et la terrasse destinées à la mère forment un porte-à-faux en haut de l'ensemble. Les jardins des côtés nord et sud sont visibles depuis le niveau inférieur qui est surélevé au-dessus de la pente. La maison est pleinement adaptée au terrain escarpé et semble parfaitement à sa place à cet emplacement spécifique. Les jardins sont accessibles depuis l'étage inférieur où vit le jeune couple.

The large sloping and completely glazed upper
space is divided by a full-height bookshelf
placed perpendicular to the long, narrow plan
of the building.

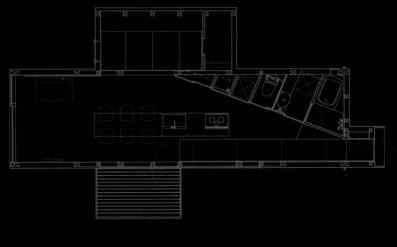

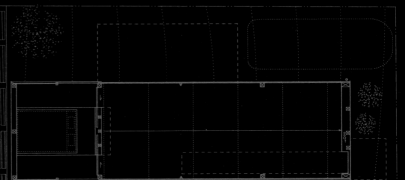

VILLA BESIDE A LAKE

GO HASEGAWA

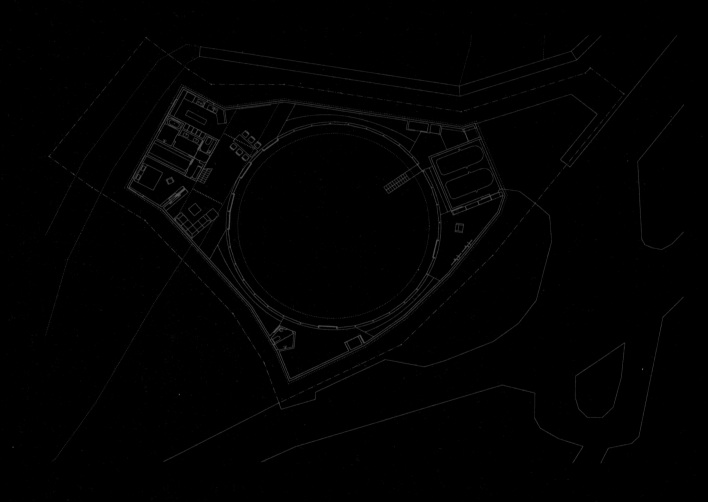

Hamamatsu, Shizuoka, 2018–20
Area: 342 m²
Collaboration: Ohno Japan
(Structural Engineer)

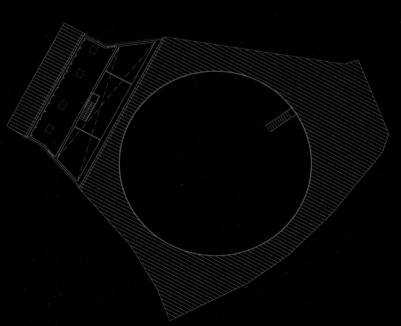

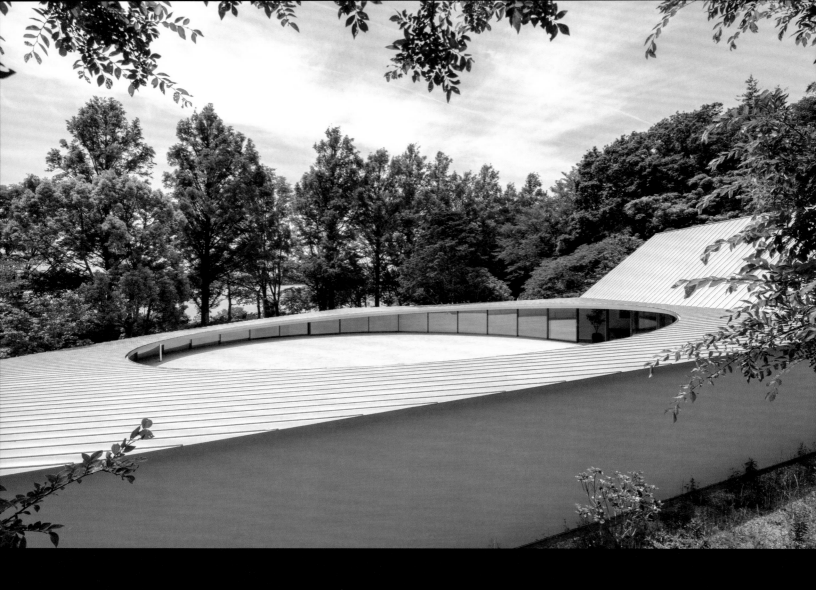

Simple lines and a gray-and-white color scheme are seen in this image, which begins to reveal the large central opening of the house.

Hamamatsu is a city of about 800 000 people located southeast of Nagoya. This house was designed for a young family for a sloped site near a lake. Views of the lake and privacy vis-à-vis a lakeside path were priorities for the clients. The house is centered on a circular inner courtyard. The living area is at the highest point of the site, where a gap in the roof frames a view of the lake while also blocking visibility from the path. The angled house is clearly designed to fit into the site, and the only curved form is that of the inner courtyard. The flat courtyard is set at the ground level of the living spaces, meaning that the opposite side of the roof of the house, closer to the lake following the terrain, is closer to the ground. The architect writes: "The project proposes a new inside/outside relationship, which creates a sense of being in an enclosed space and an open one at the same time thanks to the insertion of a courtyard—a typical form in a house—laid out in consonance with the gently sloping terrain. The project thus accentuates the sense of the body expanding to the scale of the landscape."

Hamamatsu ist eine Stadt mit etwa 800 000 Einwohnern, die südöstlich von Nagoya liegt. Dieses Haus befindet sich auf einem abschüssigen Grundstück in Nähe eines Sees und wurde für eine junge Familie entworfen. Wichtig für die Auftraggeber waren der Blick auf den See und Privatsphäre trotz eines Uferwegs. Das Haus ist um einen kreisförmigen Innenhof zentriert. Der Wohnbereich liegt auf dem höchsten Punkt des Grundstücks. Von hier aus blickt man auf den See, ohne gesehen zu werden. Das Haus ist nur auf der Innenseite zum Hof hin kurvig geformt und fügt sich in sein Umfeld ein. Der ebene Innenhof liegt auf dem Niveau der Wohnräume. Das gegenüberliegende, seeseitige Hausdach verläuft nur knapp oberhalb des Innenhofniveaus. Der Architekt schreibt: „Das Projekt schlägt eine neue Innen-Außen-Beziehung vor, die einem das Gefühl vermittelt, dass man sich in einem geschlossenen und gleichzeitig offenen Raum befindet – dies dank eines für Häuser üblichen Innenhofs, der im Einklang mit dem sanft abfallenden Gelände angelegt ist. Das Projekt betont auf diese Weise den Eindruck, dass sich der Körper dem Maßstab der Landschaft anpasst."

Hamamatsu est une ville d'environ 800 000 habitants située au sud-est de Nagoya. Cette maison a été conçue pour une jeune famille sur un site en pente près d'un lac. La vue sur le lac et l'intimité vis-à-vis d'un chemin au bord du lac étaient des priorités pour les clients. La maison est centrée sur une cour intérieure circulaire. L'espace de vie se trouve au point le plus élevé du site, où une fente dans le toit offre une vue sur le lac tout en bloquant la visibilité depuis le chemin. La maison en angle est clairement conçue pour s'intégrer dans le site, et la seule forme incurvée est celle de la cour intérieure. La cour plate est située au niveau du sol des espaces de vie, ce qui signifie que le côté opposé du toit de la maison, plus proche du lac en suivant le terrain, est plus proche du sol. L'architecte écrit : « Le projet propose une nouvelle relation intérieur/extérieur qui crée un sentiment d'être dans un espace à la fois fermé et ouvert grâce à l'insertion d'une cour – une forme typique dans une maison – aménagée en harmonie avec le terrain en pente douce. Le projet accentue ainsi le sens du corps qui s'étend à l'échelle du paysage. »

The very low-lying nature of the structure is
achieved by placing part of the space below grade,
as seen in the images on this page.

The house embraces its large central courtyard,
where full-height sliding glass walls allow interior
and exterior to become one. Wood is present on
floors and beneath the sloped roof (left, bottom).

WHITE ROSE ENGLISH SCHOOL

NAOKO HORIBE

Osaka, 2014
Area: 578 m²
Collaboration: Syunya Takahashi Structural Building
Research Institute, Grand Facility, Zealplus Inc.

Takatsuki
Castle
Historical Park

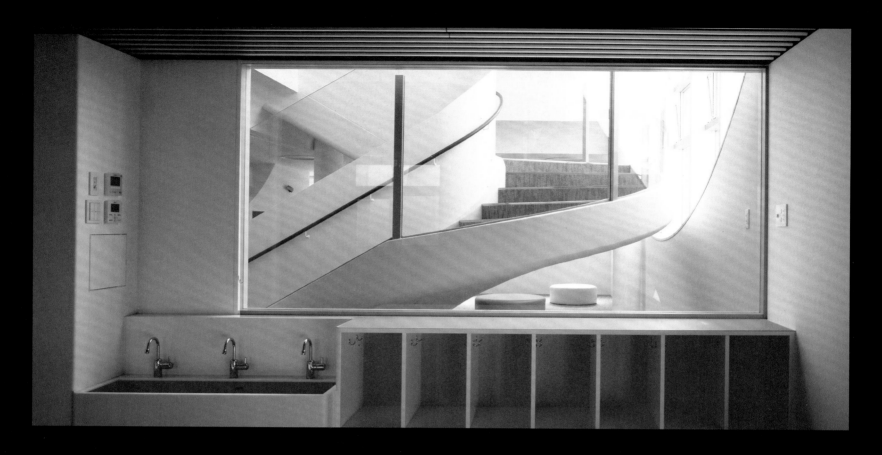

*White and concrete-gray surfaces combined with
ample glazing give interiors a light, airy feeling.*

NAOKO HORIBE was born in Osaka in 1972. She graduated from the Faculty of Architecture at Kindai University (Osaka, 1995) and established her own firm, Horibe Associates, in 2003. Her work includes the House in Mita (Mita, Osaka, 2014); the White Rose English School (Osaka, 2014, published here); House in Kisaichi (Kisaichi, Osaka, 2017); Garage House in Kawagoe (Mie, 2017) and House in Sugie (Shiga, 2018).

This school has a three-story reinforced-concrete structure. It was built on a 497-square-meter site near the historic ruins of Takatsuki Castle and has four classrooms located on the second and third floors. Built for a budget just under €1900 per square meter, the building has two large rounded gateways cut into the volume of the structure that permit parents picking up children to drive into and through the premises, avoiding congestion on the nearby road. Intended to introduce kindergarten children to the English language, the school has bright, open forms "that represent the overflowing energy and liveliness of the children." Children can be seen through the large-scale semicircular window, making it obvious when the school is in use. With a footprint of 204 square meters, the structure is just under 10 meters high. Basically consisting of a rectangular volume, what makes the school unusual is its large rounded openings, with a street-side window facing the park around the ruins of the castle. It is clad in fair-faced concrete and is located on the site of the former castle moat and shipping dock.

NAOKO HORIBE wurde 1972 in Osaka geboren und ist Absolventin der Fakultät für Architektur der Kindai-Universität (Osaka, 1995). Sie gründete 2003 Horibe Associates. Zu ihren Projekten gehören House in Mita (Mita, Osaka, 2014), White Rose English School (Osaka, 2014, hier vorgestellt), House in Kisaichi (Kisaichi, Osaka, 2017), Garage House in Kawagoe (Mie, 2017) sowie House in Sugie (Shiga, 2018).

Diese dreigeschossige Schule wurde unweit der Ruinen der Takatsuki-Wasserburg in Stahlbetonbauweise auf einem 497 m² großen Grundstück errichtet. Sie verfügt über vier, auf das zweite und dritte Geschoss verteilte Klassenzimmer. Die Baukosten lagen bei 1900 Euro pro Quadratmeter. Das Projekt zeichnet sich durch zwei abgerundete, in das Volumen eingebrachte Durchfahrtswege aus, sodass Eltern, die ihre Kinder abholen, direkt auf das Schulgelände fahren können. Auf diese Weise gerät der Verkehr auf der anliegenden Straße nicht ins Stocken. Die Institution führt Vorschulkinder an die englische Sprache heran und zeichnet sich durch eine der „überschäumenden Energie und Lebendigkeit der Kinder angemessene" Helligkeit und Offenheit aus. Durch das große halbkreisförmige Fenster kann man die Kinder sehen und weiß, wann Schulbetrieb ist. Das Gebäude hat eine Grundfläche von 204 m², ist knapp 10 m hoch und besteht im Wesentlichen aus einem quaderförmigen Volumen, das durch seine ungewöhnlichen Einschnitte auffällt. Vom straßenseitigen Fenster aus blickt man auf den Park, der sich um die Burgruinen erstreckt. Die Schule verfügt über eine Sichtbetonfassade und steht dort, wo sich einst der Burggraben und die Bootsanlegestelle befanden.

NAOKO HORIBE est née à Osaka en 1972. Elle est diplômée de la faculté d'architecture de l'université Kindai (Osaka, 1995) et a créé son agence, Horibe Associates, en 2003. Ses réalisations comprennent une maison à Mita (Mita, Osaka, 2014) ; le cours d'anglais de la Rose blanche (Osaka, 2014, publiée ici) ; une maison à Kisaichi (Kisaichi, Osaka, 2017) ; la Maison-garage à Kawagoe (Mie, 2017) et une maison à Sugie (Shiga, 2018).

La structure de l'école à trois niveaux est en béton armé. Elle a été construite sur un terrain de 497 m² près des ruines historiques du château de Takatsuki et ses quatre classes occupent le premier et le deuxième étage. Réalisé pour un budget de presque 1 900 euros le mètre carré, le bâtiment possède deux vastes entrées arrondies découpées dans le volume qui permettent aux parents d'entrer et de traverser en voiture le complexe pour venir chercher leurs enfants afin d'éviter l'engorgement de la route voisine. Destinée à apprendre l'anglais aux enfants de maternelle, l'école présente des formes claires et ouvertes « qui représentent la vivacité et l'énergie débordantes des enfants ». On les voit par l'immense fenêtre en demi-cercle qui permet de voir si l'école est occupée. L'ensemble occupe une empreinte au sol de 204 m² pour une hauteur de presque 10 m. Composée pour l'essentiel d'un volume rectangulaire, l'école tire son originalité des larges ouvertures arrondies, la fenêtre côté rue donnant sur le parc qui entoure les ruines du château. Le bâtiment est revêtu de béton de parement et occupe les anciennes douves du château et son embarcadère.

FOUR
RECTANGLES

The apparently predictable form of the lower part of the house becomes less expected with the large projecting canopy and the triple gable roof.

JUN IGARASHI was born in Hokkaido in 1970. He was educated at the Hokkaido Central Kogakuin Technical College (1990) and created his own practice, Jun Igarashi Architects, in 1997. His work includes House O (Tokoro, Hokkaido, 2009); Repository House (Asahikawa, Hokkaido, 2012); House of Density (Sapporo, 2013); House D (Asahikawa, Hokkaido, 2015); Hat H House (Engaru, Hokkaido, 2016); House Vision (Koto, Otaru, Hokkaido, 2016); Roof and Rectangular House (Tomakomai, Hokkaido, 2016); a temporary playhouse (Osaka, 2016); and Four Rectangles (Iwaki, Hokkaido, 2017, published here). He is one of only a few significant architects in Japan to live and work mostly in the northern area of Hokkaido.

JUN IGARASHI wurde 1970 in Hokkaido geboren, erhielt seine Ausbildung an der Technischen Hochschule Nihon Kogakuin Hokkaido (1990) und gründete 1997 die Firma Jun Igarashi Architects. Zu seinen Projekten gehören House O (Tokoro, Hokkaido, 2009), Repository House (Asahikawa, Hokkaido, 2012), House of Density (Sapporo, 2013), House D (Asahikawa, Hokkaido, 2015), Hat H House (Engaru, Hokkaido, 2016), House Vision (Koto, Otaru, Hokkaido, 2016), Roof and Rectangular House (Tomakomai, Hokkaido, 2016), ein temporäres Theater (Osaka, 2016) und Four Rectangles (Iwaki, Hokkaido, 2017, hier vorgestellt). Er gehört zu den wenigen bedeutenden japanischen Architekten, die vor allem auf der Insel Hokkaido im Norden des Landes leben und arbeiten.

JUN IGARASHI est né à Hokkaido en 1970. Il a été formé à l'École supérieure technique Nihon Kogakuin de Hokkaido (1990) et a ouvert son agence, Jun Igarashi Architects, en 1997. Ses réalisations comprennent la maison O (Tokoro, Hokkaido, 2009) ; la Repository House (Asahikawa, Hokkaido, 2012) ; la House of Density (Sapporo, 2013) ; la maison D (Asahikawa, Hokkaido, 2015) ; la Hat H House (Engaru, Hokkaido, 2016) ; la House Vision (Koto, Otaru, Hokkaido, 2016) ; la Roof and Rectangular House (Tomakomai, Hokkaido, 2016) ; un théâtre temporaire (Osaka, 2016) et la maison Four Rectangles (Iwaki, Hokkaido, 2017, publiée ici).Il est l'un des rares architectes influents du Japon à vivre et à travailler essentiellement dans le Nord de Hokkaido.

*Interiors openly display the wooden structure
of the house, especially in the ceilings seen here.
Ample glazing and high spaces give a feeling
of generous space despite the small (119 m²) size
of the structure.*

The architect explains that because he grew
up in the cold climate of Hokkaido, he thought
a great deal about what he calls the "middle
area" *(engawa)*, an area between inner and
outer space. In his thoughts about this important element of architecture, he refers to Alvar
Aalto, whose work, in its own way, takes into
account the severity of northern weather. In
order to prevent very cold air from penetrating
a house, one solution employed is a kind
of airlock that is often narrow and inexpensive.
Jun Igarashi decided to give a more "enjoyable"
form to this element of the FOUR RECTANGLES
house. By making the airlock as large as a
child's room, he created "a sense of distance
between outside and inside." Placed in the
center of the small site, with large eaves that
also emphasize the idea of the "in-between"
space, the house has four areas, correspond-
ing to the Four Rectangles in its name. The
first of these is in the center and is the most
"stable" part of the residence, fully open
to the wooden rafters. The second rectangle
surrounds the first. The third rectangle is the
space between the eaves, and the fourth is
formed by the band of land around the house.
These rectangles are clearly visible in plan.
The generous use of wood and natural light
makes the residence warm and agreeable.

Der Architekt ist auf Hokkaido aufgewachsen
und hat sich wegen des kühlen Klimas dort
eingehend mit dem Bereich zwischen Innen-
und Außenraum auseinandergesetzt, den er
selbst als „Zwischenzone" (Engawa) bezeichnet. In sein Nachdenken über dieses Charakte-
ristikum der japanischen Architektur bezieht
Igarashi auch Alvar Aalto mit ein, der das strenge nordische Klima ebenfalls berücksichtigte.
Damit keine, dass kalte Luft ins Haus eindringt,
werden oftmals schmale und kostengünstige
„Schleusen" eingeplant. Igarashi beschloss,
diese in seinem Projekt FOUR RECTANGLES
so zu gestalten, dass man sich an ihm „erfreu-
en" kann. Seine Schleuse hat die Größe eines
Kinderzimmers und soll „zwischen außen und
innen eine gewisse Distanz" schaffen. Das
Gebäude wurde zentral auf dem kleinen Grundstück platziert und verfügt über breite Traufen,
die den Aspekt des „Zwischenräumlichen" un-
terstreichen. Den vier namensgebenden Recht-
ecken entsprechend teilt es sich in vier Bereiche auf: Der erste, zentral gelegene Bereich mit
den offenliegenden Dachsparren ist der „sta-
bilste" Teil des Wohnhauses. Das zweite Rechteck umschließt das erste. Die äußere Grenze
des dritten Rechtecks wird durch die Traufen
gebildet, und das vierte Rechteck markiert der
Grundstücksstreifen, der um das Haus läuft. Im
Grundriss wird dieser Aufbau deutlich erkenn-
bar. Extensiver Holzeinsatz und viel natürliches
Licht erzeugen Wärme und Behaglichkeit.

L'architecte raconte qu'il a grandi dans le climat
froid de Hokkaido, ce qui explique qu'il fait
grand cas de ce qu'il appelle l'« espace du milieu » *(engawa)*, une zone située entre l'espace
intérieur et l'espace extérieur. Dans sa réflexion
sur cet élément architectural important, il cite
notamment Alvar Aalto dont le travail prend
aussi en compte à sa manière la rigueur du climat du Nord. Pour empêcher l'air très froid de
pénétrer dans une maison, l'une des solutions
consiste à construire un sas, souvent étroit
et peu onéreux. Jun Igarashi a choisi de donner
une forme plus « agréable » à cet élément de
la maison FOUR RECTANGLES. En donnant au
sas la taille d'une chambre d'enfant, il a créé
« un sentiment de distance entre l'extérieur et
l'intérieur ». Construite au milieu du petit terrain
et dotée de vastes avant-toits qui soulignent
encore l'idée de l'espace « entre deux », la maison comprend quatre parties qui correspondent
aux quatre rectangles de son nom. La première
est au centre et constitue la partie la plus
« stable » de la demeure, avec son espace entièrement ouvert sur les chevrons en bois de
la charpente. Le deuxième rectangle entoure le
premier. Le troisième rectangle est formé par
l'espace entre les avant-toits, et le quatrième
est la bande de terrain tout autour de la maison.
Ils sont particulièrement visibles sur le plan.
L'usage généreux du bois et de la lumière naturelle rend la maison chaleureuse et agréable.

STONE VILLA

YOSUKE INOUE

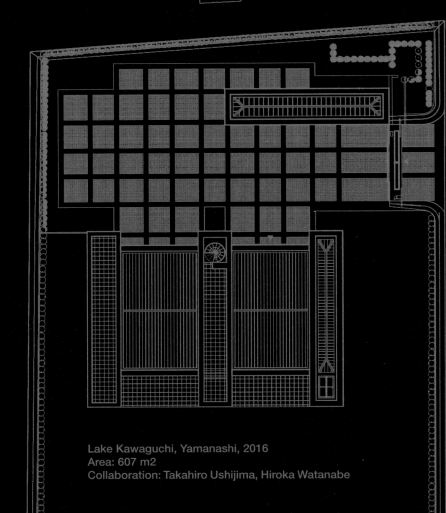

Lake Kawaguchi, Yamanashi, 2016
Area: 607 m2
Collaboration: Takahiro Ushijima, Hiroka Watanabe

The house is shielded from the shore of Lake Kawaguchi, which lies at 800 meters above sea level, by a row of cherry trees.

YOSUKE INOUE was born in Tokyo in 1966 and graduated from the Department of Architecture of Kyoto University in 1991. He worked in the office of Sakakura Associates in Tokyo from 1991 to 2000, then established his own office, Yosuke Inoue Architect & Associates. His work includes House in Setagaya-Sakura (Setagaya, Tokyo, 2004); Villa in Hayama (Hayama, Kanagawa, 2006); House in Yotsuya (Shinjyuku, Tokyo, 2008); House in Yoga (Setagaya, Tokyo, 2010); House in Daikanyama (Shibuya, Tokyo, 2013); Stone Villa at Lake Kawaguchi (Yamanashi, 2016, published here); House in Shimokitazawa (Setagaya, Tokyo, 2018); and House in Funabashi (Funabashi, Chiba, 2018).

YOSUKE INOUE wurde 1966 in Tokio geboren und schloss 1991 ein Studium im Fachbereich Architektur der Universität Kyoto ab. Von 1991 bis 2000 arbeitete er im Büro von Sakakakura Associates in Tokio. Mit Yosuke Inoue Architect & Associates gründete er sein eigenes Büro. Zu seinen Projekten zählen House in Setagaya-Sakura (Setagaya, Tokio, 2004), Villa in Hayama (Hayama, Kanagawa, 2006), House in Yotsuya (Shinjyuku, Tokio, 2008), House in Yoga (Setagaya, Tokio, 2010), House in Daikanyama (Shibuya, Tokio, 2013), Stone Villa am Kawaguchi-See (Yamanashi, 2016, hier vorgestellt), House in Shimokitazawa (Setagaya, Tokio, 2018) und House in Funabashi (Funabashi, Chiba, 2018).

YOSUKE INOUE est né à Tokyo en 1966. Il est diplômé du département d'architecture de l'université de Kyoto (1991). Il a travaillé dans l'agence Sakakura Associates à Tokyo de 1991 à 2000 avant d'ouvrir son agence, Yosuke Inoue Architect & Associates. Ses réalisations comprennent une maison à Setagaya-Sakura (Setagaya, Tokyo, 2004) ; une villa à Hayama (Hayama, Kanagawa, 2006) ; une maison à Yotsuya (Shinjyuku, Tokyo, 2008) ; une maison à Yoga (Setagaya, Tokyo, 2010) ; une maison à Daikanyama (Shibuya, Tokyo, 2013) ; la Villa de pierre du lac Kawaguchi (Yamanashi, 2016, publiée ici) ; une maison à Shimokitazawa (Setagaya, Tokyo, 2018) et une maison à Funabashi (Funabashi, Chiba, 2018).

Irregular granite surfaces within the visible concrete frame give way to very large windows taking advantage of the views of Mount Fuji, as seen on the next double page.

Lake Kawaguchi is located in southern Yamanashi Prefecture, near Mount Fuji. This residence uses the sacred mountain as its focal point, creating a panoramic view from the living and bedrooms. The composition is symmetrical with the living and bedrooms placed between three closed volumes, including staircases, storage and a wine cellar. The architect states: "It is a simple rigid-frame structure of concrete and stone, featuring pillars and beams; the interior and exterior are covered with split-face granite on concrete. A matte texture stone called Burlington slate was used for flooring, which creates a chic and luxurious finished touch." Calling on natural materials that evoke a feeling of strength, Yosuke Inoue designed the details of the structure with great care and sought to bring "universal features of beauty" to light with this house.

Der Kawaguchi-See liegt im Süden der Präfektur Yamanashi unweit des Fuji. Aus den Wohn- und Schlafräumen blickt man auf den heiligen Berg, der den wesentlichen Bezugspunkt des Wohnhauses darstellt. Der Entwurf ist symmetrisch, Wohn- und Schlafräume liegen zwischen drei geschlossenen Volumen mit Treppenaufgängen, Abstellraum und Weinkeller. Der Architekt: „Es handelt sich um eine einfache steife Rahmenkonstruktion aus Beton und Stein samt Säulen und Trägern. Sowohl innen als auch außen sind die Betonoberflächen mit Granitpaneelen verkleidet. Als Bodenbelag wurde matter Burlington-Schiefer verwendet, der dem Haus eine elegante, luxuriöse Anmutung verleiht." Yosuke Inoue entwarf das Gebäude bis ins letzte Detail mit großer Sorgfalt, es sollte „universelle Aspekte des Schönen" verkörpern.

Le lac Kawaguchi se trouve dans le sud de la préfecture de Yamanashi, près du mont Fuji. La résidence fait de la montagne sacrée son point de convergence, et offre une vue panoramique depuis le salon et les chambres. La composition est symétrique, le salon et les chambres sont placés entre trois volumes clos comprenant la cage d'escalier, un rangement et une cave à vin. L'architecte déclare : « C'est une structure simple à charpente rigide, de béton et pierre, à base de piliers et de poutres ; l'intérieur et l'extérieur sont recouverts de granit de parement ciselé sur du béton. Une pierre à la texture mate appelée ardoise Burlington a été utilisée pour le sol, ce qui confère une touche de finition chic et luxueuse. » Yosuke Inoue a eu recours à des matières naturelles qui donnent une impression de solidité et a conçu avec beaucoup de soin les détails de l'ensemble, cherchant à mettre en lumière des « caractéristiques universelles de beauté » avec cette maison.

Granite again appears as cladding on interior
walls, here in the kitchen-dining area with its
wood-topped surfaces. Below: *plans of the house.*

Poured-in-place concrete columns alternate with more granite surfaces in the very solid-looking living space. Below: a bedroom with warmer wooden walls.

BOTANICAL GARDEN ART BIOTOP / WATER GARDEN

JUNYA ISHIGAMI

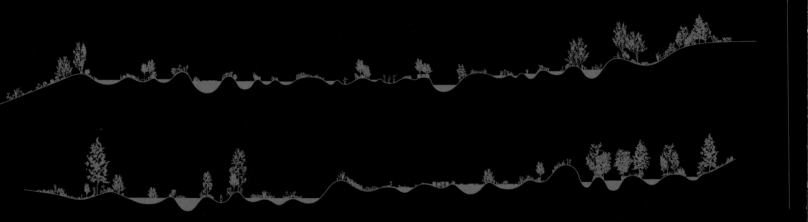

Nasu, Tochigi, 2018
Area: 16 670 m²

Although this garden is very unusual, it does to some extent follow the tradition of Japanese gardens where nature and man-made elements become difficult to distinguish from each other.

JUNYA ISHIGAMI was born in Kanagawa in 1974. He studied at the Tokyo National University of Fine Arts and Music in the Architecture Department, graduating in 2000. He worked in the office of Kazuyo Sejima & Associates (now SANAA) from 2000 to 2004, establishing Junya Ishigami+Associates in 2004. He has designed a number of tables, including one measuring 9.5 meters long and three millimeters thick made of prestressed steel (titled "Table"), and realized a project for Kaiyo Hotel and residential buildings (2007). He has designed the KAIT Workshop at the Kanagawa Institute of Technology (Kanagawa, 2008); a store for Yohji Yamamoto in New York's Meatpacking District (USA, 2008); participated in the 2008 Venice Architecture Biennale (Japanese Pavilion, Venice, Italy); and completed a house for a young couple (Tokyo, 2013). He is currently working on a house and restaurant (Yamaguchi, 2016–). Published here are his Botanical Garden Art Biotop/Water Garden (Nasu, Tochigi, 2018) and the 2019 Serpentine Gallery Summer Pavilion (Kensington Gardens, London, UK, 2019).

JUNYA ISHIGAMI wurde 1974 in Kanagawa geboren, studierte an der Nationaluniversität der Künste im Fachbereich Architektur und schloss im Jahr 2000 sein Studium ab. Von 2000 bis 2004 arbeitete er im Büro Kazuyo Sejima & Associates (heute SANAA). 2004 gründete er Junya Ishigami + Associates. Er entwarf mehrere Tische, darunter ein Modell mit einer 9,5 m langen und 3 mm dünnen Tischplatte aus Vorspannstahl (Modellname: „Table") und realisierte ein Projekt für das Kaiyo Hotel sowie Wohnungsbauten (2007). Er entwarf den KAIT-Workshop des Kanagawa Institut für Technologie (Kanagawa, 2008), einen Store für Yohji Yamamoto im Meatpacking District von New York (2008) und war 2008 im japanischen Pavillon auf der Architekturbiennale Venedig vertreten. Außerdem hat Ishigami ein Haus für ein junges Paar (Tokio, 2013) realisiert und arbeitet derzeit an House & Restaurant (Yamaguchi, 2016–). In diesem Band werden sein Botanical Garden Art Biotop/Water Garden (Nasu, Tochigi, 2018) sowie sein Sommerpavillon der Londoner Serpentine Gallery (Kensington Gardens, London, 2019) vorgestellt.

JUNYA ISHIGAMI, né en 1974 à Kanagawa, a étudié au département d'architecture de l'Université nationale des beaux-arts et de musique de Tokyo, dont il est sorti diplômé en 2000. Il a travaillé chez Kazuyo Sejima & Associates (aujourd'hui SANAA) de 2000 à 2004, et a ouvert l'agence Junya Ishigami + Associates en 2004. Il a créé de nombreuses tables, dont une de 9,5 m de long et 3 mm d'épaisseur en acier précontraint (Table), ainsi qu'un projet pour l'hôtel Kaiyo et des logements (2007). Outre l'atelier de l'Institut de technologie KAIT de Kanagawa (Kanagawa, 2008), il a conçu le magasin new-yorkais du couturier japonais Yohji Yamamoto (États-Unis, 2008) dans le Meatpacking District ; participé à la Biennale d'architecture de Venise en 2008 (Pavillon japonais) ; construit une maison pour un jeune couple (Tokyo, 2013), et il travaille actuellement sur un projet de maison et de restaurant (Yamaguchi, 2016–). Nous publions ici le projet Botanical Garden Art Biotop/Water Garden (Nasu, Tochigi, 2018) et le pavillon d'été 2019 de la Serpentine Gallery (Kensington Gardens, Londres, 2019).

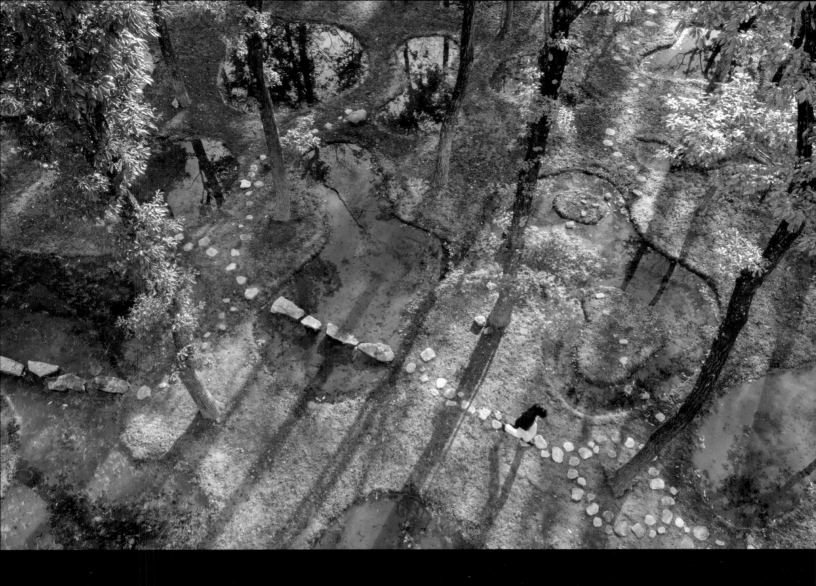

This unusual project is located on the site of farmland that functions through the leasing of plots. A hotel allows visitors to plant crops, harvest them, and then cook the produce. When he heard that hundreds of trees from the nearby hotel site were to be cut down, Junya Ishigami proposed, instead, to replant them in an adjacent meadow. Referring to the farming plots, another part of the scheme, the architect explains: "The site also needs to be enjoyable as scenery for those who do not rent the farmland but rather are spectators." Making use of the former meadow, the design seeks to prioritize crop production but also appear to be part of the existing scenery. "On the bases of such interests," says Ishigami, "I intend to create a landscape with a small environment of vegetation that is in a state of ever-changing flux, like a kaleidoscope. What I aim to achieve in this project is to realize a 'dream-like landscape.'" Rather than making use of straight lines, the environment was laid out in a complex pattern of curved elements likened to pieces of a jigsaw puzzle, forming a large number of gardens bordered by ponds. In fact, these ponds, fed by a nearby river, appear to be natural but actually provide structure for the gardens on a scale that recalls Japanese courtyard gardens, called *tsubo-niwa*. The farming allotments make use of water from the ponds. The land space of this complex and unusual design is open to visitors, who wander freely in what might be termed a kind of nature beyond nature, an artificial (natural) environment. This garden is, according to Junya Ishigami, nothing less than, "a new nature never before seen."

Dieses ungewöhnliche Projekt befindet sich inmitten einer landwirtschaftlichen Nutzfläche, die parzellenweise verpachtet wird. Gäste eines Hotels haben die Möglichkeit, Feldfrüchte anzubauen, zu ernten und anschließend zuzubereiten. Als Ishigami erfuhr, dass auf dem Grundstück Hunderte von Bäumen gefällt werden sollten, schlug er vor, diese auf eine Wiese in der Nähe umzupflanzen. Mit Bezug auf die Parzellen, die ebenfalls zu dem Projekt gehören, erklärt der Architekt: „Die Anlage muss auch für Menschen attraktiv sein, die keine Pächter, sondern lediglich Zaungäste sind." Dem Entwurf kommt das einstige Wiesenland zugute, das den Anbau von Nutzpflanzen priorisieren und gleichwohl Teil der bestehenden Landschaft werden soll. „Auf Grundlage dieser Überlegungen", so Ishigami, „beabsichtige ich, eine Landschaft mit einem kleinen Vegetationsenvironment zu schaffen, das sich ständig verändert, wie ein Kaleidoskop. Ich möchte mit diesem Projekt eine ‚traumartige Landschaft' kreieren." Das Environment kommt ohne gerade Linien aus und wird durch Muster aus geschwungenen Formen bestimmt, die Puzzleteilen ähneln und eine Vielzahl von Teichen umgebener Einzelgärten bilden. Die von einem Fluss gespeisten Teiche scheinen natürlichen Ursprungs zu sein. Sie strukturieren die Gärten auf eine Art und Weise, die an japanische *tsuboniwa*-Gärten erinnert. Die Nutzparzellen werden mit Wasser aus diesen Teichen bewässert. Das komplexe und ungewöhnliche Projekt steht Besuchern offen, die sich in einer Landschaft frei bewegen wollen, die man als Natur jenseits der Natur, als künstliches (Natur-)Environment bezeichnen könnte. Der Garten

Ce projet inédit occupe un terrain agricole et fonctionne par crédit-bail de parcelles. Un hôtel permet aux visiteurs de planter, de récolter et de cuisiner le produit de leur culture. Lorsqu'il a entendu que des centaines d'arbres de l'hôtel voisin allaient être abattus, Junya Ishigami a proposé de plutôt les replanter dans une prairie adjacente. Quant aux parcelles agricoles, l'autre partie du projet, l'architecte explique : « Le site doit aussi former un décor agréable pour ceux qui ne louent pas de terres agricoles, mais en sont spectateurs. » Le concept, qui utilise l'ancienne prairie, cherche à privilégier la culture, mais aussi à apparaître comme un élément du paysage existant. « En me basant sur ces intérêts, dit Ishigami, mon intention est de créer un paysage à l'environnement végétal réduit qui ne cesse de fluctuer, comme un kaléidoscope. Avec ce projet, je cherche à réaliser un "paysage à l'image d'un rêve". » Plutôt que des lignes droites, le décor a été composé avec un motif complexe d'éléments courbes comparés aux morceaux d'un puzzle, formant de multiples jardins bordés par des étangs. Ces derniers, alimentés par une rivière voisine, semblent naturels, mais structurent en fait les jardins à l'échelle des petits jardins aménagés dans les cours au Japon et appelés *tsubo-niwa*. Les parcelles cultivées utilisent l'eau des étangs. L'espace terrestre de ce projet complexe et original est ouvert aux visiteurs qui peuvent parcourir librement ce qu'on pourrait appeler une nature au-delà de la nature, un environnement (naturel) artificiel. Pour Junya Ishigami, ce jardin n'est rien de moins qu'« une nouvelle nature encore jamais vue ».

SERPENTINE GALLERY SUMMER PAVILION

JUNYA ISHIGAMI

Kensington Gardens,
London, 2019
Area: 350 m²

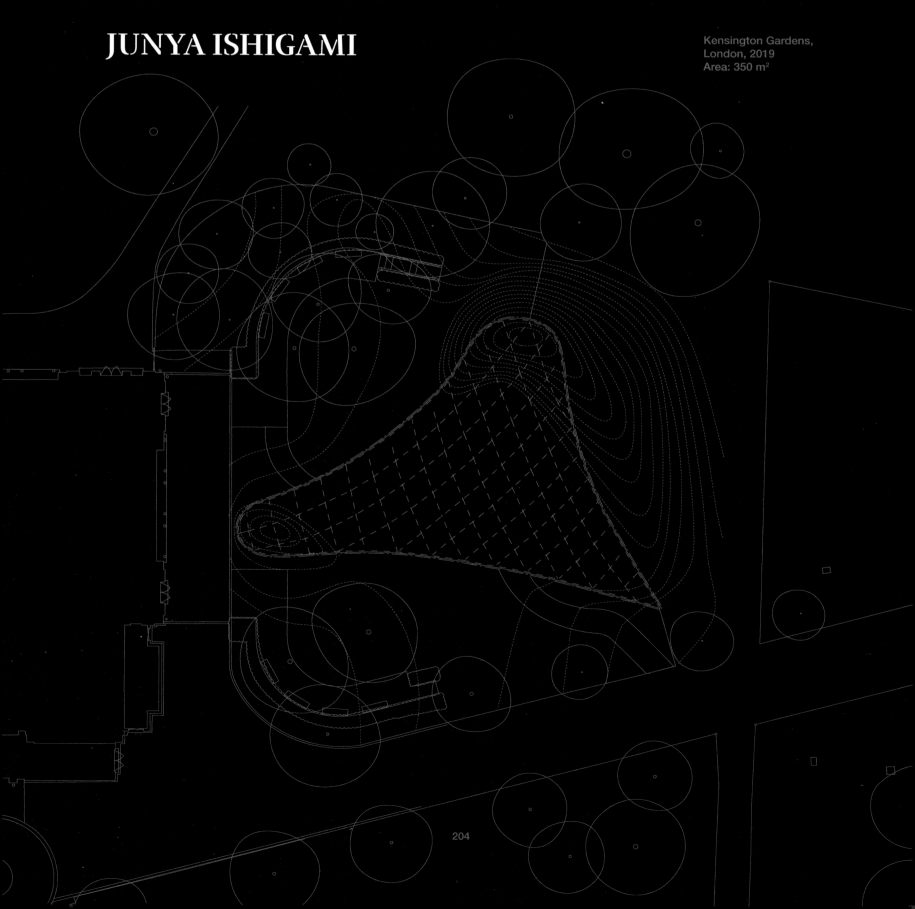

Junya Ishigami designed one of the most unusual SERPENTINE GALLERY SUMMER PAVILIONS using 48-millimeter-diameter steel columns and steel beams covered by Cumbrian slate from northern England. Junya Ishigami explains that he is looking to find ways to create a new kind of architecture using time-honored materials and contemporary technology. In this instance, he says: "Slabs of natural stone shattered into various shapes and sizes are piled up over an elegant, gauze-like structure assembled from uprights and horizontal members of very thin steel. Rain runs smoothly off the overlapping aggregation of stones; in this alone, the structure serves as a gigantic roof resembling a rocky alpine landscape. The attractively layered stone fragments, seemingly random, and without any panels or waterproofing, fulfill the function of architecture with gentle ease." He imagines the Pavilion like a "giant black bird [that] floats in the leaden London skies." Ishigami is, of course, responding to the annual Serpentine Gallery commission for a temporary structure used for talks, concerts, and other events. The freedom and openness of his design—which combines an apparently weighty but uninsulated roof with an extremely light structure—does imply a fascinating confrontation between modern materials (steel) and a kind of artificial landscape made of slate.

Der von Junya Ishigami entworfene SERPENTINE GALLERY SUMMER PAVILION ist einer der außergewöhnlichsten seiner Art. Die mit kumbrischem Schiefer eingedeckten Stahlträger ruhen auf Stahlsäulen mit einem Durchmesser von nur 48 mm. Ishigami erklärt, er suche nach Möglichkeiten, neue Formen der Architektur zu schaffen, indem er althergebrachte Materialien mit modernen Technologien verbinde. In Bezug auf den Pavillon sagt er: „In verschiedene Formen und Größen zerbrochene Natursteinplatten wurden auf eine elegante, gazeartige Konstruktion aus Säulen und horizontalen Bauelementen aus sehr dünnem Stahl geschichtet. An dem sich überlagernden Gestein perlt der Regen sanft ab. Die Konstruktion dient als ausgreifendes Dach und erinnert an eine felsige Alpenlandschaft. Die ansehnlich geschichteten Steinfragmente, die scheinbar zufällig und ohne jede Verkleidung oder Abdichtung angeordnet sind, erfüllen ihre architektonische Funktion mit Leichtigkeit." Ishigami stellt sich den Pavillon wie einen „riesigen schwarzen Vogel vor, (der) im bleiernen Londoner Himmel schwebt". Ishigami reagiert mit seinem Entwurf auf den jährlich von der Serpentine Gallery vergebenen Auftrag für einen temporären Pavillon. Die Freiheit und Offenheit seines Entwurfs, der ein schweres, nicht isoliertes Dach mit einer extrem leichten Rahmenkonstruktion verbindet, kontrastiert auf faszinierende Weise ein modernes Material

Junya Ishigami a conçu l'un des pavillons d'été les plus originaux de la SERPENTINE GALLERY en utilisant des colonnes et des poutres en acier de 48 millimètres de diamètre recouvertes d'ardoises de Cumbria provenant du nord de l'Angleterre. Junyalshigami explique qu'il cherche le moyen de créer un nouveau type d'architecture, en utilisant des matériaux anciens et des technologies contemporaines. En l'occurrence, il déclare : « Des dalles de pierre naturelle brisées, de différentes formes et tailles, sont empilées sur une élégante structure diaphane composée de montants et d'éléments horizontaux en acier très fin. La pluie s'écoule doucement de l'agrégation des pierres qui se chevauchent ; la structure sert de toit gigantesque ressemblant à un paysage rocheux alpin. Les fragments de pierre élégamment empilés, apparemment au hasard, et sans aucun panneau ni imperméabilisation, remplissent la fonction d'architecture avec une incroyable facilité. » Il imagine le Pavillon comme un « oiseau noir géant flottant dans le ciel plombé de Londres ». Ishigami répond, bien sûr, à la commande annuelle de la Serpentine Gallery pour une structure temporaire utilisée pour des conférences, des concerts et d'autres événements. La liberté et l'ouverture de sa conception – qui combine un toit apparemment lourd, mais non isolé, avec une structure extrêmement légère – impliquent une confrontation fascinante entre matériaux modernes (l'acier) et une

The surprising, low roof of Ishigami's structure is covered with roughly laid natural stone, placing it at an unexpected intersection between the surrounding gardens and the Grade II-listed former tea pavilion that houses the Serpentine Gallery itself.

'MINNA NO MORI' GIFU MEDIA COSMOS

TOYO ITO

Gifu, 2015
Area: 15 444 m²
Collaboration: ARUP (Structural Engineer),
Ohtaki E&M Consulting Office (Electrical Engineer),
ES Associates (Mechanical Engineer), University
of Tokyo Mikiko Ishikawa Lab (Landscape Design)

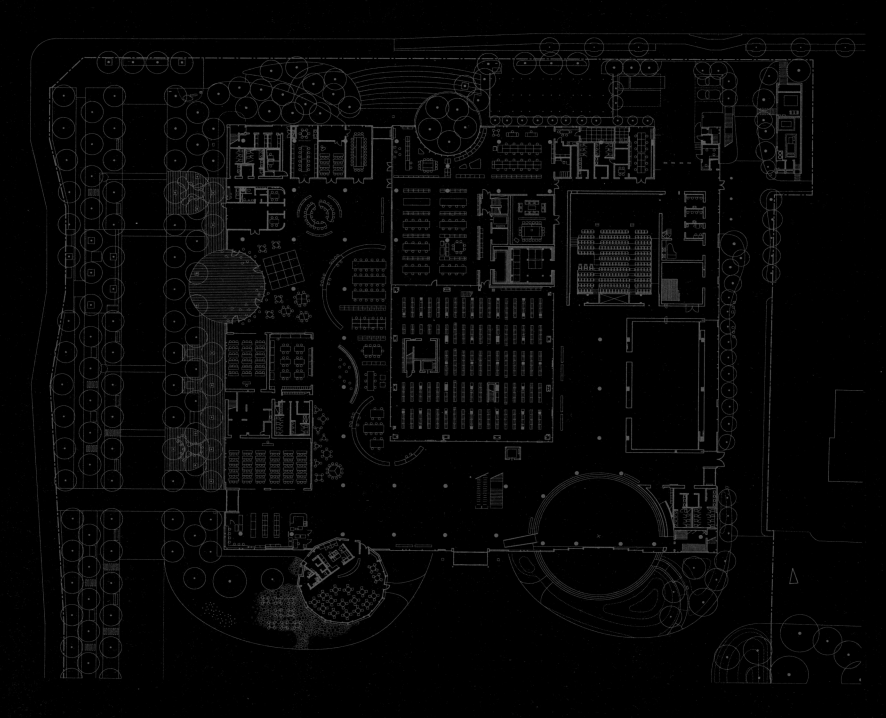

The building combines an orthogonal arrangement with the kind of structural lightness that Toyo Ito is known for. Large, round skylights sit above reading areas, such as the one on the opposite page.

Born in 1941 in Seoul under Japanese rule, TOYO ITO grew up in Shimosuwa, Nagano, Japan, and graduated from the University of Tokyo in 1965. After working in the office of Kiyonori Kikutake until 1969, he founded his own office, Urban Robot (URBOT), in Tokyo in 1971, changing its name to Toyo Ito & Associates, Architects in 1979. He was awarded the Golden Lion for Lifetime Achievement from the 8th International Venice Architecture Biennale in 2002, the RIBA Gold Medal in 2006, and the Pritzker Prize in 2013. He has designed the Sendai Mediatheque (Miyagi, 2001); the 2002 Serpentine Gallery Summer Pavilion (London, 2002); Tod's Omotesando Building (Tokyo, 2004); Tama Art University Library, Hachioji Campus (Tokyo, 2007); ZA-KOENJI Public Theater (Tokyo, 2008); Kaohsiung National Stadium (Kaohsiung, Taiwan, 2009); Toyo Ito Museum of Architecture, Imabari (Ehime, 2011); "Minna no Mori" Gifu Media Cosmos (Gifu, 2015, published here); National Taichung Theater (Taichung, Taiwan, 2016); and 'Meguri no Mori' Kawaguchi City Funeral Hall (Saitama, 2018, also published here).

TOYO ITO wurde 1941 in Seoul geboren, zu einer Zeit, als Südkorea unter japanischer Herrschaft stand. Er wuchs in Shimosuwa, Präfektur Nagano, auf. Toyo Ito schloss 1965 sein Studium an der Universität Tokio ab und arbeitete bis 1969 bei Kiyonori Kikutake. 1971 gründete er in Tokio sein Büro Urban Robot (URBOT), das seit 1979 Toyo Ito & Associates, Architects heißt. Er wurde 2002 für sein Lebenswerk mit dem Goldenen Löwen der 8. Internationalen Architekturbiennale in Venedig ausgezeichnet und erhielt die RIBA-Goldmedaille (2006) sowie den Pritzker-Preis (2013). Zu seinen Projekten gehören die Sendai Mediatheque (Miyagi, 2001), der Sommerpavillon der Londoner Serpentine Gallery (2002), das Tod's Omotesando Building (Tokio, 2004), eine Bibliothek auf dem Hachioji-Campus der Kunsthochschule Tama (Tokio, 2007), das ZA-KOENJI Public Theater (Tokio, 2008), das Nationalstadion Kaohsiung (Kaohsiung, Taiwan, 2009), das Toyo-Ito-Architekturmuseum (Imabari, Ehime, 2011), CapitaGreen (Singapur, 2014), „Minna no Mori" – Gifu Media Cosmos (Gifu, 2015, hier vorgestellt), das Nationaltheater Taichung (Taichung, Taiwan, 2016) und ‚Meguri no Mori', die städtische Trauerhalle Kawaguchi (Saitama, 2018, ebenfalls hier vorgestellt).

Né en 1941 à Séoul alors sous domination japonaise, TOYO ITO a grandi à Shimosuwa, Nagano. Il est diplômé de l'université de Tokyo (1965). Après avoir travaillé dans l'agence de Kiyonori Kikutake jusqu'en 1969. Il a fondé son agence Urban Robot (URBOT) à Tokyo en 1971, changeant son nom pour celui de Toyo Ito & Associates, Architects en 1979. Il a gagné le Lion d'or pour l'ensemble de son œuvre à la VIIIᵉ Biennale internationale d'architecture de Venise en 2002, la médaille d'or du RIBA en 2006 et le prix Pritzker en 2013. Il a réalisé la médiathèque de Sendai (Miyagi, 2001) ; le pavillon d'été de la Serpentine Gallery (Londres, 2002) ; l'immeuble Tod's d'Omotesando (Tokyo, 2004) ; la bibliothèque universitaire d'art de Tama sur le campus de Hachioji (Tokyo, 2007) ; le théâtre public ZA-KOENJI (Tokyo, 2008) ; le stade national Kaohsiung (Kaohsiung, Taïwan, 2009) ; le musée d'architecture Toyo Ito à Imabari (Ehime, 2011) ; l'immeuble CapitaGreen (Singapour, 2014) ; la bibliothèque « Minna no Mori » Media Cosmos de Gifu (Gifu, 2015, publiée ici) ; le Théâtre national Taichung (Taichung, Taïwan, 2016) ; et le funérarium municipal « Meguri no Mori » de Kawaguchi (Saitama, 2018, également publié ici).

The 'MINNA NO MORI' GIFU MEDIA COSMOS is a two-story library complex that opened in July 2015. It is located fairly close to the JR Gifu railway station and has a view of Gifu Castle. The building footprint is 80 x 90 meters with space for 600 000 books in the middle of the ground floor. An exhibition gallery, a multipurpose hall, and an array of civic activity and an exchange center surround the book storage. A further 300 000 books are located on the upper floor, where there is a reading area with 910 seats and no walls. The architect has created 11 translucent "globes" measuring between 8 and 14 meters in diameter that hang above the reading spaces. These are intended to "create gentle air movements and soft, diffused light from above, providing a comfortable indoor environment." The placement of the globes corresponds to undulations in the timber roof. Water pumped from below the site is used for radiant floor heating and cooling, and there are solar panels on the roof, with a net savings of approximately half of the energy that a similar building designed 20 years ago would have consumed. Ito continues to work with the gentle lightness and awareness of nature (be it artificial) and the environment that has always characterized his work.

Der 'MINNA NO MORI' GIFU MEDIA COSMOS ist ein zweigeschossiger Bibliothekskomplex, der im Juli 2015 eröffnet wurde. Er liegt mit Blick auf die Burg Gifu in unmittelbarer Nähe des Bahnhofs Gifu. Die Grundfläche des Gebäudes, dessen Magazin im zentralen Bereich des Erdgeschosses 600 000 Bücher fasst, beträgt 80 x 90 m. Um das Magazin herum sind Ausstellungsgalerien, eine Mehrzweckhalle sowie ein Bürger- und Begegnungszentrum angeordnet. Weitere 300 000 Bücher sowie ein offener Lesesaal mit 910 Sitzplätzen befinden sich im Obergeschoss. Der Architekt hat elf lichtdurchlässige „Sphären" mit einem Durchmesser von 8 bis 14 m geschaffen und an der Decke des Lesesaals aufgehängt. Sie sollen „für eine angenehme Atmosphäre sorgen und sanfte Luftbewegungen sowie weiches diffuses Licht erzeugen". Die Sphären sind in den Vertiefungen der Holzdecke platziert. Die Fußbodenheizung und die Klimaanlage werden mit Wasser aus dem Untergrund gespeist. Auf dem Dach wurden Solarmodule installiert. Die Nettoersparnis gegenüber einem vergleichbaren, vor 20 Jahren errichteten Gebäude beträgt etwa 50 Prozent. Ito beweist einmal mehr seinen Sinn für die Umwelt und eine (wenn auch künstlich erzeugte) zarte Natürlichkeit, die seine Arbeit seit jeher auszeichnen.

Le complexe « MINNA NO MORI » GIFU MEDIA COSMOS est une bibliothèque à deux niveaux qui a ouvert en juillet 2015, tout près de la gare JR de Gifu, avec vue sur le château de Gifu. Le bâtiment occupe une empreinte au sol de 80 x 90 m et peut accueillir 600 000 livres au centre du rez-de-chaussée. Une salle d'expositions, un hall polyvalent et un centre d'éducation à l'activité civique et d'échange sont déployés autour du magasin. Trois cent mille autres livres se trouvent à l'étage où l'espace de lecture compte 910 sièges et aucune cloison. L'architecte a imaginé onze « globes » translucides de 8 à 14 m de diamètre suspendus au-dessus des zones de lecture. Ils sont destinés à « imprimer de légers mouvements à l'air et créer une lumière douce diffusée depuis le haut pour une atmosphère intérieure douillette ». Les emplacements des globes correspondent aux ondulations de la toiture en bois d'œuvre. De l'eau pompée sous la construction est utilisée pour le chauffage par le sol à rayonnement et la climatisation, tandis que le toit est garni de panneaux solaires, pour une économie nette de la moitié de l'énergie qu'un bâtiment semblable conçu vingt ans auparavant aurait consommée. Ito poursuit ici son travail avec la clarté douce et la conscience de la nature (même artificielle) et de l'environnement qui caractérise ses réalitions.

'MEGURI NO MORI' KAWAGUCHI CITY FUNERAL HALL

TOYO ITO

Kawaguchi, Saitama, 2018
Area: 7886 m²
Collaboration: Sasaki Structural Consultants
(Structural Engineer), SOGO Consultants
(Facility Engineer), Chuo University
Mikiko Ishikawa Lab (Landscape Design)

The light, undulating roof of the building, together with the site, which combines a pond and natural grasses, creates a feeling of calm and contemplation appropriate to the function of the facility.

The architect describes this project as "a space to mourn the dead while immersed in nature." The city-operated crematorium is located in a nine-hectare park near Kawaguchi, near Tokyo in Saitama Prefecture. The area is known for having provided trees for Tokyo since the Edo period. Centers for regional products and nature information are also located on the site. The two-story design includes a "low and heavy roof" that may give the impression that it is part of a land form. The cremation furnace rises to a height of 13 meters. Inurnment rooms and the furnace are located at the center of the structure, connecting to the entrance and waiting halls. Timber-framed curtain walls allow visitors to look out over a pond and the park. The Akayama Historic Nature Park Information Center consists of three "house-like spaces" (brick, earth, and wood) connected by a foyer. Gardens between the houses are planted with local species. The Akayama Historic Nature Park Regional Products Center sells garden trees and includes a café, shop, and event space. A semi-outdoor space is used for exhibitions and the sale of trees.

Der Architekt beschreibt dieses Projekt als „Ort inmitten der Natur, um die Toten zu betrauern". Das städtische Krematorium befindet sich in einem 9 ha großen Park bei Kawaguchi in der Präfektur Saitama unweit von Tokio. Die Gegend ist seit der Edo-Zeit ein wichtiger Holzlieferant für Tokio. Auf dem Gelände befinden sich zudem ein Informationszentrum und das Zentrum für Regionalprodukte. Der zweigeschossige Entwurf verfügt über einen „niedrige und schwere Dachkonstruktion", die wie eine Landschaftsformation anmutet. Der Einäscherungsofen ist 13 m hoch. Die Urnenbeisetzungsräume sowie der Ofen sind zentral im Gebäude gelegen und über einen Eingangs- und Wartebereich miteinander verbunden. Durch die holzgerahmte Vorhangfassade blicken Besucher auf einen Teich und den Park. Das Zentrum des Naturparks Akayama besteht aus drei „hausartigen Bauten" (Ziegel, Lehm, Holz), die durch ein Foyer miteinander verbunden sind. Die Gärten zwischen den Häusern sind mit einheimischen Pflanzen bestückt. Das Zentrum für Regionalprodukte bietet Gartenbäume zum Kauf an, verfügt über ein Café, einen Shop und Veranstaltungsräume. Ein halboffener Raum wird für Ausstellungen und den Verkauf von Bäumen genutzt.

L'architecte décrit son projet comme « un espace où pleurer les morts tout en étant immergé dans la nature ». Le crématorium exploité par la municipalité est situé dans un parc de 9 ha près de Kawaguchi, dans la préfecture de Saitama proche de Tokyo. La région est célèbre pour les arbres qu'elle fournit à Tokyo depuis l'époque d'Edo. Le site comprend aussi des centres de produits régionaux et d'information sur la nature. Le complexe à deux niveaux porte un « toit bas et lourd » qui peut donner l'impression qu'il fait partie d'une forme terrestre. Le crématorium se dresse à 13 m de hauteur. Il est situé au centre de la structure avec les espaces de mise en urne des cendres et communique avec l'entrée et les salles d'attente. Des murs rideaux au cadre en bois ouvrent la vue aux visiteurs sur un étang et le parc à l'extérieur. Le Centre d'information du parc naturel historique d'Akayama est composé de trois « espaces de type maison » (briques, terre et bois) reliés par un hall. Entre eux, des jardins sont plantés de variétés locales. Le Centre de produits régionaux du parc naturel historique vend quant à lui des arbres de jardins et comprend un café, une boutique et un espace évènementiel. Une zone semi-extérieure est consacrée à l'exposition et à la vente des arbres.

...inurnment room is both closed and bathed
...ght. Below: a section drawing of the building
...ws its 13-meter-high cremation furnace.

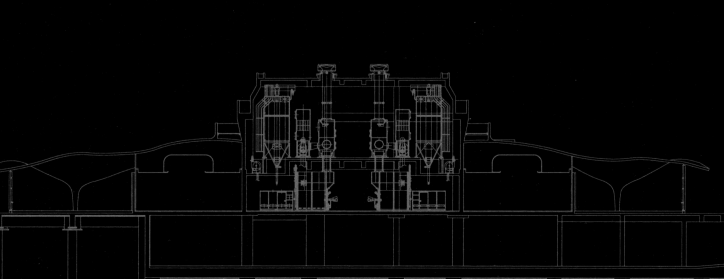

The entry space and the neighboring front of the
building with its overhanging roof emphasize
a feeling of lightness and connection to nature.

ARK NOVA LUCERNE FESTIVAL

ANISH KAPOOR + ARATA ISOZAKI

Matsushima, Miyagi, 2013
Area: 720 m²

Ark Nova is intriguing not only because of its ephemeral nature, but also because it combines the talents of the Pritzker Prize-winning architect Arata Isozaki and the celebrated artist Anish Kapoor.

The artist ANISH KAPOOR was born in Bombay, India, in 1954 and has lived and worked in London since the early 1970s. He studied at the Hornsey College of Art (1973–77) and the Chelsea School of Art (1977–78), and he held his first solo exhibition in 1980. He represented Britain at the 1990 Biennale in Venice and won the Turner Prize in 1991. His many exhibitions include architecture-scale works such as *Marsyas* (Tate Modern, London, UK, October 2002– April 2003); *Cloud Gate*, Chicago Millennium Park (Chicago, Illinois, USA, 2004); and *Leviathan*, Monumenta 2011 (Grand Palais, Paris, France, 11 May–23 June, 2011).

Der Künstler ANISH KAPOOR wurde 1954 in Bombay, Indien, geboren und lebt und arbeitet seit den frühen 1970er-Jahren in London. Dort studierte er am Hornsey College of Art (1973–1977) und an der Chelsea School of Art (1977–1978). Seine erste Einzelausstellung hatte er 1980. Er vertrat Großbritannien 1990 bei der Biennale in Venedig und erhielt 1991 den Turner-Preis. In zahlreichen Ausstellungen präsentierte er auch Arbeiten von architektonischem Ausmaß: darunter *Marsyas* (Tate Modern, London, Oktober 2002 bis April 2003), *Cloud Gate* im Chicago Millennium Park (Chicago, Illinois, USA, 2004) und *Leviathan* auf der Monumenta 2011 (Grand Palais, Paris, 11. Mai bis 23. Juni 2011).

L'artiste ANISH KAPOOR est né à Bombay en 1954, il vit et travaille à Londres depuis le début des années 1970. Il a fait ses études au Hornsey College of Art (1973–77) et à la Chelsea School of Art (1977–78). Sa première exposition personnelle date de 1980. Il a représenté la Grande-Bretagne à la Biennale de Venise en 1990 et a gagné le prix Turner en 1991. Dans ses nombreuses expositions, il a aussi présenté des œuvres à l'échelle architecturale comme *Marsyas* (Tate Modern, Londres, octobre 2002–avril 2003) ; *CloudGate*, au Chicago Millennium Park (Chicago, 2004) et *Leviathan* à la Monumenta 2011 (Grand Palais, Paris, 11 mai–23 juin 2011).

Born in Oita City on the island of Kyushu, Japan, in 1931, ARATA ISOZAKI graduated from the Architectural Faculty of the University of Tokyo in 1954 and established Arata Isozaki & Associates in 1963, having worked in the office of Kenzo Tange. Arata Isozaki has received the 1986 RIBA Gold Medal and the 2019 Pritzker Prize. His notable buildings include the Museum of Contemporary Art (Los Angeles, California, USA, 1986); Art Tower Mito (Mito, 1986–90); and the Center of Science and Industry (COSI, Columbus, Ohio, USA, 1999). His more recent work includes the Shenzhen Cultural Center (Shenzhen, China, 2007); Central Academy of Fine Art, Museum of Art (Beijing, China, 2008); Qatar National Convention Center (Doha, Qatar, 2011); Shanghai Symphony Hall (2014); and the Hunan Provincial Museum (Changsha, China, 2017). HIROSHI AOKI was born in 1952 in Tokyo. A Director at Arata Isozaki & Associates beginning in 1975, he became Representative Director of the firm Isozaki, Aoki & Associates in 2011.

ARATA ISOZAKI wurde 1931 in Oita auf der japanischen Insel Kyushu geboren. Er schloss 1954 ein Studium an der Fakultät für Architektur der Universität Tokio ab und gründete nach seiner Tätigkeit für Kenzo Tange im Jahr 1963 Arata Isozaki & Associates. Er wurde 1986 mit der RIBA Gold Medal ausgezeichnet. Wichtige Projekte sind das Museum of Contemporary Art (Los Angeles, 1986), der Art Tower Mito (Mito, Japan, 1986–1990) und das Center of Science and Industry (COSI, Columbus, Ohio, USA, 1999). Jüngere Projekte sind das Kulturzentrum Shenzhen (Shenzhen, China, 2007), ein Kunstmuseum für die Zentrale Akademie für Bildende Kunst (Peking, 2008), das Nationale Kongresszentrum Katar (Doha, Katar, 2011), die Shanghai Symphony Hall (2014) und das Provinzmuseum Hunan (Changsha, China, 2017). HIROSHI AOKI wurde 1952 in Tokio geboren und war ab 1975 Director von Arata Isozaki & Associates, 2011 wurde er Representative Director von Isozaki, Aoki & Associates. Arata Isozaki gewann 2019 den Pritzker-Preis.

Né dans la ville d'Oita, sur l'île de Kyushu, en 1931, ARATA ISOZAKI est diplômé de la faculté d'architecture de l'université de Tokyo (1954) et a fondé Arata Isozaki & Associates en 1963 après avoir d'abord travaillé dans l'agence de Kenzo Tange. Lauréat de la médaille d'or du RIBA en 1986, ses constructions les plus notables comprennent le musée d'Art contemporain (Los Angeles, 1986) ; la tour Art Tower Mito (Mito, 1986–1990) et le Center of Science and Industry (COSI, Columbus, Ohio, 1999). Plus récemment, il a construit le Centre culturel de Shenzhen (Shenzhen, Chine, 2007) ; l'Académie centrale des beaux-arts du musée d'Art (Pékin, 2008) ; le Palais des congrès du Qatar (Doha, Qatar, 2011) ; la salle de musique symphonique de Shanghai (2014) et le Musée de la province du Hunan (Changsha, Chine, 2017). Partenaire d'Arata Isozaki, HIROSHI AOKI est né en 1952 à Tokyo. Directeur d'Arata Isozaki & Associates depuis 1975, il est devenu directeur délégué de la société Isozaki, Aoki & Associates en 2011. Arata Isozaki a remporté le prix Pritzker en 2019.

At night the 18-meter-high performance space glows from within its PVC-coated polyester fabric forms.

This inflatable concert hall with a capacity for 500 people marked the first collaboration between Arata Isozaki and Anish Kapoor. The form of the structure is related to that of Kapoor's *Leviathan* (2011). Matsushima is near the areas most damaged by the 2011 Tohoku earthquake and tsunami, and the concert hall was intended to reach out to as many people affected by those events as possible. The interior and exterior structure was made with PVC-coated polyester fiber fabric, floors were made of salvaged cedar timber, and a used 12.2-meter freight container was employed as an air lock. Anish Kapoor developed the concept of the structureless shell in collaboration with the British company Aerotrope, with whom he has worked on previous projects. A freely positioned, hanging, helium-filled, acoustic reflection screen was used to ensure optimal sound inside the 18-meter-high hall.

Diese aufblasbare Konzerthalle bietet Platz für 500 Personen und ist das erste gemeinsame Projekt von Arata Izosaki und Anish Kapoor. In ihrer Form erinnert die Halle an Kapoors *Leviathan* (2011). Matsushima befindet sich in der Nähe der Region, die durch das Tohoku-Erdbeben und den Tsunami von 2011 am stärksten in Mitleidenschaft gezogen wurde. Die mobile Konzerthalle soll für möglichst viele Menschen erreichbar sein, die von der Katastrophe betroffen waren. Die Hülle besteht aus einem sowohl von innen als auch von außen mit PVC überzogenem Polyestergewebe, die Böden sind aus recyceltem Zedernholz gearbeitet, ein etwa 12 m langer Frachtcontainer dient als Luftschleuse. Das Konzept für diese Hülle ohne Tragwerk hat Anish Kapoor in Zusammenarbeit mit der britischen Firma Aerotrope entwickelt, die auch an einigen seiner früheren Projekte beteiligt war. Ein beliebig positionierbarer Heliumballon dient als Akustikschirm und sorgt in der 18 m hohen Halle für einen optimalen Klang.

Cette salle de concert gonflable d'une capacité de 500 personnes a marqué la première collaboration entre Arata Isozaki et Anish Kapoor. La forme s'apparente à celle du *Leviathan* (2011) de Kapoor. Matsushima est proche des zones les plus touchées par le tremblement de terre et le tsunami du Tohoku en 2011 et la salle de concert devait pouvoir accueillir le plus possible de victimes. La structure intérieure et extérieure est en fibres de polyester recouvertes de PVC, les sols sont en cèdre de récupération et un ancien container maritime de 40 pieds a servi de sas à air. Anish Kapoor a mis au point le concept de coque sans charpente en collaboration avec la société britannique Aerotrope avec laquelle il avait déjà travaillé à d'autres projets. Un écran de réflexion acoustique empli d'hélium est suspendu et positionné librement pour un son optimal à l'intérieur de la salle haute de 18 m.

S-HOUSE

YUUSUKE KARASAWA

Omiya, Saitama, 2013
Area: 104 m²

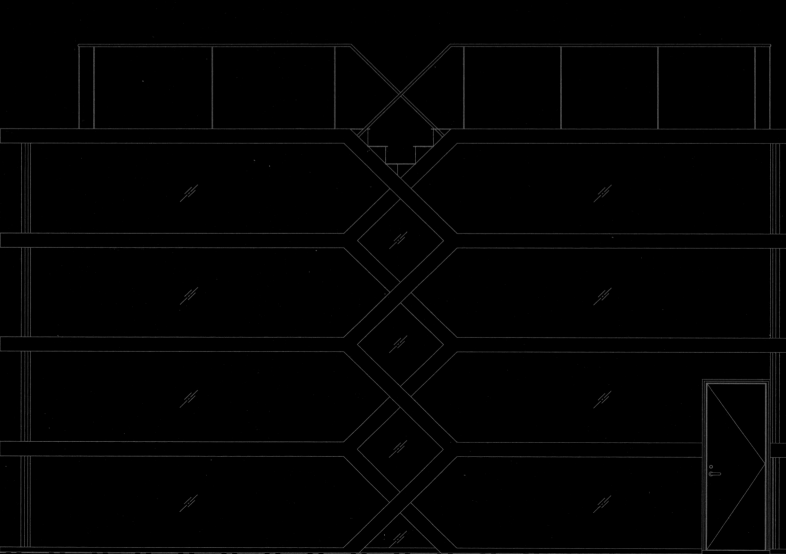

The building seems in this image to be almost impossibly light, revealing only its structure, its glazed walls, and minimal interior elements.

YUUSUKE KARASAWA was born in Tokyo in 1976. He attended the Keio University Faculty of Environment and Information Studies (1995–99) and then studied Architecture and Urban Design at the Keio University Graduate School of Media and Governance (1999–2001). He worked at MVRDV in Rotterdam as a trainee with the assistance of the Japanese Government Overseas Study Program for Artists (2002–03), before spending two years in the office of Shigeru Ban in Tokyo (2004–05). He created his own firm in 2006 in Tokyo and has taught at the Tokyo University of Science since 2012. His work includes House in Oyamadai (Tokyo, 2006); Villa Kanousan (Kimitsou, Chiba, 2009); a proposal for the Ningbo University Gymnasium (China, 2012); and S-House

YUUSUKE KARASAWA wurde 1976 in Tokio geboren und besuchte die Fakultät für Umwelt- und Informationsstudien der Keio-Universität (1995–1999). Anschließend studierte er ebendort Architektur und Städtebau an der Graduiertenschule für Medien und Governance (1999–2001). Er war mit Unterstützung des Auslandsstudien-Künstlerprogramms der japanischen Regierung in Rotterdam Trainee bei MVRDV (2002–2003), bevor er zwei Jahre im Büro von Shigeru Ban in Tokio arbeitete (2004–2005). Karasawa gründete 2006 in Tokio seine eigene Firma und unterrichtet seit 2012 an der Naturwissenschaftlichen Universität Tokio. Zu seinen Projekten gehören House in Oyamadai (Tokio, 2006), Villa Kanousan (Kimitsou, Chiba, 2009), ein Entwurf für die Sporthalle der Universität Ningbo (China, 2012) sowie S-House

YUUSUKE KARASAWA est né à Tokyo en 1976. Il a d'abord suivi les cours de la faculté des études de l'environnement et de l'information de l'université Keio (1995–1999) avant d'étudier l'architecture et l'urbanisme à l'École supérieure des médias et de la gouvernance de l'université Keio (1999–2001). Il a fait un stage à MVRDV à Rotterdam avec l'aide du Programme d'études à l'étranger pour artistes du gouvernement japonais (2002–2003), puis a passé deux ans dans l'agence de Shigeru Ban à Tokyo (2004–2005). Il a ouvert son agence en 2006 à Tokyo et enseigne à l'université des sciences de Tokyo depuis 2012. Ses réalisations comprennent une maison à Oyamadai (Tokyo, 2006) ; la villa Kanousan (Kimitsou, Chiba, 2009) ; un projet pour le gymnase de l'université de Ningbo (Chine, 2012) et la S-House (Omiya, Saitama, 2013, publiée ici)

What the architect calls "a network of complex
levels" creates intriguing spatial configurations
that bring to mind the work of M. C. Escher.
Roof space is used as well.

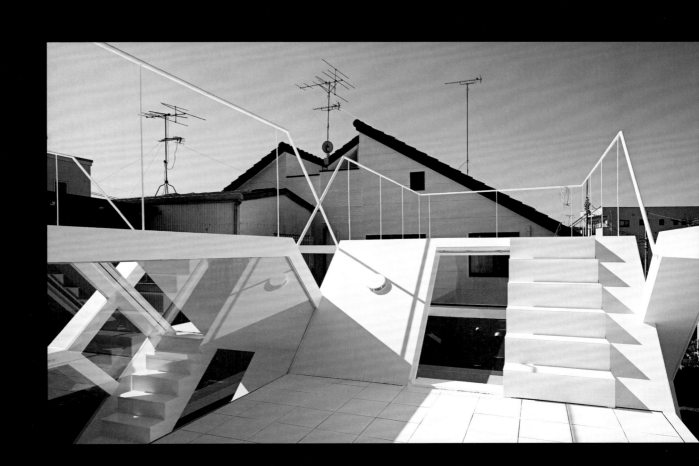

This small two-story house was built on
a 100-square-meter site for a budget
of $425 000 with steel plate, ceramic tiles,
plaster board, oak flooring, and hemp car-
pet. The staggered floors create a surprisingly complex spatial network inside the
residence, leaving the impression that there
are four levels instead of two. Karasawa
explains: "The commonly understood
three-dimensional depth and the sense of
distance are being disturbed, creating architectural spaces where various distances
become complicated, much like what is hap-
pening in infospheres like the Internet.
This architecture realizes such network-type
spaces, where various distances become
increasingly complex, as a 'network of complex levels' in which multiple levels are

Dieses kleine zweigeschossige Haus wurde
auf einem 100 m² großen Grundstück errichtet.
Das Budget betrug 425 000 Dollar. Verbaut
wurden Stahlplatten, Keramikfliesen, Gipskarton und Eichenböden. Das Projekt verfügt
zudem über Hanfteppiche. Die versetzten
Stockwerke bilden ein überraschend komplexes räumliches Netzwerk, das den Eindruck
erweckt, das Haus bestehe nicht nur aus zwei,
sondern aus vier Ebenen. Karasawa: „Das
Gefühl für dreidimensionale Tiefe und für Ent-
fernungen wird verwirrt, es entstehen Räume,
in denen die Wahrnehmung von Abständen
erschwert scheint, so wie in den Infosphären
des Internets. Dieses Gebäude realisiert solche netzwerkartigen Räume als ‚Netzwerk aus
komplexen Ebenen', in dem mehrere Ebenen
in- und übereinandergeschichtet sind", Trotz

Cette petite maison de deux étages a été
construite sur un terrain de 100 m² pour un budget de 425 000 dollars avec des plaques d'acier,
des carreaux de céramique, des panneaux de
plâtre, un plancher de chêne et une moquette
de chanvre. Les étages décalés créent à l'intérieur un réseau étonnamment complexe qui
donne l'impression de quatre étages au lieu
de deux. Karasawa explique : « La profondeur
tridimensionnelle et le sens de la distance com-
munément admis sont troublés pour donner
naissance à des espaces architecturaux où
les distances deviennent complexes, comme
ce qui se passe dans les infosphères du type
d'Internet. Cette architecture crée des espaces
de type réseau où les différentes distances
deviennent de plus en plus complexes sous
la forme d'un "réseau de niveaux complexes"

*Although emptiness is the rule, the house has
all the practical spaces, such as the kitchen seen
on the left page, that are required for daily life.*

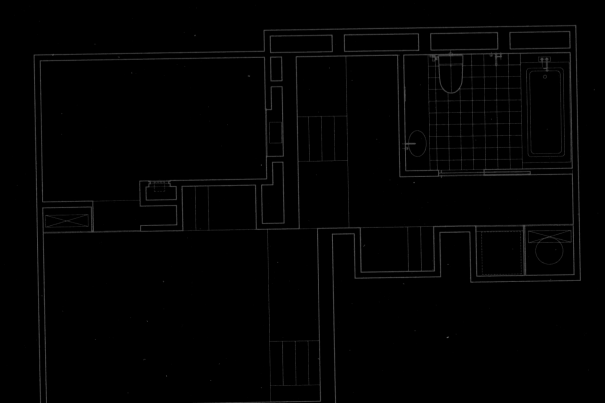

S-House

YUSUHARA WOODEN BRIDGE MUSEUM

KENGO KUMA

Yusuhara, Kochi, 2010
Area: 446 m²

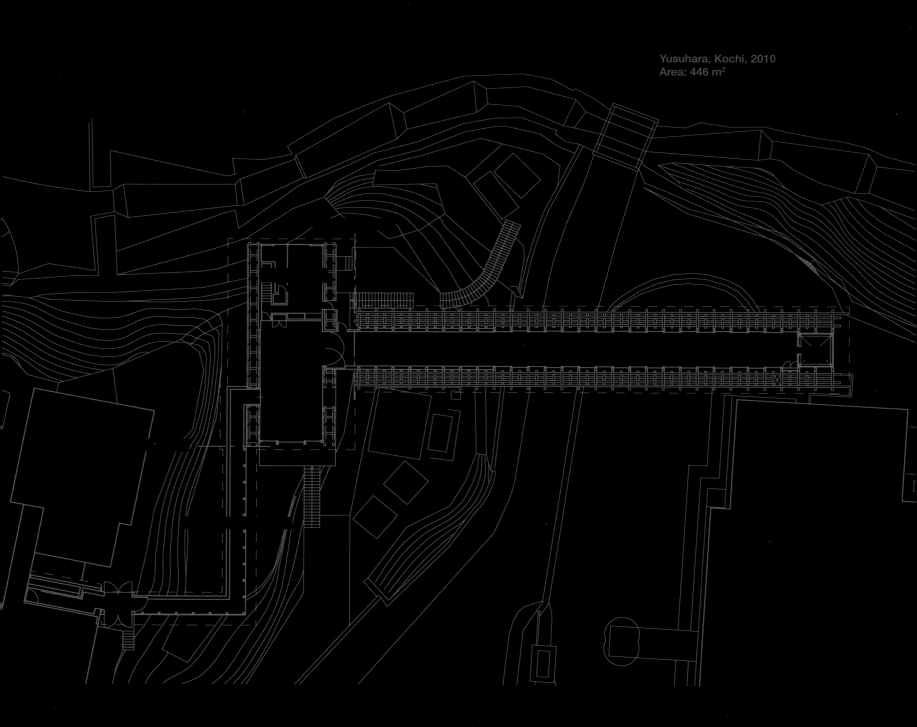

Both the elongated plan of the structure and
its design are intimately related to local history
and to the use of wood in bridge and
building construction.

Born in 1954 in Kanagawa, KENGO KUMA
graduated in 1979 from the University of Tokyo
with an M.Arch degree. In 1987, he established
the Spatial Design Studio, and in 1990 he
created Kengo Kuma & Associates. His work
includes the Great (Bamboo) Wall Guesthouse
(Beijing, China, 2002); One Omotesando
(Tokyo, 2003); LVMH Osaka (Osaka, 2004);
Nagasaki Prefectural Art Museum (Nagasaki,
2005); Zhongtai Box, Z58 building (Shanghai,
China, 2006); Tiffany Ginza (Tokyo, 2008); Nezu
Museum (Tokyo, 2009); Museum of Kanayama
Castle Ruin (Ota City, Gunma, 2009); Glass/
Wood House (New Canaan, Connecticut, USA,
2010); Yusuhara Community Market (Yusuhara,
Kochi, 2010); and the Yusuhara Wooden Bridge
Museum (Yusuhara, Kochi, 2010, published
here). The architect has also begun to work
extensively in Europe: FRAC PACA (Marseille,
France, 2013); the Darius Milhaud Conservatory
of Music (Aix-en-Provence, France, 2014);
and Under One Roof, EPFL ArtLab (Lausanne,
Switzerland, 2016). His recent work includes
the V&A Dundee (Dundee, UK, 2018) and
the Japan National Stadium (with Taisei
Corporation, Azusa Sekkei Co., Ltd.; Tokyo,
2019), both published here.

KENGO KUMA wurde 1954 in Kanagawa
geboren und schloss 1979 sein Studium an
der Universität Tokio mit einem M.Arch ab.
Er gründete 1987 das Spatial Design Studio
und 1990 Kengo Kuma & Associates. Zu seinen
Projekten gehören das Great (Bamboo) Wall
Guesthouse (Peking, 2002), One Omotesando
(Tokio, 2003), LVMH Osaka (Osaka, 2004),
das Kunstmuseum der Präfektur Nagasaki
(Nagasaki, 2005), Zhongtai Box – Gebäude Z58
(Shanghai, 2006), Tiffany Ginza (Tokio, 2008),
das Nezu-Museum (Tokio, 2009), das Museum
of Kanayama Castle Ruin (Ota, Gunma, 2009),
Glass/Wood House (New Canaan, Connecticut,
2010), Yusuhara Community Market (Yusuhara,
Kochi, 2010) und das Yusuhara Wooden Bridge
Museum (Yusuhara, Kochi, 2010, hier vorge-
stellt). Auch in Europa realisiert der Architekt
regelmäßig Projekte, darunter FRAC PACA
(Marseille, 2013), das Conservatoire Darius
Milhaud (Aix-en-Provence, 2014) sowie Under
One Roof, EPFL ArtLab (Lausanne, 2016).
Zu seinen jüngeren Arbeiten gehören zudem
V&A Dundee (Dundee, GB, 2018) und das
Japan National Stadium (in Zusammenarbeit
mit Taisei Corporation und Azusa Sekkei Co.,
Ltd., Tokio, 2019), die beide in diesem Band
vorgestellt werden.

Né en 1954 à Kanagawa, KENGO KUMA possède un M.Arch de l'université de Tokyo (1979).
En 1987, il crée le Spatial Design Studio et,
en 1990, Kengo Kuma & Associates. Ses réalisations comprennent la maison d'hôtes de
la Grande muraille (de bambou) (Pékin, 2002) ;
l'immeuble One Omotesando (Tokyo, 2003) ;
l'immeuble LVMH Osaka (2004) ; le musée d'Art
de la préfecture de Nagasaki (Nagasaki, 2005) ;
l'immeuble Zhongtai Box, Z58 (Shanghai,
2006) ; l'immeuble Tiffany Ginza (Tokyo, 2008) ;
le musée Nezu (Tokyo, 2009) ; le musée des
Ruines du château de Kanayama (Ota City,
Gunma, 2009) ; la Glass/Wood House
(New Canaan, Connecticut, 2010) ; le Marché
communautaire de Yusuhara (Yusuhara,
Kochi, 2009–10) et le musée du Pont de bois de
Yusuhara (Yusuhara, Kochi, 2010, publié ici).
Il a aussi commencé à travailler intensément en
Europe avec : la FRAC PACA (Marseille, 2013) ;
le conservatoire Darius Milhaud de musique
(Aix-en-Provence, 2014) et Under One Roof,
EPFL ArtLab (Lausanne, Suisse, 2016).
Parmi ses projets récents figurent le musée
V&A Dundee (Dundee, Royaume-Uni, 2018)
et le stade national du Japon (avec Taisei
Corporation, Azusa Sekkei Co., Ltd., Tokyo,
2019), tous les deux publiés ici.

The omnipresence of wood, here set in part
on a rough stone wall, ties the Museum to its site
even as it proposes a contemporary expression
of ancestral forms.

ual museum was built on a
...are-meter site in Yusuhara, a small
...ed on the island of Shikoku. It has
...ent level and two stories above
...e design was intended to link two
...separated public buildings with a
...e structure. Functioning as a muse-
...o housing an artist-in-residence
...nd workshop area, the design relies
...ctural system that is composed of
..., referring to cantilever design often
... in traditional architecture in Japan
..." Called *tokiyo*, the structural
...d only one existing example in
... so-called Saruhashi, Enkyo bridge
...shi Prefecture. This system allows
...ation of a substantial laminated
...ilever without recourse to large-
...ctural elements. The architect states:
...esented an attempt to create new
...hitecture capable of bridging a wide
...sues, including the rejuvenation
... culture, urban design, structural
...y, and materials and traditional
...n." This project is one example of
...quent use of Japanese tradition
...ice of contemporary structures

Dieses ungewöhnliche Museum befindet sich
auf einem 14 736 m² großen Gelände in Yusuhara, einer kleinen Stadt auf der Insel Shikoku.
Es hat ein Kellergeschoss und zwei Oberge-
schosse. Das Projekt sollte zwei zuvor getrenn-
te öffentliche Gebäude in Form einer Brücke
miteinander verbinden. Außer dem Museum
beherbergt das Projekt auch ein Artist-in-
Residence-Programm sowie Werkstätten.
Kuma: „Wir haben uns gegen ein kleinteiliges
Tragwerk und für eine auskragende Form entschieden, die in der traditionellen japanischen
und chinesischen Architektur häufig zum Einsatz kommt". Es gibt in Japan nur ein einziges
Beispiel für eine in der sogenannten *tokiyo*-
Bauweise ausgeführte Brücke: die Saruhashi-
Brücke in der Präfektur Yamanashi. Die Technik ermöglichte den Bau eines großen Auslegers
aus Schichtholz, ohne auf große Konstruktionselemente zurückgreifen zu müssen. Kuma:
„Der Entwurf war ein Versuch, eine neue Form
der öffentlichen Architektur zu schaffen,
die die Revitalisierung regionalen Kulturlebens
sowie städtebauliche, konstruktions- und
materialtechnische Aspekte berücksichtig und
traditionelle Bezüge aufweist." Kuma setzt
hier erneut traditionelle japanische Techniken

Cet étonnant musée a été construit sur un site
de 14 736 m² à Yusuhara, une petite ville de
l'île de Shikoku. Il se compose d'un niveau en
dessous du sol et de deux au-dessus. Il a été
conçu dans l'intention de relier par une structure de type pont, deux bâtiments publics
auparavant séparés. L'ensemble sert de musée
et accueille aussi un programme d'artistes
en résidence et une atelier. Il est basé sur « un
système structurel composé de petits éléments,
en référence aux structures en porte-à-faux
souvent employées par les architectures tradi-
tionnelles chinoise et japonaise ». Connu sous
le nom de *tokiyo*, il en existe un seul exemple
au Japon, le pont d'Enkyo appelé Saruhashi,
dans la préfecture de Yamanashi. Ce système
a permis la réalisation d'un pont cantilever
de grandes dimensions en bois lamellé sans
utiliser de pièces trop massives. Kuma déclare :
« C'était une tentative de créer une nouvelle
architecture publique qui soit en mesure de répondre à toute une série de questions concer-
nant le rajeunissement de la culture régionale,
l'urbanisme durable, la technologie structurelle,
les matières et l'expression traditionnelle. »
Le projet est l'un des nombreux exemples de
l'exploitation par Kuma de la tradition japonaise

Above: *a long wood and glass gallery marks the upper section of the structure. A kitchen space below also assumes the overall wooden vocabulary of the structure itself.*

*Whereas old wooden buildings might be expected
to be rather dark with fewer glazed surfaces,
this building takes advantage of modern design,
using large glass panes to integrate interior
and exterior in visual terms.*

V&A DUNDEE

KENGO KUMA

Dundee, UK, 2018
Area: 8400 m²
Collaboration: PiM.studio Architects,
James F Stephen Architects

Built for Dundee City Council for a cost of €92 million, this is a branch of London's Victoria & Albert Museum. The architect imagined the project as "a gate that connects the city back to the water." The layered and twisted precast-concrete, panel-clad building willfully reflects the forms of coastal cliffs.. Located near the water, the museum also clearly evokes a naval metaphor. A public indoor plaza overhangs another external plaza. An entrance hall, reception, café and shop form the public area of the ground floor, along with separate administrative offices and storage spaces. The main entrance space has cladding in oak panels in a similar fashion to that recalling the exterior textured concrete panels. Kuma described the main hall of the museum as a "living room for the city" at the time of the competition and believes that this was one reason he won. The upper floor houses permanent Scottish design galleries and 1100 square meters for two temporary exhibition spaces. The Oak Room, an original

Diese Außenstelle des Londoner Victoria & Albert Museum wurde im Auftrag der Stadt Dundee gebaut. Das Budget betrug 92 Millionen Euro. Der Architekt hatte ein Projekt im Sinn, „das die Stadt mit dem Wasser verbindet". Die gestuften, versetzten Volumina sind mit vorgefertigten Beton-Elementen versehen und erinnern an Küstenklippen. Darüber hinaus stellt das wasserseitig gelegene Museum unverkennbar eine Schiffsmetapher dar. Die Plaza im Inneren kragt über eine weitere Plaza im Außenbereich. Foyer, Rezeption, Café und Museumsshop bilden den öffentlichen Bereich des Erdgeschosses, nicht zugänglich sind die ebenfalls hier befindlichen Verwaltungs- und Lagerräume. Der Haupteingangsbereich ist mit Eichenholzplatten verschalt und erinnert an die Fassade mit ihren Betonlamellen. Kuma beschrieb die Haupthalle des Museums als „städtisches Wohnzimmer" und glaubt, dass hierin einer der Gründe dafür lag, dass er den Wettbewerb für sich entscheiden konnte. Das Obergeschoss beherbergt eine Dauer-

Construit pour le conseil municipal de Dundee pour 92 millions d'euros, le musée est une succursale du Victoria & Albert Museum de Londres. L'architecte a imaginé ce projet comme « une porte qui rétablit le lien entre la ville et l'eau ». Le bâtiment stratifié et torsadé revêtu de panneaux de béton précoulé reproduit délibérément les formes des falaises de la côte écossaise. Proche de l'eau, le musée évoque aussi clairement une métaphore navale. Une place intérieure publique forme un surplomb au-dessus d'une place extérieure. Le hall d'entrée, la réception, le café et la boutique constituent l'espace public du rez-de-chaussée, avec les bureaux de l'administration et des espaces de stockage séparés. L'entrée principale est recouverte de panneaux de chêne disposés d'une manière similaire aux panneaux de béton texturé de l'extérieur. Pour le concours, Kuma a décrit le hall principal du musée comme « un salon pour la ville », et il pense que c'est l'une des raisons pour lesquelles il a gagné. L'étage abrite l'exposition permanente de design écos-

The architect succeeds in giving the exterior of the building both a reminiscence of the appearance of a ship and also of natural cliff formations. Water passes in front of and under the building.

Above: the ample entrance foyer echoes the stepped exterior of the building.

Below: a section drawing and two views of exhibition galleries.

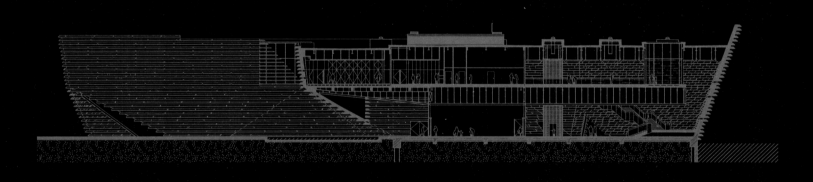

JAPAN NATIONAL STADIUM

TAISEI CORPORATION, AZUSA SEKKEI CO., LTD., AND KENGO KUMA & ASSOCIATES

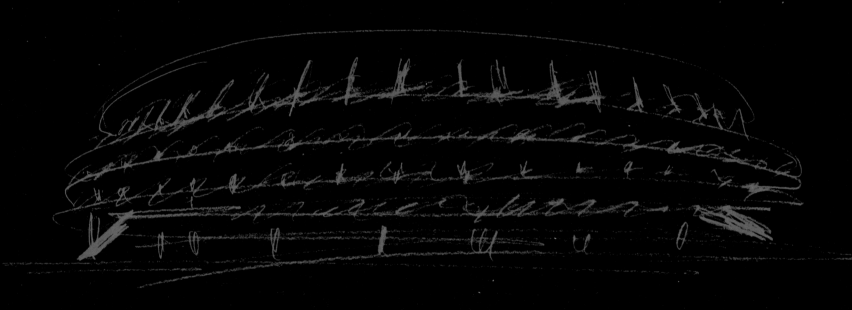

Tokyo, 2019
Area: 194 000 m²

The large roof is supported by a mixed structure made of steel and larch wood.

In Kengo Kuma's words: "This large stadium was designed as a collection of small-diameter pieces of wood. The façade consists of overlapping, multilayered eaves. Small-diameter wood louvers cover the underside of each of these eaves, aiming to evoke and express the beautiful traditional eaves characterizing Japan's architecture in an appropriate contemporary manner. The louvers were created by splitting square cedar lumber measuring 105 millimeters, the most common size in Japan, into three 50-millimeter pieces. The frequency and density of the louvers was then varied in order to endow the eaves with a human scale. The roof is made up of a truss structure that combines steel beams and laminated lumber of a medium

Mit den Worten von Kengo Kuma: „Dieses große Stadion wurde als Ansammlung dünner Holzstücke konzipiert. Die Fassade besteht aus Dachvorsprüngen, die einander in mehreren Schichten überlappen. Dünne Holzgitter bedecken die Unterseite dieser Dachvorsprünge, um auf zeitgemäße Weise an die schönen Dachvorsprünge zu erinnern, die die traditionelle japanische Architektur kennzeichnen. Zur Herstellung der Gitter wurde Zedernkantholz mit der in Japan üblichen Dicke von 105 Millimetern in jeweils drei 50 Millimeter dünne Bretter geschnitten. Die Frequenz und Dichte der Gitter ist unterschiedlich, um den Dachvorsprüngen eine menschliche Dimension zu verleihen. Das Dach besteht aus einem Tragwerk,

Selon de Kengo Kuma : « Ce grand stade a été conçu comme une collection de pièces de bois de petit diamètre. La façade est constituée d'un avant-toit composé de plusieurs couches qui se chevauchent. Des persiennes en bois de petit diamètre couvrent le dessous de chacun de ces avant-toits, visant à évoquer et à exprimer d'une manière contemporaine appropriée les beaux avant-toits traditionnels qui caractérisent l'architecture japonaise. Les persiennes ont été créées en divisant du bois de cèdre carré de 105 millimètres, la taille la plus courante au Japon, en trois morceaux de 50 millimètres. La fréquence et la densité des persiennes ont ensuite été modifiées, afin de conférer aux avant-toits une échelle humaine. Le toit est

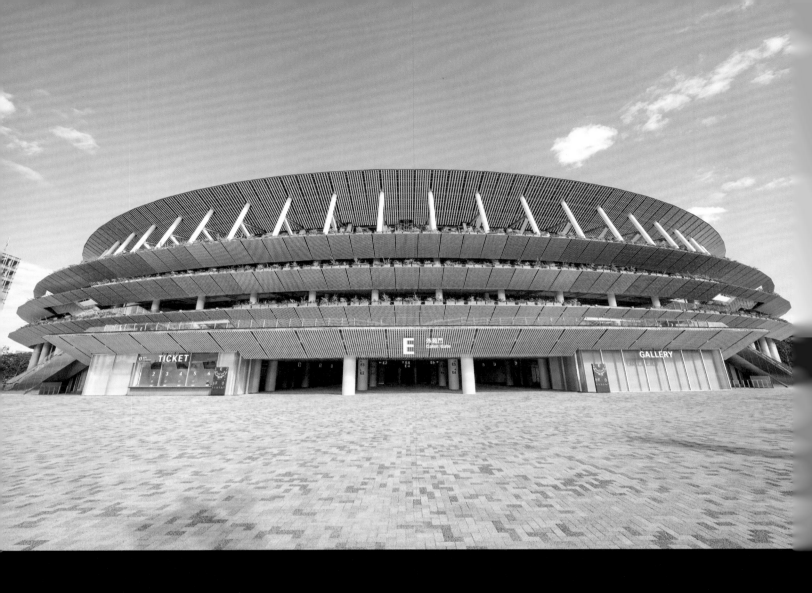

Above: the south side of the Stadium. Cedar panels with a 105 × 30-millimeter cross section were applied to the eaves at carefully calculated pitches. Below: a stream traces the same path on this site as the former Shibuya River.

4 WORLD TRADE CENTER

FUMIHIKO MAKI

New York, 2014
Area: 213 720 m²
Collaboration: AAI Architects
(Architect of Record), Beyer Blinder
Belle Architects

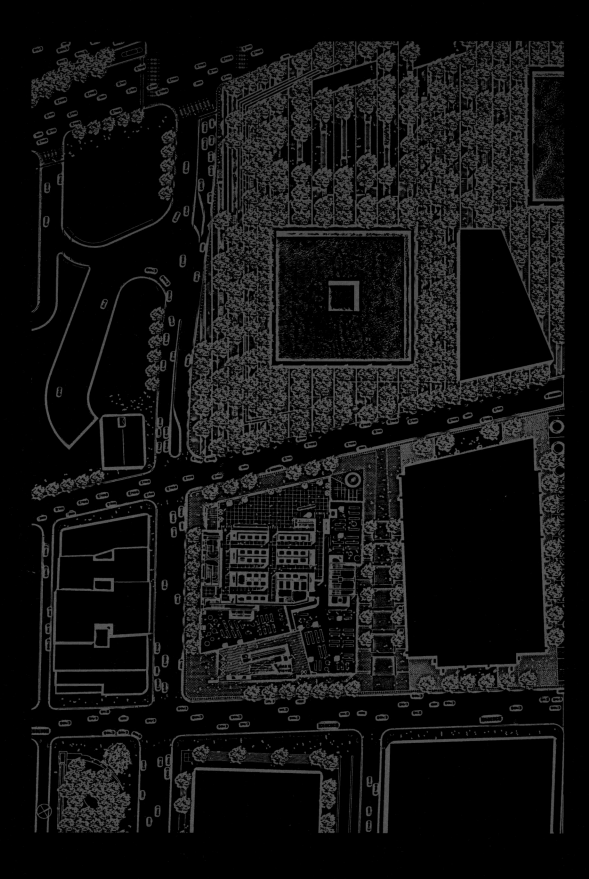

Born in Tokyo in 1928, FUMIHIKO MAKI received his B.Arch degree from the University of Tokyo in 1952, and M.Arch degrees from the Cranbrook Academy of Art (1953) and the Harvard GSD (1954). He worked for Skidmore, Owings & Merrill in New York (1954–55) and Sert Jackson and Associates in Cambridge, Massachusetts (1955–56) before starting his own firm, Maki and Associates, in Tokyo in 1965. Fumihiko Maki was awarded the Pritzker Prize in 1993. Notable buildings include the Fujisawa Municipal Gymnasium (Fujisawa, Kanagawa, 1984); Spiral (Minato, Tokyo, 1985); National Museum of Modern Art (Sakyo, Kyoto, 1986); Tepia (Minato, Tokyo, 1989); Nippon Convention Center Makuhari Messe (Chiba, Chiba, 1989); the Tokyo Metropolitan Gymnasium (Shibuya, Tokyo, 1990); and the Yerba Buena Center for the Arts (San Francisco, California, USA, 1993). Other work includes the Delegation of the Ismaili Imamat (Ottawa, Ontario, Canada, 2008); MIT Media Laboratory Expansion (Cambridge, Massachusetts, USA, 2009); and the Aga Khan Museum (Toronto, Canada, 2014). His most recent work includes the three projects published here—4 World Trade Center (New York, USA, 2014); Tokyo Denki University, Tokyo Senju Campus (Tokyo, 2012 phase 1, 2017 phase 2); and the Japanese Sword Museum (Tokyo, 2017).

FUMIHIKO MAKI wurde 1928 in Tokio geboren, erhielt seinen B.Arch-Abschluss an der Universität Tokio (1952) und seine beiden M.Arch-Abschlüsse an der Cranbrook Academy of Art (1953) und der Harvard GSD (1954). Er arbeitete für Skidmore, Owings & Merrill in New York (1954–1955) und für Sert, Jackson and Associates in Cambridge, Massachusetts (1955–1956), bevor er 1965 in Tokio seine Firma Maki and Associates gründete. Fumihiko Maki wurde 1993 mit dem Pritzker-Preis ausgezeichnet. Wichtige Projekte sind unter anderem die städtische Sporthalle Fujisawa (Fujisawa, Kanagawa, 1984), Spiral (Minato, Tokio, 1985), ein Nationalmuseum für moderne Kunst (Sakyo, Kyoto, 1986), Tepia (Minato, Tokio, 1989), Nippon Convention Center Makuhari Messe (Chiba, Chiba, 1989), die städtische Sporthalle Tokio (Shibuya, Tokio, 1990) und das Yerba Buena Center for the Arts (San Francisco, 1993). Weitere Projekte sind die Gesandtschaft des Imamats der Ismailiten (Ottawa, Ontario, Kanada, 2008), die MIT Media Laboratory Expansion (Cambridge, Massachusetts, 2009) und das Aga Khan Museum (Toronto, 2014). Zu Makis jüngeren Arbeiten gehören die drei in diesem Band vorgestellten Projekte: das 4 World Trade Center (New York, 2014), der Tokyo Senju Campus der Tokyo Denki Universität (Tokio, Phase 1: 2012, Phase 2: 2017) und das japanische Schwertmuseum (Tokio, 2017).

Né à Tokyo en 1928, FUMIHIKO MAKI est titulaire d'un B.Arch de l'université de Tokyo (1952) et de deux M.Arch de la Cranbrook Academy of Art (1953) et de la Harvard GSD (1954). Il a travaillé pour Skidmore, Owings & Merrill à New York (1954–1955) et Sert Jackson and Associates à Cambridge, Massachusetts (1955–1956), avant de fonder son agence, Maki and Associates, à Tokyo en 1965. Fumihiko Maki a été lauréat du Pritzker Prize en 1993. Les bâtiments les plus remarquables qu'il a construits sont notamment le gymnase municipal de Fujisawa (Fujisawa, Kanagawa, 1984) ; Spiral (Minato, Tokyo, 1985) ; le musée national d'Art moderne (Sakyo, Kyoto, 1986) ; Tepia (Minato, Tokyo, 1989) ; le palais des congrès Makuhari Messe (Chiba, Chiba, 1989) ; le centre sportif de Tokyo (Shibuya, Tokyo, 1990) et le Yerba Buena Center for the Arts (San Francisco, 1993). Parmi ses autres réalisations figurent la Délégation de l'imamat Ismaili (Ottawa, Ontario, Canada, 2008) ; l'extension du Media Laboratory du MIT (Cambridge, Massachusetts, 2009) et le musée Aga Khan (Toronto, Canada, 2014). Ses projets les plus récents comprennent les trois publiés ici – la tour 4 du World Trade Center (New York, 2014) ; le campus Senju de l'université Denki de Tokyo (Tokyo, 2012 pour la phase 1 et 2017 pour la phase 2) et le musée de l'Épée japonaise (Tokyo, 2017).

Maki's parallelogram-shaped tower, with its glassed set-backs and angles, shimmers and even seems to be completely evanescent at certain viewpoints, as it stands out from neighboring architecture.

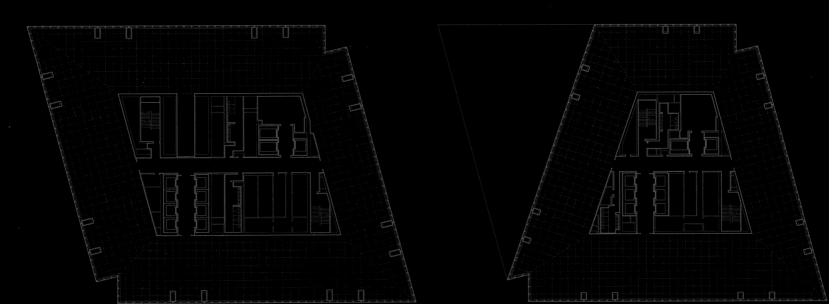

The generous lobby of 4 World Trade Center includes projected images of nature and the sky which recall the architect's idea that the tower should "disappear into the sky."

This elegant tower is part of the massive redevelopment of the former World Trade Center site, which includes the work of David Childs (1 World Trade Center, 2014), Santiago Calatrava (World Trade Center Transportation Hub, 2016), and Richard Rogers (3 World Trade Center, 2018), while a Performing Arts Center is due for completion in 2022 (Joshua Prince Ramus, REX). All of these buildings are grouped around the National World Trade Center Memorial and Museum, which includes gardens and fountains by Michael Arad and Peter Walker (*Reflecting Absence*, 2011), and the Museum by Snøhetta and Davis Brody Bond (2014). Maki's 218-meter-high tower has 65 floors above ground level, including 56 floors of office space, and received a LEED Gold energy label. The structural engineer was Leslie Robertson Associates, who worked on the original World Trade Center buildings. As the architects describe it, 4 WORLD TRADE CENTER is a "minimalistic sculpture that distinguishes itself in the skyline." It is clad in colorless silver glass which, at certain angles, blends almost entirely with the color of the sky. The building footprint is aligned with the South Reflecting Pool of the Memorial, where the original South Tower of the World Trade Center stood.

Dieses elegante Hochhaus ist Teil eines umfangreichen Neuentwicklungsprojekts auf dem Gelände des einstigen World Trade Centers, an dem auch David Childs (1 World Trade Center, 2014), Santiago Calatrava (World Trade Center Transportation Hub, 2016) und Richard Rogers (3 World Trade Center, 2018) beteiligt waren. Das Performing Arts Center von Joshua Prince-Ramus (REX) soll 2022 fertiggestellt werden. Alle genannten Gebäude gruppieren sich um das National World Trade Center Memorial and Museum, zu dem die Park- und Brunnenanlage von Michael Arad sowie Peter Walker (*Reflecting Absence*, 2011) und das Museum von Snøhetta und Davis Brody Bond (2014) gehören. Makis Turm ist 218 m hoch und verfügt über 65 oberirdische Stockwerke, 56 davon beherbergen Büros. Das Gebäude ist LEED-Gold-zertifiziert. Für die Statik zeichnen, wie bereits im Fall des alten World Trade Centers, Leslie Robertson Associates verantwortlich. Die Architekten beschreiben das 4 WORLD TRADE CENTER als „minimalistische Skulptur, die aus der Skyline hervorsticht". Das Hochhaus verfügt über eine farblos spiegelnde Fassade und verschmilzt, aus dem richtigen Blickwinkel betrachtet, vollständig mit der Farbe des Himmels. Die Grundfläche des Gebäudes wurde dem South Reflecting Pool des Memorials angeglichen, an dessen Stelle der Südturm

Cette gracieuse tour est l'un des éléments de l'important plan de réaménagement de l'ancien World Trade Center, qui comprend aussi le travail de David Childs (1 World Trade Center, 2014), Santiago Calatrava (gare World Trade Center Transportation Hub, 2016) et Richard Rogers (3 World Trade Center, 2018), ainsi qu'un centre des arts du spectacle qui doit être achevé en 2022 (Joshua Prince-Ramus, REX). Les bâtiments sont tous groupés autour du mémorial et du Musée national du World Trade Center, dont les jardins et les fontaines sont l'œuvre de Michael Arad et Peter Walker (*Reflecting Absence*, 2011), tandis que le musée a été conçu par Snøhetta et Davis Brody Bond (2014). La tour de Maki, haute de 218 m, a 65 étages au-dessus du sol, dont 56 étages de bureaux, et a reçu une certification énergétique or du LEED. L'ingénieur de la construction est Leslie Robertson Associates, qui a déjà travaillé aux immeubles du World Trade Center original. Les architectes décrivent l'immeuble du 4 WORLD TRADE CENTER comme une « sculpture minimaliste qui se distingue dans la ligne d'horizon ». Il est revêtu de verre miroir incolore qui, vu sous certains angles, se fond presque entièrement dans la couleur du ciel. L'empreinte du bâtiment est alignée sur le bassin sud du mémorial, à l'emplacement de la tour Sud du World Trade Center d'origine.

TOKYO DENKI UNIVERSITY, TOKYO SENJU CAMPUS

FUMIHIKO MAKI

Tokyo, 2012 (phase 1), 2017 (phase 2)
Area: 97 826 m²

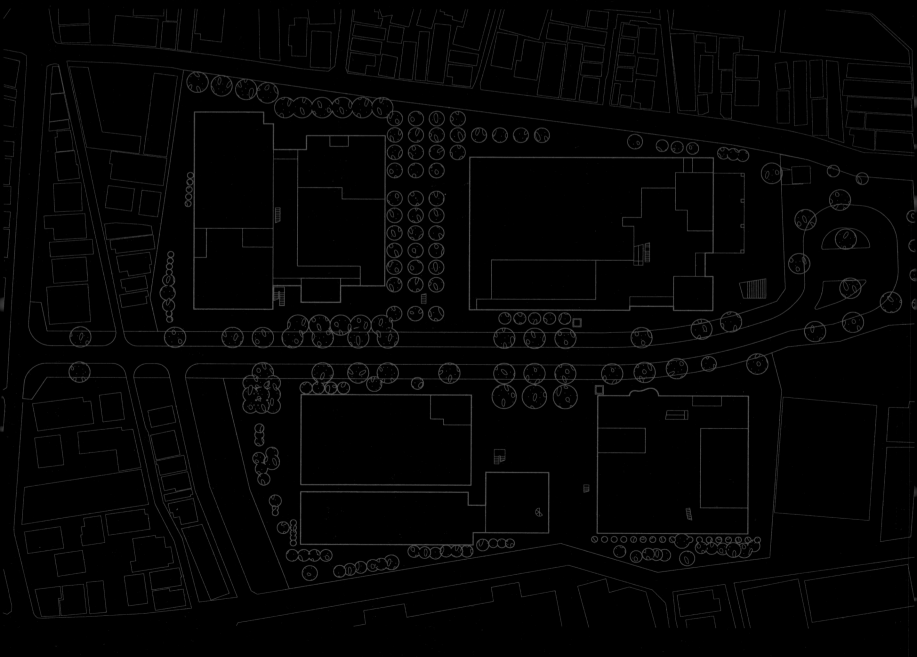

General aerial and ground-level views show the
rigor and geometric precision of Fumihiko Maki's
design and also how it fits into the dense urban
tissue of Tokyo.

Garden spaces provide some respite from the bustle of the city. Despite their large volumes, the buildings have a kind of gentle presence in the city because of their materials and colors.

In conjunction with its 100th anniversary, TOKYO DENKI UNIVERSITY moved from its original location to the Kita-Senju area of the capital on a site formerly occupied by

Anlässlich ihres hundertjährigen Bestehens zog die TOKYO DENKI UNIVERSITÄT von ihrem ursprünglichen Standort in das Viertel um den Kita-Senju-Bahnhof, auf ein Gelände,

En même temps que son 100e anniversaire, l'UNIVERSITÉ DENKI DE TOKYO a quitté sa première adresse pour aller s'installer dans le quartier de Kita-Senju, sur un site occupé aupa-

JAPANESE SWORD MUSEUM

FUMIHIKO MAKI

Tokyo, 2017
Area: 2619 m²

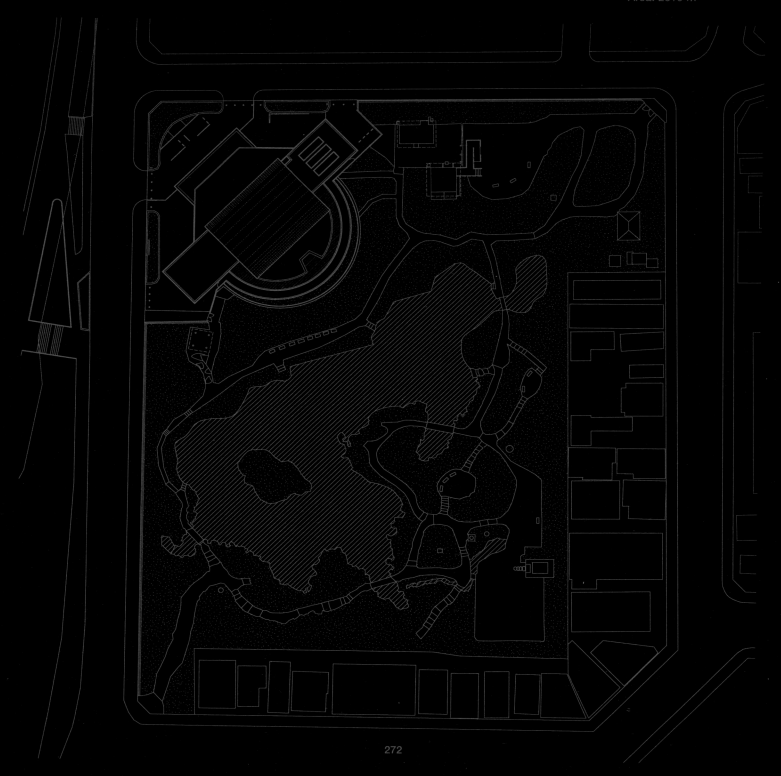

This museum, which exhibits some of the best swords in Japan, existed for 50 years on another site. Designed as weapons, the swords are today considered exceptional works of art. The SWORD MUSEUM's new site is adjacent to the Kyu-Yasuda Garden, which was part of a Daimyo (upper class Samurai) estate in the 18th century. The museum is based on a cylindrical volume that extends with two wings toward a pond. The vaulted roof of the structure houses the main exhibition gallery on the second floor. A terrace just outside the exhibition gallery offers panoramic views of the garden, while the ground floor serves as a public neighborhood amenity, including a café, lecture hall, museum shop, and information corner. These spaces can be used by garden visitors and as a meeting point for the neighborhood.

Dieses Museum, das einige der bedeutendsten Schwerter Japans präsentiert, befand sich 50 Jahre lang an einem anderen Standort. Die Schwerter, die ursprünglich zum Waffengebrauch bestimmt waren, werden in Japan als Kunstgegenstände angesehen. Das neue Domizil des SCHWERTMUSEUMS grenzt an den Kyu-Yasuda-Garten, der im 18. Jahrhundert zum Anwesen eines Daimyo (Samurai der Oberschicht) gehörte. Das Museum, ein zylindrisches Volumen mit zwei Flügeln, liegt an einem Teich. Unter der gewölbten Dachkonstruktion befindet sich im zweiten Geschoss der Hauptausstellungsraum. Eine angrenzende Terrasse mit Blick auf den Garten schließt sich an. Im Erdgeschoss befinden sich ein Café, ein Hörsaal, der Museumsshop und ein Informationsbereich. Diese können von Besuchern des Gartens und Anwohnern genutzt werden.

Ce musée qui expose des épées parmi les meilleures du Japon existe depuis cinquante ans, mais à une autre adresse. Conçues comme des armes, les épées sont aujourd'hui considérées comme des œuvres d'art d'exception. Le nouveau site du MUSÉE DE L'ÉPÉE touche au jardin Kyu-Yasuda qui faisait partie du domaine d'un daimyo (samouraï de classe supérieure) au XVIIIᵉ siècle. Le musée est formé d'un volume cylindrique avec deux ailes qui s'étendent vers un étang. Le toit voûté abrite la principale galerie d'exposition au deuxième étage. Une terrasse tout autour du toit permet de jouir d'une vue panoramique sur le jardin, tandis que le rez-de-chaussée tient lieu d'espace public pour le voisinage avec un café, une salle de lecture, la boutique du musée et un point information. Ces différents équipements sont ouverts aux visiteurs du jardin et servent de lieu de ren-

Fumihiko Maki has always mastered very subtle references to Japanese tradition in the context of his thoroughly modern buildings, as in the distant echo of a samurai helmet in the entry canopy below.

ROADSIDE STATION IN MASHIKO

MOUNT FUJI ARCHITECTS STUDIO

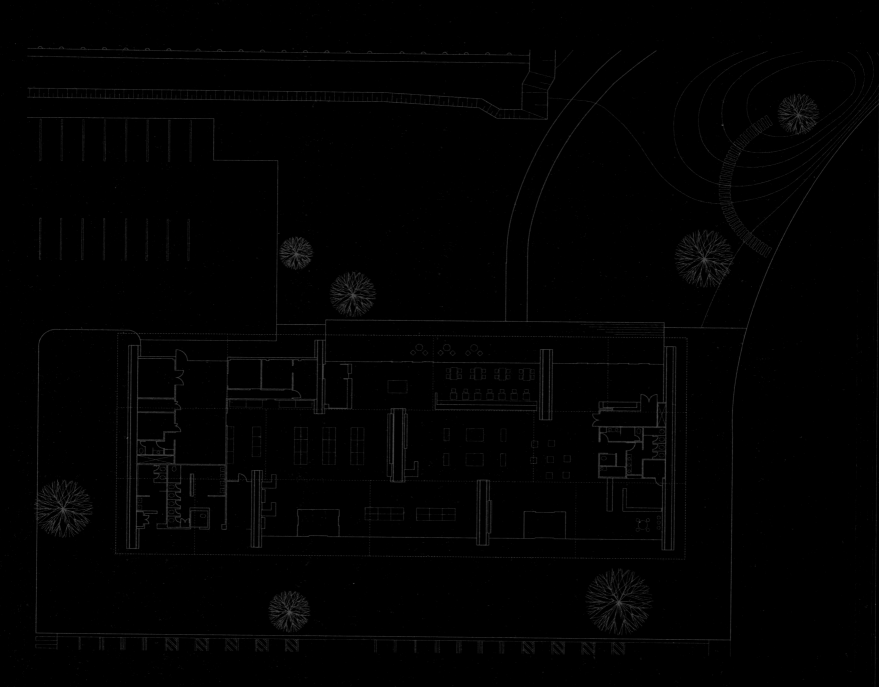

Mashiko, Tochigi, 2016
Area: 1329 m²

MASAHIRO HARADA was born in Yaizu (Shizuoka, 1973) and graduated with an M. Arch from the Shibaura Institute of Technology (Tokyo, 1997). He worked in the offices of Kengo Kuma (Tokyo, 1997–2000), José Antonio Martínez Lapeña and Elías Torres (Barcelona, 2001–02), and Arata Isozaki (Tokyo, 2003) before creating MOUNT FUJI ARCHITECTS STUDIO in Tokyo in 2004. MAO HARADA was born in Sagamihara, Kanagawa, in 1976 and graduated from the Shibaura Institute of Technology with a B.Arch degree in 1999, before cofounding MOUNT FUJI with Harada. Their recent work includes Kasa (Shizuoka, 2016); House Toward Tateyama (Toyama, 2016); Chiryu Afterschool (Aichi, 2016); Roadside Station in Mashiko (Tochigi, 2016, published here); Shoeizan Sengyoji (Tokyo, 2018); A&A LIAM FUJI (Okayama, 2019); and ROOFLAG (Tokyo, 2020).

MASAHIRO HARADA wurde 1973 in Yaizu, Shizuoka, geboren und schloss sein Studium am Shibaura Institut für Technologie mit einem M.Arch ab (Tokio, 1997). Er arbeitete in den Büros von Kengo Kuma (Tokio, 1997–2000), José Antonio Martínez Lapeña und Elías Torres (Barcelona, 2001–2002) und Arata Isozaki (Tokio, 2003), bevor er 2004 in Tokio das MOUNT FUJI ARCHITECTS STUDIO gründete. MAO HARADA wurde 1976 in Sagamihara, Kanagawa, geboren und schloss sein Studium am Shibaura Institut für Technologie mit einem B.Arch ab (1999), bevor er gemeinsam mit Harada MOUNT FUJI gründete. Zu ihren jüngsten Arbeiten gehören Kasa (Shizuoka, 2016), House Toward Tateyama (Toyama, 2016), der Chiryu Afterschool (Aichi, 2016), die Mashiko Roadside Station in Mashiko (Tochigi, 2016, hier vorgestellt), Shoeizan Sengyoji (Tokio, 2018), A&A LIAM FUJI (Okayama, 2019) und ROOFLAG (Tokio, 2020).

MASAHIRO HARADA est né à Yaizu (Shizuoka, 1973) et possède un M.Arch de l'Institut de technologie Shibaura (Tokyo, 1997). Il a travaillé dans l'agence de Kengo Kuma (Tokyo, 1997–2000), José Antonio Martínez Lapeña et Elías Torres (Barcelone, 2001–02), et l'agence d'Arata Isozaki (Tokyo, 2003) avant de créer MOUNT FUJI ARCHITECTS STUDIO à Tokyo en 2004. MAO HARADA est né à Sagamihara, Kanagawa, en 1976 et a obtenu un B.Arch de l'Institut de technologie Shibaura (1999) avant de fonder MOUNT FUJI avec Harada. Leurs réalisations récentes comprennent Kasa (Shizuoka, 2016) ; la Maison vers Tateyama (Toyama, 2016) ; la garderie Chiryu (Aichi, 2016) ; l'aire de repos Mashiko Roadside Station à Mashiko (Tochigi, 2016, publiée ici) ; ShoeizanSengyoji (Tokyo, 2018) ; A&A LIAM FUJI (Okayama, 2019) ; et ROOFLAG (Tokyo, 2020).

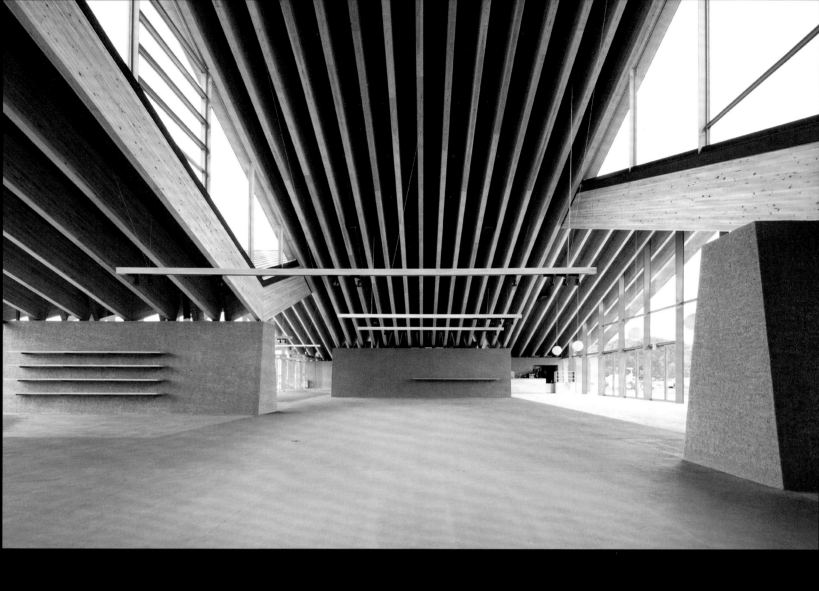

The ribbed wooden forms of the interior made with locally sourced cedar emphasize the connection between the building and its location.

Mashiko is located in central Honshu, north of Tokyo and south of Fukushima. The local economy is dependent on tourism and the ceramic craft industry. This ROADSIDE STATION was intended to promote tourism and local crafts. The interior design has a timber structure that evokes "a stroll to the folds of the mountains nearby." The roof, also inspired by nearby mountains, was made with locally processed laminated Yamizo cedar. Natural light is brought in through clerestory windows. Large openings on the gable connect the interior space with the fields and mountains that stretch in front of them, creating "a direct relation between the food being tasted and the scenery." The architect Masahiro Harada says: "Architecture made from scenery while creating scenery was exactly what we pursued." The trapezoidal walls intended to be "connected with the earth" were plastered with on-site soil. The structure of the building is in reinforced concrete with a partially wooden frame. Extruded cement board, and steel doors and windows were used, as was a locally inspired earthen floor (doma).

Mashiko liegt in Zentral-Honshu, nördlich von Tokio und südlich von Fukushima. Die Region hängt wirtschaftlich vom Tourismus und dem Keramikhandwerk ab. Die RASTSTÄTTE soll beides fördern. Die Deckenkonstruktion im Inneren lässt an „einen Spaziergang in die nahegelegenen Berge" denken. Das Dach, ebenfalls inspiriert von den nahegelegenen Bergen, besteht aus laminierter Yamizo-Zeder aus der Region. Obergadenfenster lassen Tageslicht ins Innere. Großflächige giebelseitige Fensteröffnungen verbinden den Innenraum mit den Feldern und Bergen, die sich um die Raststätte erstrecken, und „stellen einen direkten Zusammenhang zwischen dem hier angebotenen Essen und der Landschaft her". Der Architekt Masahiro Harada: „Ein Bauwerk zu erschaffen, das die Landschaft miteinbezieht und selbst zur Landschaft wird – das war es, was wir wollten". Die trapezförmigen Wände, die „mit der Erde verbunden" sein sollten, wurden mit am Standort gefördertem Lehm verputzt. Es handelt sich um eine Stahlbetonstruktur mit teils hölzernem Rahmenwerk. Verbaut wurden extrudierte Zementplatten sowie Stahltüren und -fenster. Die Inspiration für den Lehmboden fand man in der regional verbreiteten Technik (doma).

Mashiko est située dans le centre de Honshu, au nord de Tokyo et au sud de Fukushima. L'économie locale dépend du tourisme et de l'industrie de la céramique. Cette AIRE DE REPOS a également été conçue dans le but de promouvoir le tourisme et l'artisanat local. L'architecture intérieure présente une structure en bois d'œuvre qui fait écho à « une promenade dans les plis des montagnes toutes proches ».Le toit, également inspiré par ces montagnes, est en cèdre de Yamizo stratifié traité sur place. Des fenêtres à claire-voie font entrer la lumière naturelle. Les vastes ouvertures des pignons relient l'intérieur aux champs et aux montagnes qui se déploient devant, créant « un lien direct entre les mets qui sont dégustés et le paysage ». L'architecte Masahiro Harada explique : « Une architecture faite à partir du paysage même qui crée un paysage, tel était notre but précis. » Les murs trapézoïdaux conçus pour être « en connexion avec la terre » ont été recouverts de terre du sol local. La structure est en béton armé avec une charpente partiellement en bois. Elle est complétée par des panneaux de ciment extrudé, des portes et fenêtres en acier et un sol de terre d'inspiration locale (doma).

The architects have found a way to create a visibly modern building that ties into its setting and function through its materials, colors, and views.

HOUSE IN SANGENJAYA

JO NAGASAKA / SCHEMATA ARCHITECTS

Setagaya, Tokyo, 2017
Area: 217 m²

The act of preserving an original building has been taken to extremes in this project, where modern services and glazing are installed while leaving most surfaces visible in a stripped-down version of their original substance.

JO NAGASAKA graduated from Tokyo University of the Arts in 1998 and immediately established Schemata Architects. He also created the shared creative office HAPPA in 2007. Jo Nagasaka has extensive experience in areas ranging from furniture design to architecture. His main works include his epoxy-resin Flat Tables (in collaboration with Shuhei Nakamura); the Sayama Flat apartment building (Tokyo, 2008); House in Okusawa (2009); Aesop Aoyama (Tokyo, 2011); Hanare House (Isumi, Chiba, 2011); Vitra Exhibition Stand at Fiera Milano (Milan, Italy, 2015); Blue Bottle Coffee (Kyoto, 2015); and the two projects published here, House in Sangenjaya (Setagaya, Tokyo, 2017); and °C (Do-C) Ebisu (Ebisu, Shibuya, Tokyo, 2017).

JO NAGASAKA schloss 1998 sein Studium an der Universität der Künste in Tokio ab und gründete unmittelbar darauf Schemata Architects. 2007 rief er das Kreativbüro HAPPA ins Leben. Jo Nagasaka verfügt über sehr viel Erfahrung in so unterschiedlichen Bereichen wie Möbeldesign und Architektur. Zu seinen wichtigsten Arbeiten gehören seine Flat Tables aus Epoxidharz (in Zusammenarbeit mit Shuhei Nakamura), das Apartmenthaus Sayama Flat (Tokio, 2008), House in Okusawa (2009), Aesop Aoyama (Tokio, 2011), Hanare House (Isumi, Chiba, 2011), der Messestand für Vitra auf der Fiera Milano (Mailand, 2015), Blue Bottle Coffee (Kyoto, 2015) sowie die beiden hier vorgestellten Projekte, House in Sangenjaya (Setagaya, Tokio, 2017) und °C (Do-C) Ebisu (Ebisu, Shibuya, Tokio, 2017).

JO NAGASAKA a obtenu son diplôme de l'université des arts de Tokyo en 1998 et a fondé Schemata Architects immédiatement après. Il a également créé le bureau créatif partagé HAPPA en 2007. Il possède une très grande expérience dans des domaines qui vont de la conception de meubles à l'architecture. Ses principales réalisations comprennent les tables plates en résine époxyde (en collaboration avec Shuhei Nakamura) ; l'immeuble d'appartements Sayama Flat (Tokyo, 2008) ; une maison à Okusawa (2009) ; le magasin Aesop d'Aoyama (Tokyo, 2011) ; la maison Hanare (Isumi, Chiba, 2011) ; un stand pour l'exposition Vitra à la Foire de Milan (2015) ; le café Blue Bottle (Kyoto, 2015) et les deux projets publiés ici, une maison à Sangenjaya (Setagaya, Tokyo, 2017) et l'hôtel °C (Do-C) d'Ebisu (Ebisu, Shibuya, Tokyo, 2017).

Newly-installed glazed doors open onto a terrace,
allowing interior and exterior to communicate freely.
Surprisingly, the modern details lend the whole
a very contemporary feeling.

The clients for this project were the owners of a 50-year-old house located a short walk from the Sangenjaya station. As they wished to keep the residence, the architect started by preserving the structure and then planning new uses for the spaces. A small gallery to be operated by the client in the southwest corner of the ground floor was created, and the rest of the space at this level was rented to a tenant. The client's residence is on the second floor. Jo Nagasaka states: "The distinct charm of the 50-year-old structure was kept as much as possible; the exposed exterior façades were kept as they were, while all infrastructure was encased in the service core finished with painted plasterboard." Rough surfaces and exposed structure give this project a very particular feeling, where older walls are occupied with new activities and a lifestyle that has moved on since 1965, when the original structure was built.

Dieses Projekt wurde von den Eigentümern eines 50 Jahre alten Hauses, das wenige Gehminuten vom Bahnhof Sangenjaya entfernt liegt, in Auftrag gegeben. Die Eigentümer wollten ihr Wohnhaus nicht aufgeben, also bewahrte der Architekt die Bausubstanz und entwickelte ein neues Innenraumkonzept. Im Erdgeschoss auf der Südwestseite des Hauses wurde eine kleine Galerie eingerichtet, die von den Eigentümern betrieben wird. Der übrige Teil des Erdgeschosses wird als Wohnung vermietet. Die Eigentümer selbst wohnen im zweiten Geschoss. Jo Nagasaka: „Der besondere Charme des 50 Jahre alten Gebäudes wurde so weit wie möglich erhalten. Die Außenfassaden blieben unverändert. Die gesamte Infrastruktur wurde in einem mit lackiertem Gipskarton verblendeten Erschließungskern untergebracht." Unbearbeitete Oberflächen und freiliegende Konstruktionselemente verleihen dem Projekt ein besonderes Gepräge. Alte Wohnräume übernehmen neue Funktionen und sind jetzt einer Lebensweise angemessen, die sich verändert hat, seit das Gebäude 1965 errichtet wurde.

Les clients de ce projet sont les propriétaires d'une maison construite il y a cinquante ans près de la gare de Sangenjaya. Ils souhaitaient continuer à y habiter, de sorte que l'architecte a commencé par préserver la structure, avant de prévoir de nouvelles utilisations des différents espaces. Il a aménagé une petite galerie exploitée par le client dans l'angle sud-ouest du rez-de-chaussée, tandis que le reste de cet étage a été loué. Le logement du propriétaire est situé au premier étage. Jo Nagasaka explique : « Le charme propre à cette structure vieille de cinquante ans a été le plus possible conservé ; les façades ont été laissées telles quelles, tandis que toute l'infrastructure a été encastrée dans le noyau technique aux finitions de placoplâtre peint. » Les surfaces brutes et les éléments structurels apparents donnent un caractère très particulier à l'ensemble, où les murs anciens sont désormais affectés à d'autres activités car le mode de vie a évolué depuis 1965 lorsque la maison d'origine a été construite.

Aside from the updated glazing and some newly added surfaces, the architects have added numerous elements in plywood, emphasizing the industrial feeling of the whole.

Plywood partitions and very minimal furnishings
in the Japanese style give the interior of the house
something of a worksite feeling, but it is very much
a finished environment.

°C (DO-C) EBISU

JO NAGASAKA / SCHEMATA ARCHITECTS

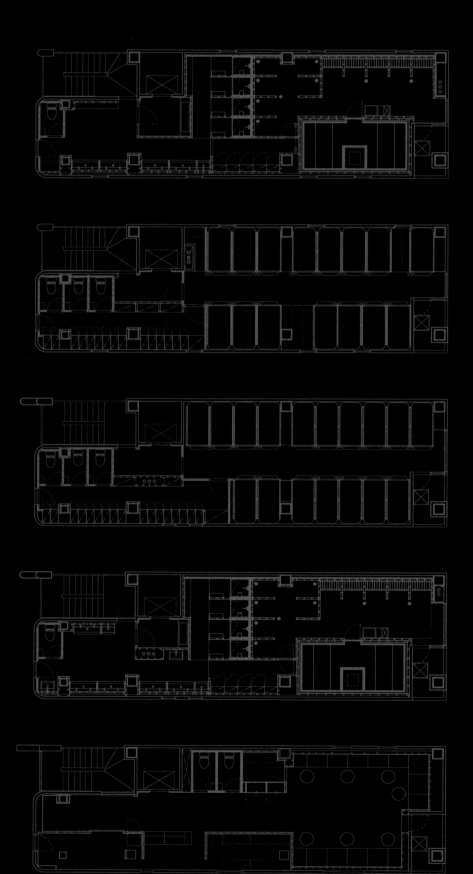

Ebisu, Shibuya, Tokyo, 2017
Area: 726 m²
Collaboration: Hiromura Design Office,
Design Studio S

Plywood and concrete form the walls, ceilings, and floors of the interiors, completely updating the "capsule hotel" décor that existed previously.

9H (Nine Hours) is a Tokyo capsule hotel chain. The client asked Jo Nagasaka to renovate an existing capsule hotel in the city center. "Our design aims to eradicate the image of the old capsule hotel by changing the interior and surroundings, while keeping the existing capsules as they were," states the architect. Saunas, often associated with capsule hotels in Japan, were added to the facility, as indicated in the °C branding. Special cooling showers manufactured by Toto use special temperature controls inspired by Finnish methods to create "authentic" saunas. The shower and sauna areas are connected by a waterproofed space that is coated from floor to ceiling in FRP (fiber-reinforced plastic). The existing surface finishes on stairs in front of the building were removed to expose structural elements that were repainted in anti-corrosion paint. The shade of this paint was designated the "signature color" of the hotel. The eight-story steel structure occupies a 125-square-meter site and has a footprint of just 105 square meters.

9H (Nine Hours) ist der Name einer Tokioter Kapselhotel-Kette. Der Kunde beauftragte Jo Nagasaka mit der Renovierung eines bereits existierenden Kapselhotels im Stadtzentrum. „Unser Entwurf zielt darauf ab, das Image früherer Kapselhotels abzustreifen, indem wir eine neue Inneneinrichtung entwerfen und die Kapseln als solche unverändert lassen", so der Architekt. Die Anlage wurde um Saunen erweitert, die in Japan üblicherweise mit Kapselhotels in Verbindung gebracht werden – das °C-Branding weist darauf hin. Die Duschen des Herstellers Toto sind mit speziellen Temperaturreglern ausgestattet und von finnischen Saunen inspiriert, sie sollen ein „authentisches" Sauna-Erlebnis ermöglichen. Dusch- und Saunabereiche sind durch einen wasserdichten Raum miteinander verbunden, der vom Boden bis zur Decke mit FVK (Faserverbundkunststoff) beschichtet ist. Der Außentreppenaufgang wurde von seiner Verblendung befreit, die auf diese Weise freigelegten Bauelemente wurden mit einem korrosionsbeständigen Anstrich versehen. Der neue Farbton wurde zur „Markenfarbe" des Hotels. Der achtgeschossi-

9H (Nine Hours) est une chaîne d'hôtels capsules de Tokyo. Le client a demandé à Jo Nagasaka de rénover un hôtel « capsule » existant dans le centre-ville. « Notre concept vise à éradiquer l'image de l'ancien hôtel capsule en modifiant l'intérieur et l'environnement des capsules, tout en les conservant », explique l'architecte. Des saunas, souvent proposés par les hôtels capsules au Japon, ont été ajoutés comme le veut la marque °C. Des douches rafraîchissantes spécialement construites par Toto y font appel à des systèmes de contrôle de la température inspirés des méthodes finlandaises pour des saunas « authentiques ». Les douches et les saunas communiquent par un espace entièrement étanchéifié recouvert du sol au plafond de FRP (plastique renforcé de fibre de verre). Les finitions de surface des escaliers à l'avant du bâtiment ont été retirées pour rendre apparents des éléments structuraux qui ont été repeints avec une peinture anticorrosion. La teinte de cette peinture a été désignée pour « signature » de l'hôtel. Le bâtiment en acier de huit étages occupe une parcelle de 125 m² et une empreinte au sol

Simple tables and benches, along with the overall
cladding, give the impression of an inexpensive
but clean space.

S
Sauna
サウナ

S → S → C
Shower → Sauna → Cool Down
シャワー　サウナ　クールダウン

x 3 Set
3セットくらいがオススメ

R
Rest
休憩

(!)

Caution 注意

タオルドライ
サウナに入る前に、身体の水分を拭いてください。

サウナマット
サウナではサウナマットをご使用ください。
使用済みのマットは、回収ボックスに入れてください。

水分補給
こまめに水分補給をしてください。

アルコール
飲酒をしているお客様は、事故防止のため
サウナのご利用をお断りします。

メガネ・貴金属
メガネやアクセサリーなどの貴金属は外してください。

心疾患・高血圧
心疾患や高血圧などの療養中の方は、
医師にご相談の上ご利用ください。

Dry Yourself
Please dry yourself with a towel
before entering the sauna.

Sauna Mat
Please use a sauna mat.
Place used mats in the collection box provided.

Hydration
Please drink frequently to stay hydrated.

Alcohol
For everyone's safety, the sauna is not open
to guests who have been drinking alcohol.

Glasses / Metal Accessories
Please remove anything metal,
such as glasses or accessories.

Heart Disease / High Blood Pressure
If you are undergoing treatment for
heart disease or high blood pressure,
please consult with a doctor before using a sauna.

*The wooden sauna areas recall more traditional
settings, while added elements like the signage
are more willfully modern.*

Wooden shower stalls are marked with their temperatures (left). Below: bathroom space also surrounded by plywood, and below, the actual refurbished capsule hotel "rooms."

RIBBON CHAPEL

HIROSHI NAKAMURA & NAP

Onomichi, Hiroshima, 2014
Area: 80 m²

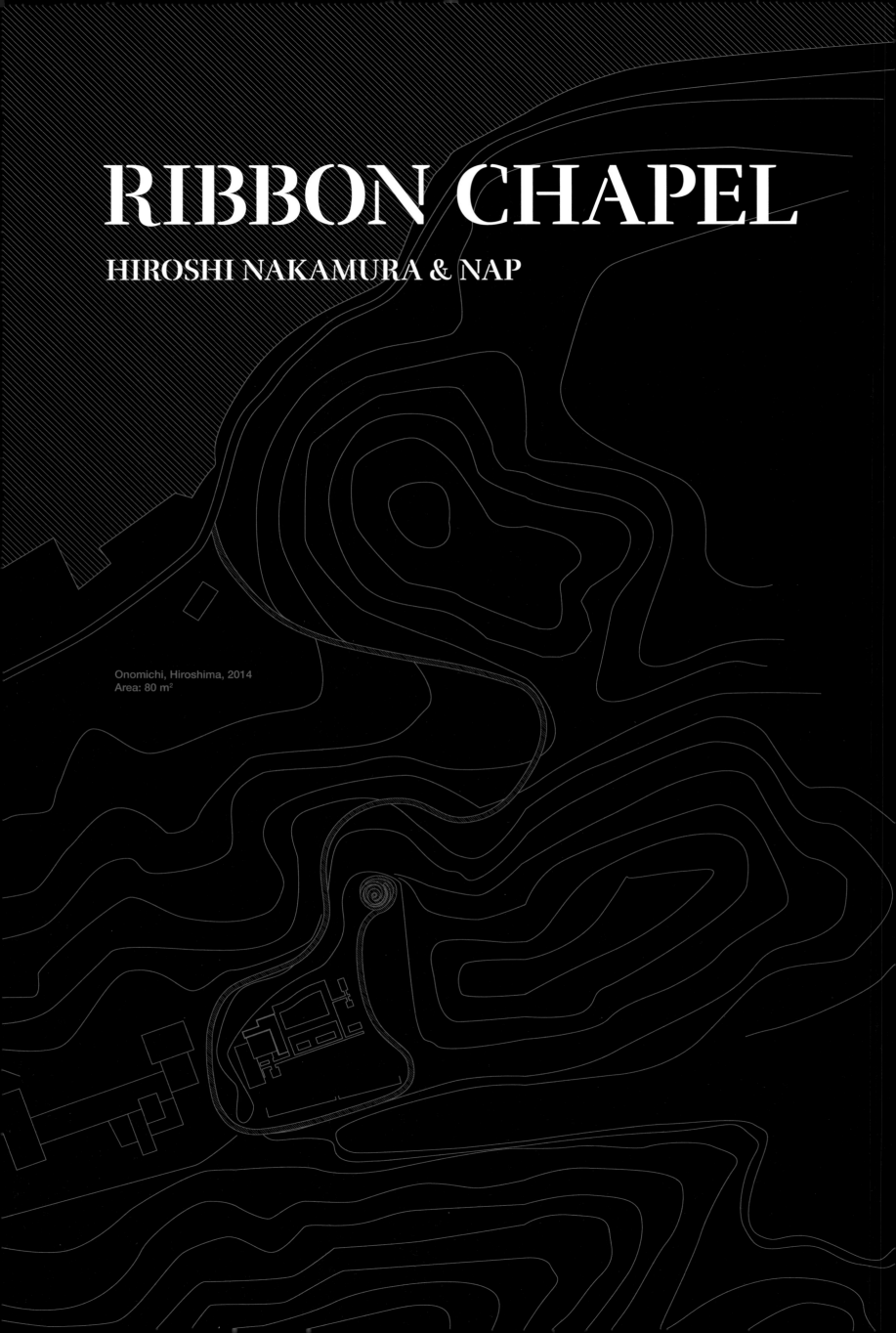

Rising from its wooded setting, the Chapel offers views of the Seto Inland Sea.

Opposite: drawings of the structure as seen in section and plan.

HIROSHI NAKAMURA was born in Tokyo in 1974. He obtained his master's degree from the Graduate School of Science and Technology of Meiji University (Tokyo, 1999). Between his graduation and 2002, Nakamura worked in the office of Kengo Kuma (Tokyo), before establishing his own office in 2003. The firm has 40 employees who work on architectural design and supervision, but also on regional urban planning and site planning, as well as industrial design. Their work includes the Sayama Lakeside Cemetery Community Hall (Sayama, Saitama, 2013); the two buildings published here, Ribbon Chapel (Onomichi, Hiroshima, 2014); and Kamikatz Public House (Kamikatsu, Tokushima, 2015); Bella Vista Spa and Marina Erretegia (Onomichi, Hiroshima, 2015); and the House of Glittering Leaves (Tokyo, 2016). Current work includes St. Mary's Cathedral (Manila, Philippines, 2020) and the Craft & Resort (Miao-Li, Taiwan, 2023).

HIROSHI NAKAMURA wurde 1974 in Tokio geboren und erwarb seinen Masterabschluss an der Graduiertenschule für Naturwissenschaften und Technologie der Meiji-Universität (Tokio, 1999). Anschließend arbeitete er bis 2002 im Büro von Kengo Kuma (Tokio), bevor er 2003 eine eigene Firma gründete. Das Unternehmen für Architekturplanung und Bauaufsicht beschäftigt 40 Mitarbeiter, die auch Stadt- und Standortplanungs- sowie Industriedesignprojekte realisieren. Zu ihren Arbeiten gehören eine Friedhofshalle am Sayama-See (Sayama, Saitama, 2013), die beiden hier veröffentlichten Arbeiten Ribbon Chapel (Onomichi, Hiroshima, 2014) und Kamikatz Public House (Kamikatsu, Tokushima, 2015), das Bella Vista-Spa und der Erretegia-Jachthaften (Onomichi, Hiroshima, 2015) sowie das House of Glittering Leaves (Tokio, 2016). Aktuelle Projekte umfassen die St. Mary's-Kathedrale (Manila, Philippinen, 2020) sowie Craft & Resort

HIROSHI NAKAMURA est né à Tokyo en 1974. Il est titulaire d'un master de l'École supérieure de sciences et de technologie de l'université Meiji (Tokyo, 1999). Entre l'obtention de son diplôme et 2002, il a travaillé dans l'agence de Kengo Kuma (Tokyo) avant d'ouvrir la sienne en 2003. Elle compte aujourd'hui 40 employés qui travaillent à des projets de design architectural et de supervision, et aussi d'urbanisme régional et d'aménagement du terrain ou de design industriel. Leurs réalisations comprennent la salle commune du cimetière du lac Sayama (Sayama, Saitama, 2013) ; les deux bâtiments publiés ici, la chapelle Ruban (Onomichi, Hiroshima, 2014) et le bar Kamikatz Public House (Kamikatsu, Tokushima, 2015) ; le spa et la marina Bella Vista (Onomichi, Hiroshima, 2015) et Marina Erretegia (Onomichi, Hiroshima, 2015) ; la House of Glittering Leaves (Tokyo, 2016). Parmi leurs projets en cours figurent la cathédrale Sainte-Marie (Manille, Philippines, 2020) et le Craft & Resort

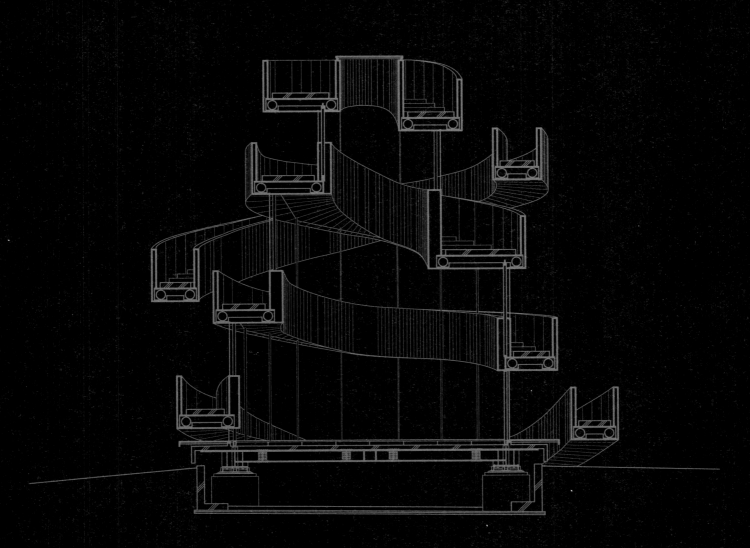

Inside the Chapel, glazing seems to surround the seating area but also the area behind the summary altar, opening both to the green garden area and to the sky.

Onomichi is a town of about 140 000 people located on the Seto Inland Sea in the prefecture of Hiroshima, known for its scenery and its numerous temples. This wedding CHAPEL designed by Hiroshi Nakamura is on a hill in the garden of the Bella Vista Sakaigahama Hotel that offers broad views of the inland sea. The architect intertwined two spiral stairways in a form intended to symbolize of marriage. Individually, the spirals would have been unstable, but joined together at four points, they rise to a height of 15.3 meters, enclosing the chapel itself, which seats 80 people. The spiral forms replace the walls and roof that one might expect. A titanium zinc alloy is used for the walls and ceilings, with white-painted wood paneling for exterior cladding. In this chapel, prior to marriage, the bride and groom walk up separate stairways and meet at the top of the structure and then come down together to join the guests. "The chapel," says Hiroshi Nakamura,"is composed only of paths, along which sceneries of ocean, mountains, sky, and distant islands successively appear and disappear."

Onomichi ist eine Stadt mit rund 140 000 Einwohnern an der Seto-Inlandsee in der Präfektur Hiroshima. Sie ist für ihren landschaftlichen Reiz und ihre zahlreichen Tempel bekannt. Diese von Hiroshi Nakamura entworfene HOCHZEITSKAPELLE liegt auf einem Hügel im Garten des Bella Vista Sakaigahama Hotels. Sie besteht aus zwei ineinander verschlungenen Wendeltreppen, die ein Symbol für den Bund der Ehe darstellen. Für sich genommen wären die Spiralen instabil gewesen, deswegen wurden sie an vier Punkten miteinander verbunden und winden sich nun bis auf eine Höhe von 15,3 m. Sie umschließen den Innenraum der Kapelle, in dem 80 Gäste Platz finden. Die Spiralformen ersetzen zudem gesonderte Wand- und Dachkonstruktionen. Innenwände und Deckenbereiche sind mit einer Titan-Zink-Legierung versehen. Von außen ist die Kapelle mit weiß lackiertem Holz verschalt. Braut und Bräutigam gehen vor der Eheschließung die separaten Treppen hinauf, treffen am höchsten Punkt der Kapelle aufeinander und steigen anschließend zu den Hochzeitsgästen hinab. „Alle Wege der Kapelle", so Hiroshi Nakamura, „führen am Meer, den Bergen, dem Himmel und den entfernten Inseln vorüber, die nacheinander erscheinen und verschwinden."

Onomichi est une ville d'environ 140 000 habitants au bord de la mer intérieure de Seto, dans la préfecture d'Hiroshima, connue pour ses paysages et ses nombreux temples. La CHAPELLE de mariage créée par Hiroshi Nakamura s'élève au sommet d'une colline dans le jardin de l'hôtel Bella Vista Sakaigahama, d'où se déploie largement la vue sur la mer. L'architecte a entrelacé deux escaliers en colimaçon en leur donnant une forme symbolisant le mariage. Aucun ne serait suffisamment stable seul, mais assemblés en quatre points, ils se dressent à une hauteur de 15,3 m et entourent la chapelle proprement dite qui peut accueillir 80 personnes. Les spirales remplacent les murs et le toit qu'on s'attendrait à trouver. Les murs et plafonds sont faits d'un alliage de titane et de zinc et revêtus à l'extérieur de panneaux de bois peints en blanc. Dans cette chapelle, avant le mariage, le marié et la mariée montent deux escaliers distincts et se retrouvent au sommet de la structure avant de redescendre ensemble pour rejoindre leurs invités. « La chapelle, explique Hiroshi Nakamura, est uniquement composée de chemins le long desquels des vues de l'océan, des montagnes, du ciel et des îles au loin apparaissent et disparaissent successivement. »

KAMIKATZ PUBLIC HOUSE

HIROSHI NAKAMURA & NAP

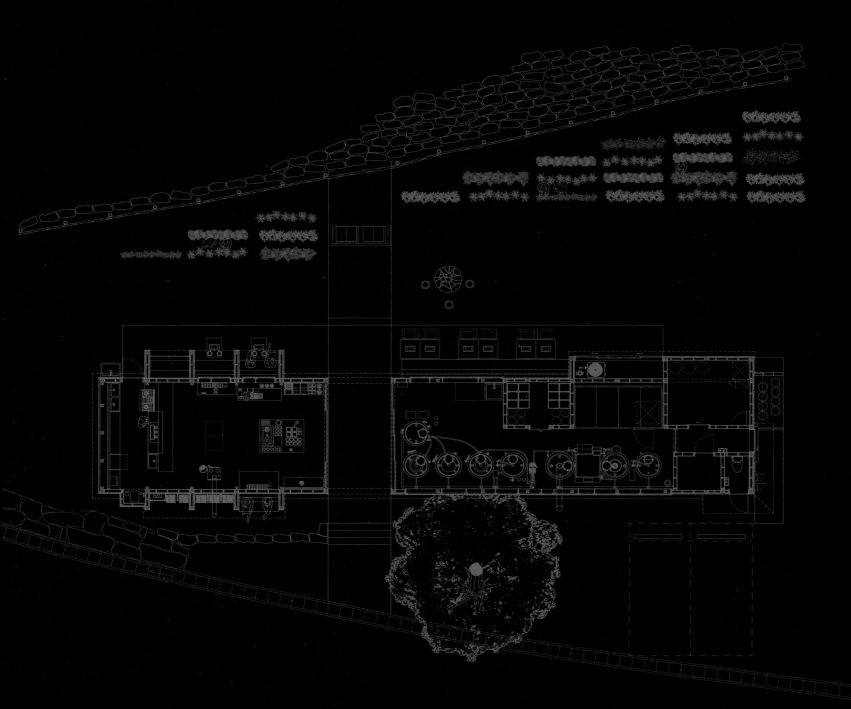

Kamikatsu, Tokushima, 2015
Area: 141 m²

Despite its unusual high-windowed façade, the building fits well into its rural mountain setting on the island of Shikoku. The timber structure and red coloring participate in this contextual insertion.

The KAMIKATZ PUBLIC HOUSE is a timber structure that functions as a micro-brewery. It is located in Kamikatsu, a town of about 1500 people on the island of Shikoku, which is known for its attempt to produce "zero waste," requiring residents to separate their garbage into 45 different categories and recycling them. Expanding on the word "pub," the architects created a shop based on the principles of the town and selling household goods, food, and beer. There is a raw materials warehouse space for the brewery and a pub that serves the beer. In order to make the structure recognizable from the town, an eight-meter-high wall was designed, using windows from local, abandoned houses. The high interior ceiling is conceived to encourage natural ventilation, along with a ceiling fan that circulates heat from a carbon-neutral heater in winter. Product displays were made with converted and restructured furniture, such as bridal chests and farm fixtures. The architects explain: "We utilized abandoned items from a tile factory for the floor, empty bottles to create a chandelier, antlers produced in the town for the draft tower, and newspapers as wallpaper. The space is full of improvisation and discoveries with this creative combination of waste material."

Das KAMIKATZ PUBLIC HOUSE ist ein Projekt in Holzbauweise, in dem eine Mikrobrauerei betrieben wird. Es befindet sich in Kamikatsu, einer Stadt mit etwa 1500 Einwohnern auf der Insel Shikoku, die für ihren Zero-Waste-Ansatz bekannt ist. Wer hier lebt, ist verpflichtet, seine Abfälle zu Recyclingzwecken kleinteilig zu trennen; es wird zwischen 45 Müllsorten unterschieden. Die Architekten haben ein Geschäft entworfen, das die Nachhaltigkeitsprinzipien der Stadt berücksichtigt. Vertrieben werden Haushaltswaren, Lebensmittel sowie Bier. Darüber hinaus gibt es ein Lager für Braurohstoffe und ein Gasthaus, in dem eigenes Bier serviert wird. Damit das Gebäude von der Stadt aus zu sehen ist, verfügt es über eine 8 m hohe Fassade, in die Fenster aus leerstehenden Häusern der Region eingebaut wurden. Der hohe Innenraum ermöglicht eine natürliche Luftzirkulation und ist mit einem Deckenventilator ausgestattet. Dieser soll gewährleisten, dass sich im Winter die klimaneutrale Heizungswärme gut verteilt. Die Produkte werden in umgebauten Möbelstücken angeboten. Die Architekten: „Wir haben Ausschussware aus einer Fliesenfabrik als Bodenbelag verwendet, aus leeren Flaschen einen Kronleuchter gebaut, die Zapfanlage mit Geweihen aus Kamikatsu dekoriert und die Wände mit Zeitungspapier tapeziert. Überall gibt es etwas zu entdecken, womit wir kreativ improvisiert haben."

La KAMIKATZ PUBLIC HOUSE abrite une micro-brasserie dans une structure en bois d'œuvre. Kamikatsu, la ville d'environ 1 500 habitants où elle se trouve, sur l'île de Shikoku, est connue pour sa politique « zéro déchet » qui consiste à trier les ordures en 45 catégories et à les recycler. Les architectes ont donné un sens élargi au mot « pub » et créé, en respectant les principes de la ville, un magasin qui vend des biens d'équipement ménager, de la nourriture et de la bière. Il comprend un entrepôt pour les matières premières destinées à la brasserie, et un pub qui sert la bière. Pour que le bâtiment se voie depuis la ville, un mur de 8 m de haut a été construit avec des fenêtres de maisons abandonnées du voisinage. À l'intérieur, la grande hauteur sous plafond doit favoriser la ventilation naturelle, de même qu'un ventilateur qui fait circuler la chaleur produite par un radiateur au bilan carbone neutre en hiver. Les étalages sont faits de meubles reconvertis et transformés, notamment des coffres de mariées et des équipements agricoles. Les architectes expliquent : « Nous avons utilisé des carreaux au rebut d'une usine de céramique pour le sol, des bouteilles vides pour le lustre, des bois produits en ville pour le refroidisseur des fûts de bière et des vieux journaux pour tapisser les murs. Cet assemblage créatif de matériaux au rebut crée un espace plein d'improvisation et de découvertes. »

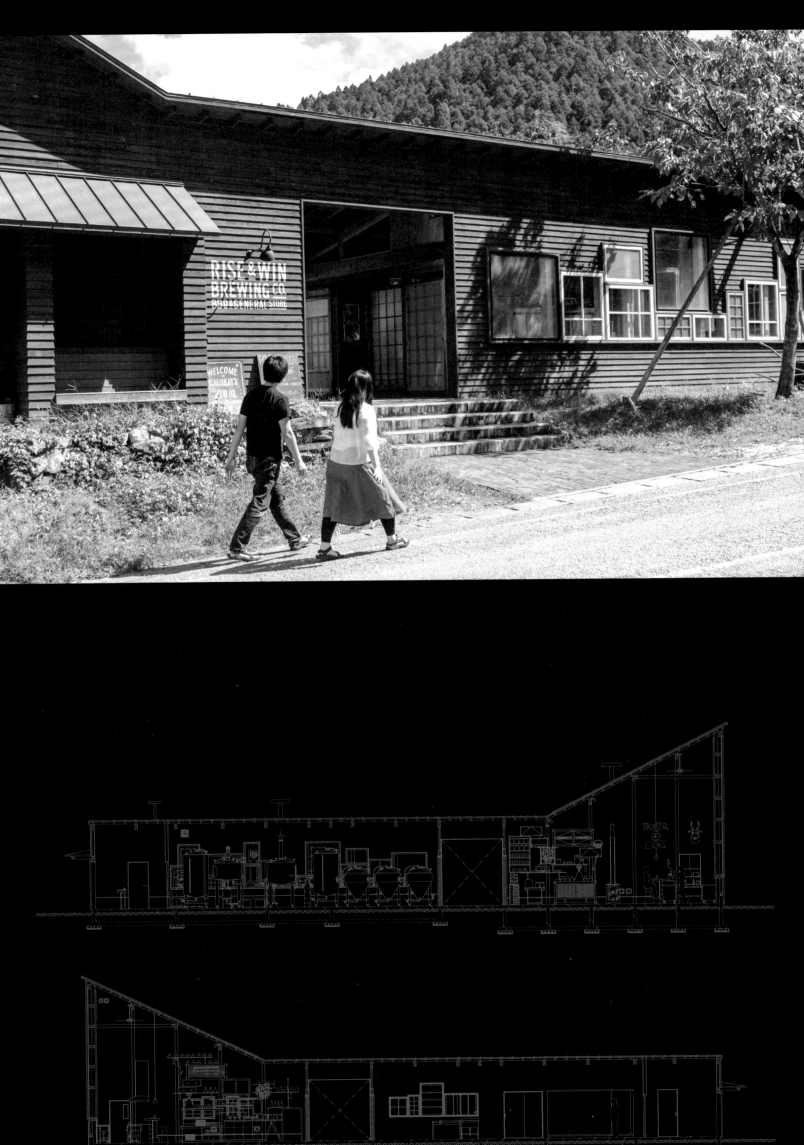

Inside, the microbrewery has a "cozy" atmosphere that might not be expected in a work by noted architects: in any case, there is warmth and ample natural light in the space.

KOHTEI

KOHEI NAWA / SANDWICH

Fukuyama, Hiroshima, 2016
Area: 793 m²
Collaboration: Yoshitaka Lee,
Yuichi Kodai (Architects)

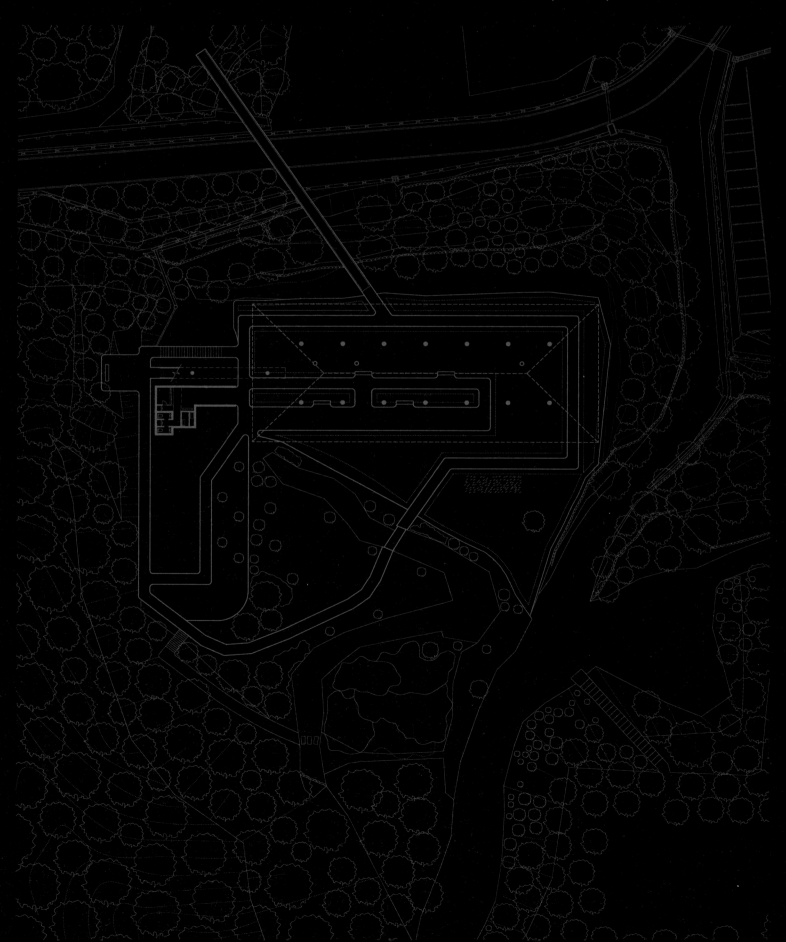

The unusual structure is lifted off the ground on thin columns. The drawing below shows the materials used, mainly a steel frame, stainless-steel eaves, wood, plaster board, and some concrete.

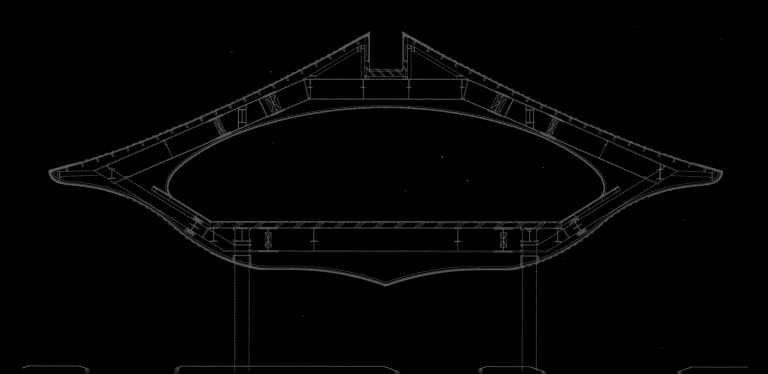

The form of the structure does bring to mind some ancient temples but even more, perhaps, a kind of science-fiction vessel, albeit one constructed with down-to-earth materials.

KOHEI NAWA was born in 1975 and is based in Kyoto. He received a Bachelor of Fine Arts in Sculpture from the Kyoto City University of Arts in 1998, and a Ph.D. from the same institution in 2003, before studying sculpture at the Royal College of Art (London). Sandwich is a multidisciplinary creative platform he created in an old sandwich factory near the Uji River in Kyoto. His architectural work with Sandwich includes the renovation of the Sandwich building (Kyoto, 2009); Nemika Hiroo store (2014); Kyodo House (Setagaya, Tokyo, with Team Low-Energy, 2015); and Kohtei (Fukuyama, Hiroshima, 2016, published here). He has also completed numerous art projects in fashion, stage design, and installation art. He is represented by SCAI the Bathhouse (Tokyo), PACE Gallery (NYC, London, Hong Kong, Seoul, Geneva, Palo Alto), and Arario Gallery (Seoul, Shanghai, Cheonan). His work *Throne* was exhibited beneath I. M. Pei's Louvre Pyramid from November 2018 to January 2019 in the context of the 2018 *Japonismes* exhibitions.

KOHEI NAWA wurde 1975 geboren und lebt in Kyoto. Er erhielt 1998 seinen Bachelor in Bildhauerei von der Städtischen Kunsthochschule Kyoto, die ihm 2003 auch einen Doktortitel verlieh, bevor er Bildhauerei am Royal College of Art in London studierte. Er gründete Sandwich, eine multidisziplinäre Kreativplattform in einer alten Sandwichfabrik in der Nähe des Flusses Uji in Kyoto. Zu den Architekturprojekten, die er mit Sandwich realisiert hat, zählen ein Umbau des Sandwich-Gebäudes (Kyoto, 2009), der Nemika Hiroo Store (2014), Kyodo House (Setagaya, Tokio, zusammen mit Team Low-Energy, 2015) sowie Kohtei (Fukuyama, Hiroshima, 2016, hier vorgestellt). Darüber hinaus hat Kohei Nawa zahlreiche Kunstprojekte in den Bereichen Mode, Bühnenbild und Installationskunst umgesetzt. Vertreten wird er durch die Galerie SCAI the Bathhouse (Tokio), PACE Gallery (New York, London, Hongkong, Seoul, Genf, Palo Alto) und Arario Gallery (Seoul, Shanghai, Cheonan). Von November 2018 bis Januar 2019 wurde seine Arbeit *Throne* im Rahmen der Ausstellung *Japonismes 2018* in der von I. M. Pei ent-

KOHEI NAWA, basé à Kyoto, est né en 1975. Il a obtenu un B.A. en sculpture d'art de l'université des arts de Kyoto en 1998 et un doctorat de la même institution en 2003, avant d'étudier la sculpture au Royal College of Art (Londres). Sandwich est une plate-forme créative multidisciplinaire qu'il a fondée dans une ancienne usine de sandwichs au bord de la rivière Uji, à Kyoto. Ses réalisations architecturales avec Sandwich comprennent la rénovation du bâtiment qui abrite Sandwich (Kyoto, 2009) ; le magasin Nemika d'Hiroo (2014) ; la maison Kyodo (Setagaya, Tokyo, avec l'équipe Low-Energy, 2015) et Kohtei (Fukuyama, Hiroshima, 2016, publié ici). Il a également réalisé de nombreux projets artistiques dans les domaines de la mode, des décors de théâtre et des installations artistiques, présentés par la galerie SCAI the Bathhouse (Tokyo), PACE Gallery (New York, Londres, Hong Kong, Séoul, Genève, Palo Alto), et Arario Gallery (Séoul, Shanghai, Cheonan). Son œuvre *Throne* a été exposée sous la Pyramide du Louvre de I. M. Pei de novembre 2018 à janvier 2019, dans le cadre de la manifestation culturelle « Japonismes 2018 ».

The Shinshoji Zen Museum and Gardens, located within the precinct of Tenshinzan Shinshoji Temple, is described as "a place for visitors to experience the spirit of Zen," including the tea ceremony, viewing Zen calligraphy, or visiting the extensive gardens. The

Das Zen-Museum Shinshoji liegt innerhalb des Tempelbezirks Tenshinzan Shinshoji und wird als Ort beschrieben, „an dem Besucher den Geist des Zen erleben können" – in Form von Teezeremonien, Zen-Kalligrafie und großen Gartenanlagen. Der Tempel wurde ursprünglich

Le musée zen Shinshoji et ses jardins, dans l'enceinte du temple Tenshinzan Shinshoji, sont décrits comme « un lieu où les visiteurs peuvent vivre l'esprit du zen », de la cérémonie du thé à la calligraphie zen, ou en visitant les vastes jardins. Le temple lui-même a été commandé

The lower surfaces of the building are clad in wooden strips. Rough stone surrounds the perimeter.

Below: a view of the interior installation which evokes the "quiet rippling ocean."

TESHIMA ART MUSEUM

RYUE NISHIZAWA

Teshima Island, Kagawa, 2010
Area: 2335 m²
Collaboration: Rei Naito (Artist)

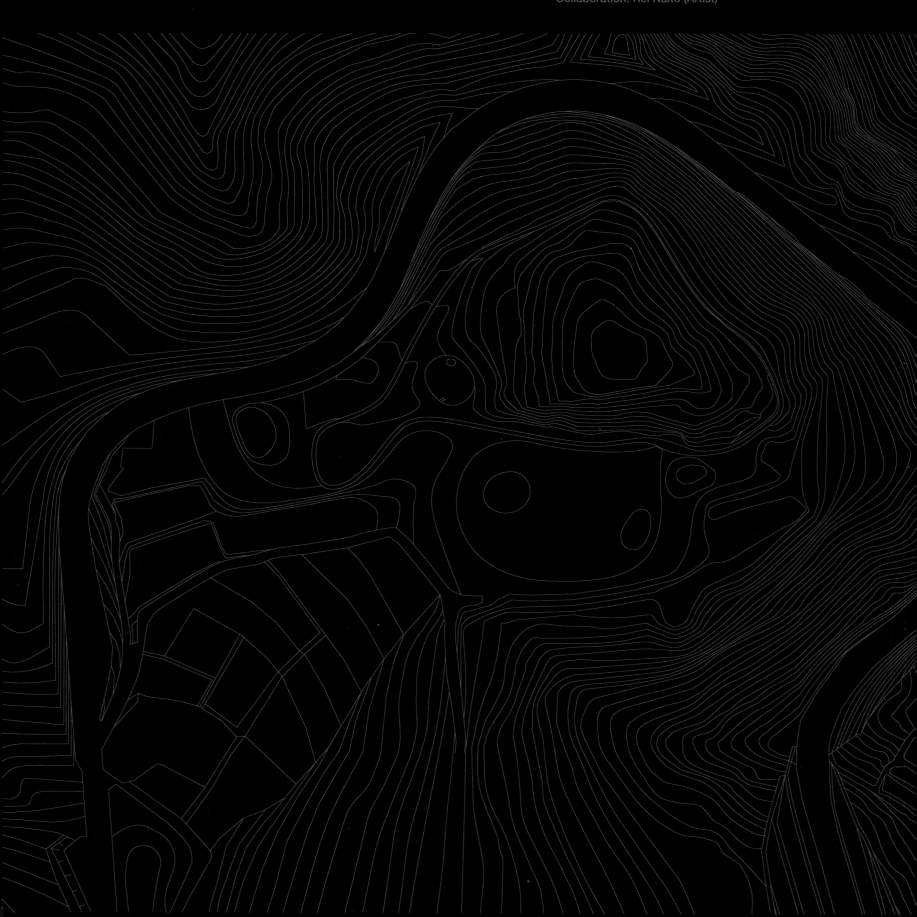

The Museum is set into the green, hilly topography of the small island of Teshima, which is essentially rural with relatively few inhabitants.

RYUE NISHIZAWA was born in Tokyo in 1966. He graduated from Yokohama National University with an M.Arch in 1990, and joined the office of Kazuyo Sejima & Associates in Tokyo the same year. In 1995, he established SANAA with Kazuyo Sejima, and two years later his own practice, the Office of Ryue Nishizawa. He has worked on all the significant projects of SANAA, and has been a Visiting Professor at Yokohama National University (2001–), the University of Singapore (2003), Princeton (2006), and Harvard GSD (2007). His work outside of SANAA includes Weekend House (Gunma, 1998); N Museum (Kagawa, 2005); Moriyama House (Tokyo, 2006); House A (East Japan, 2006); Towada Art Center (Aomori, 2008); Teshima Art Museum (Teshima Island, Kagawa, 2010, published here); Garden & House (Tokyo, 2011); Hiroshi Senju Museum (Karuizawa, Nagano, 2011); the Fukita Pavilion in Shodoshima (Shodoshima, Kagawa, 2013); Ikura Church (Kanagawa, 2014); and Terasaki House (Kanagawa, 2014).

RYUE NISHIZAWA wurde 1966 in Tokio geboren und schloss 1990 sein Studium an der Nationaluniversität Yokohama mit einem M.Arch ab. Noch im selben Jahr begann er für Kazuyo Sejima & Associates in Tokio zu arbeiten. 1995 rief er zusammen mit Kazuyo Sejima SANAA ins Leben, zwei Jahre darauf gründete er seine eigene Firma. Nishizawa war an allen wichtigen Projekten von SANAA beteiligt und ist Gastprofessor an der Nationaluniversität Yokohama (2001–), der Universität Singapur (2003), in Princeton (2006) und an der Harvard GSD (2007). Unabhängig von SANAA entstandene Projekte sind Weekend House (Gunma, 1998), N Museum (Kagawa, 2005), Moriyama House (Tokio, 2006), House A (Ostjapan, 2006), das Kunstzentrum Towada (Aomori, 2008), das Kunstmuseum Teshima (Teshima Island, Kagawa, 2010, hier vorgestellt), Garden & House (Tokio, 2011), das Hiroshi Senju Museum (Karuizawa, Nagano, 2011), der Fukita-Pavillon in Shodoshima (Shodoshima, Kagawa, 2013), die Ikura-Kirche (Kanagawa, 2014) sowie Terasaki House (Kanagawa, 2014).

RYUE NISHIZAWA, né à Tokyo en 1966, a obtenu son M.Arch à l'Université nationale de Yokohama (1990). Il a commencé à travailler dans l'agence de Kazuyo Sejima & Associates à Tokyo la même année, avant qu'ils ne fondent ensemble SANAA en 1995 et qu'il n'ouvre sa propre agence Office of RyueNishizawa deux ans plus tard. Il est intervenu sur tous les grands projets de SANAA et a été professeur invité à l'Université nationale de Yokohama (2001–), aux universités de Singapour (2003), Princeton (2006) et à la Harvard GSD (2007). Son œuvre personnelle comprend une maison de campagne (Gunma, 1998) ; le musée N (Kagawa, 2005) ; la maison Moriyama (Tokyo, 2006) ; la maison A (Japon oriental, 2006) ; le Centre d'art Towada (Aomori, 2008) ; le musée d'Art de Teshima (île de Teshima, Kagawa, 2010, publié ici) ; une Garden & House (Tokyo, 2011) ; le musée Hiroshi Senju (Karuizawa, Nagano, 2011) ; le pavillon Fukita à Shodoshima (Shodoshima, Kagawa, 2013) ; l'église d'Ikura (Kanagawa, 2014) et la maison Terasaki (Kanagawa, 2014).

The interior is entirely open to the wind and the sky, with only the silent water drops imagined by the artist Rei Naito emerging from the gently sloping concrete floor.

Teshima is a small island located in Japan's Inland Sea, not far from Naoshima, where Tadao Ando has worked for over 20 years on various projects. The same client commissioned Ryue Nishizawa to build this museum, which is part of the broader Benesse Art Site Naoshima project. The ART MUSEUM, which contains only one work, is reached mainly by bicycle from Teshima's small port. "We proposed an architectural design composed of free curves, echoing the shape of a water drop," says the architect. "Our idea was that the curved drop-like form would create a powerful architectural space in harmony with the undulating landforms around it." The remarkable thin concrete shell structure, designed with the noted engineer Mutsuro Sasaki, rises to a maximum of 4.5 meters and spans as far as 60 meters, "creating a large, organic interior space." Openings in the shell let light, air, and rain inside. Within, Rei Naito's subtle work is based on drops of water that seem to emerge from the white, very gently sloped surfaces beneath the shell, running together to form rivulets in an unpredictable pattern. Visitors walk among these rivulets and hear

Teshima ist eine kleine, unweit von Naoshima gelegene Insel in der japanischen Inlandsee, auf der Tadao Ando seit mehr als 20 Jahren Projekte realisiert. Andos Auftraggeber betraute nun Nishizawa mit dem Bau eines KUNST-MUSEUMS, das zur Benesse Art Site Naoshima gehört. Es präsentiert ein einziges Werk und wird hauptsächlich per Fahrrad von Teshimas kleinem Hafen aus erreicht. „Wir haben einen Entwurf mit fließenden Linien vorgeschlagen, dessen Form an einen Wassertropfen erinnert", sagt der Architekt. „Die geschwungene, tropfenähnliche Form sollte einen eindrucksvollen architektonischen Raum erzeugen, der mit der hügeligen Landschaft harmoniert.". Die von dem renommierten Ingenieur Mutsuro Sasaki entworfene, bemerkenswert dünne Betonhülle hat eine Höhe von maximal 4,5 m und eine Spannweite von maximal 60 m, wodurch „ein großer, organischer Innenraum entsteht". Durch Öffnungen in der Hülle gelangen Licht, Luft und Regen ins Innere. Rei Naitos raffinierte Installation inszeniert Wassertropfen, die aus dem weißen, leicht abschüssigen Boden im Inneren der Hülle austreten und in einem unvorhersehbaren Muster

Teshima est une petite île de la mer Intérieure du Japon, non loin de Naoshima où Tadao Ando a travaillé pendant plus de vingt ans à divers projets. Le même client a demandé à Ryue Nishizawa de construire ce musée qui fait partie du projet plus vaste, Benesse Art Site Naoshima. Le MUSÉE D'ART, qui n'abrite qu'une œuvre unique, est principalement accessible à vélo depuis le petit port de Teshima. « Nous avons proposé un design architectural en courbes libres dont la forme fait écho à celle d'une goutte d'eau, explique l'architecte. Notre idée était que cette forme courbe en goutte crée un espace architectural fort, en harmonie avec les ondulations du paysage tout autour. » L'étonnante coque mince en béton, conçue avec le célèbre ingénieur Mutsuro Sasaki, s'élève jusqu'à 4,5 m de haut à son point culminant pour une envergure allant jusqu'à 60 m qui « détermine un vaste volume organique intérieur ». Des ouvertures laissent passer la lumière, l'air et la pluie. À l'intérieur, l'œuvre subtile de Rei Naito, l'artiste présentée, est fondée sur des gouttes d'eau qui donnent l'impression d'émerger des surfaces blanches en pente très douce sous la coque, avant de se rejoindre

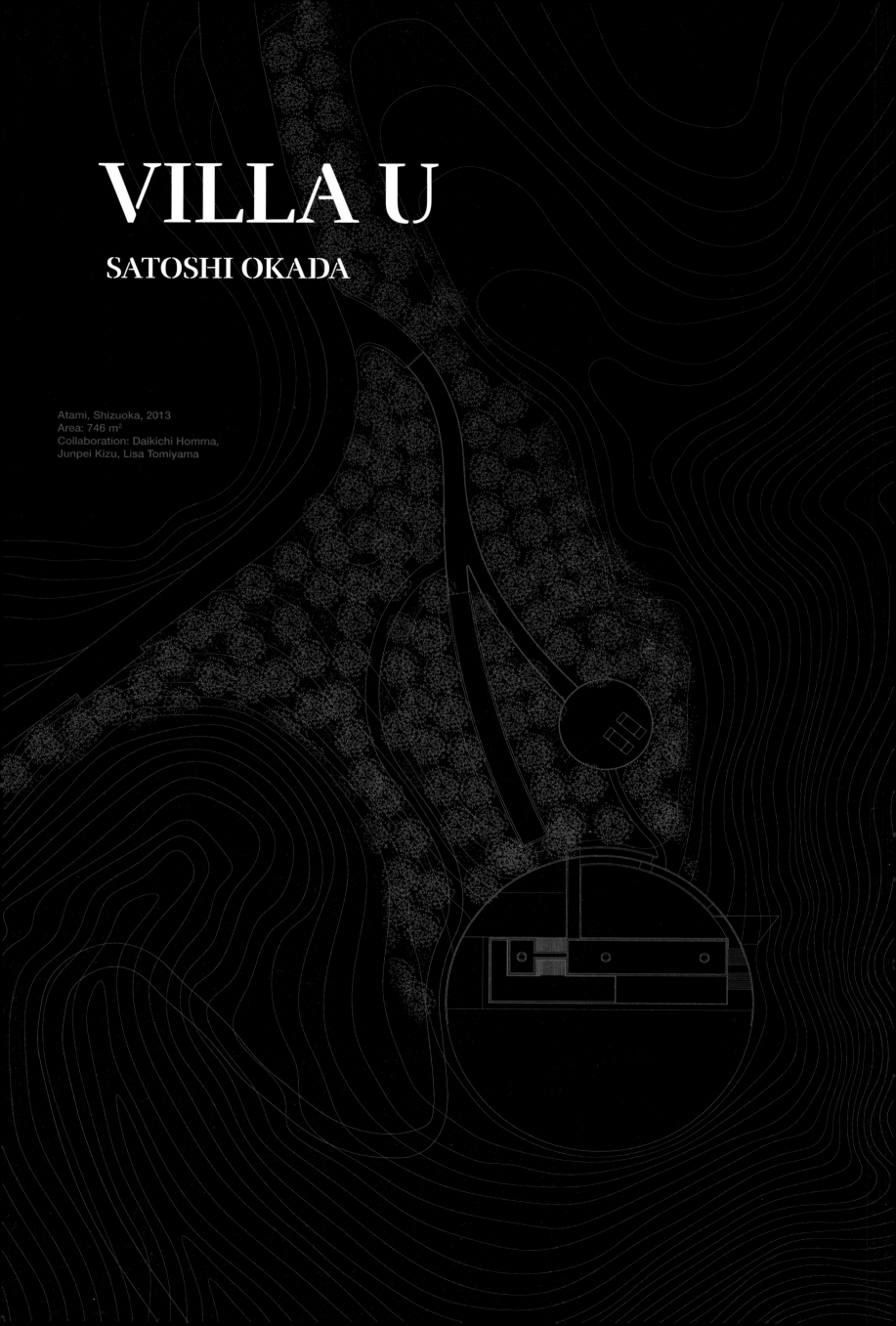

VILLA U

SATOSHI OKADA

Atami, Shizuoka, 2013
Area: 746 m²
Collaboration: Daikichi Homma,
Junpei Kizu, Lisa Tomiyama

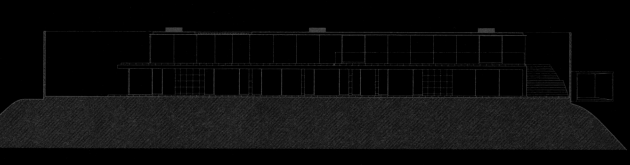

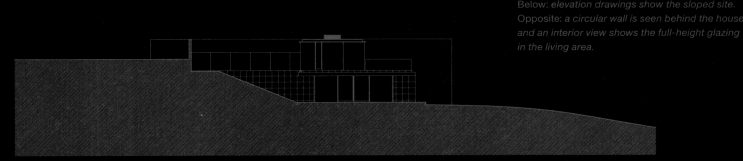

The site of this two-story house overlooks
the Pacific Ocean and, in fact, its lower level
is visible only from the ocean side. A rounded
wall at the back of the house "references
the curvy terrain lines of the coastal landscape and works as a protective enclosure
for the villa." Thus inscribed within a circle,
the house is developed as a minimal, rectangular composition. The bedrooms are on
the lower level and are finished in dark stone
and custom timber fittings. The living or public spaces are on the upper level and open
onto an ample terrace. The architect explains
that the client for this house was looking
for "timeless architecture." Okada asks:
"What does it mean to portray 'timelessness'
in architecture? We believe such architecture
intrinsically bears an unspoken character,
namely to remain unchangingly beautiful over
time: this pure and simple dignity is difficult
to achieve."

Dieses zweigeschossige Haus wurde mit Blick
auf den Pazifik errichtet. Die untere Ebene
ist nur von der Meerseite aus zu sehen. Eine
halbrunde Mauer an der Rückseite des Hauses
„verweist auf den kurvenreichen Verlauf
der Küstenlandschaft und dient der Villa als
Schutz". Das auf diese Weise in eine Kreisform
eingeschriebene Haus ist als minimale, rechteckige Komposition angelegt. Die Schlafzimmer befinden sich im unteren Geschoss und
sind mit dunklem Stein und individuellen Holz-
einbauten ausgestattet. Die Wohnräume liegen
im Obergeschoss und öffnen sich zu einer
großzügigen Terrasse. Dem Architekten zufolge war dem Bauherrn an „zeitloser Architektur" gelegen. Okada: „Was bedeutet ‚Zeitlosig-
keit' in architektonischer Hinsicht? Zeitlose
Architektur soll, auch wenn dies nicht aus-
drücklich so gesagt wird, mit dem Vergehen
der Zeit aus sich selbst heraus unverändert
schön bleiben; Etwas zu bauen, das in seiner

Le site sur lequel est construite cette maison
de deux niveaux domine l'océan Pacifique et le
niveau inférieur n'est d'ailleurs visible que
depuis la mer. Un mur arrondi à l'arrière de la
maison « rappelle les lignes courbes du littoral
et tient lieu d'enclos protecteur pour la villa ».
Ainsi inscrite dans une forme circulaire, elle
développe une composition rectangulaire minimaliste. Les chambres occupent le niveau
inférieur avec des finitions en pierre sombre et
des équipements sur mesure en bois d'œuvre.
Les espaces à vivre ou publics sont situés au
niveau supérieur et ouvrent sur une généreuse
terrasse. L'architecte explique que le client
recherchait une « architecture intemporelle. Et il
interroge : Qu'est-ce que cela veut dire, représenter l'"intemporalité" en architecture ? Nous
pensons que cette architecture porte en soi une
qualité inexprimée, celle de demeurer d'une
beauté immuable au fil du temps : une dignité
pure et simple qui est difficile à obtenir. »

MIYAJIMA MISEN OBSERVATORY

HIROSHI SAMBUICHI

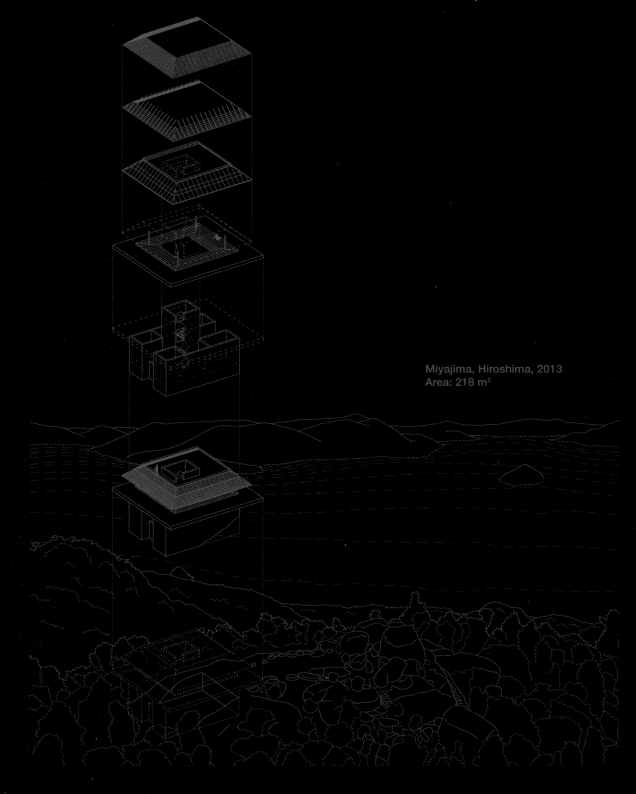

Miyajima, Hiroshima, 2013
Area: 218 m²

The design of the structure is very simple and relies on the craftsmanship of the woodworkers involved.

HIROSHI SAMBUICHI was born in 1968. He graduated from the Department of Architecture in the Faculty of Science and Technology at Tokyo University of Science. After working for Shinichi Ogawa and Associates, he established Sambuichi Architects and began design work in Hiroshima. His work includes the Running Green Project (Yamaguchi, 2001); Air House (Yamaguchi, 2001); Miwa-gama (Yamaguchi, 2002); Sloping North House (Yamaguchi, 2003); Stone House (Shimane, 2005); and the Inujima Seirensho Art Museum (Okayama, 2008), a museum located on the small island of Inujima in the Inland Sea of Japan, carried out for the same client as Tadao Ando's work on the nearby island of Naoshima. His other work includes the Miyajima Office (Hatsukaichi, Hiroshima, 2008); Miyajima Misen Observatory (Miyajima, Hiroshima, 2013, published here); Naoshima Hall (Naoshima, Kagawa, 2015, also published here); and Hiroshima Orizuru Tower (Hiroshima, 2016).

HIROSHI SAMBUICHI wurde 1968 geboren und studierte Architektur an der Fakultät für Naturwissenschaften und Technik der Naturwissenschaftlichen Universität Tokio. Nach seiner Tätigkeit für Shinichi Ogawa & Associates gründete er Sambuichi Architects und begann seine Arbeit als Designer in Hiroshima. Zu seinem Werk gehört das Running Green Project (Yamaguchi, 2001), Air House (Yamaguchi, 2001), Miwa-gama (Yamaguchi, 2002), Sloping North House (Yamaguchi, 2003), Stone House (Shimane, 2005) sowie das Inujima Seirensho Art Museum (Okayama, 2008), ein Museum auf der kleinen Insel Inujima in der Inlandsee, das von demselben Kunden in Auftrag gegeben wurde wie Tadao Andos Projekt auf der nahegelegenen Insel Naoshima. Weitere Arbeiten sind Miyajima Office – Büros für Hiroshima Project Offices (Hatsukaichi, Hiroshima, 2008), der Aussichtspunkt Miyajima Misen (Miyajima, Hiroshima, 2013, hier vorgestellt), Naoshima Hall (Naoshima, Kagawa, 2015, ebenfalls hier vorgestellt) sowie Hiroshima Orizuru Tower

HIROSHI SAMBUICHI est né en 1968. Il est diplômé du département d'architecture de la faculté de sciences et de technologie à l'université des sciences de Tokyo. Il a d'abord travaillé pour Shinichi Ogawa and Associates, avant de fonder Sambuichi Architects et de commencer à imaginer ses premiers projets à Hiroshima. Ses travaux comprennent le projet Running Green (Yamaguchi, 2001) ; Air House (Yamaguchi, 2001) ; Miwa-gama (Yamaguchi, 2002) ; Sloping North House (Yamaguchi, 2003) ; Stone House (Shimane, 2005) et Inujima Seirensho Art Museum (Okayama, 2008), un musée sur la petite île d'Inujima dans la mer intérieure du Japon pour le même client Tadao Ando sur l'île voisine de Naoshima. D'autres réalisations comprennent les bureaux du Hiroshima Project à Miyajima (Hatsukaichi, Hiroshima, 2008) ; l'observatoire du mont Misen de Miyajima (Miyajima, Hiroshima, 2013, publié ici) ; le Centre communautaire Naoshima Hall (Naoshima, Kagawa, 2015, également publié ici) et la tour Orizuru d'Hiroshima (Hiroshima, 2016).

A platform and reflecting pool overlook Hiroshima Bay and the torii of Itsukushima Shrine.

The Itsukushima or Miyajima Shrine and its 13th-century design is a UNESCO World Heritage Site. Hiroshi Sambuichi states: "I think that Miyajima Shrine is one of the world's most beautiful expressions of natural 'moving materials.' Its celestial and terrestrial beauty is manifest in the relationship between the Shrine and the ebb and flow of the tides." The Virgin Forest Misen of the 535-meter-high Mount Misen is also located on Miyajima Island. Hiroshi Sambuichi's OBSERVATORY is located here, looking toward the Shrine to the north and the Virgin Forest to the west, with the Inland Sea to the east. "Since I was a child," says the architect, "I have climbed Mount Misen annually for the New Year holidays and worshiped the view of the sunrise from the high mountaintop. Seeing its extreme beauty, faster than anyone to pray, I always decided that the mountaintop was a *za* (seat). No matter how many times I climbed to the summit of Mount Misen, I had the sense of meditating, entranced by its varied beauty. In conveying the sense that constantly changing nature—that is to say, moving materials— is a *za* (seat), my instinct was to convey Mount Misen just as it is." The Observatory was built with *hinoki* (Japanese cypress) and *sugi* (Japanese cedar) in Hiroshima Prefecture.

Der Itsukushima- oder Miyajima-Schrein aus dem 13. Jahrhundert gehört zum UNESCO-Weltkulturerbe. Hiroshi Sambuichi: „Ich halte den Miyajima-Schrein für eine der weltweit schönsten Ausdrucksformen von natürlicher ‚bewegter' Materie. Die himmlische und irdische Schönheit des Schreins manifestiert sich in seinem Verhältnis zum Kommen und Gehen der Gezeiten." Auf dem 535 m hohen Misen, der sich auf der Insel Miyajima erhebt, befindet sich Hiroshi Sambuichis AUSSICHTSPUNKT, von dem aus man im Norden den Schrein, im Westen den Urwald der Insel und im Osten die Inlandsee sieht. „Seit meiner Kindheit", so der Architekt, „bin ich an den Neujahrsfeiertagen auf den Misen gestiegen und habe vom Gipfel aus den Sonnenaufgang bewundert. Angesichts der atemberaubenden Schönheit hatte ich stets den Eindruck, dass der Gipfel ein *za* (Thron) ist. Egal wie oft ich auf dem Gipfel des Misen war, stets hatte ich das Gefühl zu meditieren, wenn mich seine vielgestaltige Schönheit für sich einnahm. Da die sich stets wandelnde Natur – bewegliche Materie also – für mich ein *za* ist, folgte ich meinem Instinkt und übersetzte den Berg selbst in die Architektur des Aussichtspunkts." Das Projekt wurde in der Präfektur Hiroshima aus *hinoki* (japanische Zypresse) und *sugi* (japanische Zeder) errichtet.

Le sanctuaire d'Itsukushima ou de Miyajima du XIIIᵉ siècle figure sur la liste du patrimoine mondial de l'UNESCO. Pour Hiroshi Sambuichi : « Je pense que le sanctuaire de Miyajima est l'une des plus belles expressions au monde de "matières mouvantes" naturelles. Sa beauté céleste et terrestre se manifeste dans le rapport du sanctuaire et des marées montante et descendante. » L'île de Miyajima abrite aussi la forêt vierge du mont Misen, d'une altitude de 535 m. C'est là qu'est situé l'OBSERVATOIRE de Hiroshi Sambuichi, avec vue sur le sanctuaire au nord et sur la forêt à l'ouest, ou encore la mer intérieure à l'est. « Depuis mon enfance, explique l'architecte, je monte sur le mont Misen tous les ans pour les congés du nouvel an et je rends un culte à la vue du soleil levant au sommet de la montagne. À la vue de cette beauté extrême, propice plus que toute autre à la prière, j'ai toujours décidé que le sommet était un *za* (siège). Peu importe le nombre de fois où j'ai gravi le mont Misen, j'avais le sens de la méditation, sous le charme de sa beauté multiple. En transmettant l'idée que la nature en perpétuelle transformation – les matières mouvantes – est un *za* (siège), mon instinct m'a dit de restituer le mont Misen lui-même, tel qu'il est. » L'observatoire a été construit en *hinoki* (cyprès du Japon) et en *sugi* (cèdre du Japon) dans la préfecture d'Hiroshima.

NAOSHIMA HALL

HIROSHI SAMBUICHI

Naoshima, Kagawa, 2015
Area: 1273 m²

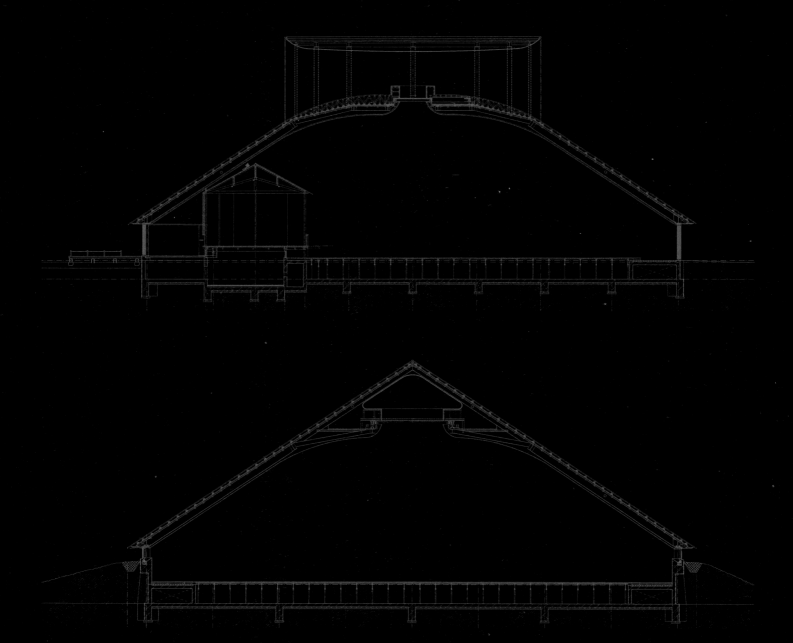

NAOSHIMA HALL is a public project located on Naoshima island, near Inujima island where Inujima Seirensho Art Museum (2008) is located, a project of the Benesse Art Site Naoshima. The new building includes a hall, a community center, and a garden—with a roof made of *hinoki* (Japanese cypress)— inspired by local traditional architecture. The hall is used as a place of practice for the Naoshima Onna Bunraku, designated an "Important Tangible and Intangible Folk Cultural Property" for Kagawa Prefecture. Clad in *hinoki*, the large roof of the hall is a traditional hipped shape that is often seen in the villages of Naoshima and has a vent opening aligned with the prevailing wind direction. The shape is a visualization of the flow of materials in Naoshima and simultaneously produces a difference in pressure that causes air to circulate in the hall. Even with the windows closed in summer, heat is removed by the gentle movements of the air—a device that allows for various activities. In the community center, four buildings are ar-

Die NAOSHIMA HALL ist ein Gemeindezentrum auf der Insel Naoshima, nahe der Insel Inujima, dem Standort des Inujima Seirensho Art Museum (2008), einem Projekt der Benesse Art Site Naoshima. Der Neubau umfasst einen Saal, ein Gemeindezentrum, einen Garten und verfügt über ein Dach aus *hinoki* (japanische Zypresse). Das Projekt ist von der traditionellen Architektur in der Region inspiriert. Unter anderem wird hier Naoshima Onna Bunraku geprobt, ein Figurentheater, das laut der Präfektur Kagawa ein „bedeutendes materielles und immaterielles Volkskulturerbe" ist. Die Form des großen, mit *hinoki* verschalten Walmdachs findet sich in den Dörfern von Naoshima häufiger; das Dach verfügt über eine der vorherrschenden Windrichtung angepasste Lüftungsöffnung. Die Dachform erzeugt ein Druckgefälle, so dass die Luft im Gebäude zirkulieren kann. Auch wenn im Sommer die Fenster geschlossen sind, entweicht die Hitze und das Gebäude bleibt kühl. Unter der großen Dachkonstruktion befinden sich vier Volumen,

NAOSHIMA HALL est un projet public situé sur l'île de Naoshima, près de l'île d'Inujima où se trouve le Inujima Seirensho Art Museum (2008), un projet du Benesse Art Site Naoshima. Le nouveau complexe comprend un hall, un centre communautaire et un jardin – au toit de *hinoki* (cyprès du Japon) – qui s'inspirent de l'architecture traditionnelle locale. La salle est destinée à la pratique du théâtre traditionnel Onna Bunraku de Naoshima, qualifié d'« important patrimoine culturel populaire tangible et intangible » par la préfecture de Kagawa. Revêtu de *hinoki*, le grand toit adopte une forme en croupe traditionnelle que l'on voit souvent dans les villages de Naoshima, et possède une ouverture de ventilation orientée vers le vent dominant. Cette forme est une visualisation du flux de matériaux à Naoshima, et produit simultanément une différence de pression qui fait circuler l'air dans la salle. Même lorsque les fenêtres sont fermées, l'été, la chaleur est évacuée par les mouvements de l'air – un dispositif qui permet d'y organiser diverses activités.

The Hall is an intriguing combination of inspiration from local traditions and a marked sense of modernity. Gardens and terraces are a prominent feature of the project.

The interior spaces of the Hall are high and filled
with light. Sliding glass walls open large parts of the
interior to the outside when weather permits.

GRACE FARMS

SANAA / KAZUYO SEJIMA + RYUE NISHIZAWA

New Canaan, USA, 2015
Area: 7513 m²
Collaboration: Shohei Yoshida,
Takayuki Hasegawa, Ichio Matsuzawa

Inscribed in the wooded land of New Canaan, Connecticut, Grace Farms occupies 32-hectare site, of which fully 31-hectares are intended to be preserved as meadows, woods, wetlands, and ponds.

Born in Ibaraki Prefecture, in 1956, KAZUYO SEJIMA received her M.Arch degree from Japan Women's University in 1981 and went on to work in the office of Toyo Ito the same year. She established Kazuyo Sejima and Associates in Tokyo in 1987. RYUE NISHIZAWA was born in Tokyo in 1966, and graduated from the National University (Yokohama, 1990). He began working with Sejima the same year, and the pair created the new firm SANAA / Kazuyo Sejima + Ryue Nishizawa in 1995. In 2010, SANAA was awarded the 2010 Pritzker Prize. The work of SANAA includes the 21st Century Museum of Contemporary Art (Kanazawa, Ishikawa, 2004), whose rectangular galleries are placed within a circular glass perimeter, as well as abroad, firstly the Glass Pavilion, the Glass Pavilion of the Toledo Museum of Art (Ohio, USA, 2006), and a theater and cultural center in Almere (Die Kunstlinie, The Netherlands, 2007). In terms of media exposure, they rose still higher with the New Museum of Contemporary Art, located on the Bowery in New York (USA, 2007), and the vast open spaces of the Rolex Learning Center at the EPFL in Lausanne (Switzerland, 2009). Recent work by SANAA includes the Louvre-Lens (Lens, France, 2012); Grace Farms (New Canaan, Connecticut, USA, 2015, published here); and Shogin Tact Tsuruoka (Tsuruoka, Yamagata, 2017, also published here).

KAZUYO SEJIMA wurde 1956 in der Präfektur Ibaraki geboren, erhielt 1981 ihren M.Arch-Abschluss von der Japanischen Frauenuniversität und begann noch im selben Jahr, für Toyo Ito zu arbeiten. Sie gründete 1987 in Tokio Kazuyo Sejima & Associates. RYUE NISHIZAWA wurde 1966 in Tokio geboren. 1990 schloss er sein Studium an der Nationaluniversität Yokohama ab und begann im selben Jahr, mit Sejima zusammenzuarbeiten. Das Paar gründete 1995 die Firma SANAA / Kazuyo Sejima + Ryue Nishizawa. 2010 wurde SANAA mit dem Pritzker-Preis ausgezeichnet. Zu ihren Projekten gehören ein Museum für zeitgenössische Kunst des 21. Jahrhunderts (Kanazawa, Ishikawa, 2004), dessen rechteckige Galerieräume innerhalb einer runden Struktur mit gläsernen Außenwänden liegen. Ihre ersten Auslandsprojekte waren ein Glaspavillon für das Toledo Museum of Art (Ohio, 2006) sowie „Die Kunstlinie", ein Theater- und Kulturzentrum in Almere (Niederlande, 2007). Die bis dato größte Medienpräsenz bescherte ihnen das New Museum of Contemporary Art an der Bowery in New York (2007) und die großen Freiflächen des Rolex Learning Center an der EPFL in Lausanne (2009). Zu den jüngsten Projekten von SANAA gehören Louvre-Lens (Lens, Frankreich, 2012), Grace Farms (New Canaan, Connecticut, 2015, hier vorgestellt) und Shogin Tact Tsuruoka (Tsuruoka, Yamagata, 2017, ebenfalls hier vorgestellt).

Née dans la préfecture d'Ibaraki en 1956, KAZUYO SEJIMA obtient son M.Arch de l'université féminine du Japon en 1981 et est engagée par Toyo Ito la même année. Elle crée l'agence Kazuyo Sejima & Associates à Tokyo en 1987. RYUE NISHIZAWA, né à Tokyo en 1966, est diplômé de l'Université nationale de Yokohama (1990). Il a commencé à travailler avec Sejima la même année avant qu'ils ne fondent ensemble SANAA / Kazuyo Sejima + Ryue Nishizawa en 1995. SANAA a reçu le prix Pritzker en 2010. Parmi les réalisations de l'agence figurent le musée d'Art contemporain du XXIᵉ siècle (Kanazawa, Ishikawa, 2004) dont les galeries rectangulaires sont disposées à l'intérieur d'un cercle de verre ; le Pavillon de verre du musée d'Art de Toledo (Ohio, États-Unis, 2006), premier de leurs projets à l'étranger, et un théâtre et centre culturel à Almere (Die Kunstlinie, Pays-Bas, 2007). Leur notoriété internationale s'est encore élargie avec des œuvres comme le New Museum of Contemporary Art sur le Bowery à New York (2007) et les vastes espaces ouverts du Rolex Learning Center à l'EPFL de Lausanne (Suisse, 2009). Leurs projets récents comprennent le Louvre-Lens (Lens, France, 2012) ; Grace Farms (New Canaan, Connecticut, États-Unis, 2015, publié ici) et Shogin Tact Tsuruoka (Tsuruoka, Yamagata, 2017, également publié ici).

The long snake-shaped canopy leading to the different facilities in the complex winds down a sloped site.

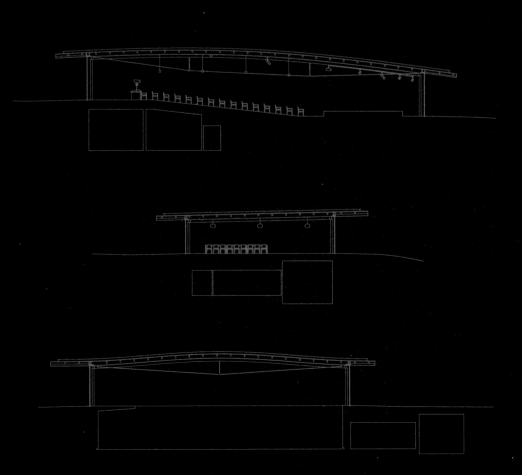

The canopy, which allows ample views of the site, is set on thin columns and has a wooden underside.

This project was carried out on a 32-hectare wooded site with lakes and wetlands. The program includes a multipurpose hall, community gathering space with food and beverages, gymnasium, and library, as well as an athletic field and courtyard for barbecueing. The GRACE FARMS Foundation is dedicated to preserving this natural landscape, and thus, logically, the architects state: "In this rich and natural environment, we sought to make a piece of architecture that becomes a part of the landscape." The winding, long roof of the wood frame structure follows the landscape. The interior programs are held under the large roof, organized and enclosed in glass volumes according to character and use. The large roof also gives way to a variety of different kinds of spaces, like a lively room facing a plaza, or a calm space with sunlight filtered through tree foliage. The main materials used for this $67-million-dollar project were timber beams, steel columns, aluminum panels, glass, concrete, wood, and brick.

Dieses Projekt wurde in einem 32 ha großen Waldgebiet mit Seen und Feuchtgebieten realisiert. Es umfasst eine Mehrzweckhalle, Gemeinschaftsräume mit Speise- und Getränkeangebot, eine Turnhalle und eine Bibliothek sowie einen Sport- und einen Grillplatz. Die GRACE FARMS Foundation widmet sich der Erhaltung der Naturlandschaft, in der es sich befindet. Die Architekten: „In einer von der Natur reich beschenkten Umgebung wollten wir ein Bauwerk erschaffen, das mit der Landschaft eine Verbindung eingeht." Das lange gewundene Dach der Holzrahmenkonstruktion folgt dem Terrain. Unter dem Dach befinden sich die je nach Nutzungsart unterschiedlich ausgestatteten Innenräume in Form verglaster Volumina. Das Dach beschirmt eine Vielzahl verschiedener Bereiche, z. B. einen viel frequentierten Raum mit Vorplatz und einen Erholungsraum, vor dem Bäume stehen, durch deren Blätterdach die Sonne scheint. Die wichtigsten Materialien für dieses 67-Millionen-Dollar-Projekt sind Holzbalken, Stahlstützen, Aluminiumplatten, Glas, Beton, Holz und Ziegel.

Le projet occupe un terrain boisé de 32 ha aux nombreux lacs et zones humides. Il comprend une salle polyvalente, un espace communautaire avec possibilité de restauration, un gymnase et une bibliothèque, ainsi qu'un terrain d'athlétisme et une cour pour les barbecues. La Fondation GRACE FARMS tient beaucoup à préserver ce paysage naturel, ce qui amène logiquement les architectes à déclarer : « Dans cet environnement naturel riche, nous avons cherché une architecture qui fasse partie intégrante du paysage. » Le long toit sinueux de la construction à charpente en bois épouse les lignes du terrain. Répartis sous ce toit, les différents espaces intérieurs sont entourés de volumes vitrés selon leur nature et leur usage. La vaste toiture ouvre aussi sur un grand nombre d'espaces de différents types, telles une salle animée face à une place ou une zone calme où la lumière du soleil est filtrée par le feuillage des arbres. Les principaux matériaux de ce projet d'un coût de 67 millions de dollars sont des poutres en bois d'œuvre, des colonnes en acier, des panneaux en aluminium, du verre, du béton, du bois et des briques.

Above: *the indoor amphitheater seats 700 people.*
Below: *the court is partially below-grade and serves as a gymnasium/multipurpose space.*

SHOGIN TACT TSURUOKA

SANAA / KAZUYO SEJIMA + RYUE NISHIZAWA

Tsuruoka, Yamagata, 2017
Area: 7846 m²
Collaboration: Rikiya Yamamoto,
Satoshi Ikeda, Takuma Yokomae

Built for the cost of 65 800 000 euro, the facility is located in Tsuruoka, a city of 125 000 people in the northwest of Honshu Island.

This complex is a multipurpose hall that serves as a base for cultural and artistic activities in the area. The project aimed to expand local civic activities, while incorporating an old hall that had been the heart of cultural activities for students and arts groups. The architects state: "We proposed a large hall wrapped by a corridor, resembling traditional Japanese *saya-do* construction. This corridor is open to the public on a daily basis. The large central hall was conceived to bring the audience and performers as close together as possible." The exterior appearance of the complex makes use of a number of small roofs, coming down to a height of one story near the road. "By controlling the volume in this way," states SANAA, "we sought to make a building that is in harmony with the adjacent historic building and the surrounding cityscape." They further sought to provide a sense of natural warmth with plastered concrete finishes or textured sheet metal. The project was carried out with a reinforced concrete foundation and a steel structure, with glass, aluminum panel and steel sheet plates for the exterior.

In diesem Komplex ist ein Mehrzwecksaal untergebracht, der für künstlerische und kulturelle Veranstaltungen in der Region zur Verfügung steht. Ziel war es, einen bereits existierenden Saal einzubinden, der von Studenten und Künstlergruppen genutzt wurde, um so eine Zunahme bürgerschaftlicher Aktivitäten zu bewirken. Die Architekten: „In Anlehnung an traditionelle japanische *saya-do*-Konstruktionen schlugen wir eine große, von einem Korridor umgebene Halle vor. Der Korridor ist jeden Tag für die Öffentlichkeit zugänglich. Der Aufbau der großen zentralen Halle sorgt für eine größtmögliche Nähe zwischen Publikum und Darstellern." Der Komplex zeichnet sich durch eine Vielzahl kleinerer Dachkonstruktionen aus, die bis auf Erdgeschossniveau hinunterreichen. „Indem wir das Volumen auf diese Weise gestalteten", so SANAA, „sollte ein Gebäude entstehen, das mit dem historischen Stadtbild in der unmittelbaren Umgebung harmoniert." Verputzter Beton und Strukturblech sollen ein Gefühl natürlicher Wärme vermitteln. Das Projekt wurde mit einem Stahlbetonfundament, einer Stahlkonstruktion und im Fassadenbereich mit Glas-, Aluminium- und Stahlblechplatten realisiert.

Ce complexe multi-usage est un centre local d'activités culturelles et artistiques. Le projet avait pour but d'encourager les activités citoyennes en incorporant une salle plus ancienne qui avait été le cœur des activités culturelles d'étudiants et de groupes artistiques. Les architectes expliquent : « Nous avons imaginé un vaste hall entouré d'un corridor qui rappelle la construction japonaise traditionnelle *saya-do*. Le corridor est ouvert au public tous les jours. Le vaste hall central a été conçu pour le rapprocher le plus possible des interprètes. » Vu de l'extérieur, le complexe présente un grand nombre de toits aux dimensions réduites qui descendent jusqu'à la hauteur d'un étage à côté de la route. « En contrôlant ainsi le volume, déclare SANAA, nous avons cherché à réaliser un bâtiment en harmonie avec les bâtiments historiques voisins et le paysage urbain environnant. » Les architectes ont aussi voulu donner au projet une chaleur naturelle avec des finitions de béton taloché ou des feuilles de métal texturé. L'ensemble possède des fondations en béton armé, une structure en acier, des panneaux de verre et d'aluminium et des feuilles d'acier à l'extérieur.

Below: *a section drawing shows the main hall where an effort was made to bring spectators and performers as close as possible.*

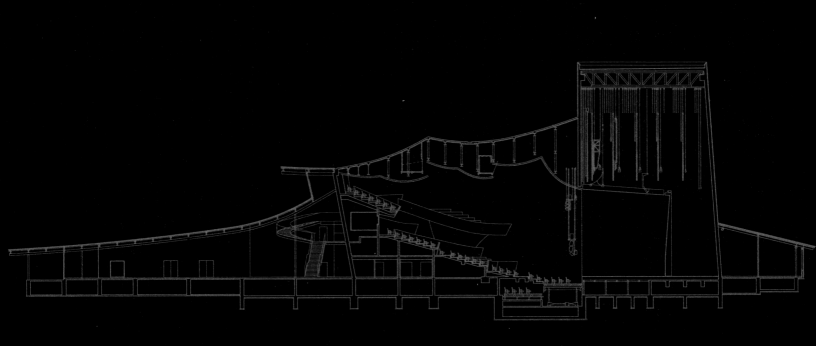

Lobby spaces are light and airy in the style of SANAA. Above: the main performance hall whose seating patterns recall to some extent the exterior of the building.

MOYAMOYA

FUMIHIKO SANO

Higashikurume, Tokyo, 2014
Area: 145 m²

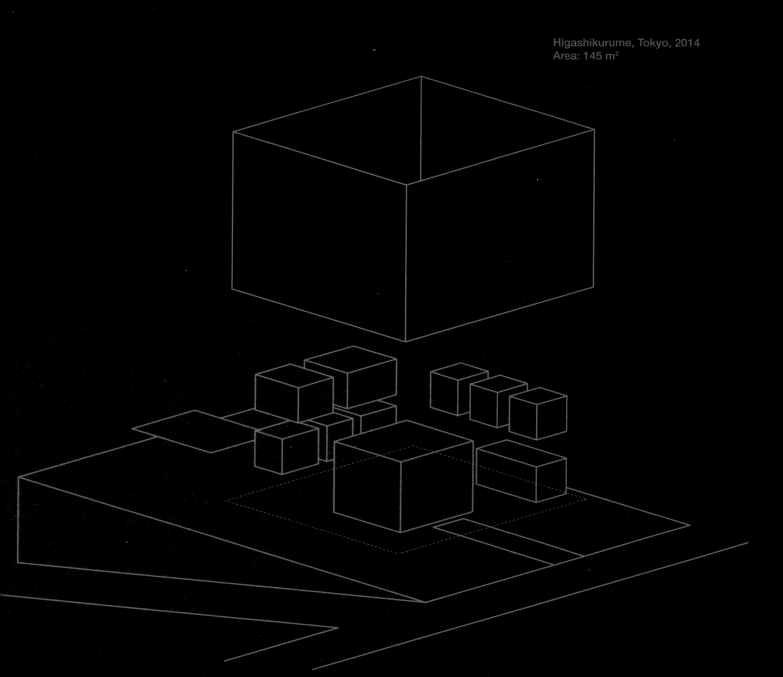

Below: *plan and section drawings show
the rigorous geometry of the design and the
allocation of interior space.*

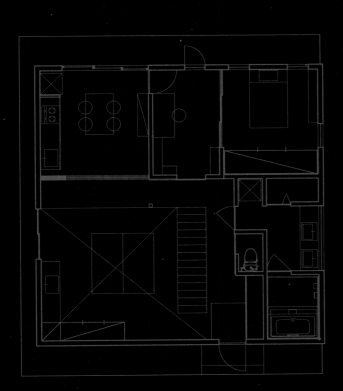

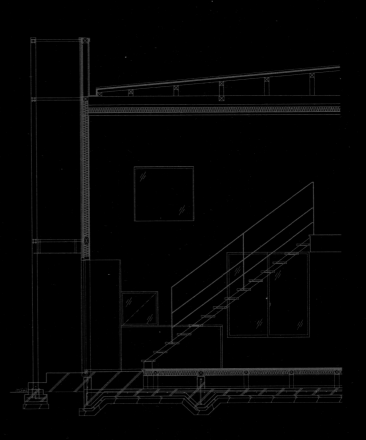

The interior of the house is finished in tones of beige (wood) and white. There is a mixture of spaces that could easily be Western or Japanese-style areas, seen opposite.

Set on a large square lot in a suburb of Tokyo, MOYAMOYA is a house and studio for a woman who dyes kimonos. Its plan also forms a square in the center of the lot. The studio is connected to a kitchen, while a bedroom and study are on the first floor. The living room and Japanese-style room are on the second floor, where there is a view of Mount Fuji. A full-height, stainless steel mesh fence surrounds the building and makes it difficult for passersby or neighbors to see inside. Fumihiko Sano emphasizes the moiré patterns that are created by the fence according to movements of the wind or the time of the day. "This is the place" he says, "where people can closely enjoy the transitions of time, seasons, and climates through the house."

Das auf einem großen quadratischen Grundstück in einem Vorort von Tokio gelegene Projekt MOYAMOYA dient einer Frau, die Kimonos färbt, als Wohnhaus und Studio. Der Grundriss des mittig auf dem Grundstück platzierten Baus ist ebenfalls quadratisch. Studio und Küche sind miteinander verbunden. Schlafzimmer und Arbeitszimmer befinden sich im ersten, das Wohnzimmer und ein Zimmer im japanischen Stil, von dem aus man den Fuji sehen kann, im zweiten Geschoss. Das Gebäude wird auf ganzer Höhe von einem feinmaschigen Edelstahlgitter umgeben, sodass Passanten und Nachbarn die Räumlichkeiten nicht einsehen können. Fumihiko Sano hebt den Moiré-Effekt hervor, den das Gitter je nach Windverhältnissen und Tageszeit in unterschiedlicher Ausprägung hervorruft. „In diesem Haus", sagt er, „können die Menschen das Vergehen der Zeit, der Jahreszeiten und Wetterverhältnisse genießen".

Construit sur une vaste parcelle carrée dans une banlieue de Tokyo, MOYAMOYA se compose d'une maison et d'un studio pour une femme qui teint des kimonos. Le plan forme un deuxième carré au centre du terrain. Le studio communique avec une cuisine, tandis que la chambre à coucher et le bureau sont situés au premier étage. Le salon et la pièce de style japonais occupent le deuxième étage qui a vue sur le mont Fuji. Une barrière protectrice en voile d'acier inoxydable recouvre le bâtiment sur toute sa hauteur et empêche les passants et les voisins de voir à l'intérieur. Fumihiko Sano souligne les effets moirés produits selon les mouvements du vent ou l'heure de la journée. « C'est un endroit, explique-t-il, où le passage du temps, des saisons et des conditions climatiques peuvent être perçues de très près dans toute la maison. »

T NOIE

KATSUTOSHI SASAKI

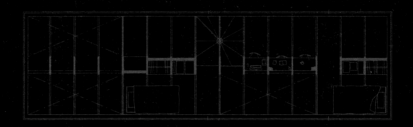

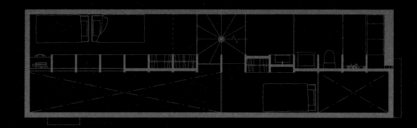

Toyota, Aichi, 2017
Area: 102 m²
Collaboration: Tatsumi Terado,
Enzo, Naoki Nakamura

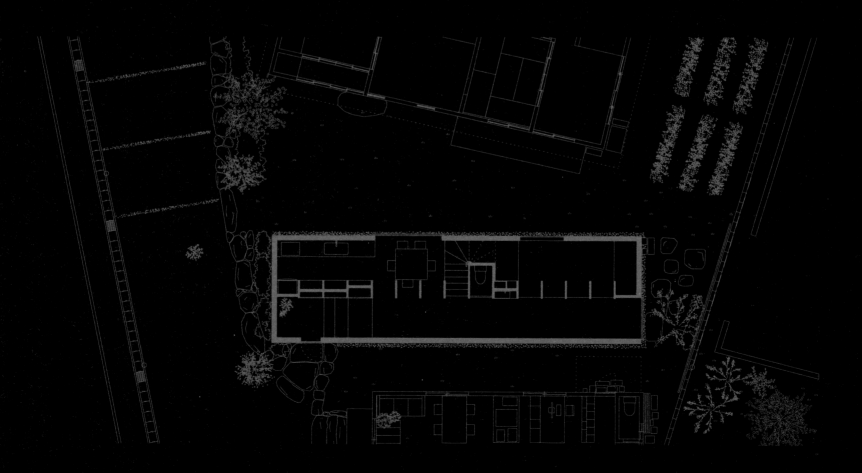

The exterior of the house is marked by vertical strips of red cedar which has aged to a uniform gray color. Glazing is limited, preserving privacy and making the structure appear to be almost monolithic.

KATSUTOSHI SASAKI was born in Toyota, Aichi, in 1976. He graduated from the Department of Architecture, Faculty of Engineering, Kindai University (Osaka, 1999). He toured 12 European countries and founded Katsutoshi Sasaki + Associates in 2008. His work includes the Ogaki House (Gifu, 2010); House in Hanekita (Okazaki, Aichi 2014); House in Yamanote (Toyota, Aichi, 2014); his own residence, T Noie (Toyota, Aichi, 2017, published here); House in Umemorizaka (Nagoya, 2018); and Uehara House (Toyota, Aichi, 2018).

KATSUTOSHI SASAKI wurde 1976 in Toyota, Aichi, geboren und studierte im Fachbereich Architektur an der Fakultät für Ingenieurwissenschaften der Kindai-Universität (Osaka, 1999). Er bereiste zwölf europäische Länder und gründete 2008 Katsutoshi Sasaki + Associates. Zu seinen Arbeiten gehören Ogaki House (Gifu, 2010), House in Hanekita (Okazaki, Aichi 2014), House in Yamanote (Toyota, Aichi, 2014), der Wohnsitz des Architekten selbst – T Noie (Toyota, Aichi, 2017, hier vorgestellt), House in Umemorizaka (Nagoya, 2018) und Uehara House (Toyota, Aichi, 2018).

KATSUTOSHI SASAKI est né à Toyota, Aichi, en 1976. Il est diplômé du département d'architecture de la faculté d'ingénierie à l'université Kindai (Osaka, 1999). Il a voyagé dans douze pays européens et a fondé Katsutoshi Sasaki + Associates en 2008. Ses réalisations comprennent la maison Ogaki (Gifu, 2010) ; une maison à Hanekita (Okazaki, Aichi, 2014) ; une maison à Yamanote (Toyota, Aichi, 2014) ; sa résidence personnelle, T Noie (Toyota, Aichi, 2017, publiée ici) ; une maison à Umemorizaka (Nagoya, 2018) et la maison Uehara (Toyota, Aichi, 2018).

*High ceilings and ample light mark interior spaces,
such as the bedroom and study areas seen above.*

Toyota, home to many of the facilities of
Toyota Motor Corporation, is located between
Shizuoka and Nagoya. It is a town of about
420 000 people. For this small house, the architect explains that he calibrated the width
from the "human perspective" and the length
and height from the "landscape perspective."
A unit size of 1.55 meters was chosen as the
"smallest common denominator" for the
house, which has a depth of 13.5 meters and
a height of eight meters. A section drawing
shows two parallel 1.55-meter areas rising up
through the house separated by a 70-centime-
ter central core. A light wooden spiral staircase winds up the interior. He says that the
narrow width of the volumes "gives the sense
of sharing the same space even when the
dwellers are actually in separate rooms." The
site area is 184 square meters, but the footprint of the structure is just 55 square meters.
Exterior cladding is in red cedar, while interior
surfaces are finished in falcata plywood.

In der zwischen Shizuoka und Nagoya gelegenen Stadt Toyota haben zahlreiche Einrichtun-
gen des gleichnamigen Automobilherstellers
ihren Sitz. Etwa 420 000 Menschen leben hier.
Die Bestimmung der Breite dieses kleinen
Hauses sei, so der Architekt, aus der „Perspektive des Menschen" erfolgt, jene der Länge
und Höhe aus der „Perspektive der Landschaft". Für das Haus, das 13,5 m tief und 8 m
hoch ist, wurde als „kleinster gemeinsamer
Nenner" eine Größeneinheit von 1,55 m gewählt. Ein Querschnitt des Hauses lässt zwei
haushohe, parallel nebeneinander verlaufende
und 1,55 m breite Teile erkennen, die durch
einen 70 cm breiten Kernbereich voneinander
getrennt sind. Eine grazile Holzwendeltreppe
erschließt das Innere. Dem Architekten zufolge
entsteht durch die geringe Breite der Volumina
„der Eindruck, denselben Raum auch dann
noch miteinander zu teilen, wenn sich die
Bewohner in unterschiedlichen Räumen auf-
halten". Das Grundstück misst 184 m², die
Grundfläche lediglich 55 m². Die Fassade ist
mit Rotzedernholz, die Innenräume sind mit
Falcata-Furnier verschalt.

La ville de Toyota, où se trouvent plusieurs
usines de Toyota Motor Corporation, est située
entre Shizuoka et Nagoya. Elle compte environ
420 000 habitants. Pour cette petite maison,
l'architecte explique qu'il a calibré la largeur
selon une « perspective humaine » et la longueur et la hauteur selon une « perspective du
paysage ». Une taille unitaire de 1,55 m a été
choisie comme « plus petit dénominateur com-
mun » pour la maison, profonde de 13,5 m
et haute de 8 m. Le schéma en coupe montre
deux parties parallèles de 1,55 m sur toute la
hauteur de la maison, séparées par un noyau
central de 70 cm. Un escalier en colimaçon en
bois léger s'enroule à l'intérieur. L'architecte
explique que l'étroitesse des volumes « donne
l'impression de partager un espace unique
même lorsque les habitants de la maison se
trouvent dans des pièces séparées ». La surface du terrain est de 184 m², mais l'empreinte
au sol de la maison ne dépasse pas 55 m². Elle
est revêtue de cèdre rouge à l'extérieur, tandis
que les finitions des surfaces intérieures sont
en contreplaqué de falcata.

The house itself is quite narrow, but an alternation
of white and wooden surfaces, as well as light
coming from different angles, creates the overall
impression of ample volumes.

SUMIDA HOKUSAI MUSEUM

KAZUYO SEJIMA

Sumida, Tokyo, 2016
Area: 3279 m²
Collaboration: Yoshitaka Tanase,
Rikiya Yamamoto, Kota Fukuhara,
Satoshi Ikeda

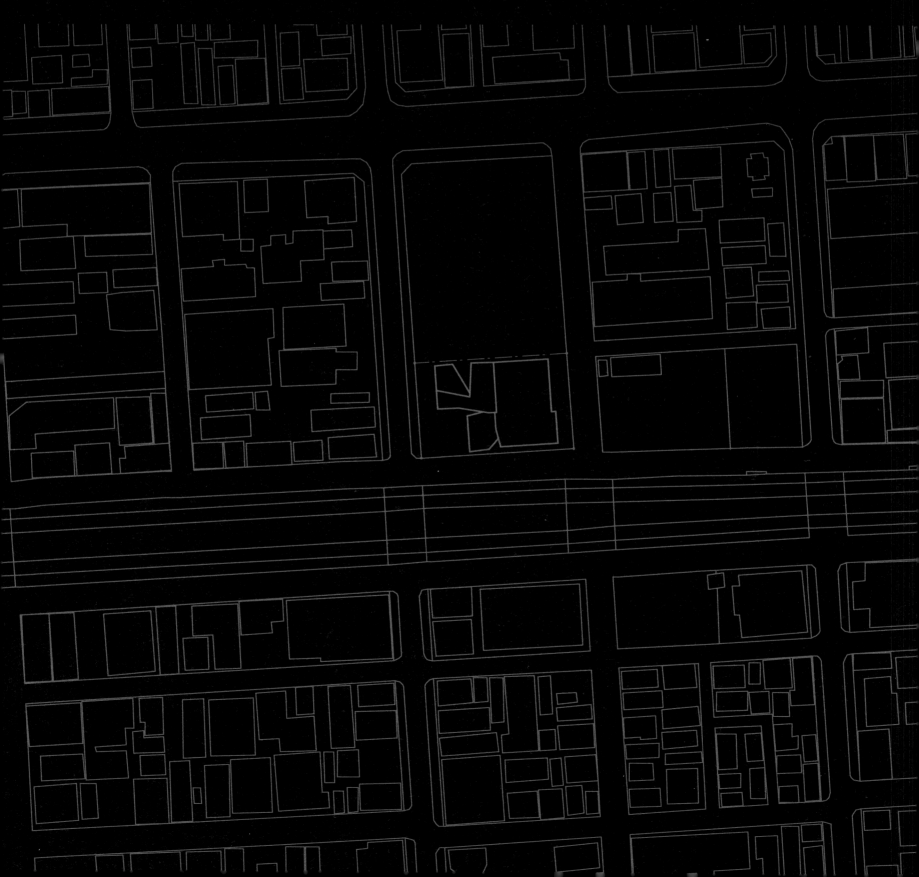

*The aluminum panel exterior of the building
and its unusual angles make it stand out instantly
from its neighborhood.*

Born in Ibaraki Prefecture in 1956, KAZUYO
SEJIMA received her M.Arch degree from
Japan Women's University in 1981 and went
on to work in the office of Toyo Ito the same
year. She established Kazuyo Sejima &
Associates in Tokyo in 1987. From the outset,
the built work of Kazuyo Sejima was widely
publicized and admired. Her Saishunkan
Seiyaku Women's Dormitory (Kumamoto,
1991) and her Pachinko Parlors in Ibaraki
Prefecture (1995) were unexpected and somehow nearly evanescent in their forms. In 1995,
she formed the 2010 Pritzker Prize-winning
practice SANAA with Ryue Nishizawa. Both
partners have maintained their own offices
since creating SANAA. Some of the work she
has completed separate from SANAA includes
the Okurayama Apartments (Kanagawa, 2008)
and the Sumida Hokusai Museum (Sumida,
Tokyo, 2016, published here). She has also
designed new mirrored express trains for
Seibu Railway (2019).

KAZUYO SEJIMA wurde 1956 in der Präfektur
Ibaraki geboren und beendete 1981 ihr Studium
an der Japanischen Frauenuniversität mit
einem M.Arch. Noch im selben Jahr nahm sie
ihre Arbeit bei Toyo Ito auf. Im Jahr 1987 gründete sie in Tokio ihr Büro Kazuyo Sejima &
Associates. Kazuyo Sejimas Architekturpro-
jekte erfuhren von Anfang an große Bewunde-
rung und wurden weit verbreitet. Ihr Frauen-
wohnheim Saishunkan Seiyaku (Kumamoto,
1991) und die Pachinko Parlors in der Präfektur
Ibaraki (1995) überraschten die Öffentlichkeit
und wirkten in formaler Hinsicht geradezu
ephemer. 1995 gründete sie zusammen mit
Ryue Nishizawa das 2010 mit dem Pritzker-
Preis ausgezeichnete Büro SANAA. Beide
gaben ihre eigenen Büros trotz der Gründung
von SANAA nicht auf. Zu den Projekten,
die Kazuyo Sejima unabhängig von SANAA
realisiert hat, gehören die Okurayama Apartments (Kanagawa, 2008) und das Hokusai-
Museum in Sumida (Sumida, Tokio, 2016, hier
vorgestellt). Für die Eisenbahngesellschaft
Seibu Testsudo hat Sejima ein neues Express-
zug-Modell entworfen (2019).

Née dans la préfecture d'Ibaraki en 1956,
KAZUYO SEJIMA obtient son M.Arch de l'université féminine du Japon en 1981 et est engagée par Toyo Ito la même année. Elle crée
l'agence Kazuyo Sejima & Associates à Tokyo
en 1987. Dès le départ, ses réalisations sont
très largement publiées et admirées. Son foyer
pour femmes Saishunkan Seiyaku (Kumamoto,
1991) et ses salles de pachinko dans la préfecture d'Ibaraki (1995) ont surpris par leurs formes
presque évanescentes. En 1995, elle fonde avec
Ryue Nishizawa l'agence SANAA qui gagnera
le prix Pritzker en 2010. Les deux partenaires
ont conservé leurs propres agences, en plus de
SANAA. Parmi les projets qu'elle a réalisés sans
SANAA figurent les appartements Okurayama
(Kanagawa, 2008) et le musée Hokusai de
Sumida (Sumida, Tokyo, 2016, publié ici). Elle
a aussi conçu les nouveaux trains express en
miroirs de Seibu Railway (2019).

Above: *looking up near the triangular entrance.*

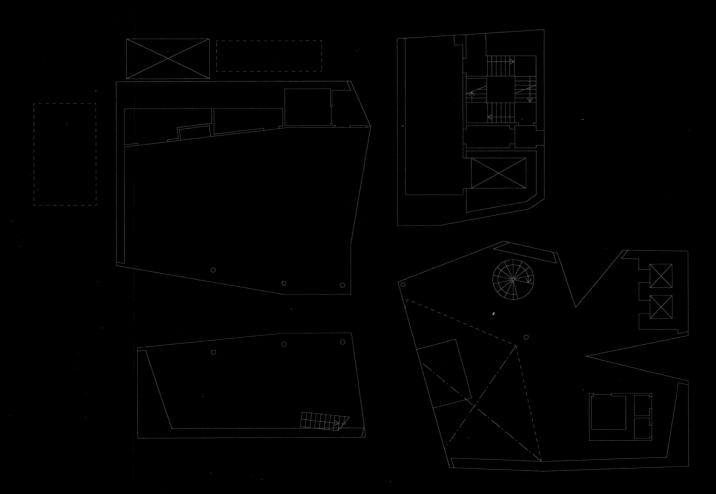

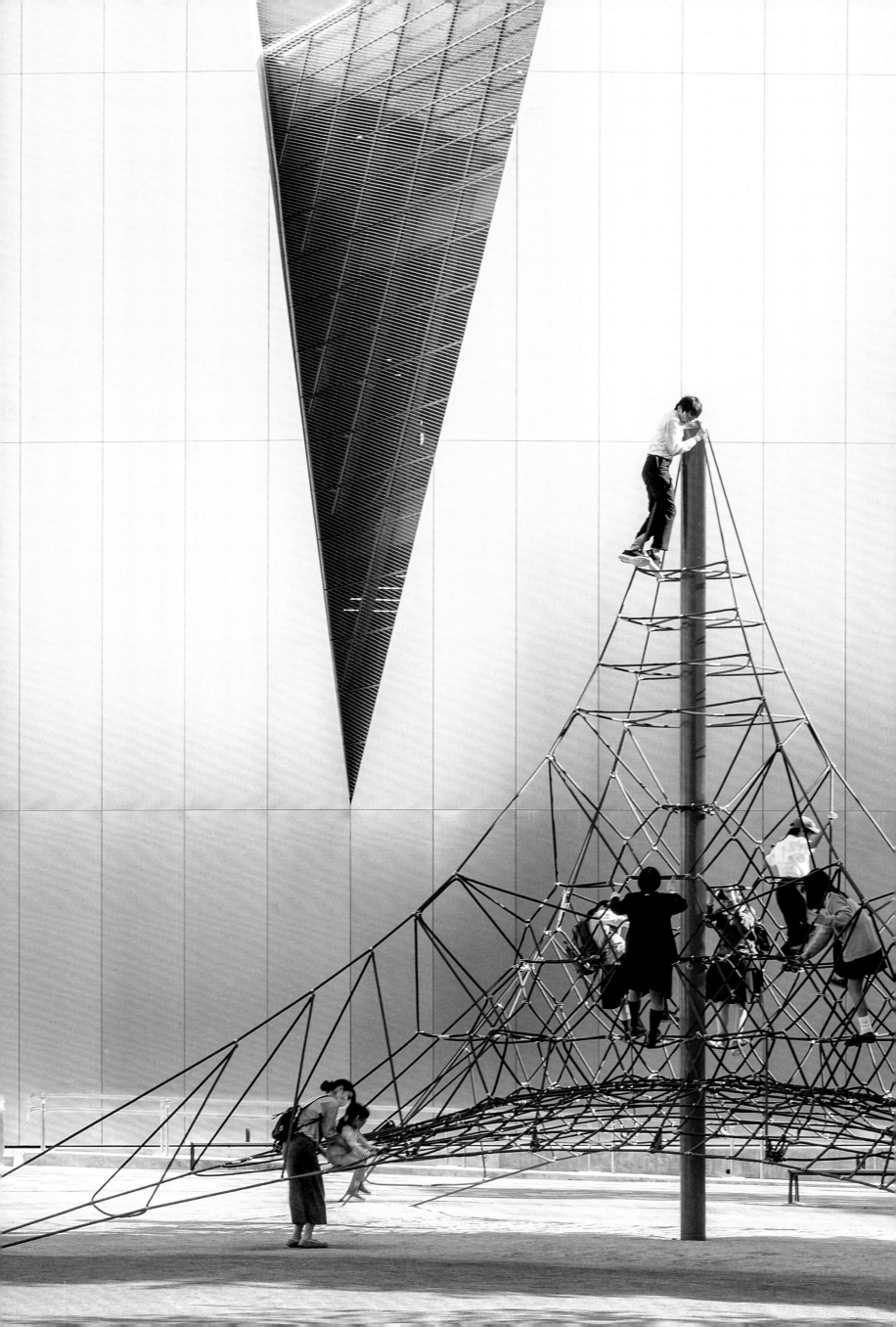

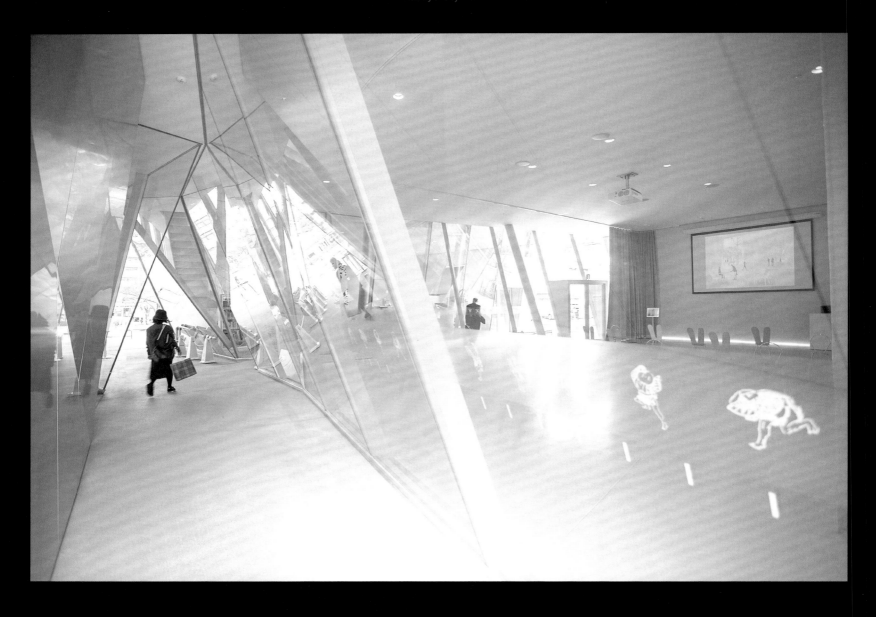

In the entrance area of the Museum, the architect's signature evanescent white volumes greet visitors.

This new museum for the work of the *ukiyo-e* painter and printmaker Katsushika Hokusai (1760–1849) is located in a park in the Sumida ward of Tokyo, which is actually in Ryogoku, the birthplace of the artist. Sejima broke her design into small volumes that come together at certain levels in order to fit into the scale of the neighborhood. The display of Hokusai's work requires low light so there are limited openings to the exterior in this design, but the architect has introduced slits between the volumes to preserve a relationship with the exterior. The plan consists of regular and special exhibition spaces, storage areas, a multi-purpose hall, a cafè, and a library. According to the architect: "The friendly scenery of surrounding townscape [is reflected in] onto the electro-polished aluminum façade of the building." Built with glass, extrusion-molded cement board, expanded aluminum, and aluminum panel, the construction cost of the museum was $26 322 380.

Dieses Museum, in dem Werke des *ukiyo-e*-Malers und Grafikers Katsushika Hokusai (1760–1849) ausgestellt werden, ist von Bäumen umgeben und befindet sich im Tokioter Bezirk Sumida, genauer in Ryogoku, dem Geburtsort des Künstlers. Damit sich der Neubau gut in die städtebaulichen Verhältnisse einfügt, hat Sejima ihren Entwurf in kleinere Volumina unterteilt, die auf einigen Ebenen miteinander verbunden sind. Da Hokusais Werke in gedämpftem Licht präsentiert werden, ist die Fassade weitgehend geschlossen. Schlitzartige Öffnungen zwischen den einzelnen Volumen wahren den Bezug nach außen. Das Museum verfügt über Flächen für Dauer- und Sonderausstellungen, Lagerräume, eine Mehrzweckhalle, eine Bibliothek und ein Café. Die Architektin: „Das freundliche Stadtbild spiegelt sich in der elektropolierten Aluminiumfassade des Gebäudes wider." Die Kosten für den Bau des Museums, bei dem Glas, stranggepresste Zementplatten, Aluminiumstreckmetall und Aluminiumplatten zum Einsatz kamen, beliefen sich auf 26 322 380 Dollar.

Ce nouveau musée destiné à l'œuvre du peintre et graveur *ukiyo-e* Katsushika Hokusai (1760–1849) est situé dans un parc du quartier de Sumida, à Tokyo, plus exactement à Ryogoku, lieu de naissance de l'artiste. Sejima a brisé l'ensemble en plusieurs petits volumes qui se rejoignent à certains niveaux pour s'adapter à l'échelle des constructions voisines. Les œuvres d'Hokusai ont besoin de peu de lumière, de sorte que les ouvertures sont limitées, mais l'architecte a conçu des fentes entre les différents volumes afin de préserver un lien avec l'extérieur. L'ensemble se compose d'espaces d'exposition permanentes et spéciales, de magasins, d'un hall polyvalent, d'un café et d'une bibliothèque. Pour l'architecte, « le décor accueillant du paysage urbain environnant (se reflète) dans la façade en aluminium électropoli du bâtiment ». Construit en verre, panneaux de ciment moulés par extrusion, aluminium expansé et panneaux d'aluminium, le musée a coûté 26 322 380 dollars.

Brighter areas given to showing elements
of the architecture (above) are contrasted with
the dark spaces (with low natural light) required
for the exhibition of original prints.

ODAWARA ART FOUNDATION: ENOURA OBSERVATORY

HIROSHI SUGIMOTO

Enoura, Odawara, Kanagawa, 2017
Area: 789 m²
Collaboration: Hiroshi Sugimoto (Concept Design), New Material Research Laboratory (Preliminary Design), Tomoyuki Sakakida, Yosai Isozaki (Project Architects)

HIROSHI SUGIMOTO was born in Tokyo in 1948, attended Saint Paul's University in Tokyo (1966–70), then studied photography at the ArtCenter College of Design in Los Angeles, receiving a B.F.A. in 1972. He moved to New York in 1974. Sugimoto won the 2009 Praemium Imperiale Award. A number of photographic series have characterized his work thus far: his pictures taken of *Dioramas* and *Wax Museums* (both since 1976); *Theaters* (since 1978); *Seascapes* (since 1980); images of *Sanjusangendo, Hall of Thirty-Three Bays* (sculptures of the Buddhist temple Sanjusangendo, 1995); and *Architecture* (since 1997). His large, usually black-and-white photos have been presented in numerous art galleries, like White Cube in London and the Sonnabend Gallery in New York, and in one-man exhibitions at numerous major museums. Hiroshi Sugimoto has shown a consistent interest in architecture, first in his photography, but also in actual works of architecture, such as his Go'O Shrine (Naoshima, 2002); Colors of Shadow (Shirogane Apartment, Tokyo, 2006); Izu Photo Museum (Mishima, Shizuoka, 2009); Glass Teahouse Mondrian (Venice, Italy, 2014); Odawara Art Foundation: Enoura Observatory (Enoura, Odawara, Kanagawa, 2017, published here); and the Hirshhorn Museum Lobby (Washington, D.C., USA, 2018).

HIROSHI SUGIMOTO wurde 1948 in Tokio geboren, studierte dort zunächst an der Saint-Paul's-Universität (Tokio, 1966–1970) und anschließend am ArtCenter College of Design in Los Angeles, wo er 1972 seinen B.F.A. in Fotografie machte. Er zog 1974 nach New York. Sugimoto gewann 2009 den Praemium Imperiale. Sein bisheriges Schaffen wird durch eine Reihe von Fotoserien geprägt: *Dioramas* und *Wax Museums* (beide ab 1976), *Theater* (ab 1978), *Seascapes* (ab 1980), *Sanjusangendo, Hall of Thirty-Three Bays* (Skulpturen des buddhistischen Sanjusangendo-Tempels, 1995) sowie *Architecture* (seit 1997). Die großformatigen Fotografien sind zumeist in Schwarzweiß gehalten und wurden in zahlreichen Galerien wie der White Cube in London und der Sonnabend Gallery in New York sowie im Rahmen von Einzelausstellungen in großen Museen präsentiert. Hiroshi Sugimoto ist seit jeher an Architektur interessiert, was zunächst in seinen fotografischen, schließlich aber auch in seinen architektonischen Arbeiten zum Ausdruck kam. Zu Letzteren gehören der Go'O-Schrein (Naoshima, 2002), Colors of Shadow (eine Wohnung in Shirogane, Tokio, 2006), das Izu-Fotomuseum (Mishima, Shizuoka, 2009), das gläserne Teehaus Mondrian (Venedig, 2014), die Kunststiftung Odawara – Aussichtspunkt Enoura (Enoura, Odawara, Kanagawa, 2017, hier vorgestellt) und eine Lobby für das Hirshhorn Museum (Washington, D.C., 2018).

HIROSHI SUGIMOTO est né à Tokyo en 1948. Il a suivi les cours de l'université de Saint-Paul à Tokyo (Tokyo, 1966–70) avant de faire des études de photographie à l'ArtCenter College of Design de Los Angeles et d'obtenir un BFA en 1972. Il s'installe à New York en 1974. Sugimoto a été en 2009 lauréat du Praemium Imperiale. Jusqu'à présent, son œuvre est surtout dominée par plusieurs séries photographiques : *Dioramas* et *Wax Museums* (depuis 1976) ; *Theaters* (depuis 1978) ; *Seascapes* (depuis 1980) ; *Sanjusangendo, Pavillon des trente-trois intervalles* (statues du temple bouddhiste du Sanjusangendo, 1995) et *Architecture* (depuis 1997). Ses photos grand format généralement en noir et blanc ont été présentées dans de nombreuses galeries, parmi lesquelles White Cube à Londres et Sonnabend Gallery à New York, et ont fait l'objet d'expositions personnelles dans bon nombre de grands musées. Hiroshi Sugimoto s'est toujours intéressé à l'architecture, d'abord dans ses photographies, mais aussi dans des réalisations concrètes, notamment le sanctuaire Go'O (Naoshima, 2002) ; Colors of Shadow (Shirogane Apartment, Tokyo, 2006) ; le musée de la Photo d'Izu (Mishima, Shizuoka, 2009) ; la maison de thé en verre Mondrian (Venise, 2014) ; la Fondation d'art Odawara : observatoire d'Enoura (Enoura, Odawara, Kanagawa, 2017, publié ici) et le hall du musée Hirshhorn (Washington, D.C., 2018).

The long main volume of the observatory is finished
in a subtle variety of stones, wood, and glazing.
Pictures by Hiroshi Sugimoto are hung inside the
space seen above and on the opposite page.

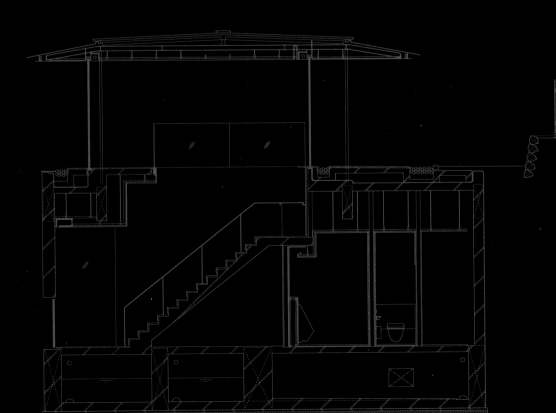

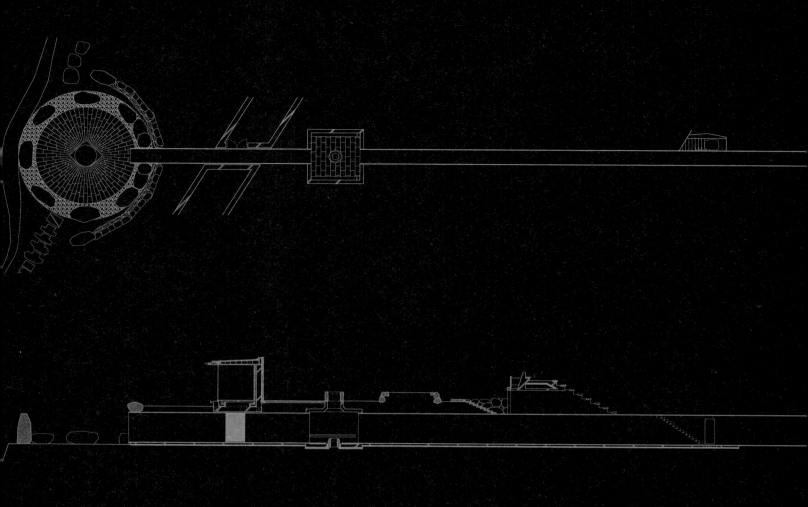

*Sugimoto employs a surprising mixture of textured
surfaces and very old stones, always placed in
a seemingly symbolic fashion.*

The ODAWARA ART FOUNDATION was
established by Hiroshi Sugimoto "with the aim
of contributing to further enhancing Japanese
culture from a global perspective by promoting
the (transmission of) traditional performing
arts to future generations and development
of contemporary art." This complex includes
a reception building, teahouse, several gates,
and an optical glass stage inserted into a
hilly site near the town of Nebukawa, looking
down on the Pacific. The main structure is
a 100-meter-long stone and glass gallery
building where seascape photos by Sugimoto
are hung. Like a Corten-steel tunnel, the gallery is placed along the axis of the rising sun
on the day of the summer solstice. Sugimoto,
convinced of the durability of his design,
states: "The buildings and the landscape
integrate with the earth and are expected to
become future ruins that may continue to
exist after 10 000 years."

Die KUNSTSTIFTUNG ODAWARA wurde von
Hiroshi Sugimoto gegründet. Sie soll „die japanische Kultur stärken – durch die Vermittlung
traditioneller darstellender Kunst an zukünftige
Generationen und durch die Förderung zeitgenössischer Kunst". Der Komplex mit Blick
auf den Pazifik liegt auf bergigem Terrain
unweit der Stadt Nebukawa und umfasst ein
Empfangsgebäude, ein Teehaus, mehrere
Tore und eine Bühne aus optischem Glas.
Im Hauptgebäude, einer 100 m langen Galerie
aus Stein und Glas, sind Meeresfotografien
von Sugimoto ausgestellt. Die Galerie ist,
so wie der Tunnel aus Corten-Stahl, entsprechend dem Sonnenlauf der Sommersonnen-
wende ausgerichtet. Sugimoto ist von der
Langlebigkeit seines Entwurfs überzeugt und
erklärt: „Das Gebäude ist eins mit der Erde
und wird in 10 000 Jahren als Ruine vielleicht
noch immer existieren."

La FONDATION D'ART ODAWARA a été
créée par Hiroshi Sugimoto « dans le but de
contribuer à développer la culture japonaise
dans une perspective mondiale par la promo-
tion (de la transmission) des arts du spectacle
traditionnels auprès des générations futures
et le développement de l'art contemporain ».
Le complexe comprend un bâtiment de réception, une maison de thé, plusieurs portes et
une scène en verre optique intégrés à un terrain
vallonné près de la ville de Nebukawa qui
domine le Pacifique. La principale structure est
une galerie de verre et de pierre longue de
100 m où sont accrochées des photos marines
de Sugimoto. Comme le tunnel en acier Corten,
elle est placée dans l'axe du soleil levant le
jour du solstice d'été. Sugimoto, convaincu
de la durabilité de son projet, déclare : « Les
bâtiments et le paysage sont intégrés à la terre
et sont destinés à devenir de futures ruines
qui existeront peut-être encore dans plus de
10 000 ans. »

JIKKA

ISSEI SUMA

Ike, Ito, Shizuoka, 2015
Area: 100 m²
Collaboration: Nawaken-jm
(Structural Engineer)

The volumes of the house are linked together to form what looks like a kind of organic community.

ISSEI SUMA was born in Tokyo in 1976. He received a B.A. in Environmental Information and Media Design from Keio University (Tokyo, 1999), and an M.Arch degree from Columbia University GSAPP (New York, 2002). He worked for the Rockwell Group (2004–07) and Voorsanger Architects (2007–10), both in New York, before founding SUMA in 2011 in Tokyo, and A Nomad Sub, Inc. in 2018. His work includes the Mika Gallery (renovation, New York, USA, 2004); House in Kamakura (Kamakura, 2012); Jikka (Hara, Ike, Shizuoka, 2015, published here); and House in Hakusan (Hakusan, Ishikawa, 2019). Ongoing work includes an elementary school for the Jinseki International School (Hiroshima, 2019).

ISSEI SUMA wurde 1976 in Tokio geboren und machte seinen B.A. in Umweltinformatik und Mediengestaltung an der Keio-Universität (Tokio, 1999) und seinen M.Arch an der Columbia University GSAPP (New York, 2002). Er arbeitete für die Rockwell Group (2004–2007) und Voorsanger Architects (2007–2010, beide in New York), bevor er 2011 in Tokio SUMA und 2018 A Nomad Sub, Inc. gründete. Zu seinen Projekten gehören ein Umbau der Mika Gallery (New York, 2004), House in Kamakura (Kamakura, 2012), Jikka (Hara, Ike, Shizuoka, 2015, hier vorgestellt) sowie House in Hakusan (Hakusan, Ishikawa, 2019). Zu seinen laufenden Projekten gehört unter anderem ein Grundschulgebäude für die Jinseki International School (Hiroshima, 2019).

ISSEI SUMA est né à Tokyo en 1976. Il possède un BA en information de l'environnement et design des médias de l'université Keio (Tokyo, 1999) et un M.Arch de la GSAPP de l'université Columbia (New York, 2002). Il a travaillé à New York pour Rockwell Group (2004–07) et Voorsanger Architects (2007–10), avant de fonder SUMA en 2011 à Tokyo et A Nomad Sub, Inc. en 2018. Ses réalisations comprennent la galerie Mika (rénovation, New York, 2004) ; une maison à Kamakura (Kamakura, 2012) ; Jikka (Hara, Ike, Shizuoka, 2015, publié ici) et une maison à Hakusan (Hakusan, Ishikawa, 2019). Parmi ses projets en cours figurent une école élémentaire pour le cours international Jinseki (Hiroshima, 2019).

Photos and drawings show how the architect combines shapes that might well be inspired by dwellings of the distant past with a clear sense of modernity and openness. Interiors (following double page) are decidedly modern.

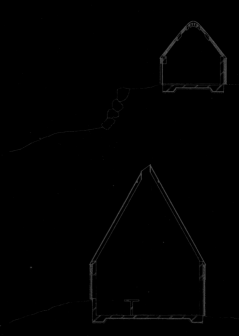

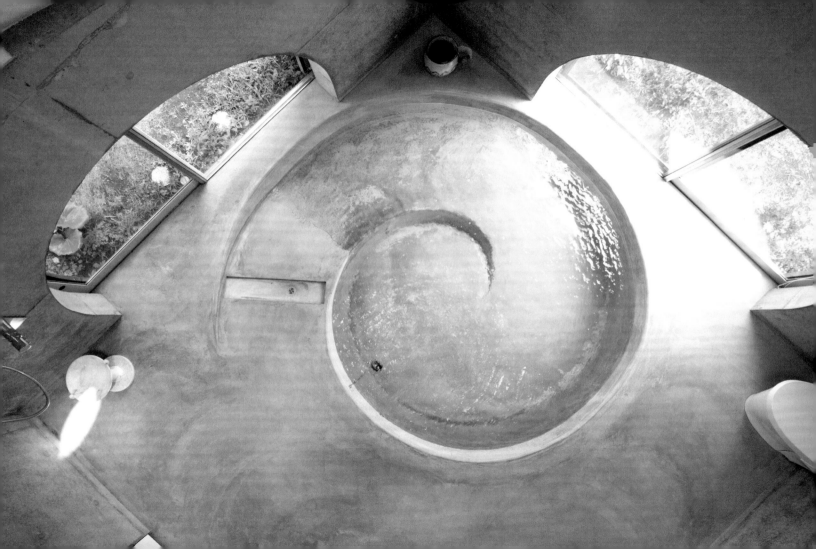

ISHIHARA DENTAL CLINIC

TAKASHI SUO

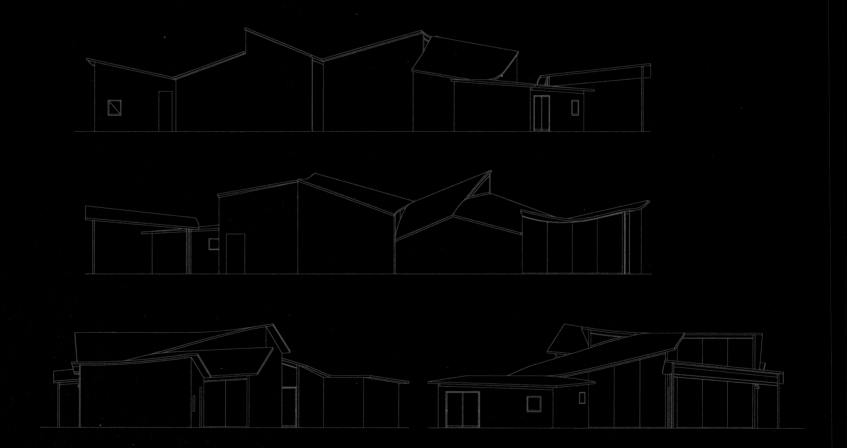

Okayama, 2017
Area: 188 m²
Collaboration: Takuya Sone (SUO),
Yoshiyuki Hiraiwa (HSC, Structural Architect),
Eiji Sato (ESA, Mechanical Equipment Design)

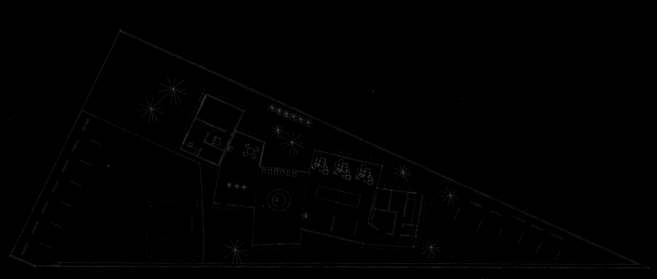

TAKASHI SUO was born in Japan in 1980 and graduated from Keio University with an M.Arch (Tokyo, 2006). After completing his studies, he worked in the office of Kazuyo Sejima & Associates, and SANAA (Tokyo). He established his own firm, SUO, in 2016. His projects include S-House Museum (Okayama, 2016); Chim↑Pom Studio (Tokyo, 2017); Kikui House (Okayama 2019); the Ishihara Dental Clinic (Okayama, 2017, published here); and Yashima Mountain Top Park (Kagawa, 2016–).

TAKASHI SUO wurde 1980 in Japan geboren und erhielt seinen M.Arch von der Keio-Universität (Tokio, 2006). Nach Ende des Studiums arbeitete er für Kazuyo Sejima & Associates und für SANAA. 2016 gründete er seine eigene Firma SUO. Zu seinen Projekten gehören das S-House Museum (Okayama, 2016), Chim↑Pom Studio (Tokio, 2017), Kikui House (Okayama 2019), die Zahnarztpraxis Ishihara (Okayama, 2017, hier vorgestellt) und der Yashima Mountain Top Park (Kagawa, 2016–).

TAKASHI SUO est né au Japon en 1980 et possède un M.Arch de l'université Keio (Tokyo, 2006). Après ses études, il a travaillé dans l'agence de Kazuyo Sejima & Associates et à SANAA (Tokyo). Il a créé sa société, SUO, en 2016. Ses projets comprennent le musée S-House (Okayama, 2016) ; le studio Chim↑Pom (Tokyo, 2017) ; la maison Kikui (Okayama, 2019) ; la clinique dentaire d'Ishihara (Okayama, 2017, publiée ici) et le parc de la montagne de Yashima (Kagawa, 2016–).

Despite its small site between a road and a parking
lot, the building boasts a great variety of angles
and forms, giving a sense of contemporary design
to an otherwise rather banal location.

Wooden walls and the angled ceilings echo the exterior forms of the building. Light-colored wood furnishings and ample filtered natural light give a welcoming feeling to the space.

This small DENTAL CLINIC is located in a suburb of the city of Okayama and was built on a narrow triangular lot near a main road. The client requested a treatment room with extra space that would allow for a future extension, and generally wanted a building that would be very flexible. The positioning of the spaces in the clinic was carefully thought out to make the best possible use of the site. The rooms of the clinic are connected to each other but shifted slightly, to ensure privacy between them. They also face some small gardens. "We carefully designed different size volumes for each room and connected them to create a sequence like the surrounding houses. When you look at the building itself, it seems to be the result of inorganic and chaotic planning, but it is, in fact, in harmony with the environment," says the architect. The steel and wood structure with exterior cladding made of pressed and anodized corrugated sheet aluminum and plywood (walls, ceilings) and linoleum (floors) inside, was built for approximately €480 000. The aluminum was chosen to harmonize the building with neighboring factories.

Diese ZAHNARZTPRAXIS befindet sich in einem Vorort der Stadt Okayama und wurde an einer Hauptstraße auf ein schmalen dreieckigen Grundstück errichtet. Der Auftraggeber wünschte sich einen Behandlungszimmer sowie räumliche Reserven, um die Praxis gegebenenfalls zu erweitern, ihm war grundsätzlich an einem flexiblen Gebäude gelegen. Um die Grundstücksfläche möglichst effizient zu nutzen, wurde die Raumanordnung sorgfältig durchdacht. Die verschiedenen Räume der Praxis sind miteinander verbunden und leicht versetzt angelegt, um Privatsphäre zu gewährleisten. Die Fenster gehen auf einen kleinen Garten hinaus. „Wir waren darauf bedacht, verschieden große Raumvolumen so aneinanderzufügen, dass sie das umliegende Stadtbild aufgreifen. Das Gebäude selbst scheint das Resultat eines unorganischen und chaotischen Planungsprozesses zu sein, tatsächlich aber steht es im Einklang mit seiner Umgebung", so der Architekt. Die Stahl- und Holzkonstruktion hat etwa 480 000 Euro gekostet, wurde mit gepresstem Wellblech sowie mit Aluminiumplatten verschalt und verfügt im Inneren über Wände und Decken aus Furnierholz sowie Linoleumböden. Das Aluminium lässt, damit

Cette petite CLINIQUE DENTAIRE située dans un faubourg de la ville d'Okayama a été construite sur une étroite parcelle triangulaire près d'une route principale. Le client avait demandé une salle de soins dotée d'un espace supplémentaire pour une future extension et, en général, un bâtiment très modulable. La disposition des différentes parties de la clinique a été soigneusement pensée afin de tirer le meilleur parti possible du site. Les pièces communiquent, mais sont légèrement décalées l'une par rapport à l'autre pour garantir l'intimité de chacune. Elles font aussi face à de petits jardins. « Nous avons soigneusement conçu des volumes différents pour chaque pièce et les avons reliés afin de créer une suite qui ressemble aux maisons environnantes. En regardant le bâtiment, on a l'impression de voir le résultat d'un plan sans ordre ni logique, mais en fait, il est parfaitement en harmonie avec le voisinage », explique l'architecte. La structure de bois et d'acier au revêtement extérieur en feuilles d'aluminium pressé ondulé ou anodisé ondulé, aux murs et plafonds en contreplaqué et aux sols en linoléum a été construite pour 480 000 euros environ. Le choix de l'aluminium s'explique par des raisons d'harmonie avec les

TODOROKI
HOUSE IN VALLEY

TSUYOSHI TANE

Setagaya, Tokyo, 2018
Area: 188 m²

In a city where views of greenery are rare, this residence offers high ceilings and urban forest views.

Born in 1979, TSUYOSHI TANE is a Japanese architect based in Paris. He created Atelier Tsuyoshi Tane Architects in 2017, after co-founding Dorell.Gotmeh.Tane / Architects in 2006, following work experience in London, Denmark, and Japan. He was born in Tokyo in 1979 and studied at Hokkaido Tokai University and at the Royal Danish Academy of Fine Arts (Copenhagen). He worked in the office of Henning Larsen (Copenhagen) and David Adjaye (London), before opening his Paris office. Aside from the Todoroki House in Valley (Setagaya, Tokyo, 2018), and the Hirosaki Museum of Contemporary Art (Hirosaki, Aomori, 2017–20), both published here, he has designed House for Oiso (Oiso, 2015); Machiya Hotel (Kyoto, 2016); the Estonian National Museum (Dorell.Gotmeh.Tane/Architects, Tartu, Estonia, 2016); Restaurant Maison (Paris, France, 2018); and the department store NewWoMan (Yokohama, 2020).

TSUYOSHI TANE ist ein japanischer Architekt mit Sitz in Paris. Nach Praktika in London, Dänemark und Japan war er 2006 Mitbegründer der Firma Dorell.Gotmeh.Tane / Architects. 2017 gründete er das Atelier Tsuyoshi Tane Architects. Tane wurde 1979 in Tokio geboren und studierte an der Tokai-Universität in Hokkaido sowie an der Königlich Dänischen Kunstakademie (Kopenhagen). Er arbeitete in den Büros von Henning Larsen (Kopenhagen) und David Adjaye (London), bevor er sein Pariser Büro eröffnete. Neben Todoroki House in Valley (Setagaya, Tokio, 2018) und dem Hirosaki Museum of Contemporary Art (Hirosaki, Aomori, 2017–20, beide hier vorgestellt) entwarf er auch das House for Oiso (Oiso, 2015), das Machiya Hotel (Kyoto, 2016), das Estonian National Museum (Dorell.Gotmeh. Tane/Architects, Tartu, 2016), das Restaurant Maison (Paris, 2018) und das Kaufhaus NewWoMan (Yokohama, 2020).

TSUYOSHI TANE est un architecte japonais basé à Paris. Il a fondé Atelier Tsuyoshi Tane Architects en 2017, après avoir participé à la fondation de Dorell.Gotmeh.Tane/Architects en 2006 à la suite d'expériences professionnelles à Londres, au Danemark et au Japon. Il est né à Tokyo en 1979 et a fait ses études à l'université Tokai de Hokkaido et à l'Académie royale danoise des beaux-arts (Copenhague). Il a travaillé dans les agences de Henning Larsen (Copenhague) et David Adjaye (Londres), avant d'ouvrir la sienne à Paris. Outre la maison dans la vallée de Todoroki (Setagaya, Tokyo, 2018) et le Hirosaki Museum of Contemporary Art (Hirosaki, Aomori, 2017–2020), publiés ici, il a conçu une maison à Oiso (Oiso, 2015) ; le Musée national estonien (Dorell.Gotmeh.Tane/Architectes, Tartu, Estonie, 2016) ; l'hôtel Machiya (Kyoto, 2016) ; le restaurant Maison (Paris, 2018) et le grand magasin NewWoMan (Yokohama, 2020).

Wood cladding and, in the bedroom above, wooden floors create comfortable, inviting spaces with numerous elements of built-in wooden furniture.

HIROSAKI MUSEUM OF CONTEMPORARY ART

TSUYOSHI TANE

Hirosaki, Aomori, 2017–20
Area: 3089 m² (museum),
498 m² (café and shop)
Collaboration: NTT Facilities Inc.,
Obayashi Corporation,
P.T. Morimura & Associates, Ltd.,
N&A Inc., Starts Corporation Inc.,
Minami Kensetsu, Yasuhirokaneda
(Structural Engineer), Izumi Okayasu
(Lighting Design), Nishimura-Gumi

The exterior walls of the former brewery buildings were stripped of coatings and restored, while volumes, such as the room at the entrance (opposite bottom) seen here, have some added brick and concrete elements, together with modern lighting.

At the upper level, the wooden rafters were
restored and had lighting installed. Wooden floors
(above), or a stairwell (opposite), blend well
with the brick surfaces, while other exhibition
areas (below) have white walls.

Interior volumes are varied both in their size and in the ways in which they are treated. The architect aimed to create a link between the past of the buildings and their present, now devoted to art instead of sake brewing.

Hirosaki is a city of about 170 000 people located in the northern Prefecture of Aomori, known for its production of apples. The museum designed by Tsuyoshi Tane opened on July 11, 2020. Brick warehouses were built in the area in the early 20th century for sake breweries. Many were then converted to produce apple cider and later became warehouses. Tane obtained the right to renovate one of these breweries, founded by Tosuke Fukushima, into a museum through a PFI competition organized by Hirosaki City in 2017. Unusual because he is based in Paris, Tsuyoshi Tane thus received his first museum commission in his native country. Plaster applied over the years was removed to reveal the original brick structure, replacing bricks as required. The intervention of the architect also concerned the required seismic upgrading and the addition of a titanium roof that he calls "Cider Gold" for its exterior coloring, with a diagonal roofing technique inspired by traditional designs. Non-combustible wood was employed in the structure as well. An effort was made to have experimental artworks interacting with the flexible design of the new warehouse museum was made. There are five exhibition galleries (one 15 meters high), three studios, and a museum shop and café. Both in terms of architectural design and function, the Hirosaki MOCA aims to create a viable link between

Hirosaki ist eine Stadt mit etwa 170 000 Einwohnern in der nördlichen Präfektur Aomori, die für ihre Apfelproduktion bekannt ist. Das von Tane entworfene Museum wurde am 11. Juli 2020 eröffnet. Anfang des 20. Jahrhunderts wurden in der Gegend Sake-Brauereien aus Backstein errichtet, die größtenteils auf die Produktion von Apfelwein umstellten und später zu Lagerhäusern wurden. Tane erhielt die Möglichkeit, eine dieser Brauereien zu einem Museum umzugestalten. Tane ist in Paris ansässig und erhielt zum ersten Mal einen Museumsauftrag in seinem Herkunftsland. Der im Laufe der Jahre aufgebrachte Putz wurde entfernt, um die ursprüngliche Ziegelstruktur freizulegen, wo nötig, wurden Ziegel ersetzt. Der Architekt musste zudem für die seismische Ertüchtigung des Gebäudes sorgen und entwarf ein Titandach, das er wegen seiner Farbgebung „Cider Gold" nennt. Das Dach wurde mit einer diagonalen Technik eingedeckt, die von traditionellen Entwürfen inspiriert ist. Feuerfestes Holz wurde ebenfalls verbaut. Das Museum ist darum bemüht, experimentelle Kunstwerke mit dem flexiblen Entwurf interagieren zu lassen. Es verfügt über fünf Ausstellungsräume (einer davon 15 m hoch), drei Ateliers und einen Museumsshop mit Café. Sowohl in Bezug auf den architektonischen Entwurf als auch in seiner Funktion zielt das Hirosaki MOCA darauf ab, eine trag-

Hirosaki est une ville d'environ 170 000 habitants, dans la préfecture nord d'Aomori, réputée pour sa production de pommes. Le musée conçu par Tane a ouvert le 11 juillet 2020. Des entrepôts en briques avaient été construits dans la région au début du XXᵉ siècle pour les brasseries de saké, dont beaucoup avaient ensuite été converties à la production de cidre de pomme, avant de devenir des entrepôts. Tane a obtenu le droit de rénover l'une de ces brasseries, fondée par Tosuke Fukushima, pour en faire un musée, grâce à un concours d'Initiative de financement public organisé par la ville d'Hirosaki en 2017. Étonnamment, car il était installé à Paris, Tane a ainsi reçu sa première commande de musée dans son pays natal. Le plâtre a été retiré pour révéler la structure originale en briques, et les briques remplacées selon les besoins. L'intervention de l'architecte a également porté sur l'adaptation antisismique requise, et l'ajout d'un toit en titane, le « Cider Gold » (en raison de sa coloration extérieure), recourant à une technique de toiture en diagonale inspirée des modèles traditionnels. Du bois non combustible a été utilisé dans la structure. Un effort a été fait pour que les œuvres d'art expérimentales interagissent avec la conception flexible du nouveau musée entrepôt, qui comprend cinq galeries d'exposition (dont une de 15 m de haut), trois ateliers, une boutique et un café. Dans sa conception architecturale

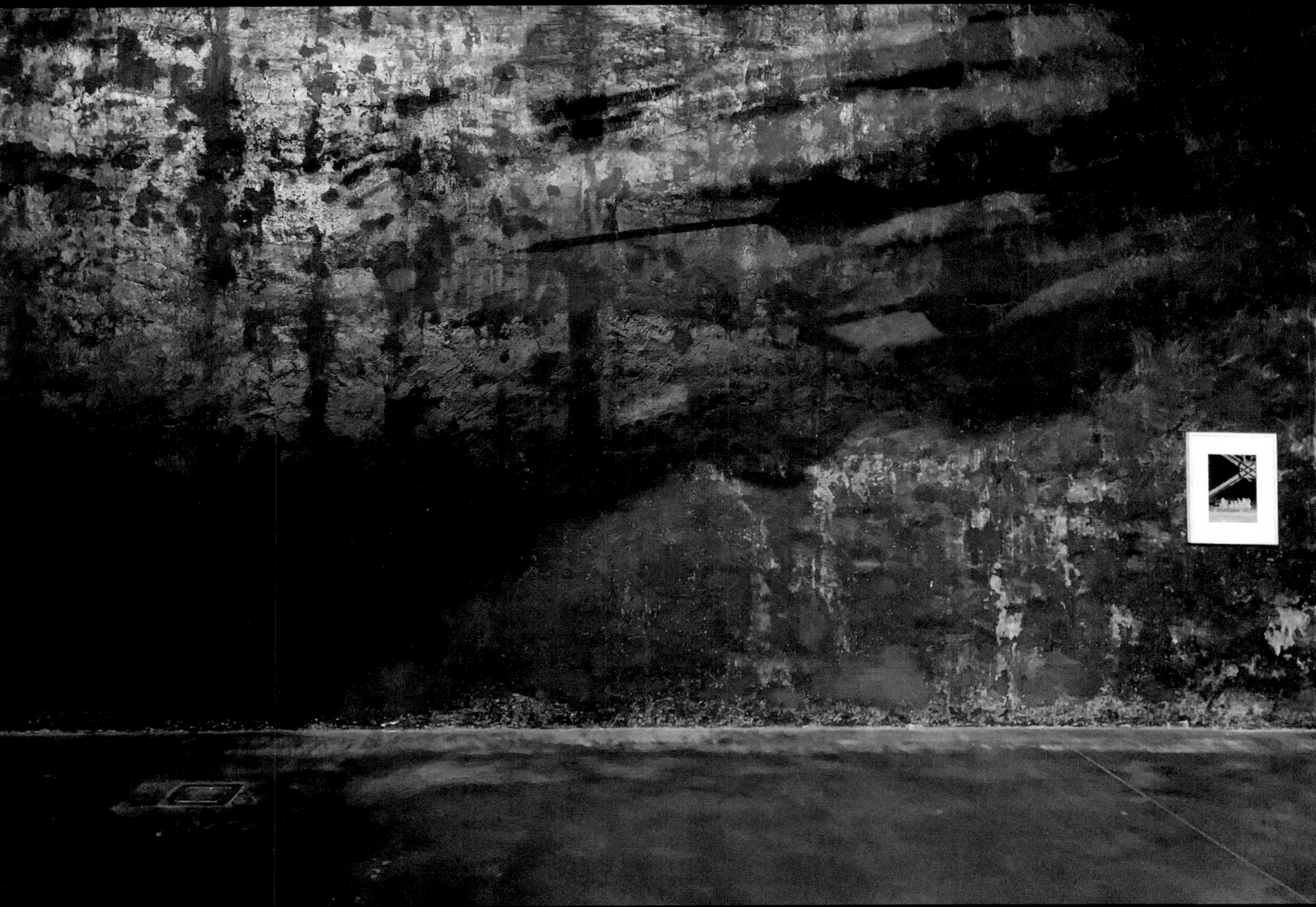

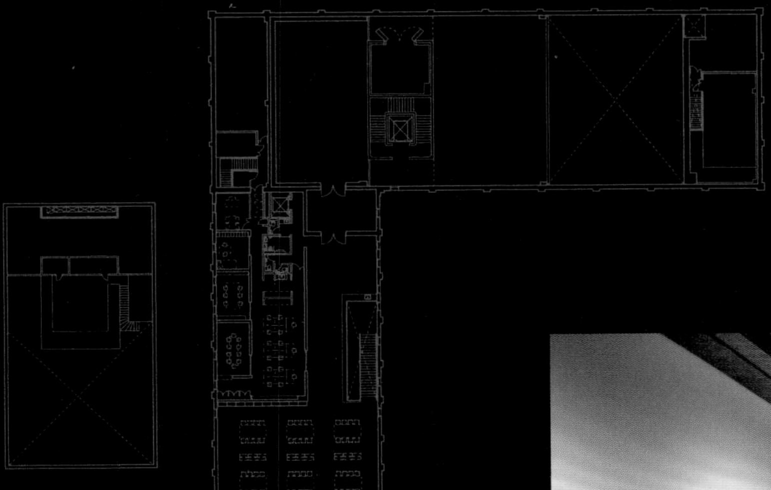

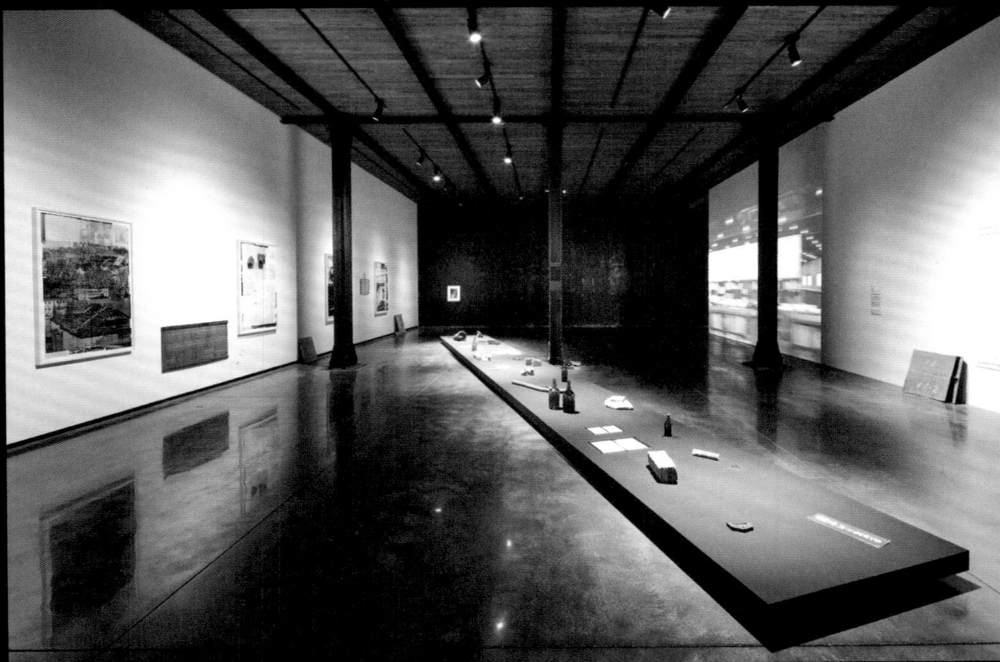

HEISEI CHISHINKAN, KYOTO NATIONAL MUSEUM

YOSHIO TANIGUCHI

Higashiyama, Kyoto, 2013
Area: 5568 m²

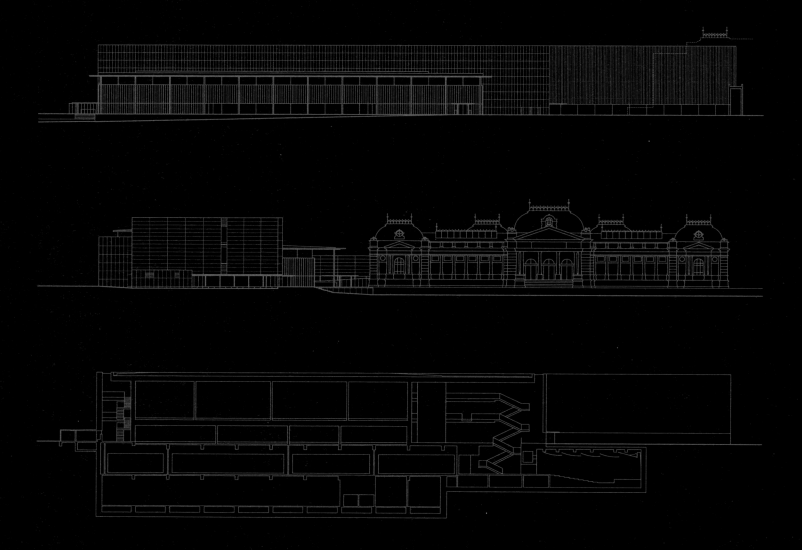

Yoshio Taniguchi is known for the precision of his work. The thin columns, reflecting pool, aligned horizontal panels, and glazing give an impression of carefully calculated geometric rigor.

YOSHIO TANIGUCHI was born in Tokyo in 1937. He received a B.A. in Mechanical Engineering from Keio University in 1960 and an M.Arch from the Harvard GSD in 1964. He worked in the office of Kenzo Tange from 1964 to 1972, then created Taniguchi, Takamiya and Associates in 1975 and Taniguchi and Associates in 1979. He was awarded the 2005 Praemium Imperiale. His built work includes the Marugame Genichiro-Inokuma Museum of Contemporary Art and City Library (Marugame, 1991); Toyota Municipal Museum of Art (Toyota City, 1995); Tokyo Kasai Rinkai Park View Point Visitors Center (Tokyo, 1995); National Museum Gallery of Horyuji Treasures (Tokyo, 1999); and the complete renovation and expansion of the Museum of Modern Art in New York (USA, 2004). He also completed the Kyoto National Museum, Centennial Hall (Kyoto, 2006); the Asia Society Texas Center (Houston, Texas, USA, 2011); and the Heisei Chishinkan wing of Kyoto National Museum (Higashiyama, Kyoto, 2013, published here).

YOSHIO TANIGUCHI wurde 1937 in Tokio geboren. Er erhielt seinen B.A. in Maschinenbau von der Keio-Universität (1960) und seinen M.Arch von der Harvard GSD (1964). Von 1964 bis 1972 arbeitete er im Büro von Kenzo Tange. Er gründete Taniguchi, Takamiya and Associates (1975) sowie Taniguchi & Associates (1979) und wurde 2005 mit dem Praemium Imperiale ausgezeichnet. Zu seinen Arbeiten gehören das Genichiro-Inokuma-Museum für zeitgenössische Kunst und die Genichiro-Inokuma-Stadtbibliothek (Marugame, 1991), das Städtische Kunstmuseum Toyota (Toyota, 1995), ein Besucherzentrum für den Aussichtspunkt im Tokioter Kasai-Rinkai-Park (Tokio, 1995), die Galerie der Horyuji-Schätze des Nationalmuseums Tokio (1999) sowie ein umfassendes Umbau- und Erweiterungsprojekt für das Museum of Modern Art in New York (2004). Taniguchi realisierte zudem die Centennial Hall des Nationalmuseums Kyoto (2006), das Asia Society Texas Center (Houston, 2011) und die Hesei-Chishinkan-Halle des Nationalmuseums Kyoto (Higashiyama, Kyoto, 2013, hier vorgestellt).

YOSHIO TANIGUCHI est né à Tokyo en 1937. Il est titulaire d'un BA en génie mécanique de l'université Keio (1960) et d'un M.Arch de la Harvard GSD (1964). Il a travaillé dans l'agence de Kenzo Tange de 1964 à 1972, avant de créer Taniguchi, Takamiya and Associates en 1975, puis Taniguchi and Associates en 1979. Il a reçu le Praemium Imperiale en 2005. Ses projets construits comprennent le musée d'Art contemporain et bibliothèque municipale Genichiro-Inokuma de Marugame (Marugame, 1991) ; le Musée municipal d'art Toyota (Toyota City, 1995) ; le Centre d'accueil des visiteurs View Point du parc Kasai Rinkai de Tokyo (Tokyo, 1995) ; la galerie des trésors d'Horyuji du Musée national (Tokyo, 1999) et la rénovation complète et l'extension du Museum of Modern Art de New York (États-Unis, 2004). Il a également réalisé la salle du centenaire du Musée national de Kyoto (Kyoto, 2006) ; la Maison de l'Asie au Texas de l'Asia Society (Houston, Texas, 2011) et l'aile Hesei Chishinkan du Musée national de Kyoto (Higashiyama, Kyoto, 2013, publiée ici).

The metal and glass volume of the entrance adjoins
an equally rigorous limestone-clad block for the
actual Museum spaces.

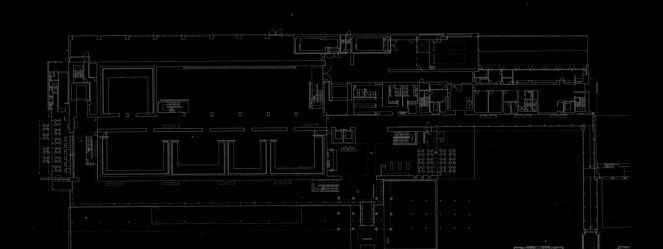

*The interior spaces echo the rigor of the exterior.
The building is, of course, designed to high seismic
standards, which explains part of its apparent
solidity, but here light and high volumes are also
brought into the equation where possible.*

MUKU NURSERY

TEZUKA ARCHITECTS

Fuji, Shizuoka, 2018
Area: 537 m²
Collaboration: Kenta Yano

TAKAHARU TEZUKA, born in Tokyo in 1964, received his degrees from the Musashi Institute of Technology (1987) and from the University of Pennsylvania (1990). He worked with Richard Rogers Partnership Ltd. (1990–94) and established Tezuka Architects the same year. He is currently a Professor at Tokyo

TAKAHARU TEZUKA wurde 1964 in Tokio geboren und erhielt seine Abschlüsse vom Musashi Institut für Technologie (1987) und von der University of Pennsylvania (1990). Er arbeitete für Richard Rogers Partnership Ltd. (1990–1994) und gründete direkt im Anschluss Tezuka Architects. Derzeit ist er Professor an

TAKAHARU TEZUKA, né à Tokyo en 1964, est diplômé de l'Institut de technologie Musashi (1987) et de l'université de Pennsylvanie (1990). Il a collaboré avec Richard Rogers Partnership Ltd. (1990–1994) et a fondé Tezuka Architects la même année. Il est actuellement professeur à l'université de Tokyo. Née à Kanagawa en 1969,

Although the architect compares the design to "bubbles," the buildings appear umbrella-like when seen from the air. Glass walls allow the spaces to communicate freely with each other.

The light wooden architecture is made even more transparent by full-height glazing. A water feature (below) allows children to play outdoors in warm weather.

The "parasol" appearance of the exterior roofs is complemented by the fully visible wooden structure that underlies them. Wood is also used for the floors and walls.

This wooden structure was designed between 2016 and 2017. Takaharu Tezuka compares the plan of this NURSERY to "bubbles slowly rising up in the air, keeping an optimum distance between each other." Each of these bubbles is imagined as having only one function and has no interior walls. He likens the bubbles to single-cell organisms. Although the architect acknowledges some of the difficulties with furniture and interior design posed by circular plans, he says: "We found there are significant advantages using this circle planning as compared to conventional modular planning." The size of the rooms can thus be freely adjusted and the design also allows for a natural 360° visibility of the premises. Finally, "the round shape provokes the endless circular movement of children. It is an endless, instinctive movement. The circles are linked with each other and create infinite combinations." One circle provides for a shallow water

Dieses Projekt in Holzbauweise wurde zwischen 2016 und 2017 entworfen. Takaharu Tezuka vergleicht den Grundriss des Kindergartens mit „Seifenblasen, die in optimalem Abstand zueinander langsam in die Luft aufsteigen". Jede der Blasen hat einen spezifischen Verwendungszweck und ist ohne Innenwände konzipiert. Der Architekt vergleicht sie mit einzelligen Organismen. Obwohl er die Schwierigkeiten nicht verleugnet, die hinsichtlich der Möblierung und der Innenarchitektur durch runde Grundrisse entstehen, sagt er: „Wir haben festgestellt, dass die kreisförmigen Grundrisse gegenüber einer herkömmlichen modularen Planung erhebliche Vorteile bieten". Nicht nur, dass so die Größe der Räume ohne jede Beschränkung gewählt werden konnte, die Form ermöglicht zudem eine Rundumsicht auf das Gelände. Außerdem „ermuntert die runde Form die Kinder instinktiv zu kreisförmigen Laufbewegungen. Die Kreise sind mitein-

La structure en bois a été conçue entre 2016 et 2017. Takaharu Tezuka compare le plan de cette CRÈCHE à des « bulles qui s'élèvent lentement dans les airs en conservant la distance idéale l'une par rapport à l'autre ». Chacune de ces bulles a été conçue pour une seule fonction et ne présente donc aucune cloison intérieure. L'architecte les compare à des organismes unicellulaires, et s'il admet certaines difficultés pour meubler et aménager des pièces rondes, il affirme aussi : « Nous avons trouvé des avantages considérables à ces plans circulaires par rapport aux concepts modulaires classiques. » La taille des pièces peut être adaptée en toute liberté et leur conception permet naturellement une vue à 360°. Enfin, « la forme ronde est la source d'un mouvement circulaire ininterrompu des enfants. C'est un mouvement continu instinctif. Les cercles sont reliés les uns aux autres pour une variété infinie de combinaisons ». L'un des cercles contient un bassin peu profond que

HELIX HOUSE

MAKOTO TAKEI +
CHIE NABESHIMA / TNA

Tokyo, 2015
Area: 126 m²

The wooden house, reached by a ramp, is set up on thin columns, offering extra space below the structure, for play or relaxation.

MAKOTO TAKEI was born in Tokyo in 1974 and graduated from the Department of Architecture of Tokai University in 1997. Between 1997 and 1999 he was at the Tsukamoto Laboratory at the Graduate School of Science and Engineering at Tokyo Institute of Technology, and he worked with Atelier Bow-Wow. Between 1999 and 2000, he worked in the office of Tezuka Architects, before establishing TNA (Takei-Nabeshima-Architects) with Chie Nabeshima. CHIE NABESHIMA was born in Kanagawa in 1975 and graduated from the course in "Habitation Space Design" at the Department of Architecture and Architectural Engineering at the College of Industrial Technology, Nihon University (1998) before working at Tezuka Architects (1998–2005) and cofounding TNA. Their projects include the Color Concrete House (Yokohama, Kanagawa, 2005); Ring House (Karuizawa, Nagano, 2006); Passage House (Karuizawa, Nagano, 2008); Division House (Nagano, 2010); Mist House (Tokyo, 2011); Ginza Natsuno Building (Tokyo, 2011); and the Kamoi Museum (Kurashiki, Okayama, 2012). Recent work includes Cube House (S-chanf, Switzerland, 2012); Joushuutomioka Station (Tomioka, Gunma, 2014); and Helix House (Tokyo, 2015, published here). They are currently working on a house in the shape of an inverted pyramid (Solo Houses, Cretas, Teruel, Spain, 2018–).

MAKOTO TAKEI wurde 1974 in Tokio geboren und schloss 1997 im Fachbereich Architektur an der Tokai-Universität sein Studium ab. Von 1997 bis 1999 arbeitete er am Tsukamoto-Labor der Graduiertenschule für Natur- und Ingenieurwissenschaften des Instituts für Technologie in Tokio, darüber hinaus arbeitete er für das Atelier Bow-Wow. Zwischen 1999 und 2000 war er bei Tezuka Architects, bevor er mit Chie Nabeshima TNA (Takei-Nabeshima-Architects) gründete. CHIE NABESHIMA wurde 1975 in Kanagawa geboren und absolvierte den Studiengang Wohnraumgestaltung im Fachbereich für Architektur und Bauingenieurwesen an der Fakultät für Industrietechnologie der Nihon-Universität (1998), bevor sie bei Tezuka Architects (1998–2005) arbeitete und TNA mitbegründete. Zu den Projekten von Takei und Nabeshima gehören Color Concrete House (Yokohama, Kanagawa, 2005), Ring House (Karuizawa, Nagano, 2006), Passage House (Karuizawa, Nagano, 2008), Division House (Nagano, 2010), Mist House (Tokio, 2011), das Ginza Natsuno Building (Tokyo, 2011) und das Kamoi-Museum (Kurashiki, Okayama, 2012). Zu ihren jüngsten Arbeiten gehören Cube House (S-chanf, Schweiz, 2012), Joshu-Tomioka Station (Tomioka, Gunma, 2014) sowie Helix House (Tokio, 2015, hier vorgestellt). Derzeit arbeiten sie an einem Haus, das die Form einer auf dem Kopf stehenden Pyramide hat (Solo Houses, Cretas, Teruel, Spanien, 2018–).

MAKOTO TAKEI est né à Tokyo en 1974. Il a obtenu son diplôme du département d'architecture de l'université Tokai en 1997. De 1997 à 1999, il a été membre du laboratoire de Tsukamoto à l'École supérieure des sciences de l'ingénieur de l'Institut de technologie de Tokyo, et a travaillé avec Atelier Bow-Wow. De 1999 à 2000, il a travaillé à l'agence Tezuka Architects, avant d'ouvrir TNA (Takei-Nabeshima-Architects) avec Chie Nabeshima. CHIE NABESHIMA est née à Kanagawa en 1975. Elle est diplômée du cours de design de l'espace d'habitation du département d'architecture et génie architectural au collège de technologie industrielle de l'université Nihon (1998) et a ensuite travaillé pour Tezuka Architects (1998–2005) et cofondé TNA. Leurs projets comprennent la Maison en béton coloré (Yokohama, Kanagawa, 2005) ; la Maison à anneaux (Karuizawa, Nagano, 2006) ; la maison Passage (Karuizawa, Nagano, 2008) ; la maison Division (Nagano, 2010) ; la maison la Brume (Tokyo, 2011) ; l'immeuble Ginza Natsuno (Tokyo, 2011) et le musée Kamoi (Kurashiki, Okayama, 2012). Ils ont réalisé récemment la Maison cube (S-chanf, Suisse, 2012) ; la gare Joshu-Tomioka (Tomioka, Gunma, 2014) et la maison Helix (Tokyo, 2015, publiée ici). Ils travaillent actuellement à une maison en forme de pyramide inversée (maisons Solo, Cretas, Teruel, Espagne, 2018–).

This small steel-frame house with Nyotah wood louvers was erected on a 174-square-meter site and set up on pilotis, which allowed the creation of a parking spot and a children's play area. It was originally designed without any stairways, only a sloping ramp linking the levels. Local building regulations limited

Diese eher kleine Stahlrahmenkonstruktion mit Jalousien aus Nyatoh-Holz wurde auf einem 174 m² großen Grundstück, auf einer Pilotis-Konstruktion errichtet, um Platz für einen Park- und einen Spielplatz zu schaffen. Das Haus wurde von Anfang an ohne Treppen entworfen, die verschiedenen Ebenen werden

Cette petite maison à charpente en acier et aux persiennes en bois de Nyatoh a été construite sur un terrain de 174 m² sur des pilotis, ce qui a permis la création d'une place de parking et d'un terrain de jeux pour les enfants. Elle était conçue à l'origine sans le moindre escalier, avec une rampe entre les différents niveaux.

ARCHITECT CONTACTS

CREDITS

**EACH AND EVERY TASCHEN
BOOK PLANTS A SEED!**
TASCHEN is a carbon neutral publisher. Each year, we offset our annual carbon emissions with carbon credits at the Instituto Terra, a reforestation program in Minas Gerais, Brazil, founded by Lélia and Sebastião Salgado. To find out more about this ecological partnership, please check: *www.taschen.com/zerocarbon*.
Inspiration: unlimited.
Carbon footprint: zero.

To stay informed about TASCHEN and our upcoming titles, please subscribe to our free magazine at *www.taschen.com/magazine*, follow us on Instagram and Facebook, or e-mail your questions to *contact@taschen.com*.

© 2022 TASCHEN GmbH
Hohenzollernring 53, D–50672 Köln
www.taschen.com

225–231 © VG Bild-Kunst Bonn 2021, for the works Anish Kapoor / 420 © Yoshitomo Nara, A to Z Memorial Dog, 2007 / 425 installation view: Hirosaki Museum of Contemporary Art, „Thank You Memory: Cidre to Contemporary Art", 2020

Design: Andy Disl, Los Angeles
Layout: Collaborate, London
Collaboration: Harriet Graham, Turin
German translation: Gregor Runge, Berlin
French translation: Claire Debard, Freiburg

Printed in Italy
ISBN 978-3-8365-7510-2